THE BEST OF

ABBIE HOFFMAN

FOREWORD BY NORMAN MAILER

EDITED BY DANIEL SIMON WITH THE AUTHOR

FOU[illegible]NDOWS

NEW YORK

First printing November, 1989.
First paperback printing October, 1990.

Library of Congress Cataloging-in-Publication Data

Hoffman, Abbie.
[Selections. 1989]
The best of Abbie Hoffman : selections from Revolution for the hell of it, Woodstock nation, Steal this book, and new writings / Abbie Hoffman ; foreword by Norman Mailer ; edited by Daniel Simon with the author.
p. cm.
ISBN 0-941423-42-5 : $14.95
1. Radicalism—United States. 2. United States--Civilization—1970- 3. United States—Popular culture. I. Simon; Daniel. II. Title.
HN90.R3H552 1989

303.48'4—dc 20 89-23585
CIP

Four Walls Eight Windows
P.O. Box 548
Village Station
New York, N.Y. 10014

Designed by Cindy LaBreacht.
Jacket Design by Cindy LaBreacht.
Printed in the U.S.A.
First edition.

DISCONTENTS

PART FOUR
NEW WRITINGS
1981–1988

PHOTOGRAPHS

FOLLOWING PAGE 185

FOREWORD

Abbie was one of the smartest—let us say, one of the quickest—people I ever met, and he was probably one of the bravest. In the land from which he originated, Worcester, Mass., they call it moxie. He had tons of moxie. He was also one of the funniest people I ever met. He was also one of the most appealing if you ask for little order in personality. Abbie had a charisma that must have come out of an immaculate conception between Fidel Castro and Groucho Marx. They went into his soul and he came out looking like an ethnic milkshake—Jewish revolutionary, Puerto Rican lord, Italian street kid, Black Panther with the old Afro haircut, even a glint of Irish gunman in the mad, green eyes. I remember them as yellow-green, like Joe Namath's gypsy green eyes. Abbie was one of the most incredible-looking people I ever met. In fact, he wasn't Twentieth Century, but Nineteenth. Might just as well have emerged out of *Oliver Twist*. You could say he used to look like a chimney sweep. In fact, I don't know what chimney sweeps looked like, but I always imagined them as having a manic integrity that glared out of their eyes through all the soot and darked-up skin. It was the knowledge that they were doing an essential job that no one else would do. Without them, everybody in the house would slowly, over the years, suffocate from the smoke.

If Abbie was a reincarnation—and after you read this book you will ask: how could he not be?—then chimney sweep is one of his past lives. It stands out in his karma. It helps to account for why he was a crazy maniac of a revolutionary, and why, therefore, we can say that this book is a document, is, indeed, the autobiography of a bona fide American revolutionary. In fact, as I went through it, large parts of the sixties lit up like areas of a stage grand enough to hold an opera company. Of course, we all think we know the sixties. To people of my generation, and the generation after us, the sixties is a private decade, a good relative of a decade, the one we believe we know the way we believe we know Humphrey Bogart. I always feel as if I can speak with authority on the sixties, and I never knew anybody my age who didn't feel the same way (whereas try to find someone who gets a light in their eyes when they speak of the seventies). Yet reading this work, I came to decide that my piece of the sixties wasn't as large as I thought. If we were going to get into comparisons, Abbie lived it, I observed it; Abbie committed his life, I merely loved the sixties because they gave life to my work.

So I enjoyed reading these pages. I learned from them, as a great many readers will. It filled empty spaces in what I thought was solid knowledge. And it left me with more respect for Abbie than I began with. I had tended to think of him as a clown. A tragic clown after the cocaine bust, and something like a ballsy wonder of a clown in the days when he was making raids on the media, but I never gave him whole credit for being serious. Reading this book lets you in on it. I began to think of Dustin Hoffman's brilliant portrait of Lenny Bruce where, at the end, broken by the courts, we realize that Lenny is enough of a closet believer in the system to throw himself on the fundamental charity of the court—he will try to make the judge believe that under it all, Lenny, too, is a good American, he, too, is doing it for patriotic reasons. So, too, goes the tone of this unique autobiography. Comrades, Abbie is saying, "under my hustle beats a hot Socialist heart. I am really not a nihilist. I am one of you—a believer in progress."

He was serious. Abbie was serious. His thousand jokes were to conceal how serious he was. It makes us uneasy. Under his satire beat a somewhat hysterical heart. It could not be otherwise. Given his life, given his immersion in a profound lack of security, in a set of identity crises that would splat most of us like cantaloupes thrown off a truck, it is prodigious how long he resisted madness and death. He had to have a monumental will. Yet it is part of the civilized trap of literature that an incredible life is not enough. The survivor must rise to heights of irony as well. This was not Abbie's forte. His heart beat too fiercely. He cared too much. He loved himself too much. All the same, we need not quibble. We have here a document of a remarkable man. In an age of contracting horizons, we do well to count our blessings. How odd that now, Abbie is one of them. Our own holy ghost of the Left. Salud!

—NORMAN MAILER
October 1989

PREFACE

Parts 1, 2, and 3 of *The Best of Abbie Hoffman* were compiled according to Abbie's express wishes as communicated to me in January, February, and March of 1989. The books that had been his most massive communications of the early years—*Revolution for the Hell of It*, *Woodstock Nation*, and *Steal This Book*—had stayed with him. Two decades later, still impelled by the same principles of social justice by which he had written them, Abbie decided he would see them in print again. He tried for two years. No publisher wanted them. It wasn't that the publishers thought they would lose money: The books had sold nearly 3 million copies in previous incarnations; there was a sixties revival going on. . . . Rather, the rejections were the expression of a basic discomfort with Abbie himself. He was incorrigible, and it irked publishers to have to deal with this yippie who was beginning to tire but wouldn't quit. In December 1988, Abbie placed an ad in the classified section of *The Nation*: "Serious publishers interested in reprinting 3 60s classics as 1 quality paperback immediately contact: Abbie Hoffman" with a post office box address in New Hope, Pennsylvania. Four

Walls Eight Windows responded. We found Abbie's enthusiasm to be mixed with vulnerability, and fear, as if the part of himself the book would represent were a part he was feeling suddenly estranged from. But mostly he was enthusiastic. Work began immediately and was going well. In January he wrote us, "I reread [the three books] & can see how original 60s language & spirit was. So many books about the 60s, so much revisionism, why not the original texts? I love this project."

At age 52 Abbie was not exactly the same person that had raised the Pentagon, dumped dollar bills from the gallery of the Wall Street Stock Exchange, and in so many other ways faced down the lumpenmilitariat that he saw corrupting this country in the 1960s. He was more mature personally, his ideas were more subtle, his world view was broader. But he stood by the young man he had been and stood by what that young man had said and written.

In conversation, Abbie was as acute as ever. Didn't he want to delete the section on drug use in *Steal This Book* in the new book, I asked him, since the innocence of turning on had given way to the violence of crack? No, he didn't. Crack was a problem of hopelessness, neglect, and poverty, not simply a drug problem, he said. Just say no with Nancy? Hell no! Didn't he want to delete the section on hijacking planes, since it is so difficult to do these days? No, he said, we shouldn't underestimate the shock value. As for the sections on explosives, they were written tongue in cheek for the most part and contained nothing any twelve year old couldn't find on the shelves at the local public library, he said. I had planned to cut *Steal This Book* by half or more. But I found in Abbie a natural respect for things as they are—a marvelous quality in a revolutionary. He preferred to add new material rather than change what was already written. In the end, *Steal This Book* was kept virtually in its entirety—not only because this was how Abbie wanted it but because finally that book is not so much a handbook as it is a provocation, an assault on rational sensibilities, and this is how it must remain.

Then in April, Abbie was gone. Any notes he had written for the introduction, overview, and annotations to this new collection were locked away in sealed trunks. Part 4, by presenting a sampling of Abbie's recent speeches and essays, offers us a glimpse of how much Abbie learned in the last twenty years, and hence, shows us the enormity of our loss in his death. Much more than the early writings, the late writings reveal that he thought almost constantly about the future and was setting his hopes on the strength and integrity of the next generation. Where he had begun, in the 1950s and 1960s, discovering and then describing, with enormous energy, what the country he called Woodstock Nation could be, he ended, in his writings of the 1980s, describing America in terms of what it is—in many ways a far more ambitious undertaking. It took enormous courage in the later years to lead the Save the River movement while he himself was on the run and endangered, or to write a reflective essay on convict-author Jack Abbott while he himself was doing a stint at the Edgecombe Correctional Facility, or to trumpet the birth of a new student activism in speeches on university campuses at the same time as he felt deeply depressed about the decline of the Left. Courage and something more. What Abbie did he did uniquely well, which was in the end to maintain a devastatingly clear vision while nonetheless continuing to *do* democracy. Let those who hear it, answer his call.

A lot of people came together in a very short time to ensure that this project saw light of day. They include Chris Buck, Lisa Callamaro, Heather Fenby, Marty Jezer, Cindy LaBreacht, Hannah Lerner, Norman Mailer, Elaine Markson, Steve Jesse Rose, Adriana Scopino, Studs Terkel, and Howard Zinn. Johanna Lawrenson saw her way through the confusion of these last months to be consistently supportive. Jack Hoffman kept making what was good, better. John Oakes offered sound insight at every critical turning.

—DANIEL SIMON
October 1989

PART ONE

FROM

REVOLUTION FOR THE HELL OF IT

1968

1

REVOLUTION FOR THE HELL OF IT

"In a Revolution one wins or dies."
—MAJOR ERNESTO "CHE" GUEVARA

"Dash: A revolution in cleansing powder."
—FROM A TV COMMERCIAL

Revolution for the hell of it? Why not? It's all a bunch of phony words anyway. Once one has experienced LSD, existential revolution, fought the intellectual game-playing of the individual in society, of one's identity, one realizes that action is the only reality; not only reality but morality as well. One learns reality is a subjective experience. It exists in my head. I am the Revolution. The other day I took some LSD somewhere in the Florida Keys, where I've come to try to write a book. It's an interesting setting: exactly equidistant from Havana and Miami Beach. You are always reminded of the fact because Radio Havana is one of the clearest radio stations. They play terrible crap music and you wonder why they don't play Country Joe and the Fish or the Beatles. That would be good propaganda. It seems as if they are trying to convert all the retirees who waddle around in Bermuda shorts. You wonder what they have in mind. Anyway, all of a sudden a tropical storm hit and the sky turned black. I thought (felt) it was a tornado and before I knew it the house had become unfastened and was spinning wildly in the air like a scene from *The Wizard of Oz*. Paul Krassner, who was watching television, shouted that Stokely had just returned and had been grabbed by the FBI. Everybody is hallucinating a mile a minute. "Shit, Tim Leary, I'm sorry I said LSD was a fake." I'm laughing away, dreaming of the house getting blown to Cuba with the floor shaking like a son-of-a-bitch. "The Revolution Is On!" I scream and grab a cap pistol, preparing to shoot the first cop that comes along. My wife joins the game and we have this whole *Bonnie and Clyde* thing going. It's all hilarious, really. One big revolution for the hell of it. The point is, if it were a real gun and a cop walked in, I would have shot him dead. BANG! What are the guidelines for revolution when the house has been cast adrift in a tornado? What of the debates between Marat and Sade when the inmates run wild? Listen to Fidel Castro:

> There are those who believe that it is necessary for ideas to triumph among the greater part of the masses before initiating action, and there are others who understand that action is one of the most efficient instruments for bringing about the triumph of ideas among the masses. Whoever hestitates while waiting for ideas to triumph among the masses before initiating revolutionary action will never be a revolutionary. Humanity will, of course, change; human society will, of course, continue to develop—in spite of men and the errors of men. But that is not a revolutionary attitude.
>
> —MAJOR FIDEL CASTRO RUIZ
> *Speech delivered at the closing of the First Conference of the Latin American Organization of Solidarity (OLAS), August 10, 1967*

Revolution is in my head. I am the Revolution.
Do your thing
Do your thing

Do your thing
Do your thing
Do your thing
Be your thing

Practice. Rehearsals come after the act. Act. Act. One practices by acting. Billy the Kid strides with 6 guns blazing, receding into his inner space. What does he find? Another Billy the Kid striding with 6 guns blazing, receding into his inner space. There are no rules, only images. Only a System has boundaries. Eichmann lives by the rules. Eichmann, machine-like, twitching nervously, pushes at his steel-rimmed glasses, takes his neatly folded handkerchief from the breast pocket of his gray-flannel suit and mops his sweating bald forehead (An electrical engineer: "*My goal in life is to make myself replaceable*"—DOT—DOT—BEEP—BEEP).

"My God was a pink memo. Uh . . ." he stutters, "excuse me, my God was a pink memo on Tuesdays, on Wednesdays it was a blue memo. . . . It's hard to remember exactly. Yes, yes, that was it. Pink memo on Tuesdays, blue memo on Wednesdays."

Eichmann lets out a huge sigh of relief, smiles a little pince-nez smile, carefully refolds his handkerchief and replaces it in his pocket.

"I was a careerist. (slow) I was only doing my death."

Behind Billy the Kid stands Abraham. Grand old man of 9,000 years, striding across the desert lands, sweat crushed against his brow by a huge sun-baked forearm of golden fleece, the same golden fleece that hung from his head and face in cascading waves of hard times.

God says, "Abraham, take your beloved son Isaac to the land of Moriah and place him upon an altar and make of him a sacrifice."

And Abraham tightens his fists and gnarls his teeth and cries out, "How do I know that is the God that has guided me and my people all these years?"

Inside he knows because He is God, which is to say, a Man and not a machine. He bids goodbye to Sarah, whom he truly loves, and he walks, holding his young son's tender hand, the three miles to Moriah. Placing his son upon the carefully constructed altar, he binds and gags him to let his son know that he loves him, and yet he does not need to do that because the boy too loves his father and needs no bindings. There would be no pain. Then Abraham dabs the boy with holy water that he had carried from his holy well and recites a few ritual prayers, mumbling them rotely because three days ago when he talked to God, he had already decided he would do what he must do. He holds his left hand over his son's eyes and raises the long well-used knife in the air, poising it for that final plunge. One plunge, quickly, for the steel in his mighty arm-sword will need but one thrust upon the young lad's frail body.

"Abraham, I am your God."

He slumps, exhausted with joy. It was an orgasm of consciousness, pulsating down rows upon rows of mankind.

Trust your impulses. Trust your impulses. TRUST — TRUST — TRUST — TRUST — TRUST — TRUST — TRUST — TRUST — TRUST — TRUST — TRUST

Test

Test

Test

Relax

The trouble with liberalism and bull-shit American middle class DOT—DOT—BEEP—BEEPs is that they run the myth backwards.

"God is dead," they cry, "and we did it for the kids."

A true revolutionist carves the revolution out of Granite Rock. Ho Chi Minh crawls through the Mekong Delta rice-paddy mud and comes to a fork in the road. A road, by the way, that he and he alone constructed. Environment is in your head. Your head is a granite rock of neural impulses, get some dynamite if you need it.

Billy the Kid blazes his motorcycle down that neural impulse road and thrashes madly, gears lock, guns fall from his side in the jolt, the chrome-plated Harley-Davidson rears on its hind legs. Oop! He sails from the sturdy bike, hurled into inner space.

People said he was such a nice young kid.

"Why, I remember the time young Billy used to like to run naked from the swimmin' hole down through town, still dripping wet."

Not exactly Lady Godiva, I'll admit. Billy sure was a hot shit in those days.

"Can't figger him out now, he must have flipped."

Yeah, sure, that was it, he must have flipped out. Crazy motherfucker Billy.

"Billy come back, come back, Billy, Billy, Billy."

Go Billy! Go! Go! Billy Go. We don't need leaders. We need cheerleaders. Go Billy Go!! Do your thing! Sock it to 'em!

Fidel sits on the side of a tank rumbling into Havana on New Year's day. His green army fatigues swiped from Batista's Free Store, sent down by John Foster Dulles, who, adding a touch of creativity to his cousin Eichmann's idea, decided that if everyone in Latin America wore American Army fatigues, all the problems would be solved. Clever Yankee was John Foster Dulles. Fidel's rifle lies like a feather cradled in his strong arms. Girls throw flowers at the tank and rush to tug playfully at his black beard. He laughs joyously and pinches a few rumps, for he is a soldier and they like to do that sort of thing, you know. The tank stops in the city square. Fidel lets the gun drop to the ground, slaps his thighs and stands erect. He is like a mighty penis coming to life, and when he is tall and straight, the crowd immediately is transformed.

NOW THE REVOLUTION BEGINS

He goes to a friend's house, collapses on the floor, snoring loudly, exhausted from five days without sleep, and sleeps for twenty straight hours.

For ten long years he builds a country. Makes love. Steals Russian rubles. Sticks a finger in Uncle Sam's nose.

"We are going to do away with money, people should relate to each other as human beings."

Go Fidel Go! Go Fidel Go! Go Fidel Go! Do your thing! Sock it to 'em!

He fires Commie Dean Ruskies who say he is going mad (not publicly of course) and makes the revolution.

> This Byzantine discussion about the ways and means of struggle, whether it should be peaceful or non-peaceful, armed or unarmed—the essence of this discussion, which we call Byzantine because it is like an argument between two deaf and dumb people, is what distinguishes those who want to promote revolution and those who do not want to promote it. Let no one be fooled.*

*Castro speech at closing of OLAS conference, Aug. 10, 1967.

And again he "meditates" like Siddhartha sitting cross-legged under the flower-blossomed Bo tree . . .

> These years have taught us all to meditate more and analyze better. We no longer accept any "self-evident" truths. "Self-evident" truths belong to bourgeois philosophy. A whole series of old clichés must be abolished. Marxist literature itself, revolutionary political literature itself, should be renewed because repeating the same old clichés, phraseology and verbiage that have been repeated for 35 years wins over no one, convinces no one at all. There are times when political documents, called Marxist, give the impression that someone has gone to an archive and asked for a form: form 14, form 13, form 12; they are all alike, with the same empty words, in language incapable of expressing real situations. Very often, these documents are divorced from real life. And then many people are told that this is Marxism . . . and in what way is this different from a catechism, and in what way is it different from a litany, from a rosary?*

And finally, shooting down communism, Christianityism, Lyndon Baines Johnsonism, Old Ageism, he says,

> The communist movement developed a method, a style, and in some aspects, even took on the characteristics of a religion. And we sincerely believe that the character should be left behind. Of course, to some of these "illustrious revolutionary thinkers" we are only petit bourgeois adventurers without revolutionary maturity. We are lucky that the Revolution came before maturity!†

All this while still sitting cross-legged under the flower-blossomed Bo tree in the center of Havana.

*Ibid.
†Ibid.

AN EXPLANATION: What does free speech mean to you? To me it is an image like all things.

ME: Yes, I believe in total free speech.
INTERVIEWER: Well, surely you don't believe in the right to cry "fire" in a crowded theatre?
ME: F I R E !

CONVERSATION WITH THE READER: What goes through your head when you read this pudding? Images? Images of who? Me? You? I am a myth. Besides I can't write and words are all bullshit anyway. I don't know how to write. Here is an example of what I mean. It is called a poem. I didn't call it that, someone else did. I called it a brown manila envelope. It is a manila envelope about meetings. It was fun to write.

DIGGER CREED FOR HEAD MEETINGS

MEETINGS ARE

INFORMATION
MEDITATION
EXPERIENCE
FUN
TRUST
REHEARSALS
DRAMA
HORSESHIT

MEETINGS ARE NOT

PUTTING PEOPLE DOWN

Shhhh! LISTEN AT MEETINGS Shhhhhh!

LISTEN TO eye movements
LISTEN TO scratching
LISTEN TO your head
LISTEN TO smells
LISTEN TO singing
LISTEN TO touches
LISTEN TO silence
LISTEN TO gestalt vibrations
LISTEN TO a baby born in the sea
LISTEN TO the writing on the wall

DON'T LISTEN TO WORDS
DON'T LISTEN TO WORDS
DON'T LISTEN TO WORDS
meetings are life
surrender to the meeting . . . the meeting is the message
MEETINGS ARE CONFRONTATION—
MEETINGS ARE RELAXATION—
DIG OTHER HEADS—
DIG YOUR HEAD

dig disrupters, dig poets, dig peacemakers, dig heads who mumble, dig heads who don't go to meetings, dig heads who fall asleep, dig andy kent, dig clowns, dig street fighters, dig heads who scribble on paper, dig hustlers, dig heads that admit they are wrong, dig heads that know they are right, dig doing, dig changes, dig holy men, DIG HEADS who do everything

AT MEETINGS DIG HEADS WHO DIG MEETINGS

all meetings are the same same same same same same same same same same same same same—DIFFERENT meetings are rivers—don't build dams

BEWARE OF STRUCTURE FREAKS
BEWARE OF RULES
BEWARE OF "AT THE LAST MEETING WE DECIDED . . ."

DON'T GO BACK—THERE WAS NO LAST MEETING
DON'T GO FORWARD—THERE IS NOTHING
meetings are Now you are the meeting we are Now
WITHOUT MEETINGS THERE IS NO COMMUNITY
COMMUNITY IS UNITY
AVOID GANGBANGS . . . RAPE IDEAS NOT PEOPLE
MAKE LOVE AT ALL MEETINGS
MEETINGS TAKE A MOMENT—Time is Fantasy—
MEETINGS TAKE FOREVER
there is no WAY to run a meeting
use meetings to help you DO YOUR THING
Go naked to meetings—Go high to meetings
BE PREPARED
PREPARE BY meditation
PREPARE BY doing
COME PREPARED TO DROP OUT—COME PREPARED TO STAY FOREVER

IF YOU ARE NOT PREPARED MEETINGS ARE NOT YOUR THING ONLY DO YOUR THING

mene, mene, tekel, upharsin

(meetings are a pain in the ass)

Once about three months ago, or four or five, I got a call that there was "trouble" on the streets. There was a knock on the door and a nervous young kid whom I like stammered out things like "Ninth Precinct" and "arrests." I got dressed in my cowboy clothes and walked three blocks down to the Ninth Precinct. The night air was chilly. It was Saturday night and the streets were teeming with the run-of-the-mill chaos. Paul, Anita, Barry, Phyllis, and I strode along. I was headed for a revolutionary encounter. "Here we all go to the Ninth Precinct, Ninth Precinct, Ninth Precinct." When we finally reached the station house entrance all sorts of information was flying around the air. We had come on some issue regarding a rock band called Salvation that had got busted for something or other, or so Barry said and Captain Fink concurred.

Captain Fink and I are old friends. "Friends," I had said to him, "ain't got nothing to do with it. Some of my best friends are enemies." He has a copy of a poem I wrote. He confessed to me he didn't understand Allen Ginsberg. Captain Fink is Jewish sometimes, just like me. Once I said to him what my relatives always said to me: "What's a nice Jewish guy like you doing in a place like this." I like to talk Yiddish in front of him, especially if there are goy cops in hearing distance. He doesn't understand Yiddish. I speak only a few lines, but he thinks I'm a Talmudic scholar. It's a funny little game. This time, however, I am here on "business."

The fact that Fink is here on Saturday night is heavy information. Other information is flying around the air. Lots of black people are running back and forth. I'm very interested in this because I'm trying to build links with people outside the system. I guess it's called being an organizer or a missing link. It seems, upon talking to a group of very young black kids, that 20 or so of their friends have just been arrested in a large pot bust. This is what I call bad news/good news.

> **BAD NEWS**: Cops bust black people; hippies won't get busted when they smoke pot in large groups because of racism (hippies in strange way better organized than

> blacks in the power politics pressure game on the Lower East Side); blacks will be pissed at hippies. *Cops manipulate intergroup frictions through politics.*
>
> **GOOD NEWS**: I'm there and there is a chance to play missing link, to join forces with blacks. I have a stage.

While everybody is shaking their heads and advising and huddling and yelling, I lie down in front of the station-house door. Nobody can get out of the police station. People, cops, spades, Captain Fink are all confused.

Phyllis yells, "He's been stabbed!"

A tug of war develops between us and them, with me as the rope. I'm in meditation, just lying there smiling while the cops drag me into the station house. Fink confronts me.

"FREE, this isn't your business. They aren't hippies. Why don't you go home."

"What do you mean, 'hippie'? I'm a nigger and I was smoking pot with them. Arrest me or let them go."

The cops put me in the back room. I'm jiving with the spades. I bum a cigarette from one. We're all brothers. Most think I'm crazy, same as Fink and the cops, but one little kid they picked up, he must have been twelve years old, is smiling and winking. You know the smile I mean? Fink comes in and tries again to get me to go home. I tell him I'm just doing my job and he'd better place me under arrest before I burn down the police station. He walks out of the room, sweating. I'm getting restless.

"What is this bullshit. Am I under arrest or not. Asshole cops, you don't know your job." I follow Fink into the main lobby of the station. Everybody's farting around.

"Am I under arrest or not?" I shout. Nobody answers.

I raise my cowboy boot and kick in Captain Fink's trophy case window. The glass flies all over the place and Fink, turning red in the face (he seemed to be losing his temper for some reason), shouts, "You're under arrest."

"It's about fuckin' time," I respond. Even the cops are laughing at the "Ol' Man," as they call him.

I'm led away and booked. The rest is anticlimax. A night in the Tombs.

Court scene. Judge: "Do you realize that this leads to anarchy?" (That's as good a word as any, so I smile.)

People have asked me why I did what I did at the station house and I told them a story similar to the one I just told here, but it was all bullshit. I really did it because it was fun. That's what I tell my friends. To my brothers I tell the real truth, which is that I don't know why I did it. They smile because they know any explanation I give is made up.

2

THE RISING OF THE PENTAGON

MARCH 30, 1967: Spring is here and things are popping. On Easter Sunday there was a huge Be-In in Central Park. There were probably 30,000 people that Was-In. It was hard to tell—it was all over the place. Everybody high on something: balloons, acid, bananas, kids, sky, flowers, dancing, kissing. I had a ball—totally *zonked*. People kept giving away things free—fruit, jelly beans, clothes, flowers, chicken, Easter eggs, poems. Leaving the park, I strolled down Fifth Avenue singing "In your Easter bonnet . . ." and every once in a while yelling "Draft Cardinal Spellman." All of a sudden there it was, St. Patrick's Cathedral, a huge gray mouldering bastion, loudspeakers urging "Come on in." I'm very calm now, cross the street when it says WALK, mount the steps and then—"Hey, you, buddy!" A line of cops wiggling their index fingers. "You can't go in with that uniform" (flowers, gold paint, Easter bunny).

"Why not, officer? You can go in with yours."

"You can't go in the church with flowers in your hair. It's the Cardinal's orders."

"It's my Easter suit—I want to go in the church." Assume the stance. Crowd gathers. Have to work tonight, Freedom, goals, what's important . . . Silence . . . Staring . . . "Keep your damn church, we got the park anyway." Angry at self later—chickened out—who knows . . . There's time to get them later.

APRIL 29, 1967: There we sat in a corner of Central Park going through all the changes that you go through before direct action. Sixteen members of the Flower Brigade preparing to march in the Support Our Boys in Vietnam parade. "Shit, I'm scared. I almost didn't make it up on the subway," says one kid. Joe Flaherty of the *Village Voice* drops by to tell us it's like walking into the lion's den. Jim Fouratt says he's definitely marching. He called the parade committee and was assured we were an officially designated group in the parade and he has this marvelous cherub look that says "we got to show them our love." The *Daily News* reporter comes by: "Where are all your members?"

"They went AWOL," someone quips. "If Jim goes I guess we all go." No one cops out. Since I'm supposed to know about this stuff I do my OK-I-think-we're-gonna-get-the-shit-kicked-out-of-us speech. It's a quickie on non-violent defense, about removing earrings, protecting genitals and base of the head, staying together as a group, etc. Jim talks to the cops. They are going to escort us to Lexington and 93rd, our assembly point. They try to talk us out of going. Some cop's on a walkie-talkie and orders are that we get no escort. Just then a patrol car rides by with a "Support Our Boys" sticker on the windshield.

We figure it's safer without the cops. Off come as many identifying items as possible. All we got are flowers. We march the five blocks without incident and form behind a Boy Scout group from Queens. It's sunny and we're really grooving. Glad there's no trouble, we wait for about an hour. Some bystanders who like what we're doing buy us more flowers to carry. We all have American flags, some guys have official Support Our Boys banners that they bought from vendors who came by. I have a beautifully colored cape that says "FREEDOM" all over it. Anita is dressed in red, white and blue. Three people have pink posters that say "Love" on them. A few college hawkniks come by. One guy swings, wants to get laid, takes a flower and says he'll even march with us. The Boy Scouts are really digging us goofing around: "Hey, they're kissing, look at that."

The Scout leaders are having a real time controlling the kids. They make them line up with their right arms extended two inches below Heil Hitler position. They order them to face front. Everything looks cool. We're all impatient to get going. The word goes out: "We're movin' out." OK. "Left, Right, Left, Right, Left, Right" or "Right, Left." The Boy Scouts are really showing us up. We march a half block to Park Avenue. You can really hear the bands now. It's John Philip Sousa Day in Fun City. Man, I dig parades. A busty mother walks by with her four-year-old twins dressed in Army clothes, each with a plastic machine gun. Two Bircher type women see us. They ask the cops what's going on. The cop shrugs his shoulders. They confer with the Boy Scout leaders.

They decide that we are a corrupting influence. They march the Scouts around the Flatbush Conservative Club contingent. We follow. We get cut off from the Boy Scouts. "Be Prepared!" Zonk! Fists, red paint, kicks, beer cans, spitting—the whole American Welcome Wagon treatment. They grab our American flags and rip them up. Quite an interesting bit, since this parade was formed chiefly because of the flag-burning at the April 15 peace march. Daisy petals flying all over like chicken feathers. A mother drops her baby in order to get in a few well-placed kick punches. The baby's getting crushed along with the flower people. The baby's one of us, while Mom does her patriotic thing. Two girls are stomped on. We sound the retreat. "Get those bearded creeps!" (No one had a beard.) "Cowards! Cowards!" "Go back to the Village!" Cops appear out of nowhere. There is a flying wedge. We are marched to Second Avenue and get a police escort to St. Marks Place.

The Flower Brigade lost its first battle, but watch out, America. We were poorly equipped with flowers from uptown florists. Already there is talk of growing our own. Plans are being made to mine the East River with daffodils. Dandelion chains are being wrapped around induction centers. Holes are being dug in street pavements with seeds dropped in and covered. The cry of "Flower Power" echoes through the land. We shall not wilt. Let a thousand flowers bloom.

SKULLDIGGERY: This Digger phenomenon deserves a close examination by the peace movement—not that these jottings will necessarily make things clearer; clarity, alas, is not one of our goals. Confusion is mightier than the sword!

First it is important to distinguish between hippies and Diggers. Both are myths: that is, there is no definition, there is no organized conspiracy; both are in one sense a huge put-on. Hippies, however, are a myth created by media and as such they are forced to play certain media-oriented roles. They are media-manipulated. Diggers too are myth, but a grass-roots myth created from within. We have learned to manipulate media. Diggers are more politically oriented but at the same time bigger fuckoffs. Diggers are zenlike in that we have totally destroyed words and replaced them with "doing"—action becomes the only reality. Like Lao-tzu: "*The way to do is to be.*" We cry, "No one understands us," while at the same time, winking out of the corner of our eye, recognizing that if the straight world understood all this Digger shit, it would render us impotent, because understanding is the first step to control and control is the secret to our extinction.

This reluctance to define ourselves gives us glorious freedom in which to fuck with the system. We become communist-racist-acid-headed freaks, holding flowers in one hand and bombs in the other. The Old Left says we work for the CIA. Ex-Marines stomp on us as Pinkos. Newport police jail us as smut peddlars. Newark cops arrest us as riot inciters. (These four events were all triggered by passing out free copies of the same poem.) So what the hell are we doing, you ask? We are dynamiting brain cells. We are putting people through changes. The key to the puzzle lies in theater. We are theater in the streets: total and committed. We aim to involve people and use (unlike other movements locked in ideology) any weapon (prop) we can find. The aim is not to earn the respect, admiration, and love of everybody—it's to get people to do, to participate, whether positively or negatively. All is relevant, only "the play's the thing."

. . . Stand on a street corner with 500 leaflets and explode. Give some to a sad-looking female. Tell guys that pass, "Hey, can you help her out? She can't do it by herself and her father's a communist cell leader and will beat her up if she doesn't pass them out." Recruit a person to read the leaflet aloud while all this distribution is going on. Run around tearing the leaflets, selling them, trading them. Rip one in half and give half to one person and half to another and tell them to make love. Do it all fast. Like slapstick movies. Make sure everyone has a good time. People love to laugh—it's a riot. Riot—that's an interesting word-game if you want to play it.

Don't be for or against. Riots—environmental and psychological—are Holy, so don't screw around with explanations. Theater also has some advantages. It is involving for those people that are ready for it while at the same time dismissed as nonthreatening by those that could potentially wreck the stage. It's dynamite. By allowing all: loving, cheating, anger, violence, stealing, trading, you become situation-oriented and as such become more effective. You believe in participatory democracy (especially when talking to a New Left audience), only you call it "everyone doing his thing." You let people decide, no strings attached. During the riots in Newark we smuggled in food, giving it to our underground soul brothers SNCC and NCUP (Newark Community Union Project).

"We brought a lot of canned goods, Tom, so the people can eat them or throw them at the cops."

Like many of the people in the riot, we dug the scene. Had a ball passing out food. Seven truckloads in all. And that's another key to the riddle: Dig what you're doing! Make war on paranoia. Don't be afraid. Don't get uptight. There's a war against property going on. I ask an old black woman in Newark, "What's going on?" and she tells me they stole her shoes and she's roaring with laughter. Spades and Diggers are one. Diggersareniggers. Both stand for the destruction of property. There are many ways to destroy property: to change is to destroy—give it away free. The free thing (another clue) is the most revolutionary thing in America today. Free dances, free food, free theater (constantly), free stores, free bus rides, free dope, free housing, and most important, free money. Theater will capture the attention of the country, the destruction of the monetary system will bring it to its knees. Really fuck with money. Burn it, smoke it to get high, trade with it, set up boxes of it in the streets marked "Free Money," panhandle it, steal it, throw it away.

SCENE: *Washington Square Park. Actors: one very nicely dressed white liberal, one down-and-out-looking Digger. Audience: a large crowd of similar liberals, of various sexes. The title of the play:* Food for Newark Spades.

DIG.: Sir, could you please spare a dollar for some food for Negroes in Newark?

LIB.: Gee, I'm sorry, I don't have much money on me.

DIG.: (still pleading, hat in hand) We're collecting food

at Liberty House.* Couldn't you buy a dollar's worth and bring it over?

LIB.: If I had a dollar, I certainly would.

DIG.: (exploding) I think you're full of shit. Here's ten dollars (pulling out real American money and shoving it in his face); go buy some food and bring it over to Liberty House.

LIB.: (getting a bit annoyed but still wanting to be polite) Oh no, I couldn't take money from you.

DIG.: (throwing the money on the ground) Well, there it is on the ground, do something with it.

The Digger walks away dropping clues to understanding the street drama: Liberty House, Black, Newark, Food, Free, Money.

The rumors begin to fly as rumors always do. Rumors have power. Like myths, people become involved in them, adding, subtracting, multiplying. Get them involved. Let them participate. If it's spelled out to the letter there is no room for participation. Nobody participates in ideology. Never lie—Diggers never lie. Once committed in a street drama, never turn back. Be prepared to die if it's necessary to gain your point.

! ! ! ! ! ! ! ! !

Don't rely on words. Words are the absolute in horseshit. Rely on doing—go all the way every time. Move fast. If you spend too long on one play, it becomes boring to you and the audience. When they get bored, they are turned off. They are not receiving information. Get their attention, leave a few clues and vanish. Change your costume, use the props around you. Each morning begin naked. Destroy your name, become unlisted, go underground. Find brothers. Soul brothers. Black people, Puerto Ricans,

---

*Liberty House is what first brought me to New York. It was set up in the West Village to serve as a retail outlet for crafts made in cooperatives in Mississippi. It is a branch of the SNCC operations; some of us under the leadership of Jesse Morris formed the Poor People's Corporation and quickly trained poor blacks in craft skills and business management. We were told by all sorts of fancy economic experts that it was impossible to train these people, never mind giving them control of the business. The experts might be interested in knowing that the program not only has survived three years but has expanded quite successfully without help from the government and in an extremely hostile environment (Mississippi). This type of program is next best to *free* and we are developing a similar one for the Lower East Side.

Dropouts, Bowery Bums. Find out where they're at. Don't fuck with their thing. P.R.s dig manhood, don't play sissy. Black people dig pot, don't give them acid. Dropouts dig flowers, don't give them I. F. Stone weeklies. Bowery bums dig wine, don't give them Bibles. Become aware of the most effective props. On the Lower East Side pot is an effective prop, it is the least common denominator. It makes us all outlaws, brothers, niggers. Smoke it in public. It really has an effect on P.R.s, really challenges their concept of courage.

"Hey man, you're brave enough to kill someone, and not brave enough to smoke pot in the park!"

That kind of thing is a good deal more effective than sermons on the holiness of passive resistance. Use non-verbal props and media. Music is another denominator. Conga-Rock, get together. The Diggers and Pee Wee's gang (largest P.R. gang on New York's Lower East Side) threw a large dance at the Cheetah, a discotheque, on August 15. *Conga-Rock. Something for everybody. Do your thing. Don't give speeches. Don't have meetings. Don't have panel shows. They are all dead. Drama is anything you can get away with.* Remember that last peace demonstration? Do you recall the speeches of the Bread and Puppet Theater and Stokely yelling "Hell no, we won't go!" That was drama, not explanation. The point is nobody gives a shit anymore about troop strength, escalation, crying over napalm. A peace rally speech to me is like reading the *National Guardian* which is like watching the TV reports on Highway Fatalities which is like praying for riots to end which is like BULLSHIT! Herbert Marcuse says flower children have the answer. He smoked hashish at the big world happening in London in early August. Pray tell, what is a good Marxist to do?

Accept contradictions, that's what life is all about. Have a good time. Scrawled on the wall of the American pavilion at Expo '67 is our slogan in bright Day-glo: "It is the duty of all revolutionists to make love." Do weird things. Silly-putty sabotage and monkey warfare. John Roche, who is now intellectual-in-residence fink at the White House, once said that if Hitler had been captured in 1937, brought to Trafalgar Square, and had his pants pulled down, he could never have risen to power. Every time he tried one of those spectacular speeches the people would have just laughed at him because the image of "Mein Fuhrer" with his pants down around his ankles would have been too much.

Think about it.

PROPERTY is THEFT
PROPERTY is ROBBERY
(Choose one of the three—
choose the one that rhymes)

MAY 20, 1967: At first I thought throwing out money at the Stock Exchange was just a minor bit of theater. I had more important things to do, like raising bail money for a busted brother. Reluctantly, I called up and made arrangements for a tour under the name of George Metesky, Chairman of East Side Service Organization (ESSO). We didn't even bother to call the press. About eighteen of us showed up. When we went in the guards immediately confronted us. "You are hippies here to have a demonstration and we cannot allow that in the Stock Exchange." "Who's a hippie? I'm Jewish and besides we don't do demonstrations, see we have no picket signs," I shot back. The guards decided it was not a good idea to keep a Jew out of the Stock Exchange, so they agreed we could go in. We stood in line with all the other tourists, exchanging stories. When the line moved around the corner, we saw more newsmen than I've ever seen in such a small area. We started clowning. Eating money, kissing and hugging, and that sort of stuff. The newsmen were told by the guards that they could not enter the gallery with us. We were ushered in and immediately started throwing money over the railing. The big tickertape stopped and the brokers let out a mighty cheer. The guards started pushing us and the brokers booed. When we got out, I carried on in front of the press.

"Who are you?"

"I'm Cardinal Spellman."

"Where did you get the money?"

"I'm Cardinal Spellman, you don't ask me where I get my money."

"How much did you throw out?"

"A thousand dollars in small bills."

"How many of you are there?"

"Two, three, we don't even exist! We don't even exist!"

We danced in front of the Stock Exchange, celebrating the end of money. I burned a fiver. Some guy said it was disgusting and I agree with him, calling my comrades "Filthy Commies."

The TV show that night was fantastic. It went all over the world. TV news shows always have a pattern. First the "serious" news, all made up, of course, a few commercials, often constructed better than the news, then the Stock Market Report. Then the upswing human interest story to keep everybody happy as cows. Our thing came after the Stock Market Report, it was a natural. CBS, which is the most creative network, left in references to Cardinal Spellman; I was surprised at that. Every news report differed. Some said we threw out monopoly money, some said twenty–thirty dollars, some said over $100, some said the bills were all ripped up first. It was a perfect mythical event, since every reporter, not being allowed to actually witness the scene, had to make up his own fantasy. Some had interesting fantasies, some boring. One tourist who joined the exorcism got the point: "I'm from Missouri and I've been throwing away money in New York for five days now. This is sure a hell of a lot quicker and more fun."

JUNE 24, 1967: Last week we went to a New Left–Old Left Conference in Denton, Michigan: Paul Krassner, Jim Fouratt, Keith Lampe, Bob O'Keene and I. We were met by San Francisco Diggers Emmett Grogan, Peter Berg, Billy Tumbleweed, and a beautiful cat who just played a tambourine and smiled. It was a monumental meeting, probably never to be repeated. Jim and I were the only outwardly identifiable hippies from New York. Jim in his beautiful Goldilocks hair and purple pants, I in beads, boots, bellbottoms, and a cocky Mexican cowboy hat. Sitting in the Kalamazoo airport you sense the vibrations. Hippies are the new minority group. Diggersare-niggers. I'm getting to understand what a black person goes through on a level not even reached by getting kicked around in the civil rights movement for four years. Anita and I were in Times Square the other night in costume. We panhandled a few cigarettes, which is really a gas. Panhandling really blows the mind when it's carried on by middle class drop-outs. A little guy full of *Daily News* bitterness shakes his fist at me. "You fuckin' coward, won't defend our country, won't go and fight, you cocksucker." I didn't even have one teeny-weeny peace button. He knew. The sides are drawn. When you meet another hippie in the street, especially outside the Village, you smile and say hello—a kind of comradeship that I've seen black people show when they are alone in the white world.

Back to the meeting: As we entered you could sense the vibrations as very mixed. You just have to walk around freaky-looking and you can tell where people's heads are. Tom Hayden was speaking. He was talking of the hard decision that faced NCUP over whether or not to join the poverty program in Newark. He carefully outlined the pros and cons and said that in the end there was no correct answer, there was no ideology you could turn to for reference. Then in came the Diggers. Tom is finished and all hell breaks out. We are hugging the Diggers, Grogan's yelling "One of us is in the can, is there a fuckin' lawyer here? What the hell you faggots looking at, get off your asses, we need help." They grab some fat cat who identifies himself as a lawyer and go off to the local pokey to bail out fellow Digger. Peter Berg, ex-San Francisco Mime Trooper, founder of the Digger Free Store, "Trip Without a Ticket," starts to talk. He looks like a young angry Sitting Bull, only different . . . unique, a white Snick nigger. Rambling on—wow! It's pouring out like honey and vinegar, all mixed up. Scatalogical.* He's on a trip! Holy Shit. Excitement, Drama, Revolution. The message: Property is the enemy—burn it, destroy it, give it away. Don't let them make a machine out of you, get out of the system, do your thing. Don't organize students, teachers, Negroes, organize your head. Find out where you are, what you want to do and go out and do it. Johnson's a commie, the Kremlin is more fucked up than Alabama. Get out. Don't organize the schools, burn them. Leave them, they will rot. . . . The kids are getting stoned. We're all talking now. Lots of resistance. Kid says to me, "I like what you're saying and I'm going to drop out in a year." "What the hell you waiting for?" "Well, I want to finish school first." Reminded me of an SDS picket line I saw on a campus last year, protesting the tests used to determine draft status. Most of the demonstrators put their signs down and went in to take the test. These are the potential revolutionists? *Eich meir* a revolution!

Grogan re-enters, reconvenes the meeting single-handed. He climbs up on the table. Starts slow, sucks everyone in by answering a few questions. I'm sitting next to him, sleepy from sitting on my ass in Kalamazoo. All of a sudden he erupts and kicks the fuckin' table over. He knocks down a girl, slapping SDS'ers right and left. "Faggots! Fags! Take off your ties, they are chains around your necks. You haven't got the balls to go mad. You're gonna make a revolution?—you'll piss in your pants when the violence erupts. You, spade—you're a nigger, what are you doing here? Your people

*It's funny—I'd always thought that word meant "in small pieces" like "scattered," but Krassner told me it meant "dirty." I think it fits both ways.

need you. There's a war on. They got fuckin' concentration camps ready, the world's going to end any day. Shut up and listen, I'll read a poem, 'Day of Judgment Upon Us,'"—Gary Snyder read by Elmer Gantry. Now we're all into it. The Old Left is very up tight. They say we are sent by the CIA.

The kids laugh. "Why don't you guys give away acid the way you do food?"

"Well, we gave out 5,000 capsules at the Be-In last month."

The Old Left is shitting, really scared of acid. They are losing control, Marx with flowers in his hair, can't deal with contradictory stimuli, simultaneous bombardment. Marxism is irrelevant to the U.S.A., as irrelevant as Capitalism.

The Diggers left after we had talked the whole night. The SDS'ers slept all night very soundly. They had nothing to talk about in those wee morning hours when you rap on and on and a dialogue of non-verbal vibrations begins. You Relate!! You Plan!! You Think!! You get Stoned!! You Feel!! And SDS sleeps in beds with clean sheets they have brought because they know how to "do" conferences. The Old Left snoozes in the best beds in the house. They have to get their sleep so they can run back to their nice fat system jobs, "burrowing from within," asking the Negroes (now called Blacks) to do it for them. They want to discuss "Yankee Imperialism." All the old Jewish Leftists are a little nervous about the Middle East business. It was obvious by the way it was avoided. Lost a lot of Jewish pacifists in the last few weeks.

The seminars drag on . . . a total bore . . . Jim and I are avoided, except by a small group. They do socialism, we blow pot in the grass, they do imperialism, we go swimming, they do racism, we do flowers for everybody and clean up the rooms.

Back to the Conference: Hayden asked, "How do you make it stick, how do you prevent cooptation?" I thought he said *copulation*. I answered that you build a better system. Assume America is already dead, dead for those kids who are flocking to the Lower East Side and Haight-Ashbury, and give them a new, positive, authentic frame of reference. If it's done effectively they won't go back. What is there to go back to? And the kids are flocking in or dropping out by the droves, on their way to San Francisco, on their way to New York. The media does it for us. Wow! "If you're going to San Francisco, be sure to wear a flower in your hair." That's Number 1 in the country. The media is the message. Use it! No fundraising, no full-page ads in *The New York Times*, no press releases. Just do your thing; the press eats it up. MAKE NEWS.

Quote: POT FEELS GOOD, IT'S FUN TO TURN ON.

They print it, not aware of the disruption they cause. The press spreads the word, tells them where the action is and they leave America. They stream to its two shores, can't go any further, up against the ocean, what to do, down and out. "There's a new world somewhere, if you will only hold my hand," sings the radio just as I write this line. Man, it's all around us. Total bombardment . . . can it lead to total commitment? New forms emerge. S.F. and N.Y. become the schools. The streets are the classrooms, religion's in your head.

We sit on the tribal council, Indian circle, incense burning, soft lights. The first person speaks for as long as he wants, then the next, no interruptions, consensus is reached, respect for other heads is achieved, we can do, we can be community. There are no problems, only things to do. Tribes give inner guidance, activists give helping hands to newcomers. We grow, we multiply, we build on the ashes of the old. The structure of the meeting (read Paul Goodman, *Utopian Ideas and Practical Proposals*) gives a clue to where its collective head is at. Ours is a circle: respect, love, trust, delicate. A black meeting image: sweat, yelling, stomping, "Burn, baby, burn."

Two nights ago spoke at the *Catholic Worker*. Loved it, converts to be won, dialogue to be opened. Structure sloppy, irregular tables, people on floor, on tables, image—dedication, doing, primitive. Dorothy Day [editor of the *Catholic Worker*] is a Digger. Last night at Hudson Institute think tank. Herman Kahn's brain session: long tables arranged in a square panel. We sit apart in the back of the room—niggers to the end. Angry at myself for going. Collaborating with the enemy for ego purposes. They want to know how strong we are, we put them on; we are ridiculous, ignore us, Herman Kahn. Look how freaky we are with our flowers and bells. We know we're right. One of the members confesses to me, "We're glad you brought your girl friends. They are a lot prettier than ours." Of course they are, they are beautiful women, we are beautiful men. You guys are fags, machines. We end up at a drive-in movie digging Elvis Presley.

SEPTEMBER 28, 1967: Writing on the run or rather fly as I speed back from San Francisco across America. John Wayne in *El Dorado* just ended and my mind is filled with guns—long guns, shotguns, derringers, machine guns. "You bettah get yourself a gun, boy . . ." Rap Brown, John Wayne, Diggers. Even Marvin Garson [founder, editor and publisher of the *San Francisco Express Times*] got himself a rifle, and he points it out in the bay at huge aircraft carriers filled with death bound for the war out there. "Is there really a war out there?" I sit in this airplane on imitation leather seats, looking up plastic stewardesses' skirts, at executive playing out his fantasy in the *Wall Street Journal*, at triple chins of tight-assed old hag who gobbles her dietary ulcer lunch. You bet your ass this country is involved in an evil war. I'd never have to leave this seat to know that, never have to read a newspaper.

We are throwing everything we've got at the Pentagon—evil hulk that sits like a cancerous death-trap on the beautiful Potomac. An Exorcism to cast out the evil spirits on October 21st. The Pentagon shall not survive, neither for that matter will the fag-ridden peace movement. "Ring-around-the-Pentagon-a-pocket-full-of-pot." Wrote a beautiful poem that I lost last week when Marty Carey and I got arrested there. Met a Digger in San Francisco who went to the Chicago New Politics mess. He sat on the stage with a flute in one hand and a tire iron in the other, drawing an imaginary circle around himself. "I declare this area a liberated zone. Anyone enters and I'll kill him." A total political stance. I am ready for the struggle. As far as the revolution goes, it started when I was born. Broke with the Mobilization coalition for Washington (which means I don't go to their meetings anymore). At one meeting I declared, "The truth lies through insanity." They are scared shitless of the mystery. They suppressed an article on Keith Lampe because of the word "SUCK." My Lord, what fucking prudes. Our suck magic is much too strong medicine for the middle-class peace movement.

Many wild happenings are planned in preparation: circling of Washington Monument, Empire State Building (vertically), Make Love Day orgy leading up to October 21st. On Columbus Day a mighty caravan of wagons will roll East out of San Francisco to rediscover America complete with real live Indian scouts, compliments of Chief Rolling Thunder of the Shoshone. Junk cars, stolen buses, motorcycles, rock bands, flower banners, dope, incense, and enough food for the long journey. Wagon train East. Yahoo! We will dye the Potomac red, burn the cherry trees, panhandle embassies, attack with water pistols, marbles, bubble gum wrappers, bazookas, girls will run naked and piss on the Pentagon walls, sorcerers, swamis, witches, voodoo, warlocks, medicine men, and speed freaks will hurl their magic at the faded brown walls. Rock bands will bomb out with "Joshua fit the Battle of Jericho." We will dance and sing and chant the mighty OM. We will fuck on the grass and beat ourselves against the doors. Everyone will scream "VOTE FOR ME." We shall raise the flag of nothingness over the Pentagon and a mighty cheer of liberation will echo through the land. "We are Free, Great God Almighty, Free at last." Schoolchildren will rip out their desks and throw ink at stunned instructors, office secretaries will disrobe and run into the streets, newsboys will rip up their newspapers and sit on the curbstones masturbating, storekeepers will throw open their doors making everything free, accountants will all collapse in one mighty heart attack, soldiers will throw down their guns. "The War is over. Let's get some ass." No permits, no *New York Times* ads, no mailing lists, no meetings. It will happen because the time is ripe. Come to the Day of Judgment. Forget about degrees, they are useless scraps of paper. Turn them into Litter Art. Don't hold back. Let the baby-Beatles shut your mouth and open your mind. On October 6th the Diggers in S.F. will present the Death of the Hippie and the Birth of the Free Man. S.F. will become the first Free City extending the boundaries of the Haight-Ashbury ghetto. Extend all boundaries, blow your mind. Conversation between me and other:

OTHER: What do you want?
ME: To win.
OTHER: To win what?
ME: Fuck you!

Skulldiggery shoots up the media. Chaos. Riots, earthquakes, black men grabbed in Philadelphia with enough poison for 4,000 people or cops, Digger hurls pie at colonel at University of California. "Splash." Last night at the Straight Theater in Haight-Ashbury sheer beauty of mind-body dancers acting out fears of paranoid America, huddled in a corner and casual as can be they take their clothes off and continue the dance. "We are free, we are Men, we are Women, we love, we hate, we are real"—plastic-coated America. America let's see your balls, America can I only see them on a tiny screen in a superjet acted out by John Wayne and Robert Mitchum in a land called El Dorado. El Dorado is now at the Straight Theater and it's all free.

OCTOBER 21, 1967

Don't miss *Bonnie and Clyde*
Don't miss STP
Don't miss getting laid
Don't miss lion steak
Don't miss Allen Ginsberg
Don't miss Billy the Kid
Don't miss Che Guevara
Don't miss the Exorcism of the
in living color

NOVEMBER 18, 1967: Artaud is alive at the walls of the Pentagon, bursting the seams of conventional protest, injecting new blood into the peace movement. Real blood, symbolic blood and—for camouflage—Day-glo blood. Something for everybody.

Homecoming Day at the Pentagon and the cheerleaders chant "Beat Army! Beat Army!" It's SDS at the 30-yard line and third down. Robin cuts the rope with a hunting knife and the Charge of the Flower Brigade is on.

One longhair smashes a window and is beaten to the ground. The Pentagon vibrates and begins to rise in the air. Someone gives a marshal a leaflet on U.S. imperialism, another squirts him with LACE, a high potency sex juice that makes you "pull your clothes off and make love" (according to *Time* magazine), people are stuffing flowers in rifle barrels, protesters throw tear gas at each other (according to the *Washington Post*).

A girl unzips an MP's fly and Sergeant Pepper asks the band to play *The Star Spangled Banner*. They lay down their Viet Cong flags and pick up their instruments. "*Oh, say, can you see . . .*" When it's over someone yells, "Play ball!"—and the pushing and shoving begins again.

FLASHBACK: Baby and I, complete with Uncle Sam hats and Flower Flags, jump a barbed-wire fence and are quickly surrounded by marshals and soldiers.

"We're Mr. and Mrs. America, and we claim this land in the name of Free America."

We plant the Flag and hold our ground. The troops are really shook. Do you club Uncle Sam? We're screaming incantations.

"You're under arrest. What's your name?"

"Mr. and Mrs. America, and Mrs. America's pregnant."

The troops lower their clubs in respect. A marshal writes in his book: "Mr. and Mrs. America—Trespassing." We sit down and make love. Another marshal unarrests us. A lieutenant arrests us. A corporal unarrests us. We continue making love.

After about 20 minutes we stand and offer to shake hands with the marshals. They refuse. We walk away glowing, off to liberate another zone. The crowd cheers. "You can do anything you want, baby, it's a free country. Just do it, don't bullshit."

The peace movement has gone crazy and it's about time. Our alternative fantasy will match in zaniness the war in Vietnam. Fantasy is Freedom. Anybody can do anything. "The Pentagon will rise 300 feet in the air."

No rules, speeches won't do, leaders are all full of shit. Pull your clothes off (MAKE LOVE, NOT WAR), punch a marshal, jump a wall, do a dance, sing a song, paint the building, blow it up, charge and get inside.

FLASHBACK: "67-68-69-70-"

"What do you think you guys are doing?"

"Measuring the Pentagon. We have to see how many people we'll need to form a ring around it."

"You're what!"

"It's very simple. You see, the Pentagon is a symbol of evil in most religions. You're religious, aren't you?"

"Unh."

"Well, the only way to exorcise the evil spirits here is to form a circle around the Pentagon. *87-88-89 . . .*"

The two scouts are soon surrounded by a corps of guards, FBI agents, soldiers and some mighty impressive brass.

"112-113-114-"

"Are you guys serious? It's against the law to measure the Pentagon."

"Are you guys serious? Show us the law. *237-238-239-240.* That does it. Colonel, how much is *240* times *5?"*

"What? What the hell's going on here!"

"1200," answers Bruce, an impressive-looking agent who tells us later he works in a security department that doesn't even have a name yet.

We show them our exorcism flyers. They bust us for littering.

"Shades of Alice's Restaurant. Are you guys kidding? That ain't litter, it's art."

"Litter."

"Art."

"Litter."

"How about Litter Art?" says Bruce after two hours.

We are free to go, but have to be very sneaky and ditch Bruce somewhere inside the Pentagon maze so he won't find the Acapulco Gold in the car.

The magic is beginning to work, but the media must be convinced. You simply cannot call them up and say, "Pardon me, but the Pentagon will rise in the air on October 21st." You've got to show them.

Friday, the 13th, Village Theater, warlocks, witches, speed freaks, Fugs and assorted kooks plus one non-believer named Krassner. "Out, Demons, Out!"—and, *zip,* up goes the mock Pentagon. "Higher! Higher! Higher!"

(Is it legal to cry *Higher* in a crowded theater?)

We burn the model and will use its ashes on Big Daddy the following week. Media is free. Use it. Don't pay for it. Don't buy ads. Make news.

FLASHBACK: "Give me the City Desk . . . Hello. I've defected from the Diggers because they have this new sex drug called LACE. They plan to use it at the Pentagon. It's against my morals to use it on people against their will, so I want to confess. It's got LSD and DMSO, a penetrating agent. It's lysergic acid crypto ethelene and it's purple. Why don't you come over and I'll show you how it works."

The press conference is at 8 P.M. Two couples sit on a couch. The four are squirted with the purple liquid. It disappears into their skin. They look dazed. Like robots they slowly peel off their clothes. The reporters pant. Like non-robots they begin to fuck. After a half hour the drug has worn off.

"Any questions, gentlemen?"

LACE, the new love drug, goes to the Pentagon.

This exorcism business is getting pretty exciting. Let's see *Progressive Labor* match LACE. The Pentagon happening transcended the issue of the War. "*The War Is Over*," sings Phil Ochs, and the protest becomes directed to the entire fabric of a restrictive, dull, brutal society.

The protesters become total political animals.

A totality emerges that renders the word *political* meaningless. "The war is over." Everybody's yelling and screaming. Someone writes LBJ LOVES HO CHI MINH on the wall.

> Ring around the Pentagon, a pocket full of pot
> Four and twenty generals all begin to rot.
> All the evil spirits start to tumble out
> Now the war is over, we all begin to shout.

The soldiers have a choice. "Join us! Join us!"—the cry goes up. Three do. Drop their helmets and guns and break ranks. They are caught by the marshals and dragged away into oblivion and the third degree.

It's the sixth hour of my trip. A super one, helped by large doses of revolution, no food or water, and a small purple tablet popped in my mouth by Charlie from the San Francisco *Oracle*.

A sense of integration possesses me that comes from pissing on the Pentagon: combining biological necessity with emotional feeling.

Baby and I retreat to the bowels of D.C. and grab a night's sleep after an orgy of champagne poured from an MP's helmet. It sure is one hell of a revolution.

Worried parents call the Defense Department to see if their children have been arrested and are given the number of the National Mobilization's office.

We come prepared to give our lives and debate the morality of parking on a crosswalk.

FLASHBACK: Sunday at the Pentagon is a different scene. A mind trip working on the troops. Ex-soldiers talk to MPs. So do girls, college kids and priests, for twelve long hours. Talking, singing, sharing, contrasting Free America vs. the Uniformed Machine. At midnight the Pentagon speaks after two days of silence.

"Your permit has expired. If you do not leave the area you will be arrested. All demonstrators are requested to leave the area at once. This is a recorded announcement."

"Fuck you, Pentagon. I'm not a demonstrator. I'm a tourist."

Everybody is herded into vans. The door slams shut but the lock doesn't work.

"The New Action Army sure is a pisser."

The MPs laugh and finally get the bolt in place. Off we go to Occoquan and jail land. "Carry me back to Ol' Virginny . . ." I hate jail. I try to chew my way through the van door and am doing pretty well when some of the girls get scared.

I get processed through as FREE Digger. "I'm a girl," I insist when one of the marshals gives me the clue. A matron peeks and discovers differently. "No, honey, I'm just flatchested, honest."

Jail is a goof. Easiest jailing of all time. The Army is into brainwashing. Clean sheets, good breakfast, propaganda radio station.

We call the guard and demand to be treated as prisoners of war. He listens patiently as we ask for the International Red Cross and other courtesies accorded under the Geneva Convention. He scratches his head and walks away.

Three guys begin to dig a tunnel. Everybody's trying to remember Stalag 17. At four o'clock I'm led out, meet my baby and we go to court. "The family that disobeys together stays together." Even the judge laughs, says ten bucks each and we're free.

Everybody's making the sign of the V. The battle is over. The question everyone's asking is when's the next happening?

Small battles will occur in countless communities around the country; most centered at local induction centers.

Two days after the Pentagon three clergymen walk into the induction center in Baltimore and dump blood in the files. Blood! "You bet your ass—that's what war's about, isn't it?"

New York treated Dean Rusk to a bloodbath on November 14th at the Hilton Hotel. Organized by the newly formed Protesters, Troublemakers and Anarchists. Headlines blare: "Cops Bust Up PTA Meeting."

Jesus visits St. Patrick's Cathedral. How about running Shirley Temple for Congress again? Pickets at Bellevue shout "Free LBJ!" A scenario at campus recruiting tables might include a tent with soft music and girls in bikinis. That's a real alternative.

Oh, by the way, January is Alien Registration Month. See you at the Post Office.

Get ready for a big event at the Democratic National Convention in Chicago next August. How about a truly open convention? Thousands of VOTE FOR ME buttons, everybody prints his own campaign literature and distributes pictures of themselves. Then we all rush the convention, get to the rostrum and nominate ourselves.

After all, it seems the only cat who lives for nothing in this country is LBJ. I've never met anyone who has ever seen him pay for anything. He doesn't even have a wallet. So if you want to live free, then stand up proudly on that convention platform, but don't start your speech with "My friends, come, let us reason together,"or you'll lose the election.

DECEMBER 10, 1967: I'm sitting here in Room 219, 100 Centre Street, waiting to go to trial. I've been here so often, the Security guards call me by my first name. It's the usual northern courtroom scene: Ninety-year-old judge hunched over the bench; lawyers scuttling around the pit with paper and briefcases, all got brown suits (whatever happened to gray flannels?); the pews are filled with the usual number of Puerto Ricans, black people, and a scattering of longhairs. The wall behind the judge says, in gold letters (so help me dog) IN GOD WE RUST.

Yesterday down the hall Allen Ginsberg read a blistering poem, to the disgust of the cops and the cheers of the peace demonstrators, pickpockets, prostitutes, dope pushers, and card hustlers. In Newark I hear they go one better and the judge reads the defendant's poetry to him. (Leroi Jones's trial.) After waiting six hours for a hearing I get a postponement because the judge came two hours late to court. I'm in no hurry. The charge is hitting a cop with a bottle. . . .

It is a chilly night. Dean Rusk has come to town. We rendezvous at 57th Street and Seventh Avenue, blocks away from the Hilton. Some of us recognize each other. Demonstrations always have a reunion atmosphere. Most people got army jackets; there are more longhairs than I expected. Everybody's got a prop: plastic bags filled with blood, smoke bombs, flares. Scouts run down the blocks scouting the enemy's position, and report back. There are about a hundred of us now, and the scouts also report bands of rovers at three or four other intersections. We decide to hit the intersection at 6 P.M. sharp. Someone suggests attacking only limousines and Cadillacs. Suddenly the intersection erupts. Cars jam up. Horns beep. Smoke bombs go off. Flares are lit. A straight couple ask me what's going on? I shout, "There's a WAR on! Can't you see?" A long black limousine has blood splattered on its window and *Peace* in Day-glo letters sprayed on its trunk lid. "Let's get out of here," someone yells and everyone runs toward Sixth Avenue. It's a wild scene. Cops charging people, demonstrators, Christmas shoppers, people going to hear Dean Rusk. Cops in formation wading into crowds, clubbing away. The crowd retreats to the sidewalk and cops on horses move right in on them. Crunch! Kids lying in the street bleeding all over. One's out colder than a mackerel. We rush out to pull him in when out of nowhere this guy grabs me from behind.

I think he is a right-wing heckler, and we're having a fist fight when the blue boys arrive. It seems he is a plain-clothes-man. Before I know it I'm standing in the 16th Precinct, and Badge #26466, who has missed some of the action, kicks me in the nuts. In the back room three cops are working over one demonstrator who has his arms handcuffed behind his back. They beat him for a good ten minutes with fists and clubs. All the cops are aching for blood. One is yelling how his brother got killed in Vietnam and challenges anybody to a fight in the back alley. They call us "scum-bags" and "fairies" and "Jew-bastards" and "commies" and one says, "You pull dese guys' pants off and they ain't got no pecker, just a little piece of flesh." There are other swears that I couldn't even recognize because of the culture gap but it seems they sure got this sex hang-up. Pretty soon we're all herded into a van. All except the guy who got beat up real bad. They want to clean him up a bit before sending him down. In the Tombs we are put in a special block with other demonstrators. It's old home week and everybody's cheering and making the V sign and singing old freedom songs and Beatle tunes. I'm sitting next to a seventeen-year-old kid.

"What they grab you for?"

"Breaking a window. I just jumped up on this Cadillac and kicked in the window."

"That's pretty far out. You go to the Pentagon?"

"No, this is my first demonstration."

I kind of nodded and leaned my aching head back against the wall. Ron Carver, from Columbia SDS, was leading an old one, "We'll never turn back.'' It sort of separates the veterans from the newcomers, it being the theme song of the Mississippi Project and all that. It sure made a body reminisce. I knew Ron in SNCC and then up in a peace campaign in Massachusetts in '66. He's like about a hundred other veterans I know who are still active. We rarely see each other except at demonstrations. This isn't some vast organized conspiracy, like some people think, just a lot of guys whose heads are in the same place but with different styles. Ron and I talk with our eyes. We're brothers. We've been through this so many times it's routine. We're both working out the strategy for our next street scene even as we finish the sad ''We'll never turn back'' and swing into ''This little light of mine.''

''You hair's gettin' longer,'' he jokes.

''Yeah, I'm a flower child.''

3

TALKING IN MY SLEEP —AN EXERCISE IN SELF-CRITICISM

A mythical interview of questions that are asked and answers that are given. Interviews are always going on. Here's one with myself.

Do you have an ideology?
No. Ideology is a brain disease.

Do you have a movement?
Yes. It's called Dancing.

Isn't that a put-on?
No.

Can you explain that?
Suppose we start the questions again.

OK. Do you have an ideology?
We are for peace, equal rights, and brotherhood.

Now I understand.
I don't. That was a put-on. I don't understand what I said.

I'm getting confused.
Well, let's go on.

Are you for anything? Do you have a vision of this new society you talk of?
Yes. We are for a free society.

Could you spell that out?
F-R-E-E.

What do you mean free?
You know what that means. America: the land of the free. Free means you don't pay, doesn't it?

Yes, I guess so. Do you mean all the goods and services would be free?
Precisely. That's what the technological revolution would produce if we let it run unchecked. If we stopped trying to control it.

Who controls it?
The profit incentive, I guess. Property hang-ups. One task we have is to separate the concept of productivity from work. Work is money. Work is postponement of pleasure. Work is always done for someone else: the boss, the kids, the guy next door. Work is competition. Work was linked to productivity to serve the Industrial Revolution. We must separate the two. We must abolish work and all the drudgery it represents.

Who will do what we now call dirty work, like picking up the garbage?
Well, there are a lot of possibilities. There won't be any dirty work. If you're involved in a revolution you have a different attitude toward work. It is not separate from your vision . . . All work now is dirty work. Lots of

people might dig dealing with garbage. Maybe there won't be any garbage. Maybe we'll just let it pile up. Maybe everybody will have a garbage disposal. There are numerous possibilities.

Don't you think competition leads to productivity?
Well, I think it did during the Industrial Revolution but it won't do for the future. Competition also leads to war. Cooperation will be the motivating factor in a free society. I think cooperation is more akin to the human spirit. Competition is grafted on by institutions, by a capitalist economy, by religion, by schools. Every institution I can think of in this country promotes competition.

Are you a communist?
Are you an anti-communist?

Does it matter?
Well, I'm tempted to say Yes if I sense you are. I remember when I was young I would only say I was Jewish if I thought the person asking the question was anti-Semitic.

What do you think of Russia?
Ugh! Same as here. Dull, bureaucratic-sterile-puritanical. Do you remember when Kosygin came here and met with Johnson in New Jersey? They looked the same. They think the same. Neither was the wave of the future. Johnson is a communist.

What is the wave of the future?
The National Liberation Front, the Cuban Revolution, the young here and around the world.

Doesn't everybody always place great hope in the young?
Yes, I think so. But young people today are very different from previous generations. I think generational revolt has gone on throughout history. Oretga y Gasset in *Man and Crisis* shows that very dramatically. But there are significant differences. The hydrogen bomb, TV, satellites, jet planes—everything is more immediate, more involving. We are the first internationalists. Vietnam rice paddies are as real to me as the Empire State Building. If

you don't live in New York, maybe they are more real. We live in a global village.

Do you like McLuhan?
Let's say I think he is more relevant than Marx. Quentin Fiore, his assistant, is more McLuhan than McLuhan. He's the one who puts the ideas into action. McLuhan still struggles with the printed word. But he is an explorer. He experiments. For an old guy he does well. He understands how to communicate information. It's just that his living style—Catholic, university life, grants, the risks that he takes—is merely academic. Let's say I respect him, but don't love him. What we seek are new living styles. We don't want to talk about them. We want to live them.

Do you consider what you are doing politically relevant?
No.

Is that the best answer you can think of?
Well, when you ask a question like that you trigger off umpteen responses in my head. I believe in the politics of ecstasy.

Can you explain that a little more?
No, but I can touch it, I can smell it, I can even dance it. I can even fight it. Politics to me is the way somebody lives his life. Not what they vote for or support or even believe in. I'm more interested in art than politics but, well, see, we are all caught in a word box. I find it difficult to make these kinds of divisions. Northrop, in *Meeting of East and West*, said, "Life is an undifferentiated aesthetic continuum." Let me say that the Vietcong attacking the U.S. Embassy in Saigon is a work of art. I guess I like revolutionary art.

This word game, as you call it. Doesn't that present problems in conveying what you want to say?
Yes, but not in what I want to do. Let me say . . . Did you ever hear Andy Warhol talk?

Yes, or at least I think it was him.
Well, I would like to combine his style and Castro's. Warhol understands

modern media. Castro has the passion for social change. It's not easy. One's a fag and the other is the epitome of virility. If I was forced to make the choice I would choose Castro, but right now in this period of change in the country the styles of the two can be blended. It's not guerrilla warfare but, well, maybe a good term is monkey warfare. If the country becomes more repressive we must become Castros. If it becomes more tolerant we must become Warhols.

Do you see the country becoming more repressive?
Well, it's very hard to be objective about that. The cops around here are certainly a bunch of bastards. It's winter now and traditionally that's a time of paranoia because it's a time of less action than the summer. Everything has always been geared to the summer. School's out. People in the streets. More action. When you are involved you don't get paranoid. It's when you sit back and try to figure out what's going on, or what you should do. The winter is the hardest time for revolutionists in this country. We probably should hibernate. Everything builds toward the summer. This year it seems more so. Every day we talk of Chicago and the Festival. Every day the news carries a prediction of the "long hot summer." The other day I saw a report from Detroit. People, one white line, one black line, lining up at a gun shop. Meanwhile the mayor is trying to cool things with a nice friendly speech on brotherhood. It was some contrast. Every day has a new report on some new police weapon system. Then there is uncertainty and the tendency to re-examine your tactics. Right now I feel like Dwight Eisenhower on an acid trip. "On the one hand this—on the other hand that." I think it's a case of information overload. See, I am conditioned to perform well in chaos—actual chaos. Say a riot. In a riot I know exactly what to do. I'm not good for the winter. This is my last winter in the North. I have to live in total summer if I am to survive.

Will the summer action bring on more repression?
Oh, I suppose so. I see this country as getting simultaneously more repressive and more tolerant. People run off to Hanoi to collaborate with the enemy. Everybody's smoking pot on the streets. People go on TV and radio shows and spell out in detail plans of sabotage. And simultaneously there is repression. The combination of the two is going to produce highly volatile conditions and that's why many different tactics are needed. Right

now revolution is anything you can get away with. It has to be that way because of the nature of the opposition.

What is going to accelerate that process?
Well, Vietnam, the black revolution, and most importantly, WE ARE! All three present this system with more unsolvable problems than it can deal with. You see, there is no solution to the Vietnam war. To leave or to stay is a defeat. No matter what the government does in the ghettos it loses. More aid programs increase the appetite for more demands. More repression produces more anger and defensive violence. The same with the young. I know a girl, Peggy Dobbins, who was a teacher at Brooklyn College. She let the students determine the curriculum; before you knew it, the students wanted to grade themselves. She agreed to go along and of course got the ax from the administration. The more you get, the more you want. The more you are prevented from getting what you want, the more you fight to get it. These are trends that are irreversible, because the government cannot deal with these problems—I mean, the government "deals" with problems rather than solving them.

That's pretty political in its analysis. It's New Left in its wording.
Ah, well, it's a regression. I haven't presented any new ideas. But, well, that's the point. All the ideas are in and have been for some time. I guess I just rap on that from force of habit. I was once in the New Left but I outgrew it. Or perhaps it outgrew me. We differ on many things.

Like what?
Fun. I think fun and leisure are great. I don't like the concept of a movement built on sacrifice, dedication, responsibility, anger, frustration and guilt. All those down things. I would say, Look, you want to have more fun, you want to get laid more, you want to turn on with friends, you want an outlet for your creativity, then get out of school, quit your job. Come on out and help build and defend the society you want. Stop trying to organize everybody but yourself. Begin to live your vision. For example, the other night I was at a benefit for a peace group. Great music, light shows, friends all over the place. It was a good time. Some of the money raised goes to arrange rallies at which speakers give boring political speeches. People think it's a drag but that's the sacrifice to get out the politically relevant

statement. The point is, nobody listens to politically relevant statements. In Chicago we'll have a huge free music festival. Everyone already knows our feelings on the issues because we are there. It will have a tremendous impact if we can also project the image that we are having all the fun too. When I say fun, I mean an experience so intense that you actualize your full potential. You become LIFE. LIFE IS FUN. Political irrelevance is more effective than political relevance.

I notice as we get further into the interview that your answers get more linear and longer.
You're observant. I'm getting tired.

A few more: I hear you're writing a book. What's it about?
Well, it's called *Revolution for the Hell of It*. Sometimes I think I'm writing it just to see that title on a book jacket. Actually, if I have my way, the book jacket won't have the title on it. The book jacket will have two sleeves, a collar, buttons down the front, and the word *book* on the back.

Why are you writing it?
Well, 'cause I have no idea how to make a movie. It has some parts I like but the book form is difficult and I write on the run. There is also the time gap. You know, months of delay before it comes out. By then it's a whole new ball game. As far as the medium of print is concerned, I would say I like free street leaflets the best.

Which medium do you like the best of all?
Making love.

Anything else?
Well, I like to experience pleasure, to have fun, I enjoy blowing people's minds. You know, walking up to somebody and saying, "Would you hold this dollar for me while I go in that store and steal something?" The crazier the better. I like being crazy. Letting go. Losing control. Just doing what pops into my mind. I trust my impulses. I find the less I try to think through a situation, the better it comes off.

I've seen things you've written under other names. Is that part of the put-on?
I do that a lot. It is fun because I really get pleasure in doing the act or helping to see it come off. Using false names or other people's names makes sense to me. I'm not so sure about it now. You get known. As soon as you do anything in this country you become a celebrity. It's not really the same as being a leader. You can only stimulate actions. Stopping them or controlling them is something leaders can do. I'm not a leader. Nobody is under my command. I haven't the vaguest idea how to stop a demonstration, say, except to go home. I'm really not interested in stopping anything, so I'm not a leader. But this celebrity thing has certain problems. Using false names just tends to increase the myth after a while. Sometimes I do now, and sometimes I don't. If I can get away with it, I do.

Will you use a false name on the book?
If I can get away with it.

Isn't this celebrity or star system alien to your visions of a new society?
Most definitely. I find as you get more and more well known you get less personal freedom. You spend more time doing other people's things than your own. You know, people calling in the middle of the night with their problems. Imagine this scene: You are trying to steal some groceries and some old lady comes up and says how much she likes what you're doing. That's why I use disguises, so I can keep in shape by having to hustle without the myth. The day I can't shoplift, panhandle, or pass out leaflets on my own is the day I'll retire. The myth, like everything else, is free. Anybody can claim he is it and use it to hustle.

What's the solution? Is there any to the celebrity game?
I don't know. I envision a new life after Chicago. I don't intend to deal with symbolic confrontations. I'm interested in just living with a few friends and building a community. If there is to be confrontation, let it be with the local sheriff rather than LBJ. Maybe this is just a fantasy, though. Maybe it won't happen. I guess everyone dreams of a peaceful life in the country. Especially in the winter.

You're planning to drop out?
Well, dropping out is a continual process. I don't see anything really definite in the future. I just don't want to get boxed-in to playing a predetermined role. Let's say, so much of what we do is theater—in life I just don't want to get caught in a Broadway show that lasts five years, even if it is a success. The celebrity bag is another form of careerism. But you see, celebrity status is very helpful in working with media. It's my problem and I'll deal with it just like any other problem. I'll do the best I can.

Is that why the Yippies were created? To manipulate the media?
Exactly. You see, we are faced with this task of getting huge numbers of people to come to Chicago along with hundreds of performers, artists, theater groups, engineers. Essentially, people involved in trying to work out a new society. How do you do this starting from scratch, with no organization, no money, nothing? Well, the answer is that you create a myth. Something that people can play a role in, can relate to. This is especially true of media people. I'll give you an example. A reporter was interviewing us once and he liked what we were doing. He said "I'm going to tell what good ideas you guys really have. I'm going to tell the truth about the Yippies." We said, "That won't help a bit. Lie about us." It doesn't matter as long as he gets Yippie! and Chicago linked together in a magical way. The myth is about LIFE vs. DEATH. That's why we are headed for a powerful clash.

You don't want the truth told?
Well, I don't want to get philosophical but there is really no such animal. Especially when one talks of creating a myth. How can you have a true myth? When newspapers distort a story they become participants in the creation of the myth. We love distortions. Those papers that claim to be accurate, *i.e.*, *The New York Times*, *Village Voice*, *Ramparts*, *The Nation*, *Commentary*, that whole academic word scene is a total bore. In the end they probably distort things more than the *Daily News*. *The New York Times* is the American Establishment, not the *Daily News*. The *Daily News* creates a living style. You know: "Pot-smoking, dirty, beatnik, pinko, sex-crazy, Vietnik, so-called Yippies." Compare that to *The New York Times*: "Members of the newly formed Youth International Party (YIP)." *The New York Times* is death. The *Daily News* is the closest thing to TV. Look at its front page,

always a big picture. It looks like a TV set. I could go on and on about this. It's a very important point. Distortion is essential to myth-making.

Are you saying that you actually like the *Daily News*?
Not exactly, but I don't consider it the enemy, in the same way that I don't consider George Wallace the enemy. Corporate liberalism, Robert Kennedy, Xerox, David Susskind, *The New York Times*, Harvard University—that is where the real power in America lies, and it is the rejection of those institutions and symbols that distinguishes radicals. That is not to say that I love the *Daily News* but that I consider it more honest than *The New York Times*. I once wanted to start a newspaper called the *New York Liar*. It would be the most honest paper in the country. I would sit in a dark closet and write all the news. The paper would be printed with lemon juice, which is invisible until you heat it with an iron, hence involving the reader. I would write about events without ever leaving the closet. The point is, we all live in dark closets. We all see things through a closet darkly.

That's some fantasy.
Of course. It'll come true, though. Fantasy is the only truth. Once we had a demonstration at the *Daily News* Building. About three hundred people smoked pot, danced, sprayed the reporters with body deodorant, burned money, handed out leaflets to all the employees that began: "Dear fellow member of the Communist conspiracy . . ." We called it an "Alternative Fantasy." It worked great.

What do you mean, it worked great?
Nobody understood it. That is, nobody could explain what it all meant yet everyone was fascinated. It was pure information, pure imagery, which in the end is truth. You see, *The New York Times* can get into very theoretical discussions on the critical level of what we are doing. The *Daily News* responds on a gut level. That's it. *The New York Times* has no guts.

Then being understood is not your goal?
Of course not. The only way you can understand is to join, to become involved. Our goal is to remain a mystery. Pure theater. Free, with no boundaries except your own. Throwing money onto the floor of the Stock

Exchange is pure information. It needs no explanation. It says more than thousands of anticapitalist tracts and essays. It's so obvious that I hesitate to discuss it, since everyone reading this already has an image of what happened there. I respect their images. Anything I said would come on like expertise. "Now, this is what *really* happened." In point of fact nothing happened. Neither we nor the Stock Exchange exist. We are both rumors. That's it. That's what happened that day. Two different rumors collided.

Can you think of any people in theater that influence you?
W. C. Fields, Ernie Kovacs, Che Guevara, Antonin Artaud, Alfred Hitchcock, Lenny Bruce, the Marx Brothers—probably the Beatles have the most influence. I think they have the perfect model for the new family. They have unlimited creativity. They are a continual process, always changing, always burying the old Beatles, always dropping out.

Can you pursue that a little?
Well, the Beatles are a new family group. They are organized around the way they create. They are communal art. They are brothers and, along with their wives and girl friends, form a family unit that is horizontal rather than vertical, in that it extends across a peer group rather than descending vertically like grandparents–parents–children. More than horizontal, it's circular with the four Beatles the inner circle, then their wives and kids and friends. The Beatles are a small circle of friends, a tribe. They are far more than simply a musical band. Let's say, if you want to begin to understand our culture, you can start by comparing Frank Sinatra and the Beatles. It wouldn't be perfect but it would be a good beginning. Music is always a good place to start.

Why is that?
Well, a revolution always has rhythm. Whether it's songs of the Lincoln Brigade, black soul music, Cuban love songs by José Martí, or white psychedelic rock. I once heard songs of the Algerian rebels that consisted mostly of people beating guns on wooden cases. It was fantastic. What is the music of the system? Kate Smith singing the National Anthem. Maybe that's Camp, but it's not Soul.

What about dancing?

There too. Arthur Murray. Dance lessons. What a joke. If you need lessons you haven't got the message. Dancing for us is doing anything you want. You have to see a huge throbbing light-rock show. Especially one that is free, because the free-est people only go to free events. You will see people doing all sorts of fantastic dances. Frenzied and smooth. Butterflies and antelopes. Indians and spiders. Swimming and jumping. Lots of people just sit or lie on the floor, which is a nice step too. Nobody takes lessons. In fact, if you liked the way somebody danced and asked them where they learned to do it, they would laugh. Dance schools are about as outmoded as public schools, which really are archaic. In fact, I wouldn't be surprised to find out that Arthur Murray was a U.S. Commissioner of Education, and high school was just a training ground for millions of foxtrotters. You can see the difference if you look at one of those silly dance books with the shoe prints. One-Two-Three, One-Two-Three. You know. It would be funny to make one for the new dances, which, by the way, don't have names anymore. I think about two years ago dances stopped having names. Anyway, one of those books would have shoe-prints all over the walls and ceilings. A possible title for this book I'm working on could be *The Three Basic Steps in Modern Dance.* One—Two—FREE . . . One-Three—T . . . O . . . net wo . . . 10—9—8—7—6—5—4—3—2—1 NOW! That's it. Now you've got it. Turn your motor on and fly. You can go forever.

Forever?

Haven't you heard of nuclear energy? Yes, you can dance forever. That's the Beatles' message. That's why I said before that our movement was called Dancing.

Doesn't all this dancing present a problem for society?

Not for ours, but for the parent culture, the one decaying, most definitely. The cops hate us.

How do you feel about cops?

Cops are our enemy. Not each one as a person, naked, say. We're all brothers when we are naked. Did you ever see a fight in a steam bath? But cops in uniform are a different story. Actually, all uniforms are enemies.

Just another extension of machine living. The way we dress—in costumes—is in direct opposition to a uniform culture. Costumes are the opposite of uniforms. Since the cops' uniforms also include clubs, handcuffs, guns, etc., they are particularly hated uniforms. I should also add that I've been arrested seventeen times and beaten by police on at least five occasions. I would no more think of asking a cop for help than shooting arsenic to get high.

Who would you ask for help?
My brothers. None of my brothers are cops. You see a cop's principal role is to protect private property. Our goal is the abolition of property. How could I ever call a cop?

Don't they do more than protect property?
Yeah, they kick the shit out of people who have none. Listen. You should have seen Grand Central Station last week during the YIP-IN. Picture this, thousands, maybe ten thousand people, dancing, singing, throwing balloons in the air. Some people decided to climb on top of the information booth; while they were up there they pulled the hands off the clock. This triggered a police riot, with maybe two hundred cops swinging nightsticks charging into people. No warning. No order to clear. About one hundred people were hospitalized, including my wife and me, and over sixty people arrested. There were the police lined up around the clock, guarding it while others smashed skulls. One kid, Ron Shea, tried to come to my rescue while I was being beaten. He was thrown through a glass door and had both hands broken. He may never be able to use one again. Which hands do you think the cops cared more about, the hands on the clock or Ron Shea's hands?

Why did the kids rip the hands off the clock?
I don't know. Maybe they hate time and schedules. Maybe they thought the clock was ugly. They also decorated the clock with sketches. Maybe they were having fun. When we put on a large celebration the aim is to create a liberated area. People can do whatever they want. They can begin to live the revolution even if only within a confined area. We will learn how to govern ourselves. By the way, this goes on in every revolution. Take Vietnam. In liberated zones the National Liberation Front has schools and

theater troupes and hospitals and building programs. The revolutionary experience is far more than just the fighting units.

Do you read revolutionary writings?
Yes, Guevara, Debray, Mao, Giap, McLuhan. I find Giap and McLuhan the most interesting. But of course I am totally caught up with Che as a hero. His death moved me far more than, say, that of Martin Luther King. Although King's was a shock also.

What do you think of death?
Well, I must say I have no fear of death. I faced it once about two years ago on an internal level. This is hard to explain. I've actually faced the risk of death a number of times but this one time I actually became paranoid. I was overcome with anxiety. It was unclear what was going on. I overcame that state purely on a mind level and realized that I had the power in me not to become paranoid. It's the paranoia, the living in constant fear of death, that is the real bad trip, not the death itself. I will be surprised if I get a chance to live out my life. Gleefully surprised, but surprised none the less.

Isn't that sort of gloomy?
No! Not really. You can't deny there is a tremendous amount of violence in this country. People who are engaged daily in radical social change are always exposed to that violence. I would rather die fighting for change than surrender. Death in a physical sense is just not seen as the worst of all possible things.

What is?
I don't know. Going to jail. Surrendering. . . . Maybe nothing is really bad, since I am so convinced that we will win the future.

4

YIPPIE!—THE MEDIA MYTH

A lion walks unnoticed down Wall Street. Slump. Slump. Slump. Strong, determined, with a sense of the future. You are the lion amid the sterile world around you. Where are you going? The lion jumps onto the word *Dreyfus*. "*Growl.*" He is satisfied. INVEST IN DREYFUS. Few words are needed. Words confuse. Words are hot. A lion in a street of people is worth a thousand words. It is a wonderful ad, fantastically filmed. A lion walking in a crowded street is totally absorbing. There is an underlying tension of course, but overall coolness. No chaos. No anarchy. No risks. Just give us your dough. Maybe we should run a lion for President?

Projecting cool images is not our goal. We do not wish to project a calm secure future. We are disruption. We are hot. In our ad the lion cracks. Races through the streets. We are cannibals, cowboys, Indians, witches, warlocks. Weird-looking freaks that crawl out of the cracks in America's nightmare. Very visible and, as everyone knows, straight from the white middle-class suburban life. We are a pain in the ass to America because we cannot be explained. Blacks riot because they are oppressed. An Italian cabdriver told me, "If I was black, I'd be pissed, too." America understands the blacks.

We are alienated. What's that all about? Existential lovers in a plastic society. Our very existence is disruptive. Long hair and freaky clothes are total information. It is not necessary to say we are opposed to the — — — —. Everybody already knows. It is a mistake to tell people what they already know. We alienate people. We involve people. Attract—Repel. We play on the generation gap. Parents shit. They are baffled, confused. They want the cool lion. We tear through the streets. Kids love it. They understand it on an internal level. We are living TV ads, movies. Yippie! There is no program. Program would make our movement sterile. We are living contradictions. I cannot really explain it. I do not even understand it myself.

Blank space, the interrupted statement, the unsolved puzzle, they are all involving. There is a classic experiment in psychology. Subjects are given problems to solve. Some tasks they complete; others are interrupted. Six months later they are given a memory test. They consistently remember the problems that were interrupted. Let's postulate a third setting, in which the subject is shown how to solve the problem by an instructor. It would probably be the least remembered of the three. It is called "going to school" and is the least involving relationship.

When we opened the FREE STORE we circulated a leaflet with a beautiful work of art, and under it in Spanish was the line: *Everything is free at the store of the Diggers*. No address. No store hours. No list of items and services. It was tremendously effective. Puerto Ricans began asking questions. Puerto Ricans talked to hippies. Everybody searched for the FREE STORE together.

I stare at a button. Bright pink on purple background: Yippie! It pops right out. It's misspelled. Good. Misspelling can be a creative act. What does Yippie! mean? Energy—excitement—fun—fierceness—exclamation point! Last December three of us sat in a room discussing plans to bring people to Chicago to make a statement about the Democratic Convention. Hippies are dead. Youth International Party—Y.I.P.—YIP—YIPPIE!. We're all jumping around the room, Paul Krassner, Jerry Rubin, and I. Playing Yippie! games. "Y." "Right." That's your symbol. That's our question. "Join the Y." "God, Nixon will attack us in three months for confusing the image of the YMCA." Within fifteen minutes we have created a myth. Head for the media. "Hello, my name is Paul Yippie, what's yours!" Within two weeks every underground paper has a Yippie!

story. In a month *Newsweek* writes "The Yippies Are Coming." Lawrence Lipton, in the L.A. *Free Press*, analyzes Yippie! origins. *Y*'s appear magically on walls around the country. All the while, the excitement and energy are focused on Chicago and people get involved. A Yippie! button produces a question. The wearer must answer. He tells a little story. He mentions Chicago, a festival of music, violence (Americans love to go to accidents and fires), guerrilla theater, Democrats. Each story is told in a different way. There is mass participation in the Yippie! myth. Can we change an H to a Y? Can myths involve people to the extent that they will make the journey to far-off Chicago? Can magic media succeed where organizing has failed? Y not?

Blank space is the transmission of information whereby the viewer has an opportunity

to become involved as a participant.

In Saigon, the newspapers are censored. Various pages have sections of blank news articles. There is more information in those blank articles than you might suspect. I go on television and make a point of swearing. I know the little fuckers don't get through, but the image of me blabbing away with the enthusiasm and excitement of a future world better than this while being sliced up by the puritanical, sterile culture of the Establishment is information worth conveying.

Words

can

be

used

to

create.

TV images flash in my head. Vietnam news pictured in terms of old World War II movies and they are not the Japanese but tiny bands of underdog heroes like beautiful Filipinos I once saw sabotage Japanese Military Might in surprise attack and now nineteen Vietcong guerrillas on heroic mission attack the U.S. Embassy when they said it couldn't be done. Who would have believed that crew-cut generals in shiny limousines and million-dollar planes that zoom by, dropping latest university developments brewed by those institutions we were taught as children to awe, could be whipped by nineteen gooks? America will lose more than its face in Vietnam rice paddies hunting jackknife warriors with napalm machines. Where will be our Alamos? Where even our brave men planting flag on Iwo Jima hilltop? America is a mythic land. Dreamed up by European beatniks, religious fanatics, draft dodgers, assorted hippie kooks, and runaways from servitude off to the New World of milk and honey. Europe said, "If you don't like it here, why don't you leave." Echoed three hundred years later by a middle-aged veteran with sagging ass and sagging belly hunched over sign reading IF YOUR HEART IS NOT IN AMERICA GET YOUR ASS OUT. Sagging crudeness of Joe McCarthy national policy. And even as we slaughtered the Indians, as children we could accept the encircled group of covered wagons fighting to defend themselves and wanting simply to make it to a little pastureland in the green hills and valleys of California.

The myths of America are strong and good but the institutional machine is a trap of death. Can you believe I was eighteen before I even knew this country had a Depression but at thirteen I could list with correct dates all Revolutionary War battles and discuss in detail the battle of Lexington and Concord which took place just thirty miles from my hometown? *Just last summer I stood on that bridge at 6 A.M. with a follower of Transcendental Meditation and described the battle, joining myself with imaginary musket to the ragged guerrillas that shot from those peaceful hills in Concord on that April morning. The previous day we had stood in Harvard Square passing out free poems hurling curses at the Pentagon gone mad and were attacked by drunk Marines as Harvard fairy professors stood in a circle of Adlai Stevenson-nothingness and watched and appealed to His Majesty's protectors of law and order, who finally did something. They took down our names and told us to get our asses out of Cambridge. I came away from sitting on the Concord Bridge that night knowing that some day I might just have to shoot a few of His Majesty's gendarmes and forgetting those nights of practicing how to protect my head and nuts in pacifist utero position and believing in the Second American Revolution.* America lost its balls in the frontier and since then there have been no mighty myths and now we hunt for them in lonely balconies, watching *Bonnie and Clyde*. Tragic figures, born out of rejection of a machine-mad American sterility, like James Dean and Marilyn Monroe crushed by plastic Hollywood. And later through a drugged comedian named Lenny, who had more balls by far than the stream of district attorneys that chased him with outmoded statutes. Now I can write *FUCK* and nobody's prurient interests stir and no one gets upset except maybe the DAR, which is so drugged on *The Sound of Music* that it only dreams in paranoid fantasies that such words are written, not to even mention the fact that the daughters of the Daughters are getting fucked all the time even if they are just panty raids. There are other heroes also, not home-grown, for the bowels of corporate success do not easily give birth to champions like Fidel. *I remember in the winter of '59 as we thousands cheered Fidel in Harvard Stadium as we had on New Year's day (even if he did interrupt the Rose Bowl game), Julius Lester told me of a trip he was on with him in the Cuban countryside. When the helicopter landed with the newspapers from Havana, Fidel quickly turned to the baseball scores and then threw the paper into the trash barrel. Cuba Si, Yankee No. Up in Boston we would yell the same sort of thing from the bleachers in Fenway Park. How the hell would anybody ever beat the Yankees?*

The Cubans finally did and last year so did the Red Sox. Even New Yorkers now abandon the old beaten men of the Yankees and root for the Mets. In those days of Yankee might we would go out to Fenway Park just to see Jim Piersall sit down in the middle of the game or get in a fight with the umpire. All the umpires secretly worked for the Yankees. Jim Piersall lives and so does the Revolution! *Venceremos!* Up against the wall, Mickey Mantle!

The only pure revolution in the end is technology. Yet that is the same as the revolution in consciousness. Funny, one thing just buttons, light bulbs, needles and thread. The other totally internal, spiritual, personal, emotional—*al* (do all those words end in *al* or is that just individual). It is in the fusion of that and endless other dichotomies that the road to revolution lies.

Today was a typical day. Today everything happened. The moon is full, an Aries moon, I'm told by revolutionary astrologers, and in three days the YIP-Out and thousands upon thousands will gather together in Central Park and meet each other and smile and some will ask why they are there and others will know. Some will tell others. Others will nod. Skeptics meet true believers. Left meets Right. Mao Tse-tung of the People's Republic of China will bump into Cousin Clyde of the Hell's Angels. "Let a thousand flowers bloom" meets "I jes' like to blow minds." A Be-In is an emotional United Nations. It works where the intellectual one ten blocks to the east enclosed in glass and concrete fails . . .

Today I asked Joel, the perpetual runaway, scared kid, to go and buy three flowers: one chrysanthemum, one daffodil, and one daisy—and he did and returned with the change. We had a technological problem. Which flowers would be best suited to throw out of an airplane into the YIP-Out? This was a problem, if you had visions of 10,000 stems *sans* blossoms descending on 50,000 bewildered heads. So up the twelve flights of stairs I trudged, three flowers in hand, exhausted, puffing, out of breath as if I had climbed the Himalayas (which I had in fact done). Up on the roof the sun shone brightly, pigeons were flying about. To the right lay the street, with dutiful Joel waiting to see which flower stood up the best.

There were two men on the roof. Two old men, one in his late forties, the other about sixty-five. Old Italian men with old ways and old hats feeding pigeons, hundreds of them. It was their thing. "You can't come up here" one started screaming. It was weird, they started yelling all kinds of shit like "the landlord said . . ." and "you can't come here . . ." and calling me all kinds of names "You people . . ." and I got mad and started yelling things like "I live in this fuckin' building, what do you mean 'you people' . . ." And there they were defending their territory, birds, governments, who knows what . . . We did not speak the same language and one old man ran into a little wooden shed on the roof and came out with a butcher knife and the younger one restrained me as I stood with three flowers raised over my head ready to attack and after we had all shouted I went down the stairs and there was Joel staring upward and I said, "Joel, we'll try it from across the street." I climbed six flights to the roof of the Electric Circus, signaled to Joel, and threw the flowers down. First the chrysanthemum, then the daffodil, and finally the white daisy. Klunch, klunch, klunch. Each hit the sidewalk intact. I ran down the stairs and Joel, puffing, met me halfway and said "A kid stole the chrysanthemum and somebody stepped on the daffodil." He was clutching a white daisy in both hands. He was smiling. The Scientific Method leads to Joy. Daisies would make it to the YIP-Out.

That wasn't all that happened today. Today Anita and I applied for passports. Just in case. That wasn't all either. Today was 10,000 years wide.

America is Racist.
America is Imperialistic.
Police are Brutal.
Mass media distort.

Bah—Bah—Bah—Bah—Bah—Bah—Bah—Bah—Bah Sheep talking rhetoric. People on the Left spend most of their time telling each other things like that. The point is, everybody already knows, so call it Rhetoric. The Left masturbates continuously because it is essentially rooted in an academic tradition.* It is the rhetoric of the Left, its insistence on ideological exactness rather than action, that has held the revolution back in this country as much as the actions of the people in power. The Left has the same smugness as *The New York Times*. I remember about four months ago attending a Mobilization meeting as part of Yippie! They did not want to include us in their coalition because they said we had no real constituency. We didn't even request to be included and made a point of asking them not to support us. We just wanted to let people know we would be there. For two days the MOB debated whether or not they should go to Chicago in August. We laughed at them but not in a hostile way, sort of like Buddhas smiling in the corner. While they argued back and forth we got stoned, made love to all the pretty girls, offered resolutions, like demanding an end to pay toilets and support of the Polish student rebellion (just to upset the Russian-linked U.S. Communist Party), refused to pay for our meals, and in general carried on like bad, crazy niggers. After two days of bullshit they postponed a decision until sometime in July. We came into the hall and passed out huge posters (a picture of the U.S.A. as a jigsaw puzzle all mixed up with an arrow saying Yippie! pointing to Chicago. It said Festival of Life, Chicago, August 25–30—Lights-Theater-Magic-Free-Music). We gave everyone a Yippie! button. All free of course. Then we left, knowing full well they'd all be in Chicago anyway. There was no point meeting with them again and we didn't. No Constituency! HA! The five of us† represented the most important underground magazine, the two most important figures on the N.Y. Hippie Scene, the most important movement radio personality, and the hero of the Pentagon (see Mailer's *Armies of the Night*). We had on our team the most dynamic people in the white drop-out movement: Leary, Ginsberg, and more importantly the rock musicians and

*This, of course, wasn't true of the left movement in the thirties, when it was rooted in the labor movement. Dock workers don't waste time at conferences and ideological debates. They were also ready to use any means necessary . . . that's how they got what they wanted.

†Myself, Jim Fouratt, Paul Krassner, Jerry Rubin, and Bob Fass.

most of the underground editors, especially Liberation News Service, the most exciting figures in guerrilla theater as well as the most original people on Broadway, and even more. Essentially what we had was information control, tremendous ability to manipulate the media, and enough balls to break every rule in the book. We could act like Buddhas, we had in six weeks already told the whole world we were going to the Democratic Convention. The night before we had come from the Grand Central Station Massacre of the Yippies.

In one week, on fifteen dollars cash, we had attracted five to eight thousand people to a party at midnight, for no reason, in Grand Central Station. It is debatable whether the Grand Central Massacre helped or hurt our chances in Chicago. I maintain it helped tremendously. It put Yippie! on the map. I know that sounds cold-blooded. Revolutionists are cold-blooded bastards (the best are also good lovers). I can say this honestly because I run the same, if not more risks, than anyone. I was knocked unconscious by some dumb pig in Grand Central; besides, nobody was under orders to come. (Only people in business really manipulate people because they have money-power and, as everyone knows, money IS power in America.) Besides, I was the only one who tried to cool out the scene. I asked the head cops and the Mayor's assistant, Barry Gottehrer, to let me use the P.A. system. Like dumb cops they refused, in fact they refused even to use it themselves. The Mayor's assistant had an interesting response. "They are not our police," he replied. Asking to use the P.A. system was a very difficult decision which very few people in this country can even begin to comprehend. It means a conscious, deliberate attempt to assert leadership. It's nice in a sense that the cops, as they did later in Chicago, always take over the leadership at such critical moments. "The pigs are our leaders" is the kind of information that is truer than true.

Anyway, a revolutionary artist, which is shorthand for either Revolutionist or Artist, just does it. Life-actors, all play their roles according to their backgrounds, talents, costumes, and props. The Grand Central Station Massacre knocked out the hippie image of Chicago and let the whole world know there would be blood on the streets of Chicago. It didn't matter what we predicted, what story we made up, how much we talked of fun and games. The medium is the message and the message was Theater of Cruelty. The rumor of Grand Central Station and the statements of Shoot-to-Kill

Daley and Sheriff Joe Woods ("We'll stick them in underground mud tunnels and organize white vigilante groups") were powerful enough magic to separate the hippies from the Yippies.

No one who came to Chicago because of our influence had any doubts that they were risking their life. I don't know about McCarthy kids; to use a Mother term, they were not our "responsibility." The hippie end of our mythical coalition dropped out. They failed to trust the Yippie! myth. There was a lot of name-calling but in the end it didn't matter; almost all the original hippies could be found on the streets of Chicago and they were all fighting in the style of their choice, all stoned out of their heads and all having a ball. The reason for this is that the energy centers that gravitated to the center of the myth were tough as all hell. Also a myth has a tendency to always pick the right symbols and strategy, it is in a real sense self-perpetuating.

For example, we held only one formal press conference until Chicago actually happened. It was arranged by one of the country's best publicists, held in the Americana Hotel (which of course we got FREE) and only the stars spoke, Ginsberg, Judy Collins, Phil Ochs, Jacques Levy (Broadway director), Joe Byrd (head of U.S.A. band), Al Cooper (Blood, Sweat & Tears), Bob Fass (WBAI-FM), Michael Goldstein (top P.R. man in the rock field), Paul Krassner, and Ed Sanders. Jerry Rubin and I did not speak. Except for Paul and Ed, all the others later dropped out of Yippie! until the Festival began. Some played secondary roles, not the least of which was to criticize Yippie! Maybe for this reason the press conference got very little coverage in the media? Maybe it was because of the Americana setting, maybe because of other news that day? By the rules, this press conference should have gotten into every paper in the country and on every TV station. It didn't, and it didn't precisely because it wasn't right. It didn't fit the truth of what would happen in Chicago. The media in a real sense never lie when you relate to them in a non-linear mythical manner. In similar fashion the YIP-Out on Easter Sunday, with over 40,000 people in Central Park and fifteen rock groups and flowers from the sky, didn't fit the myth (as well as being a lousy spectator event) and was soon forgotten. It was Grand Central Station that stuck, and talk of not telling the truth is pigshit for a myth always tells the truth.

Another case in point is the Pig. Introduced fairly early in the game by Hugh Romney, spiritual leader of the Hogfarm, a commune outside Los

Angeles, the Pig gravitated to the center of the myth. It took a long time, probably because of Hugh's vacillation about coming, and the fact that he was bringing the Pig probably held the myth back. During the week before the thing happened we noticed the media picking up on the Pig; with the cold-bloodedness of Madison Avenue we rammed in the Pigshit. It took only four days. When I went out to get the Pig on some American farm in Northern Illinois, the Pig had already become famous.

This particular pig was finally rejected by the myth—with a good deal of help from Jerry Rubin and Stu Albert. The meeting at which this decision was made was quite heated and actually our only "meeting" in Chicago. They wanted a meaner pig. I thought it didn't matter, sort of liked the pig we had, was worried about the technical problems of managing a large pig, and had doubts that Jerry, Stu, and Phil Ochs could find another pig in time. They were not the resource people, who were all in my gang by that time. Jerry and I had a huge fight and didn't speak to each other the rest of the time. Which upset everybody except probably Jerry and me, since we were both so determined to make our Chicago in our own style. We would not let a personal fight upset anything. Besides, we were both so dedicated that I, at least, realized that Jerry would cry at my funeral and make the right speech and that I would do the same at his. But I deliberately told my police tail and everyone else except the reporters about the fight we had. I wanted to destroy a charge of conspiracy and thought this was the best way. It fitted my pattern of Not Getting Caught. Even though we fought, we were all together.

The first blood I saw in Chicago was the blood of Stu Albert, Jerry's closest friend. It happened in the first Sunday afternoon police riot in Lincoln Park. I embraced Stu, crying and swearing—sharing his blood. I went up to the cops and shook my fist. I made a haranguing speech, standing between rows of pig cops and scared spectators of the music festival, which of course by now was over. That kind of unity that Stu and I have, even though he is a Marxist-Leninist and I am a fuck-off, is impossible to explain. We are united in our determination to smash this system by using any means at our disposal and build a new world. In any event it didn't matter. Jerry's big Pig hit the Civic Center and Mrs. Pig was let loose in the park hours later, screaming that her thirty sons would avenge her husband's arrest. I dropped the hint that we were considering running a lion. In the end thousands of pigs were used, real pigs, pig buttons, nice pigs like Mr.

and Mrs. Pig (see wonderful photo in Chicago *Daily News* entitled "Mr. & Mrs. Pig Re-United in the Pokey") and bad pigs like the cops, Daley, Humphrey and the politicians. It was shades of *Animal Farm* and you couldn't tell the pigs from the farmers or the farmers from the pigs. On the last day, I knew we had won when I saw Humphrey and Daley on TV and in photos. Everyone could see they were coming up Pig as all hell. As a familiar chant, one that I had never heard at any demonstration, put it—"The Whole World Is Watching! The Whole World is Watching!" Thanks again to Mayor Daley for beating up Walter Cronkite.

5

ON TO CHICAGO (AUGUST 25–30, 1968)

"The medium is the mess." —MARSHALL MCLU

"The policeman isn't there to create disorder. He's there to preserve disorder." —MAYOR RICHARD J. DALEY
Press Conference, September 10, 1968

"Theater of Cruelty proposes to resort to a mass spectacle; to seek in the agitation of tremendous masses, convulsed and hurled against each other, a little of that poetry of festivals and crowds when, all too rarely nowadays, the people pour out into the streets . . . The theater must give us everything that is in crime, love, war or madness if it wants to recover its necessity . . . We want to create a believable reality which gives the heart and senses that kind of concrete bite which all true sensation requires . . . We wish to address the entire organism through an intensive mobilization of objects, gestures and signs, used in a new spirit. The Theater of Cruelty has been created in order to restore a passionate and convulsive conception of life and it is in this sense of violent rigor and extreme condensation of scenic elements that the cruelty on which it is based must be understood. This cruelty, which will be bloody when necessary but not systematically so, can thus be identified with a kind of severe moral purity which is not afraid to pay life the price it must be paid."

—ANTONIN ARTAUD
The Theater and Its Double

Last December a group of us in New York conceived the Yippie! idea. We had four main objectives:

1. The blending of pot and politics into a political grass leaves movement—a cross-fertilization of the hippie and New Left philosophies.
2. A connecting link that would tie together as much of the underground as was willing into some gigantic national get-together.
3. The development of a model for an alternative society.
4. The need to make some statement, especially in revolutionary action-theater terms, about LBJ, the Democratic Party, electoral politics, and the state of the nation.

To accomplish these tasks required the construction of a vast myth, for through the notion of myth large numbers of people could get turned on and, in that process of getting turned on, begin to participate in Yippie! and start to focus on Chicago. Precision was sacrificed for a greater degree of suggestion. *People took off in all directions in the most sensational manner possible:*

"We will burn Chicago to the ground!"

"We will fuck on the beaches!"

"We demand the Politics of Ecstasy!"

"Acid for all!"

"Abandon the Creeping Meatball!"

And, all the time: "Yippie! Chicago—August 25–30."

Reporters would play their preconceived roles: "What is the difference between a hippie and a Yippie?" A hundred different answers would fly out, forcing the reporter to make up his own answers; to distort. And distortion became the life-blood of the Yippies.

Yippie! was in the eye of the beholder.

JULY 7, 1968: Remember a guy named Lyndon Johnson? He was so predictable when Yippie! began. And then *pow!* He really fucked us. He did the one thing no one had counted on. He dropped out. "My God," we exclaimed. "Lyndon is out-flanking us on our hippie side."

Then Go-Clean-for-Gene and Hollywood-Bobby. Well, Gene wasn't much. One could secretly cheer for him the way you cheer for the Mets. It's easy, knowing he can never win. But Bobby, there was the real threat. A direct challenge to our theater-in-the-streets, a challenge to the charisma of Yippie!

Remember Bobby's Christmas card: psychedelic blank space with a big question mark—"Santa in '68?" Remember Bobby on television stuttering at certain questions, leaving room for the audience to jump in and help him agonize, to battle the cold interviewer who knew all the questions and never made a mistake.

"Come on," Bobby said, "join the mystery battle against the television machine." Participation mystique. Theater-in-the-streets. He played it to the hilt. And what was worse, Bobby had the money and power to build the stage. We had to steal ours. It was no contest.

Yippie stock went down quicker than the money we had dumped on the Stock Exchange floor. Every night we would turn on the TV set and there was the young knight with long hair, holding out his hand (a gesture he learned from the Pope): "Give me your hand—it is a long road ahead."

When young longhairs told you how they'd heard that Bobby turned on, you knew Yippie! was *really* in trouble.

We took to drinking and praying for LBJ to strike back, but he kept melting. Then Hubert came along exclaiming the "Politics of Joy" and Yippie! passed into a state of catatonia which resulted in near permanent brain damage.

Yippie! grew irrelevant.

National action seemed meaningless.

Everybody began the tough task of developing new battlegrounds. Columbia, the Lower East Side, Free City in San Francisco. Local action became the focus and by the end of May we had decided to disband Yippie! and cancel the Chicago festival.

It took two full weeks of debate to arrive at a method of dropping-out which would not further demoralize the troops. The statement was all ready when up stepped Sirhan Sirhan, and in ten seconds he made it a whole new ball game.

We postponed calling off Chicago and tried to make some sense out of what the hell had just happened. It was not easy to think clearly. Yippie!, still in a state of critical shock because of LBJ's pullout, hovered close to death somewhere between the 50/50 state of Andy Warhol and the 0/0 state of Bobby Kennedy.

The United States political system was proving more insane than Yippie!.

Reality and unreality had in six months switched sides.

It was *America* that was on a trip; we were just standing still.

How could we pull our pants down? America was already naked.

What could we disrupt? America was falling apart at the seams.

Yet Chicago seemed more relevant than ever. Hubert had a lock on the convention: it was more closed than ever. Even the squares who vote in primaries had expressed a mandate for change. Hubert canned the "Politics of Joy" and instituted the "Politics of Hope"—some switch—but none of the slogans mattered. We were back to power politics, the politics of big-city machines and back-room deals.

The Democrats had finally got their thing together by hook or crook and there it was for all to see—fat, ugly, and full of shit. The calls began pouring into our office. They wanted to know only one thing: "When do we leave for Chicago?"

What we need now, however, is the direct opposite approach from the one we began with. We must sacrifice suggestion for a greater degree of precision. We need a reality in the face of the American political myth. We have to kill Yippie! and still bring huge numbers to Chicago.

SEPTEMBER 1, 1968: Perhaps the best way to begin to relate to Chicago is to clear your throat of the tear-gas fumes, flex your muscles, stiff from cop punches, write lying down, collapsing from fifteen solid days on no more than three hours sleep each night, mouth OM, smile, and then roll on the floor laughing hysterically. I can only relate to Chicago as a personal anarchist, a revolutionary artist. If that sounds egotistical, tough shit. My concept of reality comes from what I see, touch, and feel. The rest, as far as I'm concerned, didn't happen. If it did, so what, then it happened. Great! I am my own leader. I make my own rules. The revolution is wherever my boots hit the ground. If the Left considers this adventurism, fuck 'em, they are a total bureaucratic bore. SDS came to Chicago to talk to the McCarthy kids. We came to have the McCarthy kids experience what we as long-hairs experience all the time—the experience of living in a police state and the beauty of our alternative society. Today I stand safe on the corner of St. Marx Place and the headline reads: POLICE INVADE McCARTHY HEADQUARTERS AND CLUB CAMPAIGN WORKERS. It is the final scene in the Theater of Cruelty played out in Chicago. Another week and we could have gotten the cops to assassinate Humphrey.

We had won the battle of Chicago. As I watched the acceptance speech of Hump-Free (new slogan: Dump the Hump and Vote for Free) I knew we had smashed the Democrats' chances and destroyed the two-party system in this country and perhaps with it electoral politics. Nixon-Agnew vs. Humphrey-Muskie. Four deuces. HA! HA! Losers ALL!* There was no doubt in my mind when I saw that acceptance speech that we had won. There would be a Pig in the White House in '69. I went out for champagne, brought it up to the MOB office, and toasted the Revolution. Put on my dark glasses, tucked my hair under my hat, pasted on my mustache, and called my wife. Told her to ditch the Chicago police tailing us and pick me up. I checked my phony identification cards and my youth ticket. In a half hour we were at O'Hare Airport, two hours later back on the Lower East Side.

All the way on the plane I kept wondering what the fuck we would have done if they had let us stay in Lincoln Park at night. As usual the cops took care of the difficult decisions. The concept of the Pig as our leader was truer than reality. It was the perfect symbol. We love the Pig! (our candidate and leader). We hate the Pig! (Daley, cops, authority). Everything is Pig . . . Chicago is total garbage and the pigs ate like politicians. The pigs that attacked us in the park lived in the Zoo, housed in the Lincoln Cultural and Arts Center. One of the pigs that killed Dean Johnson, a seventeen-year-old Indian brother from Sioux City, our only martyr, in what was

*See McLuhan's brilliant article in a recent *Saturday Evening Post* entitled "All the Candidates Are Asleep."

allegedly self-defense, was called Officer Manley.* The liberal schmuck deputy mayor who stalled for four months on our permit application was named David Stahl. The federal judge who was to hear our lawsuit was named Lynch (we whipped him by taking back the suit and remarking that we had as little faith in the judicial system of this country as we did in the political). The names and coincidences were beyond belief.

Symbols and myths is what it's all about. Headlines: NATIONAL GUARD VS. THE HIPPIES AT CONRAD HILTON. My God, the overground press looked like the *East Village Other*. It was impossible to tell who was who. A perfect and total mess. The cops drove us out in the street each night, teaching us how to survive and fight. How could city Yippies totally unorganized (although very together) take on superior armed forces in unfamiliar territory resembling the countryside? We had to leave but we never retreated! Let us make that point crystal clear. We dispersed. We persisted in fighting for our right to stay in the park the total time we were in Chicago. In fact we were really fighting for our right to be in Grant Park, which was our original intention (check our first articles as well as the original permit applications filed on March 25th). For it was Grant Park, right across from the Headquarters of the Chief Pigs, the Conrad Hitler, largest hotel in the world, that was Circus Ring Number One.

Fifteen days ago I was left in Chicago by the other troublemakers who had things to put together in New York before heading back. I had a dollar in my pocket, which I ceremoniously burned in the *Seed* office, and said, "Now I am ready for the battle." I bummed a few bucks from Abe Peck, the editor, and was off and running. I bought a little red book in Woolworths which incidentally fell apart, revealing scraps of Chinese newspapers which I later showed to police to prove conclusively that the Yippies were linked directly to Red China. By the time I was through I had the home phone numbers of the Chief of Police, Deputy Mayor, Hubert Humphrey's credit card number (also the address where he was really staying—the Astor Tower Hotel—his office staff and aides stayed at the Hilton) and information on all the key people in Yippie!, MOB, press, police and resource people (those who had trucks, food, banners, pigs, buttons). I had a lot of information. Information is the key to survival. Information is what the

*Mayor Daley's unbelievable 70-page whitewash of what happened in Chicago states, "No one was killed or seriously injured." There seem to be a number of realities floating around.

struggle is all about. As long as I knew what I was doing better than the people I encountered knew what they were doing, I would survive. If not, I would die. I had no doubts about that. Knowing what to do was the way not to get caught. As I said to the cops who came to arrest me Wednesday as I was sitting in the Lincoln Hotel Restaurant waiting for breakfast, "The first duty of a revolutionist is to get away with it. The second duty is to eat breakfast. I ain't going." It was a bust written by a Hollywood screenwriter. I had painted the word *fuck* on my forehead as part of my costume. I didn't feel like having my picture in the mass media that day and that is the only way to do it and still be able to do your thing. Especially if your thing is heavy. My hat was drawn low over the word because I didn't feel like pissing off the waitress (we had already played out a number of theater pieces in that restaurant). Two cops came in and said, "We have a tip you have something under your hat, will you please remove it?" (Information: a phony cop. A real cop never says please. Information: he won't be rough on you.)

"I'm going to eat. Want to join us?"

They had a conference.

"You guys better call Commander Brash." (Information: cops are afraid only of losing their jobs; always call for their superior, it shakes the shit out of them. I had noticed they were from the 18th Precinct.) They left. Soon they returned with six other cops. Outside were four patrol cars. Out came their guns. "Take off your hat." I lifted the gray ranger hat, one of the hundred different disguises I had used that week, and shouted "BANG-BANG." Krassner went hysterical, even my wife, who usually worries, was smiling. The cops reached over and pulled me out across the table, with me clutching a slice of bacon (oink!), dragged me out of the restaurant, slammed me against a car, handcuffed me, and took me in. I was kept incommunicado for thirteen hours with no phone calls, no lawyers, no food (five hours without water). I was transported from precinct house to precinct house while fat dumb cops beat the shit out of me. One cop, Officer Henley, showed me a gold bullet that he said had my name on it. I fired back, "I have your name on a silver bullet and I'm the Lone Ranger." Throughout the beatings I kept laughing hysterically, "We whipped you fucking pigs, we whipped your asses. You cocksuckers are afraid to lose your jobs and we ain't afraid to die." The courtroom scene was a shambles. I swore at the ACLU lawyer and told him to get his liberal lawyers up here for a sit-in and forget about defending me. In the hall I ripped up the arrest papers with all the charges. It was all *Catch-22* bullshit anyway. I was really mad though because they had succeeded in keeping me out of the battle of Michigan Avenue. Actually I had worked out a perfect plan not to get caught and still do my thing. At midnight the night before, a girl with a brown cowboy hat covered with blood was supposed to have run into the Lincoln Park area, screaming that I had been killed. It would have worked too. Lincoln Park at midnight just before the tear gas hit was the best place in the country to begin that sort of spook story. It was the hour of Paranoid's delight. (I remember hearing a kid scream "the cops are coming" as he stared into a vacant field with only trees. "Cops are blue, kid, and they come in large numbers. Don't fire 'til you see the whites of their eyes.") Anyway, the girl didn't do it. Later she told me it was one of the toughest decisions she ever made. She, more than most, realized the power of myth. Anyway, the next day I really was flying. It was the best. I rapped in Lincoln Park thanking Ho Chi Minh for bringing the medical supplies, thanking Bob Dylan for playing in the park, thanking Chairman Mao for the secret plans ("Always have three plans—two from column A and one from column B." Stage note: when the actor says Two he holds up two fingers in the sign of the V, when he exclaims One he jams one finger into the air, making the "up your ass" sign). I thanked Marshall McLuhan for bringing his television set, I thanked the Chicago cops and Mayor Daley, the founders of the Yippies, for without their help none of this would have been possible. I rapped about how leaders were full of shit, how the MOB marshals were all cops, and how the politicians, McCarthy included, who came to the park to speak were fake prophets. I told them the only way we could get to the amphitheater was to go as a community, to just ask the guy next to you how to get there, if they didn't already know, and put your arm around his shoulder and go with him. About five thousand of us just headed for the Amphitheater down Michigan Avenue. No leader, nothing. Just people. It was beautiful. Then the chickenshit marshals took over. They are always the ones who bring the megaphones and should never be trusted. In fact, if I ever see Eric Weinberger again I'm going to slice not only his megaphone but his throat as well. About ten blocks down Michigan Avenue the troops came out. It was unbelievable. Out comes the biggest fuckin' tank I ever saw. Me and this spade cat were in the middle of the block about then. (I had remembered Dana Beal's brilliant advice to a huge crowd:

"When the shit hits the fan, the safest place is in the middle of the crowd.") I said to Frankie, my spade buddy, "Let's go up and fuck around." Eric was up there pissing in his pants, telling the people to sit down, which of course is the worst advice possible. I said, "Eric, put someone on the bullhorn who is not afraid to die, you are panicking people." I showed him. I went up and stretched out in front of the tank with one finger up in the air laughing like a son-of-a-bitch, while Frankie Spade slapped his thighs and roared.* Then I shouted out over the bullhorn, "You cops out there cool it, you hear! We just sent for the head cop and he'll be here in five minutes. You guys don't want to lose your jobs, do you?" Eric, even while I was speaking, would not give up the mike. Meanwhile Dick Gregory was having a most difficult time. He's a very funny guy but his politics are for shit and his street strategy is worse. I knew what was in his head all along. You know, front of the line, easy bust, suffer-jail-we-shall-overcome-fast-bullshit-masochistic theater—very manipulative. Because he only came out after the battle and also after he had tried his damnedest to scare people out of coming. I like him a lot but he's not ready for "any means necessary," at least not now on Michigan Avenue. I told him the rap to the cops was a bluff and my strategy was to get the head cop down here, grab him, and get us through. The other pigs (having a leader-follower head) wouldn't touch us. He said what if they did? I replied I would kill the Top Pig and I meant it. In three minutes, lo and behold a black limousine pulls up in the center of the crowd. I go up and say I want to see Chief Lynsky right away or there will be more blood spilled here than in all the other days together. A pig said, "I'm Lynsky's boss." I wasn't sure but he sure had a lot of gold braid on. Pig Rocheford was his name. He tried to get me to go with him in the car and discuss this rationally. (Information: Top Pigs always act like liberals.) "Oh no, I'm no leader. I'm just a wise-ass punk. We all have to go or nobody goes." Meanwhile Eric hustles the Big Pig to the mike, announcing, "We can go back to the park." The Chief Pig and Eric are arm in arm, leading the sheep back to the meadow. I'm going crazy but I think I can still win. I run back to the park and hustle another bullhorn. Frankie Spade is the only guy I can count on but he's passed out on the grass from the Super Honey that came from our underground lab. So

*A mistake. Better theater would have been to punch the tank or at least stand up roaring with laughter. I got co-opted by the pacifists.

there we are on the hilltop, Eric and the Chief Pig explaining very chummy how we can all stay in the park and me announcing publicly the plan to kidnap the Head Pig and snuff him if they touch us. I'm also yelling for the Motherfuckers* because when the chips are really down it's the Motherfuckers who would have the balls to do it. (They had all vanished into the night, figuring it had all been done.) Of course Gregory won out. He worked a deal with the Chief, invited everyone up to his house, walking on the sidewalk. He got control of the bullhorns and monitors as fast as cops had the people line up in threes; he put himself in front with delegates from the Convention and marched the sheep off to his house. I ran up and down the line laughing at the sheep, telling them they were being taken for a ride, they'd get in trouble following leaders, especially politicians. Even Gregory's a politician. That's why he's running for President and not voting for the Pig. I panhandled $80 in twenty minutes from the sheep, telling them it was for Dope (even though it would have been easier to tell them it was for Bail Money. I bumped into one other cat named Tom who was working the other side of the line with the Bail Bit—he made $150 and he's coming to the Lower East Side. I had finally found a brother.) Actually the money was to fly out of Chicago, 'cause it was over for me. I had seen that theater piece before; leaders with press buzzing around like flies get helped into the paddy wagons just before the sheep get slaughtered. As I walked away a kid said, "You afraid to join us?"

"You bet your ass I am. Besides, my leader is the Pig. I'll see you at the Inauguration."

"Are the Yippies going?"

"I doubt it."

There never were any Yippies and there never will be. It was a slogan YIPPIE! and that exclamation point was what it was all about. It was the biggest put-on of all time. If you believe Yippies existed, you are nothing but a sheep. The Brothers and Sisters who came and fought and made love weren't hustled. Everyone's Chicago came true. You know how I knew? Nobody was disappointed Bob Dylan didn't show up. You know he did, though it was just that the fuckin' Pigs wouldn't let him play in the park. I saw him. Sunday night we sat up in a tree near the Church of the Free Spirit

*The Up-Against-the-Wall Motherfuckers are a group of life-actor anarchists who inhabit the cellars on the Lower East Side. They enjoy scaring tourists and torturing pigs.

in Lincoln Park smoking grass. If you don't believe me, go up to Woodstock and ask him.

Jerry Rubin was the chief ideologist or scenario designer for the Festival of Life (Sunday, August 25). My task was to design the symbols and gather up the props. We spoke recently about Chicago and again it was an argument about whose trip occurred. My position was that everyone's trip occurred. It was a do-your-own-thing theatrical mess. Jerry feels nothing happened in the park. I claim the park gave the movement its soul, its spiritual quality. Our differences stem from our personalities and our attitude toward words. Maybe it's a debate between the red and the black. Jerry is much more serious. Ours might prove to be the greatest debate at this point in the Movement. Jerry wants to show the clenched fist. I want to show the clenched fist and the smile. He wants the gun. I want the gun and the flower.

It's interesting, for example, that he thinks the music festival did *not* occur on Sunday as the schedule indicates. Incidentally the *Ramparts Daily Wall Poster* (which I thought fantastic, especially the first few editions) and the *Guardian* also stated that it did not occur. In truth, MC5 from Detroit played fantastic music for over an hour and Ginsberg followed with chanting and a guerrilla theater group did a mock rally with our own LBJ and Hump. At this point the fight over the truck ensued. I was for immediately bringing the truck, which was to serve as the stage, into the park despite police orders to the contrary. Ed Sanders was for sticking with what we had, namely, the band on the ground. My general approach was to try to use every prop that I had found. I hate waste. The guy who owned the truck was against bringing it in. I had to use a lawyer, a pretty girl, myself, and a lot of other tricks to convince him that not much could happen to the truck if the police confiscated it. He finally agreed. Ed Sanders had passed out from too much Honey. I rounded up Super Joel, who was dressed like a race-car driver with crash helmet and overalls. He had already been busted twice and was the guy who stuck the flower in a paratrooper's rifle at the Pentagon. He was perfect (as of course was everyone else in Chicago). I gave him the key to the truck and as it changed hands I knew he'd do it right. Peter Rabbit, a non-existent Yippie from the Lower East Side, climbed on the back with about seventy other Yippies. A whole crowd swarmed around fences and the truck. Police formed their first pig wall. I immediately called for the head cop. We were standing next to the front of the truck with Stu Albert. I explained the situation. "People in the back of the crowd can't see the musicians. The band has to be elevated. The people will all bunch up to the front and crush each other. It will be a very dangerous social problem" (a phase I often use with city officials and head cops). "Well, Chief Lynsky will have to settle this," he replied. "He's got five minutes to get down here," I shot back. Stu loved it. Meanwhile the truck was allowed to go as close as it could get to the bandstand area, and two things occurred that were important. First, MC5 wanted to pack their equipment and leave because of the trouble they saw coming. Then, while I was working on that deal, I heard on my walkie-talkie that the cops were entering the park in the area south of the Free Zoo and the first battle of Lincoln Park had begun. The rest of the night was a series of forays by the cops into groups in the park. The official music festival was over. Police anarchy really broke loose.

For example, about 9 P.M. that night I was training a group of seven Yippies in developing gang strategy and unity (the Left calls these affinity groups, again showing their academic orientation) when I saw a crowd of people getting smashed near the fieldhouse. I went over to investigate, only to be clubbed and kicked by two cops. I returned to my original location and sent a runner to find Commander Brash, head of the 18th Precinct and currently on duty in the park. He came back telling me that Brash wanted to meet me at the Communication Center. I told him to go back and tell Brash to come over here. Two minutes later, Brash appeared. I said, "We have a legal right to be in the park until 11 P.M., isn't that correct?" "Yes," he replied. "Well, what the fuck are all these cops doing smashing us so soon? Can't you wait two hours? Where the hell's law and order in this town!" He agreed to pull the cops back until 11 P.M. Twenty minutes later a group of cops came charging around the fieldhouse and pushed and kicked us, ordering us out of the park. This was only one case of police anarchy. Either the cop in charge always broke his word or he never had control over his men; it made no difference—every agreement was broken. It made Chicago a moral as well as strategic victory for us. I considered it much better strategy to have the cops drive us out of the park each night. SDS and other groups which support Confrontation Politics rather than Being Politics tried to get people out in the streets sooner. Patience was at times a virtue.

Anyway, my strategy was to fight for every inch. That was the only way you could find out what was possible in Chicago. We had a two-hour fight, which we won, over plugging the electrical cable into the refreshment stand and finally there was MUSIC. Each little battle was exciting. The electric-cable fight was a big victory. Only the day before Chief Lynsky himself in the Pig Station (Lincoln Art and Culture Center) had sworn there would be no music in the park. He also swore that he would arrest me if I did anything wrong. He challenged me to kick him in the shins and I replied, "Only in front of NBC." I also gave a pep talk to the cops in the headquarters, saying "Don't let the National Guard steal your thunder." As I walked out of the building with my two cop tails I told them that all high level cops were phony liberals and full of shit. What I didn't tell them was two pieces of information that I picked up on this trip: 1) The cops were in a total state of disarray; walkie-talkies didn't work, they all had trouble with their different signals. I knew we would have better communication than they even if all our walkie-talkies were busted. 2) When I entered the police station, I noticed it was directly opposite 2100 North Lincoln Avenue. Up till then that building had been an ace in the hole. It had an interesting history. Four years ago the millionaire who had just renovated it went bankrupt. The apartment building was tied up in a court fight. It was totally empty and I had examined it through a cellar entrance five nights before in a very straight disguise. There was no electricity, the elevators didn't work, but it was totally habitable. It had one chain lock on the front door, which could be cut in 10 seconds. It could hold, counting the halls and everything, about 50,000 people, I estimated. There were two possible scenarios: 1) Grab it if it rained, which of course it never did. 2) Grab it on the last day and turn it over to the poor people of Chicago, making a statement about FREE RENT. However, I saw now that the location of the Police Headquarters rendered the building useless and I never thought about it again.

I guess we were discussing whether Jerry's trip or my trip happened. Jerry's original article spelled YIPPEE! thus. The button I designed spelled it YIPPIE! Let the people decide. It sure will be a hell of a debate. Jerry's a tough-son-of-a-bitch. He's got a hell of a fuckin' ego. Almost as big as mine but not quite. The debate will go on in print only, for Jerry is a writer. I know I can whip him publicly because I'll use any means necessary. I also know he reads his speeches. It's knowing shit like that which makes me such a cocky punk. Also knowing that I have a flower in my fist helps.

SCENE: Press conference held by MOB on Tuesday morning. I burst in with karate jacket, helmet, and heavy club made from the branch of a tree. I announce to the press that we are arming the Yippies and whatever the pigs dish into the park, we'll dish out. I keep slamming the club against my other palm.

REPORTER: Are you armed?
ME: I'm always armed.
REPORTER: Is that your weapon?
ME: This (holding club in the air and smiling), this is part of a tree. It symbolizes my love for nature.

Tuesday morning is chilly. I hustle my cop tails into driving me to North Beach. I walk across the sands and kneel next to Ginsberg and pick up the Indian chant "Hara—Hara, Hara—Krishna." I'm in my karate jacket and my club and helmet are at my side. I feel like the Samurai warrior in Church. The group is small and shivering under ragged blankets. I watch the gray waves of Lake Michigan roll against the beach. I notice the four patrol cars stationed on the roadway nearby. I cry real tears for about 10 minutes. I make a short speech about how this wasn't News in America. About how this wouldn't be on television that night but instead it would be shots of violence in the streets. I was very sad about that and cursed this fuckin' country. When I left, my tails said, "That's really strange, how can you go to that?" "A good politician always goes to church in the morning," I replied.

Advertisements, especially the best ones, have a fantastic amount of information. Watch, for example, *Meet the Press*, *Issues and Answers*, *Face the Nation*, or any of those boring, intellectual church-visitations on Sunday morning. Here is a typical one: a debate between a liberal and a conservative (not Vidal and Buckley—they are much more than rhetoric). The dry debate lasts about fifty minutes of the sixty allotted to the show. The other ten minutes are devoted to previews of the shows, station identification, and most importantly, commercials. Notice the way this ten minutes is treated as compared to the other fifty minutes. Notice the camera angles, cuts, flashes, zooms. Notice the play to the viewers' needs. Notice the appeal to "do what you've always wanted." The commercial is information. The program is rhetoric. The commercial is the figure. The program is the ground. What happens at the end of the program? Do you think any one of the millions of people watching the show switched from being a liberal to a conservative or vice versa? I doubt it. One thing is certain, though . . . a lot of people are going to buy that fuckin' soap or whatever else they were pushing in the commercial.

What would happen if a whole hour were filled with a soap commercial? That's a very interesting question and I will speculate that it would not work as well, which means that not as much information would be conveyed, that not much soap would be sold. It's only when you establish a figure–ground relationship that you can convey information. It is the only perceptual dynamic that involves the spectator.

Our actions in Chicago established a brilliant figure–ground relationship. The rhetoric of the Convention was allotted the fifty minutes of the hour, we were given the ten or less usually reserved for the commercials. *We were an advertisement for revolution*. We were a high degree of involvement played out against the dull field of establishment rhetoric. Watching the Convention play out its boring drama, one could not help but be conscious of the revolution being played out in the streets.

That underlying tension builds up and the viewer becomes totally involved with what we are doing EVEN IF HE CANNOT SEE OR EXPERIENCE IT DIRECTLY. He makes up what's going on in the streets. He creates the Yippies, cops, and other participants in his own image. He constructs his own play. He fabricates his own myth. Even if the media had decided on a total blackout of our activities, our message would have gotten through and perhaps with even more power. All people had to know was that America's children were getting slaughtered in the streets of Chicago and the networks were refusing to show it. WE CAN NEVER BE SHUT OUT. Not only would the public rebel against that form of censorship but also against the attempt to impose a dull ground upon an exciting figure. I'm sure what pissed off a good number of viewers was the fact that they were being forced to watch a dull, *Meet-the-Press*, Democratic Convention when, in fact, what they wanted to see was the Cops vs. Yippies football game taking place on the streets of Chicago.

> THE KEY TO ORGANIZING AN ALTERNATIVE SOCIETY IS TO ORGANIZE PEOPLE AROUND WHAT THEY CAN DO AND MORE IMPORTANTLY WHAT THEY WANT TO DO.

It is this principle that differentiates Yippie! from IBM and from the Mobilization as well. There is no ideology except that which each individual brings with him. The role he plays in building the alternative society will shape in some way its ideology. If he plays a role of total involvement, he will develop a feeling that he created the myth in his own image. He will also recognize that others have created it in their image and that in reality the myth becomes a Gestalt. The myth is greater than the sum of its parts. Energy-centers that originate or gravitate to the center of the myth have to trust not only the myth, but also the vast numbers of participants who want to add their garbage to the pile. If it is bad garbage it will quickly rot, if it is good garbage it will help transform the pile into a shrine of holiness.

6

FREE IS THE REVOLUTION

Free is the essence of Yippie! We operated Yippie! on less than $4,000 that we raised at a benefit and that we burned in a month. By the end of March we had no money, never used our bank account, had no meetings, had an office with no lock on the door and typewriters that would be liberated hours after they were donated. The non-leaders rarely visited the office, people who dropped in found themselves in a vacuum. They were forced to become leaders and spokesmen. They would answer the phones, distribute the leaflets, posters, stickers, and buttons. Everyone would answer the mail and Mitch Yippie would pick up the envelopes and sneak them through the postage meter at the place where he worked (he got caught and fired). The best article I read on Yippie! was written in a sex magazine called *Jaguar* and titled "an interview with the Queen of the Yippies." Most of us think it was totally fictitious, which, of course, makes it accurate. In Chicago we never really had an office although we used the *Seed*, Chicago's underground newspaper, as a coordination point (I was able to chisel two extra phones out of the phone company for the *Seed*, which was something

McCarthy couldn't even do because of the telephone strike), and the Free Theater on North Lincoln Street as another center. After Sunday night, the Free Theater was turned into the Communication Center, hospital, sleeping area, music theater, and FREE STORE on a twenty-four-hour basis. Paul Sills, its director, told me how the whole experience has changed his ideas. If I ever go back to Chicago it will only be to see what's going on at the Free Theater.

The concept of FREE is one of the chief differences we had with the MOB. Tuesday night we had a benefit at the Coliseum. We were to split the profits but we gave our share to the MOB—we would have burned it anyway. If I met people with money I would just ask them to come out to the park and dig what was happening. Some gave money, which we immediately "burned."

Thursday morning I visited the MOB office and found 20,000 copies of the *Rat* newspaper still wrapped up in one of the rooms. I asked this guy Lee what the fuck they were still doing there. "We want to sell them," he replied.

"To who? The whole thing's almost over. Why don't you just give them away?"

"How do you give them away?" he queried.

Slapping my forehead, I exclaimed, "Just throw them out the window!"

Late that night, just before I left Chicago, I stopped at the MOB office with the champagne. The newspapers are still there for all I know.

The FREE STORE lies at the center of our revolutionary vision. It is the key to organizing longhairs on the Lower East Side. Today there are hundreds who will fight to defend it, tomorrow there will be thousands. It breaks all the rules because it has only one: THOU SHALT NOT STEAL FROM THE FREE STORE.

Everything is given away free at the FREE STORE and so it is inundated with garbage. When you open a FREE STORE America cleans out her cellar and dumps it in front of your door. America calls this charity and a FREE STORE is not about charity. A FREE STORE accepts no garbage. Return all garbage to its original owner with a map to the nearest garbage dump. Old clothes and books are garbage. Accept old clothes only if you have facilities (sewing machines or tie-dye operations) to turn the garbage into art. A FREE

STORE dispenses ART, it does not dispense politics and it does not dispense garbage. For that you can always shop next door.

Everyone asks, "Who runs the FREE STORE?" There can only be one answer: "What do you want?" If you can help the customer then respond, "I run the FREE STORE." If you cannot help the customer then respond, "You run the FREE STORE."

There should be art on the windows and walls. The front should be particularly beautiful, to attract new customers. Making the store beautiful is the first order of business, keeping it beautiful is the second. The store can be called HEAVEN. HEAVEN is where you get whatever you want. You don't spit on the floor in HEAVEN. Paint stars on the ceiling, suspend fluffy clouds from the walls. Construct planets in the aisles. There should always be a supply of sandals, robes, wings and harps for those who wish to play clerk. Use Mylar on the walls. When you look at Mylar walls you look into your soul and smile. Cover the front with phosphorescent paint. It absorbs light and will glow at night. When people ask how the store is run, tell them "by the rays of the sun." In a FREE STORE there are no problems, there are only things to do. It is a free forum of theater in which the forces of art battle the forces of garbage. Who wins is unimportant, for the FREE STORE is a school and the student is repeatedly forced by the vacuum to choose sides. Which side are you on? Are you a garbage collector or are you an artist? The choice is always yours in a FREE STORE.

Last fall I spoke at Cornell and announced, "The food here is free!" and twenty of us walked into the cafeteria, loaded our trays with hamburgers, Cokes, and pies and walked out without paying. We sat in the dining hall laughing and slapping each other on the back stuffing our faces with Digger shit. I told them of epoxy glue and what a great invention it was. And at another school we asked them why they were there and they said just to get a diploma and so we passed out mimeographed sheets that said "This is a diploma," and asked the question again.

We appeared at Brooklyn College and announced, "The classroom environment is free," unscrewed desk tops and transformed them into guns, passed out incense and art, wrote Black Board on the door, switched off the lights and continued in darkness, announcing that the security guard was one of us, freeing him through the destruction of his identity, and in general doing whatever spontaneously came to mind. Our message is always: Do what you want. Take chances. Extend your boundaries. Break the rules. Protest is anything you can get away with. Don't get paranoid. Don't be uptight. We are a gang of theatrical cheerleaders, yelling Go! Go! Go! We serve as symbols of liberation. That does not mean that at times we do not get caught. Everyone's been arrested or stomped on or censored or shot at or fired from a job or kicked out of school or all that and more. "We've all been snuffed," as Ed Sanders says. It is not the snuffing but the notion that we can get away with taking chances that keeps us going. The reason I believe world revolution is inevitable is because the National Liberation Front is doing so well, not because they are getting slaughtered. Che Guevara went to Bolivia because they got away with it in Cuba. The Movement grows through successes, not through frustration. The ability to withstand frustration is what keeps us alive.

Our brothers and sisters are in the prisons of the universities. It is our duty to rescue them. Free men draw a line in Harvard Yard and dare President Pusey to "cross over the line." Students burst into the dean's office and when he asks them what they want they all hold a finger in the air. At San Francisco State, Black Panthers and even White Panthers wait on the rooftop ready to shoot if the administration calls the police onto campus. Make war on bells in school. Bring alarm clocks to class and have them ring on the half hour instead of the hour. You can buy a small Japanese tape recorder and a few speakers from a junkyard for about twenty-five dollars. Some careful camouflaging and you can suddenly turn the school into a huge discothèque.

Learning karate on the run. Pick up a move here, a move there. Practicing on the streets. I tried to close down this bad news commune on 11th Street run by Spade Charlie, a real amphetamine, V.D., clap headquarters. I stormed in the door screaming "Clean the place up." I gave some girl huddled in the corner two dollars and told her to go home. Spade Charlie, 250 pounds of blubber, dropped his amphetamine snort and picked up a bread knife in a rage. "Who said that?" "I did, motherfucker." It worked. He backed down.

The headline of the *Daily News* today reads BRUNETTE STABBED TO DEATH. Underneath in lower case letters: "6,000 Killed in Iranian Earthquake" . . . I wonder what color hair they had?

What happened in Chicago can be viewed in terms of a game. Football serves as the best model. (See McLuhan's *Understanding Media* and Norman Mailer's discussion of the Single Wing vs. the T-formation in his book *Advertisements for Myself.*) Cops vs. Yippies, YIP vs. MOB, Cops vs. Newsmen, Newsmen vs. Yippies. I would have loved to see the headline "Cops vs. National Guard." My money would have been on the Guard. One night in Chicago I heard part of a live broadcast of a football game. "The guards smashed through the center, Taylor is now running around end, he's really flying—SMASH! They nailed him good. It's a fumble . . ." I listened for about two minutes before I realized it wasn't the Battle of Michigan Avenue they were describing.

The only things I own are my books and a silver wedding ring. Anita bought me a portable tape recorder for our wedding. A month later I gave the tape recorder to Tom Hayden during the Newark Revolt when we brought over the truckloads of food. Anita never said a word. In a way, I guess we still have it.

Once in Japan there existed a group of warriors called the "No-Swordsmen." A Samurai and a No-Swordsman were riding on a raft with some people when the Samurai challenged the No-Swordsman to a duel. The No-Swordsman replied, "Let's jump out when we get to the next island rather than fight on the raft and possibly hurt the others." When the raft drifted by an island, the Samurai jumped out. The No-Swordsman didn't and the raft moved on. I wonder who won the duel? Funny about the word "duel," if you change one letter it becomes "duet."

And so you ask, "What about the innocent bystanders?" But we are in a time of revolution. If you are a bystander, you are not innocent.

Guerrilla theater is only a transitional step in the development of total life-actors. Life-actors never rehearse and need no script. *A life-actor uses whatever he has available,* nothing more, nothing less.

Guns are an interesting prop. Five months ago I got my first gun from a Hell's Angel friend. It was a 22-caliber pearlhandled pistol. I shot it into the wall of my living room. It made a hell of a racket. I kept it loaded under the bureau. When Jerry got busted I got rid of it along with the dope, fireworks, fuses, and various other assorted props. Although I admire the revolutionary art of the Black Panthers, I feel guns alone will never change this System. You don't use a gun on an IBM computer. You pull the plug out.

A Yippie believes only what he sees with his own two eyes, he accepts the rest as bullshit. A Yippie should examine his eyes once a month.

One night before it all happened I rode out to Bridgeport to see where Mayor Daley lived. It was a simple, sturdy bungalow no different from the others on the block, except for the guards. On the corner of the block, not fifty feet from Daley's house, was a huge, dull building with a sign over the door that said POLICE HEADQUARTERS. After seeing the rugged way he lived, there was no doubt in my mind that we would ever get a permit for anything.

One of my favorite quotes appeared in the Chicago *Tribune* on the Thursday before the Sunday: "According to Colonel Jack Reilley, the man chiefly responsible for the defense and security of Chicago and the Convention, there are no groups planning demonstrations during Convention Week."

THE PROBLEM IS NOT WHAT TO DO IN
THE REVOLUTION BUT
WHAT TO DO IN-BETWEEN THE REVOLUTION

Remembering about how you won the Battle of Chicago is not going to win the war.

PREDICTION: Because of our actions in Chicago, Richard Nixon will be elected President. Furthermore, Nixon will end the war in Vietnam. He will not only have a better chance than Humphrey but even than McCarthy of achieving a solution. Nixon will find it easier to deal with the National Liberation Front in Vietnam than to deal with the American Liberation Front here at home.

We present America with her most difficult problem. For America to burn innocent countries abroad is no problem, for America to commit genocide on the blacks that live in her cellar is no problem, for America to kill her children, that is her most difficult problem.

We have often been accused of being media-oriented. As with all criticism, it is both true and not true. The Mobilization had five times the number of press conferences that we did but we received five times the amount of coverage. The impression that we are media freaks is created by our ability to make news. *MEDIA is Communication*. The concept of getting it all out there applies whether you are speaking to one person or two hundred million.

We are printing 20,000 buttons that say YIPPIE! LEADER.

I believe in compulsory cannibalism. If people were forced to eat what they killed, there would be no more wars.

I read in the *New York Post* today that my bail bond has been increased to $5,000 and a warrant issued for my arrest—all this because of a naughty four-letter word. The honkie that tried to kill me, with an unregistered, loaded pistol, was held only three hours and released on $300 bail. I guess America is getting more prepared for guns than fucking.

The Street has always been an intriguing symbol in middle-class American life. It was always the place to avoid. There is "violence in the streets," "bad people in the streets," and "danger in the streets." It was always "let's keep the kids off the streets" as honkie America rushed from inside to inside. It is in the streets that we will make our struggle. The streets belong to the people! Long live the flower-cong of the gutters!

The FBI visited me this morning. As usual I bummed cigarettes, breakfast, and information. I found out they were having a difficult time proving conspiracy charges because of the Chicago police's mishandling of the situation. I also discovered their names, the fact that they have my phone tapped, and other valuable information. I told them I needed $20,000 to help me get to Prague, and inquired why they never asked if I was clubbed by cops, which is what the papers said they were investigating. I gave them an analysis of J. Edgar Hoover's latent homosexuality and other important information.

Never be afraid to talk to your enemy. If you are good you can always find out more about them then they can about you. If you are not good keep your mouth shut. When the FBI visits you they already know the answers to the questions anyway. Never attribute more intelligence to your enemy than to yourself and your brothers. Always trust your brothers and yourself.

THE GROUND YOU ARE STANDING ON IS A LIBERATED ZONE, DEFEND IT.

I have just visited the future. One cannot really talk of revolution without visiting "Man and his World" (formerly Expo '67) in Montreal. It is fantastic on a weekday morning when there are few tourists. It's magic to walk the mahogany boardwalks, ride streamlined tramways and flashing escalators. All Day-glos, purples, pinks, and greens. Twisting copper cobwebs, stretches of steel pillars, flowing concrete wings, and plastic tunnels. Cubes, triangles, bubbles, spaghetti nets, circles of light, fountains of energy; these are the shapes of things to come. One cannot tell the church from the fun house. "Is this the roller coaster or the subway, sir?" It is a perfect blend of harmony and excitement. I watched the people carefully as they laughed and danced through Future City . . . No one threw his garbage on the floor.

7

EGO TRIPPING

"I saw a man making love to his wife in Chicago . . ."
—WORDS TO AN OLD FAVORITE

About a year and a half ago, while I was working at Liberty House, a girl came in to volunteer. We got to talking about civil rights, the South and so on. She asked me about drugs. I asked if she had ever taken LSD. When she responded that she hadn't, I threw her a white capsule. She juggled it the way you would a lighted firecracker. That night we made love and we've been doing it ever since. Three months later we got married in Central Park. It was a beautiful June day. Linn House, on STP, played the part of the Boo-Hoo priest. Marty was best man, Fouratt, flower boy, and lots of our friends came. We were dressed all in white with daisies in our hair.

We live without conflict in a small apartment that we designed ourselves in the exact center of the busiest street (Saint Marx Place) on the Lower East Side. We spend most of our time in a bed we built seven feet off the floor.

There are no railings on the bed. Our love is strong enough to keep us suspended even if the bed collapsed.

Love is doing what you want to do, it's not all that give-and-take horseshit we were taught to believe. Anita has a Masters in psychology; once she entered Dorian Grey into a mental hospital. Now she spends most of her time stringing beads. I fell in love with her when she told me she didn't want to do anything. She is a true drop-out, a drop-out that could have made it, and made it big in the other world.

Thursday afternoon in Chicago, Ron (who had driven me around most of the time in Chicago, guarding me like a mother hen—even saving my life one night when he found his landlord at the front door of our apartment with a pistol), Anita and I walked along Michigan Avenue in front of the Conrad Hitler Hotel. I said I was going to march to the Amphitheater. Anita, who would rather sleep than march, said she was going back to the apartment. We kissed and parted. Ron came with me, reluctantly though, he didn't want to go on the march. He criticized me for not having more regard for Anita's feelings. "Ron," I said, "the reason you and I are just friends, and Anita and I are in love, is that Anita and I both do what we want." I think he finally understood because he left me and I didn't see him again that day.*

At eleven I could deal off the bottom of the deck in poker; by thirteen I didn't have to, I was so good. I have beaten everyone I've played in gin rummy. For a few years I used to play the horses every day and I still occasionally glance at the *Morning Telegraph*, one of the best papers in America. I've been in six-day crap games, where you develop a certain pacing that helps in situations like Chicago. I lost in Las Vegas, though. Gambling for high stakes, free and loose, taught me that money is only a prop, only a stake in the game. I guess all Diggers are gamblers.

At fifteen I learned how to steal cars. I have always been good at shoplifting. At seventeen I got thrown out of high school for hitting a teacher and got stabbed in the leg in a gang fight. It was sort of weird, being a nice Jewish boy and all. Then I went to prep school and later Brandeis and Berkeley, where I think I got a Masters in psychology—at least I got the

*This is the only section of the book I am dissatisfied with. I am tempted to discard it, but I won't. Love is the one thing easiest to do and the most difficult to talk about.

credits to become a state psychologist in Massachusetts. I did testing and research in a mental hospital for two years. I experienced a bum marriage (help stamp out first marriages) which produced two beautiful kids. I am a natural cook, which means I don't use a measuring cup. I have been a: drug salesman, ghetto organizer, campaign coordinator (peace campaign of Stuart Hughes and Thomas Adams, both in Massachusetts), SNCC field worker, movie theater manager, grinder in an airplane factory, camp counselor, cook.

I came to New York to start Liberty House in the West Village, which I designed, hustled the bread for, painted, and got sore fingers banging in the nails. I worked there seven days a week for $40.

I was always better at games than working. I was a Duncan Yo-Yo champion (remember the Filipino that came around with all the fancy tricks. He would carve initials in your yo-yo if you were good). My parents' house is cluttered with trophies from bowling, tennis, ping-pong, and autocar racing. I was captain of the tennis team in college, member of the wrestling team, and a member of a modern dance class. I played halfback on the junior varsity football team at Worcester Academy (the team played all the high schools around) and at 135 pounds that was an accomplishment. I broke my arm in one game. I did the Mississippi and Georgia tour of duty. I can roller skate fantastically as well as dance and fuck like no one I've ever met. I am good at golf, chess, bridge, basketball, and baseball. I have burned my draft card. I can pitch very good softball and play third base well. Last year in Newark I played tackle football with some black guys without any equipment and knew I was a hot shit. I can do all sorts of somersaults and acrobatic things, know party tricks galore and can hypnotize almost anyone. I have run with the bulls in Pamplona. I wear out six pairs of heels on my boots each year. I can ride a motorcycle. I never sit still and contrary to rumor don't use speed. I run on piss and vinegar. This is my form of meditation. I studied French for about seven years, including three weeks at the Institut d'Etudion Français, and I can speak practically none at all. I took music lessons on a variety of instruments each for about a week and can't play a one. The Group Image used to let me get up on stage and sing with Sheila Shelby, but now they want to make money. The Doors are my favorite rock group. They are the only group I can sit and listen to; the rest require dancing. I get bored at concerts and plays and only movies keep me totally absorbed. Some movies like *Viking Queen*, *Rosemary's Baby*, *2001*, *The*

Professionals, *Wild in the Streets*, *Battle of Algiers* I find fantastically compelling. I walked out of *La Chinoise* and in general find American movies better than foreign ones except for Fellini. I have been disappointed with Truffaut and Bergman lately. Bob Dylan and the Beatles are so great I hesitate to even mention them. I have what psychologists call eidetic imagery and an I.Q. of 78, resulting from over seventy LSD trips. I love Marvel comics and Moxie is my favorite drink, but unfortunately you can get it only in Massachusetts.

That ain't half of it, but if I wanted to be known for anything I guess it would be for my ability to hustle pool. Pool-hustling is a fine and delicate art. I'm one of the best there is. That doesn't mean I'm necessarily one of the best pool players. There are thousands of better players than me. A pool-hustler is a guy who plays only people he can beat. I was very young when I began hanging around pool halls. I used to bowl a lot and I became fascinated by the poolhall scene in the back of most bowling alleys: the old Buddhas sitting around the tables, following each shot, rarely making a sound; the ritualistic dances the players made; the pool-talk language; the battlefield of green felt, sixteen cannon balls of multicolored ivory, and rifle butts of long straight cue sticks. I was especially impressed, of course, by super hustlers who carried their own pool sticks. In a religious ceremony that would rival the Eucharist they would unpack and screw together the various parts of their cue sticks, powder their hands, spit in the corner, and be ready. The act of being "ready" in a pool game is the act of being ready in the world. After a year of solid practice, I finally earned the privilege of having a cue stick with my name on it placed in a special rack on the wall. For the next few years I practiced hustling. You know, walking into a pool hall, running a few racks fairly well, not as good as you really are. For the art of pool-hustling is to be only good enough to win. When some guy comes up and says, "Hey kid, how about some nine-ball?" that's the point at which you have to know everything there is to know. Examine the way he walks, how he grabs the stick out of the rack. Estimate the cost of his shoes (a clue to how much money he has in his pocket). Should it be money up front or can he be trusted? Do you beat him straight out or lose the first game or two? How much time has he got? Can you learn anything from him even if he's better than you? (Play for low stakes.) Most importantly, can he beat you? It's the knack of answering that question that makes the difference between a good hustler and a fish. It's being a good pool-hustler that has kept me alive.

One night in Chicago Anita and I went into a pool hall. One of these fancy family billiard parlors with mostly lousy players and Muzak. I shot two racks without missing—rat-tat-tat, like a machine gunner bouncing around the table. I made fancy show-off shots like behind-the-backers and one where you roll the ball down the table and then slam it into the corner pocket with the cue ball. I didn't miss a trick. It was the best pool I had ever played in my entire life.

8

EPILOGUE

Tuesday, September 17, 1968, was one hell of a day. I returned to Chicago with my attorney, Jerry Lefcourt, to stand trial for the infamous four-letter WORD on my forehead. I wanted to clear this matter up because I expected trouble at Customs when I attempted to leave to go to Prague. As we stepped off the airplane at O'Hare Airport, we were met by six of Chicago's finest. I was immediately handcuffed and arrested on a charge of jumping bail even though it was obvious to everyone I had only come back to Chicago to appear in court that afternoon. I was questioned in a special room in the airport and when asked to empty my pockets, I produced a pen knife I had purchased the day before in New York. It is a knife that is legal in every state of the union. The cops couldn't figure out how to open it so dubbed it a switchblade. After I was taken to court to stand trial for the WORD and to be arraigned on bail-jumping charges (these charges were dropped), I was again arrested by the Chicago police for carrying a concealed weapon. When bail was produced on this charge, I was then arrested by the FBI and charged with "crimes aboard an aircraft." The FBI is the only agency in the country that arrests you and makes it seem like they are doing you a favor. The dialogue went something like this:

FBI: You are now being placed under arrest for crimes aboard an aircraft.

ME: Are you kidding? All I did was goose the stewardess, what crimes?

FBI: Our instructions are to tell you only that. We must warn you that anything you say may be used against you. We'll just settle this before the U.S. Commissioner, it won't take long. We are sorry to inconvenience you this way.

ME: Can I call my wife and tell her I'll be home late from work?

FBI: Yes, we think that is certainly a most reasonable request.

In the car, driving to the Federal Building, they asked if I used any aliases. I gave them enough for three sheets of paper. They recorded them all diligently, including Casey Stengel, George Metesky, Spiro Agnew, and Muriel Humphrey. Lo and behold, the Commissioner wasn't home and it was into the jail for the night. Chicago city jails, by the way, have the worst food of any jails I have ever been in. That morning I appeared before a U.S. Commissioner who looked like the guy who played the telephone booth in *The President's Analyst*. The "crimes aboard an aircraft" revolved around the mysterious pen knife and the judge was very serious. Here is some of the dialogue:

COMMISSIONER: When you came to Chicago you said you were unemployed?

ME: Well, thanks to the Chicago police, I've become a very successful writer. I just finished a book about Chicago, a children's book, and I'm in a movie. I made $10,000 this week, but I plan to burn it all.

COMMISSIONER: Have you ever been arrested?

ME: I've been arrested over twenty times, but I've never been convicted. There are a lot of cops breaking the law in this country.

COMMISSIONER: Have you ever jumped bail?

ME: Only once, in Mississippi, but it was under unusual circumstances.

COMMISSIONER: What were they?

ME: The Ku Klux Klan was organizing a lynching party and my attorney thought it wise if I blew town.

COMMISSIONER: Does the District Attorney demand bail?

D.A.: The People ask $1500 bail, your honor.

COMMISSIONER: I think I'll make that $2500 and you are confined to Chicago and the Federal District of Manhattan.

ME: Can I go to Prague?

COMMISSIONER: No.

ME: Well, if you think the U.S. Government can handle the Czechoslovakian mess better than the Yippies, you can have that one. Can I go to Massachusetts to visit my mother?

COMMISSIONER: No.

ME: Can I go above 14th Street?

COMMISSIONER: Yes, but you cannot leave Manhattan except to return to Chicago.

ME: I want you to know that I accuse you and the Federal Government of committing an unjust act of revenge.

I turned around and walked out of the courtroom. Much to my surprise, the Commissioner did nothing.

It had been some day. I had been fingerprinted no less than seventeen times and spent most of the time in various sets of handcuffs. As I was sitting in the airplane waiting to fly back to New York, the pilot made an announcement that the flight would be delayed fifteen minutes. Five men entered the airplane. Four, I recognized as members of the Chicago Intelligence Division that had been following me throughout the Convention, the other identified himself as a U.S. Marshal. He handed me a piece of paper which began, "Greetings: You are hereby commanded to appear before the House Un-American Activities Committee . . ." It was like receiving a high school diploma.

The time since Chicago has been filled with persistent government harassment. On three occasions a phony Brink's truck has stopped outside our FREE STORE on the Lower East Side, a panel opens up and a camera begins taking photographs. I have been visited no less than five times by FBI agents, twice by Justice Department officials and once by the Internal Revenue Service.

On Tuesday, October 2, 1968, we appeared before HUAC. Jerry wore a one-man, world-conspiracy, guerrilla costume complete with toy M-16 and live ammunition. I went as an Indian with feathers, hunting knife, and a bullwhip. I also carried an electric yoyo and dazzled the Committee with tricks like, "Around-the-Capitalist-World," "Split-the-Southern-Cracker," and "Burning-Down-the-Town." On the first day, the hearing was very dull. HUAC missed Joe Pool and at one point I suggested we have five minutes of silence in his memory. When the Committee refused, I accused them of being "soft on Communism." I persisted in asking permission to go to the bathroom and pointing out to the Committee the different people in the room who were carrying guns (all Capitol guards, of course, but you never can tell, some sneaky Yippie might have rented a cop suit). Jerry walked around waving his gun and rattling his bells, his girlfriend Nancy was dressed as a Halloween witch and passed out incense. The Committee dragged on with boring testimony trying to link us to Communists (many of whom were active before we were born), and even at one point to Lee Harvey Oswald. The acting chairman of the Committee made repeated warnings against "emotional outbursts." By about three o'clock, I was so bored I couldn't take it any longer. I asked permission to make an emotional outburst. They said not in the room, so I retired to the hall and shouted, "You're full of shit" so loud it shook the Capitol Building. When the cops tried to jump me, I told them the Committee requested I do it in the hall. They let me go. Thirty minutes later, the lawyers who had been raising objections throughout the day stood in protest with their clients. They were hustled out by the cops and that ended Act I.

Wednesday, we broke for Yom Kippur or the World Series, and the Committee carried on in closed session. They heard all about the Yippie plans to assassinate Mayor Daley and blow up a baseball diamond in Lincoln

Park. A secret "deal" was revealed that showed we had arranged with the Headhunter Motorcycle Club to provide them with girls and dope if they would furnish us ammunition. At one point, we were accused of going to Chicago "to perform magic."

Thursday, I appeared in a commercially made shirt that has red and white stripes and stars on a blue background. Capitol police arrested me for mutilating the flag and proceeded to rip the shirt off my back. Anita screamed and was arrested for felonious assault on a policeman. Anita's charges were later dropped. I had to spend the night in jail (the judge originally set bail at $3000, which kind of shocked everyone) and then I was detained an extra five hours by U.S. Marshalls illegally. Of course, the terms "legal" and "illegal" are phrases lawyers throw back and forth and have nothing to do with the reality of what's happening in the judicial system in this country. The law I was arrested under would make everyone who dresses in an Uncle Sam costume and most drum majorettes criminals. The other night, I watched Phyllis Diller perform on national television in a miniskirt that looked more like an American flag than the shirt I wore.

The hearings were adjourned to Thursday and we were ordered to return December 2, 1968 to begin our testimony. I plan to reveal everything. But I must warn the Committee that there will be a continuing language barrier. I requested permission to bring an interpreter to the October hearings, but permission was denied. I brought her anyway, but it was still difficult to understand them. They spoke of Marx and I thought they meant Groucho. My interpreter said, "No, they mean Karl Marx." They spoke of Lenin and I thought they meant John Lennon of the Beatles. My interpreter said, "No, they mean the guy without a first name." It was all getting very confusing, but what's to be expected when CHROMOSOME DAMAGE meets the DINOSAURS. One thing I will state, however, before I even testify is that "I am not now nor have I ever been a member of the House Un-American Activities Committee."

A final basic question is: "What would happen if large numbers of people really do decide to fuck the system?" What would happen if large numbers of people in the country started getting together, forming communities, hustling free fish on Fulton Street, and passing out brass washers to use in the laundromats and phones? What if people living in slums started moving into abandoned buildings and refusing to move even to the point of defending them with guns? What if this movement grew and busy salesmen sweating under the collar on a hot summer day decided to say fuck the system and headed for welfare? What if secretaries got tired of typing memos to the boss's girlfriend in triplicate and took to panhandling in the streets? What if when they called a war, no one went? What if people who wanted to get educated just went to a college classroom and sat-in without paying and without caring about a degree? Well, you know what? We'd have ourselves one hell of a revolution, that's what.

PART TWO

FROM

WOODSTOCK NATION

1969

9

FOREPLAY

During the past few years I have straddled the line between "the movement" and "the community," between "the left" and "the hip," between the world of "the street" and the world of "media." I have doubts that I can go on balancing these forces in my head much longer.

I emerged exhausted, broke and bleeding from the WOODSTOCK NATION [Woodstock had ended two days prior to this writing, in late August, 1969]. It was an awesome experience but one that made me have a clearer picture of myself as a cultural revolutionary—not a cultural nationalist, for that would embrace a concept of hip capitalism which I reject—and not a political revolutionary either. Political revolution leads people into support for other revolutions rather than having them get involved in making their own. Cultural revolution requires people to change the way they live and act in the revolution rather than passing judgments on how the other folks are proceeding. The cultural view creates outlaws, politics breeds organizers.

Certainly some jabs will be taken here at my cousin revolutionaries, especially those identified in the mind of the public as the "New Left," but these are meant in the spirit of free interchange and to get a sense of the fluidity and contradictions in the total revolution going on today. I feel certain I have emerged a cultural revolutionary concerned with building and defending the new NATION that gave us a glimpse of its beauty on the shores of White Lake in the Catskill mountains.

When I appear in the Chicago courtroom [the Chicago 7 trial for conspiracy with intent to incite riots during the Democratic Convention in Chicago was due to begin on September 24, 1969], I want to be tried not because I support the National Liberation Front—which I do—but because I have long hair. Not because I support the Black Liberation Movement, but because I smoke dope. Not because I am against a capitalist system, but because I think property eats shit. Not because I believe in student power, but that the schools should be destroyed. Not because I'm against corporate liberalism, but because I think people should do whatever the fuck they want, and not because I am trying to organize the working class, but because I think kids should kill their parents. Finally, I want to be tried for having a good time and not for being serious. I'm not angry over Vietnam and racism and imperialism. Naturally, I'm against all that shit but I'm *really* pissed cause my friends are in prison for dope and cops stop me on the street cause I have long hair. I'm guilty of a conspiracy, all right. Guilty of creating liberated land in which we can do whatever the fuck we decide. Guilty of helping to bring the WOODSTOCK NATION to the whole earth. Guilty of trying to overthrow the motherfuckin senile government of the U.S. of A. I just thought you ought to know where my head was at, PIG NATION. Just thought I'd let you know what I mean when I say, "I'm just doin my thing."

Enough of this bullshit! Light up your joint, inhale and proceed to the next song.

10

LANDING A MAN ON THE EARTH WITHOUT THE HELP OF NORMAN MAILER

When I finished *Revolution for the Hell of It* in three days the first thing I did was fly up to Provincetown to armwrestle Norman Mailer. I sure looked a sight coming up that road barefoot, my Medusa-like long hair flying mad all over my grinnin puss. I knew my Chicago battle-crazy face was staring out at Mailer from the center of *The New York Times* magazine section that had been delivered that morning. It was some feat writing the book that quick, quicker by weeks than even Mailer who was damn fast and damn fuckin good even if he was getting a little too clinical and even though his Negro maid answered the door. He was the best all right, the best writer in *their* NATION. In WOODSTOCK NATION there are no writers—only poet-warriors.

WOODSTOCK NATION is built on ELECTRICITY. It is our energy, music, politics, school, religion, play, battleground and our sensuality. I hesitate only in using the word Morality, for Morality means soul and ELECTRICITY lacks soul but so too does this wooden pen I scratch against the yellow pad. Morality rests in God's imagination and if we see ourselves as gods I guess we alone make those choices. Moral decisions never rest in our tools, be they electricity or pencils, flowers or guns.

I suppose Mailer also had such thoughts; after all, he has a good mind and is always testing his environment. In the year following Chicago, I too tried to experiment: a book and a half, three quick movies, one to design and edit, the other two to improvise-act in, and lots more to get absorbed into like "The Wild Bunch," "Savage Seven" (brilliant sleeper about bikers and Indians joining together to rip off a fat capitalist named Fillmore), "Midnight Cowboy," and of course, the almost perfect propaganda film, "Easy Rider." I also did a unique Yippie calendar, ten or so street theater events, wasted time battling SDS, gave about seventy speech-performances, had hepatitis and almost died, flew about eighty thousand miles, spent a lot of time in court with my lawyer Jerry Lefcourt, helped paint the apartment, take out the garbage and cooked a lot (Women's Liberation take note in case you get pissed later when I use the word "chick"). In between I managed to write about thirty articles, mostly under other names, for the underground press, and a few children's stories. I founded the Movement Speakers' Bureau—a very good idea—and helped to hustle bread and spread the word on the conspiracy trial. I took about twenty acid trips, fucked about 856 times and did a few things that only the FBI knows about and lots of other stuff they don't. I managed to get busted only ten times and face a possible thirty-seven years or so in prison. I also quit smoking of which I am proudest of all. It ain't been too busy a year, but maybe that's cause I was zonked with the hep for three months, so for a nine-month year it ain't bad, especially since the in-fighting between movement groups and factions had reached grating proportions. I suppose all this energy results from being an anarchist, Jewish, bottle-fed, stubborn, beautiful, white, spoiled brat, dedicated, male, young, old, optimistic, Sagittarius, schmuck, revolutionist, communist, god, self-destructive, egotistical, horny, show-off, paranoid-schizophrenic, naive, fucked-up, big-mouth, not serious, brilliant, honest Yippie leader and non-leader and a whole lot more from Concord, Mass., and the Bronx, New York.*

Well, anyway, there I was on my way to see Mailer for an arm-wrestling contest, something at which I was pretty damn good considering I am a

*Each descriptive phrase appeared in somebody's review of me. I wonder what critics see when they get up in the morning and look in the mirror.

lightweight. Three months later I was to fight a draw with MIT Professor of Communications, Jerome Lettvin, on his television show in Boston. That was some trip. He weighed about twice as much as me and smoked a cigar while he grunted and I swore out phrases at him in Yiddish like *alta kaka* as I strained. Paul Krassner sort of refereed. I was on acid and had just driven a car through the Concord Bridge parking lot fence. Lettvin's wife, who teaches gym classes for early-morning viewers, cheered him on, and my two kids, age eight and six, cheered me on. It was a draw and each of us developed a certain measure of respect for the other. I saw this cat debate Leary and thought that battle was a draw. I figured I'd lay the professor out by doing whatever the fuck came along, just act out answers instead of playing interviewer word-game mish-mash.

LETTVIN: (*Alta kaka voice*) Why do you insist on calling policemen pigs?

ABBIE: (*Spoiled brat*) Cause on TV we can't call them cocksuckers.

LETTVIN: (*For the third time*) Yes, yes, I've heard that, but what is this revolution going to accomplish?

ABBIE: (*Smiles and kicks over the table, smashing two ashtrays and making a general mess*)

LETTVIN: (*Excited*) I knew it! Violence! Violence! You'll never win.

ABBIE: (*Pulling out a ten dollar bill and holding it up*) Wanna bet ten bucks?

LETTVIN: (*Reaching for the bill*) Let me see that.

ABBIE: (*Pulling it back and ripping it slowly into pieces*) Hey man, we've already won.

Well, I never cracked Norman Mailer's defenses, never even saw him that day, but when I glimpsed the way he lived an all I wasn't interested any more in armwrestling him. It was sort of the feeling I had later when I told one of his campaign aides in the primary that Norman should swim the East River in Brooklyn, Mao-style, to make the point that if he were elected he would clean the river so everyone could swim in it by 1974 (which, incidentally, could be done). That aide just gave me this Eugene McCarthy-liberal look that spelled C-R-A-Z-Y. Guess me and that bit just ain't his scene. Like booze and Negro maids ain't mine.

Anyway, Mailer is off writing his book on the space program for $1,000,000 for *Life* magazine, while I try to sort out the most remarkable event in *our* history (as opposed to *their* history), the creation of WOODSTOCK NATION. It was a phenomenal burst of human energy and spirit that came and went like a tidal wave up there in White Lake, Bethel, Woodstock, Aquarian Exposition, Music Festival, Happening, Monster, or whatever you called the fuckin thing. I took a trip to our future. That's how I saw it. Functional anarchy, primitive tribalism, gathering of the tribes. Right on! What did it all mean? Sheet, what can I say, brother, it blew my mind out. It blew it in the way I guess Mailer's mind is now gettin blown out in Houston, Texas, while he tries to rationalize the meaning of men walking around on the moon. To each his own cup of TEA.

If I had to sum up the totality of the Woodstock experience I would say it was the first attempt to land a man on the earth. It took an awful lot of people to pull it off, but pull it off we did. Welcome to the Aquarian Age.

11

THORNS OF THE FLOWER CHILDREN

Once upon a time, about a generation ago, right after the thirteen-thousand-seven-hundred-and-sixty-fourth demonstration against the war in Vietnam, young people started to congregate in an area of San Francisco known as the Haight-Ashbury. They were sick of being programmed by an educational system void of excitement, creativity and sensuality. A system that channeled human beings like so many laboratory rats with electrodes rammed up their asses into a highly mechanized maze of class rankings, degrees, careers, neon supermarkets, military-industrial complexes, suburbs, repressed sexuality, hypocrisy, ulcers and psychoanalysts. The world they came from was a world of Double Speak. A world where Lyndon Johnson and his fabulous wife Lady Bird sat in their Miami-modern ranch house, drank their bourbon, and led the nation in a marathon game of Scrabble. The victor, naturally, would donate the winnings to his or her favorite charity.

"Mah fellow Pigs, this land of ours is the most peace-loving nation in the history of the world. This government stands for peace. It does not believe social change can come about through violence. Oink-oink."

> Saigon, Vietnam: Colonel James Rivers, a veteran of World War II, Korea, and now in Vietnam, stated that the American fighting man never had it so good as in Vietnam. Just back from supervising a raid in the Mekong Delta in which over 5,000 of the enemy were killed in three days of heavy fighting, Rivers admitted, "This is the only war in history where the fighting man can sleep in a warm bed, eat a good breakfast, take a helicopter ride to battle, pause for a lunch break and return to the base in a helicopter in time for supper and a look at the day's fighting on the evening's telecast. Vietnam is the first commuter war," he explained.

And, when the game was over, Latin America, "our partners in progress," was selected as PIG NATION'S favorite charity.

> Rio de Janeiro, Brazil: Top sources in the U.S. Foreign Aid Program revealed today that of the 25,000 tons of meat shipped to Brazil under the Alliance for Progress, 85 per cent ended up in the hands of wealthy ranch owners.

Meanwhile back on the ranch, the Boob-Tube was filling our heads with all kinds of cotton-candy news.

> New York, New York: WPIX-TV (Channel 11) was reprimanded today by the Federal Communications Commission for showing pictures of maneuvers in Fort Belvoir, Virginia and labeling them Central Highlands and Danang. They also were accused of showing old footage depicting crowd scenes from Budapest and renaming them Prague. When reached, the station had no comment.

So the kids had heard a lot of stuff and had made their minds up. They saw their fathers disappear behind the corn flakes box and hurry off to their other lives in a distant land called DOWNTOWN. On weekends they saw them mowing the lawn with a dumb-looking gadget that broke down more than it worked. They saw them load up station wagons with golf clubs and run off to stand in lines for five hours to have fun (?) on the golf course running around in Bermuda shorts and silly little shoes. They heard from their mothers over and over again about being *respectable* and *responsible* and, above all, *reasonable*.

They would say things like:

> What's going on is simply terrible. You never can be too white . . . What's the matter with kids these days? When I was your age . . . I think you'll straighten out once you get into college . . . Your views would be O.K. if only you would cut your hair . . .

They monopolized the TV set with Bob Hope, baseball games, situation comedies about people like them and of course Ed Sullivan. They liked to "keep up" so they read *Time* Magazine and the N.Y. *Times* on Sunday. When some politician came on TV they would say things like, "That fellah makes damn good sense." It sure was a drag. If there ever was a Desolation Row it climbed into the front seat of the Oldsmobile on Monday morning, checked its passport and headed DOWNTOWN and not the one that Petula Clark sang about, no sir not that DOWNTOWN. Downtown Desolation Row is Wall Street not Times Square. The old men get their rocks off in the Stock Exchange, not in the balcony of the Apollo or the Guild or even the De Mille or Loew's State. . . .

And the music told it over and over:

> See my daddy in bed a-dyin,
> See his hair turnin gray,
> He's been workin and slavin his life away,
> He's been workin, workin, work-work.
>
> —THE ANIMALS

The work that the kids saw around them was so odious, so boring, so worthless that they came to regard WORK as the only dirty four-letter word in the English language.

So the kids took off for the hills of Vermont and the deserts of New Mexico and the slums of the Lower East Side and lots of places in between. Millions more took the trip. Millions ran away with flowers in their hair. Maybe they just took off for a couple days, maybe they took off forever. Some even died on the road. But they took off from Desolation Row every time they snuck a joint in the afternoon when Mom was down at the laundromat.

The ones who made it were tough. Tough as all hell. Like bare feet that had crawled through glass-jagged streets like Tenth Street and the Haight. People that can keep their minds together amid slum chaos.

> See that girl, barefoot (doeeyoumoo)
> Whistlin and a-singin
> She's a carryin on
> Laughin in her eyes, dancin in her feet,
> She a (neonwhirrwhirrmoo)
> And she can live on the street.
>
> —GRATEFUL DEAD

A new culture with psychedelic wings and big ears for hearing heavy sounds was perched up on the telephone wires. "Hey Prudence, come on out and pla-aaay." "Hey brother! Hey sister!" "Break on through to the other side." "Turn on, tune in, drop out," sang the Leary singers and although the parents were leery of Reverend Tim the kids weren't leery at all. Not one bit.

Then it happened. PIG NATION came to collect its kids, some sad-looking, tweed-suited, boney dude named George and a bitchy wife he called Delilah. Behind them was this huge motherfuckin steel-and-chrome Moloch called BIG BUSINESS. George had a straightjacket and Delilah, you guessed it, a pair of scissors. BIG BUSINESS had the biggest mouth you ever saw and loads of teeth, flat like cows' teeth for grinding. It was said that Moloch regurgitated his food. You would have believed anything if you had seen him comin.

So what did the kids do? Well, everybody made up stories. Like they went to Bellevue, or went home or got killed in the cellar on Avenue B, or went back to school, or went to the country. In the land of the hippies everybody was always "going to the country" even if they were already there.

The cops didn't buy the peace-and-flower shit, no sir, a lot of folks mostly liberals bought that crap but not the cops, hell no. They didn't see the "beautiful people," the "gentle generation," they saw commie-drug-addict-sex-crazy-dirty-homosexual-nigger-draft-card-burner-runaway-spoiled-brats. What they also saw was *their* kids, for they too were letting their hair grow a little longer and putting up those weird posters that stared out at them as they cruised past the local head shop. And that music! Why did it have to be so loud? It wasn't just the cops though, cause cops are part of a paid army and soldiers in a non-revolutionary force take orders. So people higher up, even if they didn't scream it as they charged in a flying wedge, felt the pressure and thought it. "Kill those fuckin hippies, my kid'll be with em next." "Get em quick; before you know it they'll be in Chicago throwing bags of shit." "Isn't it about time we had some LAW and ORDER?" Which is simply a more polite way of saying "Kill those fuckin hippies."

Hippies took a lot of crap. Illegal busts of crash pads and communes in the Lower East Side. Arbitrary curfews in Cambridge. Signs saying BAREFOOT PEOPLE KEEP OUT and WE DO NOT SERVE HIPPIES HERE in the Big Sur area of California. Tear gas raids on Haight-Ashbury. Heavy fighting at a music festival in Palm Springs and, at that crossroad of all movements, Telegraph Avenue, pitched battles over a people's park. Here the Berkeley Pigs earned their nickname well, as they pumped tear gas and buckshot into kids and killed a twenty-five-year-old long-hair watching from a roof. His name was and still is James Rector. You ought to take your hat off when you hear his name.

WOODSTOCK NATION wept the night Ronald Reagan, "the fascist gun in the West," sent the Pigs into Berkeley. Not everyone wept though. Three thousand miles away in the part of the NATION called the Lower East Side, someone tried to firebomb the Fillmore in retaliation. They missed and burned down the building next door. Too bad in a way cause most of us used to rip off the Lion Supermarket there when we had to eat and had no dough. Fans poured out into the streets even though The Who (who else) kept playin away. They were so zonked into their thing that Peter Townshend kicked a plainclothes cop in the balls when he tried to make an announcement and got arrested. I think it might be helpful if you know about this stuff before you judge the WOODSTOCK NATION. It didn't just happen in those three days, it was a long time comin.

This is something else you should know:

> Stamford, Connecticut: Today the publisher of *Reader's Digest* was stabbed by his sixteen-year-old son. He had just returned from a businessman's luncheon in which he delivered what was termed an ''anti-hippie'' speech.

12

½ OF ELVIS PRESLEY

People of all shapes and sizes are always coming up to me and asking me why I do what I do or am what I am. As I explained in the first book I can lay a hundred explanations all at once on em or just drop the Bomb. The Bomb meaning that one punch line. That put-on that turns everything you just said upside down. Like dig this, for example. The first book has a paragraph missing at the end. Can you imagine that? The publishers cut out the punch line because it would mean using a whole new page. Anyway, here it is:

> Well, I guess I'm getting a little tired so I think
> I'll buzz over to the Gem Spa for an egg cream
> and end it. See you after the Revolution when,
> of course, it'll be business as usual.

See, it's the "humbler" when you really let people know you're only in it for kicks and stuff and it keeps them off that follower-nagging-trip that makes you feel like a martyr, and an itchy martyr at that! It keeps down the "Dear Abbie" mail.

So when people ask a lead-in question like that, they are kind of open for a Zen jab that might help them see that they're really just like me and me like them, the only difference being that I love my work. Often when they ask those questions they ask, "How come you're a radical?" or "How come a hippie?" or "How can you say things like 'Kids should kill their parents?'" I make up a lot of stories, but now for the first time I'm about to tell the TRUTH, the whole TRUTH and nothing but the TRUTH.

Back during the 1950's me and the guys I bummed around with when I got thrown out of school wore pegged pants, had DA haircuts, blue suede shoes, and hung around pool halls swearing and spitting a lot. The music we listened to was called race-records and then rhythm and blues. Varetta Dillard singing "Mercy Mister Percy" was the first race-record I ever heard. We dug stuff like Earl Bostic, James Moody, the Midnighters, Joe Turner, and later the Drifters and Fats Domino. It was all 45 rpm stuff which made for easy swipin, simple under-the-jacket stuff. The trouble was that very few stores carried the stuff cause Patti Page singing about porcelain "Old Cape Cod" and Frankie Laine moaning "I Believe" religious hymns and Tony Bennett singing funky Tony Bennett Blues was all the stores knew. On the radio too there was just Symphony Sid out of Boston and later Moondog out of New York. We were two hundred and fifty miles from New York and had to rig up a roof antenna to hear ol Alan Freed bang a telephone book on the table while he spun out the Sound. The Sound was SAXOPHONE and it was "Unh—unh—stick—it—in—wa—doo—was." Dances were all grunts and belts with names like the Ginny-Crawl and Roxbury Mule, and there were a very few of us doing it. You just didn't do the Dirty Boogie to Theresa Brewer, no sir, and not at the Totem Pole in Newton, Mass., no man, definitely not. The whole scene except for a few of us hoods—I think that's what we preferred to be called especially if we had read *A Stone for Danny Fisher* and *The Amboy Dukes*—so except for us hoods and Bill Haley and his Comets, the whole fuckin scene was Black. Black-Ass sockin it out and humpin a sax while sweat poured out in buckets. "Shake, baby, shake, baby, shake, till the meat rolls off your bones" and "I'm gonna roll like a big wheel through the Georgia cotton fields, Honey Hush"—God that music sure gave you a boner and gettin laid then wasn't like it is today so you'd slick your hair with grease and learn how to pick your teeth with a toothpick instead.

Then it happened. It was the first taste I got of the Culture-Vultures. I didn't know the term then, in fact I knew shit about any kind of politics, except whether or not you were gonna pay up if you lost the game of nine ball like you said you would. "I didn't know nothin" (to coin a popular phrase of the time). But somehow I smelled a fish. "Sh-boom, Sh-boom, eya-ta-ta-ta-ta-ta, Sh-boom, Sh-boom, if I could take you home again, Sh-boom, Sh-boom. . ." All of a sudden you heard it not being sung by the Chords, but by a strange group that didn't sing it from the guts out. They sang it obscene, fake, commercial, phony. I don't know what it was, but the group, they were clean as hell, whiter than Ivory Snow and Grace Kelly and they were called the CREWCUTS. Motherfuckin WASPS. We were soon to learn there was a whole fuckin pack of WASPS buzzin around and they were all related to that bitch Patti Page and worse, Ezio Pinza and Mary Martin. Their leader was a lean corn flake named Pat Boone who ran around ripping off black-ass rock-and-roll and dressin it up with white bucks! WHITE BUCKS! Stepping on punks' white bucks as they came home from school was in fact among my first political acts, but even this didn't repay the feeling of wretched puke you felt when you pictured Snookie Lanson singing "Earth Angel" on the Lucky Strike Hit Parade.

Nothing else more than that rip-off of black music made me more ashamed of being white than anything, not even the "woman who came in on Thursdays." But all of a sudden, some dude came struttin up from down in the South somewhere. He dug bikes like in "The Wild One" and he smirked like James Dean in everything. He was a tough-ass motherfucker and he sang from the inside out and yet he was white. He belted it out and what he said was get the fuck off my blue suede shoes, get your fuckin crew-cut, white-buck, sissy boots off my blues. Get your big dynaflo Buick off the fuckin road and let my chopped and channeled '49 Merc fly. Get those fuckin tweeds out of Ware Pratt's and let me see those sweet talkin pegs. And baby, you better move quick or you won't just be cryin in the chapel, you'll be dyin.

Then event two happened in the life of said Communist-Bastard. Ed Sullivan, you know Ed Sullivan, well, he owned the whole plantation in those days. If you weren't on the Sullivan Shooow you didn't exist. Ed Sullivan, the Rock of Ages, who two months ago said when introducing James Earl Jones, "Ladies and gentlemen, a credit to anybody's race." Now Big Ed after much hassle had agreed to put Elvis on live. Wow! Elvis was gonna do "Heartbreak Hotel" and "Blue Suede Shoes" and all the gang came over to watch. It was Sunday night about 8:30 p.m. sometime in the late fifties.

You know what? We never did get to see his blue suedes, in fact the truth of it is, we never got to see anything below Elvis' navel! It was only the bottom half of Elvis that mattered, and fucking Ed Sullivan and CBS-TV and Madison Avenue and FCC and the Pentagon could never understand that. I got a little dizzy watching the top half of Elvis bobbin around like a fishin cork in a bathtub and staggered into the john, pukin up all the booze and Devil Dogs and with it a lot more. "Hey man, you O.K.?" asked my buddy, Hack. "Yeh, sure, how the hell can they do that? If I see that Sullivan I'm gonna push his fuckin face in."

13

HOW TWA, BEVO FRANCIS, CHE GUEVARA, AND THE YIPPIES CONSPIRED TO CROSS STATE LINES TO COMMIT CAMPUS RIOTS

Up in the sky fellow conspirators! What would we do without airplanes? Sterile lobbies, tunnel sleeves, steel Howard Johnson bellies of great birds. So natural for us, our horizontal elevators, as McLuhan would say. I wondered where Bruce and J.D. were, two FBI agents that usually accompany me with a tape recorder—Mechanical Boswells recording that great Conspiracy in the Sky. They would have dug the plane ride out of Buffalo after the hugest Dope Conference in history. See, I have this thing about not fastening my seat belt. It's against my religion to tie myself up. Anyway I was so high from Free Buffalo that even if the plane went down I'd keep on flyin. Well, usually stewardesses won't do much after I explain that I will not hold them responsible for my death. That is if they don't ball me and stuff like that. This one was a real bitch though, and it's early Sunday morning hang-over time and she says, "We have radioed ahead to the FBI who are going to arrest you for not obeying Federal Aviation Code 27-2B" something or other. Well, she was only half bluffin cause it was only local Rochester cops.

But that's ancient history and now we were headed for Antioch. Antioch in Asia Minor where Paul got mobbed out of town for provocative gestures like crossing himself. Nah, I'm only kiddin—this Antioch is Hippie Haven. It's our version of R & R (rest and recreation for you who weren't in the army). Each time we flew over another state line I thought of the Attorney General standing on the Justice Department roof with a giant telescope keeping count and playing Monopoly. "Go directly to jail. Do not pass Pennsylvania. Do not collect $200 from the Student Union." I was exhausted. Four of us potential conspirators met all night before leaving to cross state lines again. We were trying to puzzle out the Chicago mess. We were to be indicted on March 11th by the Federal Grand Jury, and on March 10th the Supreme Court socked in a decision on wire-tapping which, on the surface, appeared to fuck the Justice Department right up the ass. Seems we had a right to see the transcripts of all those secret coded telephone calls we make.

Well, PIG NATION says it doesn't want to admit that it is bugging a certain foreign embassy that we call from time to time to check on the sugar crop. It's weird because it's admitting it right on the front page of *The New York Times*! Nobody understood what the Supreme Court decision meant but everyone thought without the wire-tapping evidence we'd best the conspiracy indictments about to come out of Chicago.

Attorney General Mitchell must really have been pissed. He had been on every TV set yakkin about professional agitators crossing state lines to get their college degrees, and if it wasn't the conspiracy rap for Chicago, he'd soon get something else on us.

If the phone was bugged and the government was afraid to have it come out in court maybe we had immunity from all Federal laws? I made a note to call my lawyer and get a list of every Federal law and another note to return by way of Washington to ask Edward Bennett Williams, who argued the case, "What the fuck is going on?" Not that I really cared; spring was coming and it had been a rotten yellow winter filled with hepatitis the Government injected in me during captivity in the D.C. jail.

I checked my bag—one Yippie film, ten copies of *Fuck the System*; Mao's little red book; recipes for Molotov cocktails, electric Koolaid and digger stew; a children's game manufactured in Albania called "Kick the Yankees in the Balls"; five hundred YIPPIE! buttons and ten million dollars worth of pot which I was furiously trying to smoke up before we were commanded to move into an upright position, seeing as how I can't get vertically stoned.

Eric, Yippie Agent in charge of Ohio, was smiling in the airport lobby. I coughed all the way to Antioch explaining that my lungs were not accustomed to fresh air. It didn't take long to figure out where Antioch's head was at. There are lots of progressive nursery schools, but there the kiddies are so big!

Most issues that are being fought for at other schools were won at Antioch ten years ago. Perhaps won is not the right word, they were liberally given. Like the big sheet of paper over the men's pissing stall for grafitti. But, well Antioch would be the dream school for most students given what they now have. No ROTC, close teacher-student community relations, people turn on and fuck everywhere, naked swim-ins in the gym pool, a black dorm, nice woods, co-ed dorms, Sunday tourists who drive through to stare at the commie-hippies, and so much love and identity-searching. It was all "Who am I?" stuff. Everything was so beautiful, I was completely bored after three hours. The school lacked the energy that comes from struggle. When I was leaving the next day Eric remarked, "You know surveys show that 55 per cent of us end up in large corporations." What "Hair" is to Broadway, Antioch is to the universities. That's not really a put-down. If you can't fuck you might as well jerk off. Antioch is the best play going, that is, if you've got about $25,000 for an orchestra seat.

Next stop was Wright State, owned by the National Cash Register Company. I rapped to a group on the grass doing my little jive-ass pitch when a big NO SALE flashed on the Science Building and I decided to split. I was already preparing for the night show; I didn't want to waste the juice. A battle was brewing and I was aching for a fight.

We were headed for Rio (Rye-O) Grande College and two kids, one the school's only hippy, had driven three hours to Antioch to get me to come. Seems their favorite teacher was getting bounced for "immaturity." There had never been a demonstration there, demonstrations are forbidden. The school is so bad it doesn't even have accreditation. Its only claim to fame is a 7-foot basketball player named Bevo Francis who fifteen years ago got them in *Life* magazine when he scored a hundred points in a game against Pygmy U. Bevo was in high school when he played for Rio Grande, no one knows whether he actually graduated from Rio Grande, but they're namin a dorm after him anyway. He used to run around the country like some Mountain of White Blubber while the Harlem Globe Trotters ran circles around him. Some say Bevo is now running the State Department but the truth is the sorry big fella is driving a dump truck in Pennsylvania.

Rio Grande College is in Rio Grande, Ohio (population: 300), ten miles west of West Virginia. The barber is the mayor. There is one cop in town. He got the job for winning a pheasant hunt. I was invited by the most radical group on campus (the Young Democrats) which had been formed the day before. As we bounced along through the empty cornfields in the old Ford the troublemakers filled me in on all the shit. The Klan had promised a cross-burning. The jocks were pissed and capable of trouble. They had just hung a cat to celebrate my coming and dropped lighted cherry bombs inside some dogs. Alphus Christiansen, President and Supreme Ruler, had left unexpectedly for parts unknown when he heard the news. The teacher, Bill Christopher, a nice gentle guy, was being thrown out for three reasons:

1. Writing a letter to the campus newspaper criticizing local cultural apathy and recommending an Appalachia studies program.
2. Eating cupcakes at a faculty meeting.
3. Using profanity in front of another teacher (the exact word was "bitch").

I had trouble believing all this! I mean with all the shit flying around colleges and high schools these days. I wondered if Rio Grande, or Postdam U. or New Paltz, or Richmond or any of the fifty or so small schools I visited were important to Mitchell and NATIONAL SECURITY? I wondered if Mitchell had his telescope on Rio Grande? He might though, cause there is an amazing article in the April, 1969 *True* magazine about how PIG NATION nailed Che. They have developed aerial reconnaissance planes that at fifteen hundred feet can take pictures of a guy and tell how long it's been since he shaved. I wonder how Che would have responded to the news that you couldn't eat cupcakes at Rio Grande? I love you Che . . . Che . . . Che . . . Che . . .

My head filled with images of machine-gunning Batista as we passed a pig farm. It's very poor land out there. A special kind of poverty different from Mississippi and the Lower East Side. I had never seen that kind before—

well, yeah, in Boone, Kentucky—but that was a good time ago and I wasn't really looking. Seems there is coal under the ground there and around the early 1900's the mine owners signed contracts with the farmers allowing them the right to get the coal out of the ground by "any means necessary." In those days it worked O.K. Shit! What's a little hole here and there? But then came huge Trucks and Steam Shovels and Bulldozers. The Capitalist Pigs chewed up all the hills. They dug up the crops just to get at the coal. The farmers fought back but got fucked by the courts. In the end they were forced to lease out their land to the mining syndicates and go to work in the mines, still paying taxes on their own land. Each year they went deeper in debt. With each new debt came another kid and tuberculosis and hook-worm and that Ben Shahn 1930's look of hunger. It is the saddest poverty in the nation. The kind you used to cry about when Pete Seeger sang Union songs.

When we arrived I met Bill Christopher and asked him what the fuck he wanted to stay here for. He said, "I think I have something to teach the kids." Shit! It was all gettin so country honest. I was feeling a bit hardened by long complicated discussions at Antioch about confrontational politics, cybernetic revolution and real high-falutin theoretical bullshit. It was good to be with real people again. Bill showed me the faculty handbook with such gems as "nothing controversial that is not related to the subject matter shall be discussed in class."

The recreation hall was packed when we walked in. It was a clankety old wooden building that I immediately loved, having just spoken in about a hundred ultramodern paneled, soft-lighted mechanical mind-traps designed to rot your brain. The guys I was with, Steve Troyanovich and Jeff Gleiss, were shaking with ecstasy. Everybody had come out, even the mayor. It was as if Bevo was back in town! They didn't believe their eyes but there were ball players, black students (ten of them) . . . hillbillies, hippies (one), straights, ex-marines, teachers, six or seven hundred out of a one thousand student body. A teacher who had been thrown out last year even came back. They had never seen a conspiring yippie-hippie-communist-drugged-sex-maniac, never mind one who had done all that in Chicago and gone to Russia for instructions and punched the head of HUAC and was taking LSD and they say he's gonna show obscene movies! "This we gotta see!" And they settled back in their seats ready for the show. I turned down an introduction (which I always do), jumped up on the stage and announced,

"This is a fuckin movie about Pigs and Yippies. If you're stoned real good you can see the people fuckin in the grass. It cost me and my friends twelve bucks to make it and it ain't won no awards." Lights out, "Here's Yippie!" Bong! Mayor Daley appears. There is applause but wait—here come the Yippies pouring through the gates of the city, jumping to Phil Ochs and "I Ain't Marching Anymore." The crowd was yelling for the Freaks. By the end of the film, everybody was jumpin up and down, hissing the cops, laughing their asses off. There ain't nothing SDS got that coulda worked that night at Rio Grande but that raggedy-ass movie did it. I jumped up at the end. They were all cheering like it was a basketball game. "I'm Huey Newton and I'm here to burn down the school!" It's a wild-ass rap, throwing away the mike, ripping off my shirt, yelling about how we are getting stepped on. "This is General Motors and you are the cars. Does General Motors ask the cars if they want all that fuckin chrome?" Dig it! Fun and sadness and sittin on the edge of the stage, cryin about how we are gettin gassed and beaten and arrested. Somebody held up the sissy V sign and I yelled, "Fuck that! We are at war!" I challenged the Klan, calling them chicken shit.

It's sweet talking about cupcakes and freedom and new ways of living the FUTURE. Because WE ARE THE FUTURE! It was the best since in Lincoln Park and I was happy cause I knew the winter was over. It ended on a down-beat suspenseful-like-hanging-slow-in-the-air, "The freak show is over . . . what are you going to do??? Hum???" I mumbled as I walked down the steps of the stage and up and down the rows of stunned students . . . "What you going to do now, hum? Why don't somebody else get up there and say what is on his mind! . . . no commies in this school? . . . No agitators? . . . No cat hangers? . . . SILENCE . . . then one kid stuttered up to the front and the place went wild. "I'm gonna take a few books out of the library tomorrow and sit out on the steps and read em and if they don't let Mr. Christopher stay . . . (gulp) . . . I might just not bring em back." Yippie! Then another and another got up. A jock even. A hillbilly drawled out one of the most beautiful raps I ever heard. A teacher gave an old-fashioned rap about what education means; then a kid got up and challenged one of the members of the Administration who was sitting in the audience to answer the complaints. Everyone was screamin and stompin but he didn't say a word. A black cat got up on the stage. A chubby guy with his shirt hanging out . . . "I'm one of those drunken niggers you see around here every once in a while . . . you gotta be drunk to go to this school . . ." Everybody's hootin and yellin. Another black got up, an athlete, "I'm goin out to the library and take some books out too . . . I gotta two-thousand-dollar-a-year scholarship at stake but they can shove it if I can't have my dignity." And then the call for commitment. "How many comin out tomorrow?" and four hundred Freemen jumped up with their fists in the air. Steve and Jeff were ballin and I must admit I ain't felt that good for quite a while either and I was ballin too.

We talked most of the night in some pad and started out at 6:00 a.m.—two hours to the airport.

On the way little kids in their yellow submarine bus were going to school. They spotted my long hair and started all crowdin up to the windows. They got one open and a skinny arm juts out with two fingers making the sign of the V and we were all laughin and waving to the kids. "I wonder if we got some time to visit their school," I said, "they might dig that Yippie film . . ." "Aw, come on," Steve said, "leave some stuff for us. This conspiracy is good smokin shit."

So I got up on the plane, me and all the other executives, and I sang em "Who made the mine owners, sing the proud bells of Dum-dum" and counted the state lines as we hummed back East. "1 Boundary—2 Boundary—3 Boundary," John Mitchell, we just dig to play Monopoly, wait until we get to Park Place!

14

MOONSHINE

Dear Earth and especially that section of it
referred to as "outside the free world":

Last night a group of us weirdos sat up all night and watched what has to be the greatest TV show, in fact, the "Greatest Show on Earth," as old John Ringling North of circus fame would have put it. "Armstrong slithers out of the capsule . . . " One really can't help but get caught up in the majesty of it all, the holiness, this birth of the New Age. There they are now. Wow! Is it real? Or is it one of those back-lot Hollywood sets . . . it's too bad Walt Disney didn't live to see this one . . . Yep! It's beyond 2001! Stanley Kubrick's gotta be head of NASA . . . did some weird gremlin decide just one week before the moon-shot to play Dr. Strangelove on the Late Show? Look at em jumping around. When they leap it's poetry, when they talk, even some number-jumbo, you're aware that in one hundred years, one thousand years, this will endure as an art form.

One tries not to be cynical; after all, they are jumping around on the fuckin moon and no matter what you think of PIG NATION, you have to admit that it does have a good special effects department. Whee! Look at em bounce around. What is he gonna do? Will he piss on the moon? Will he say, "Send up some booze and broads, we don't want to go back?" Nah, no bits . . . well, what do you expect? This albino crewcut has been selected with more precision than the American Machine selects a president. Man, this cat is the unknown soldier from Arlington Cemetery, resurrected just for this special mission. A number-one-all-Amerikan cracker. I mean did you dig his parents. Mr. and Mrs. A-OK Armstrong—the Mom and Pop of Moonman . . . Moonman, the all-time comic strip hero. No, this ain't a comic strip. It's a radio show from the late forties, that's it! "Wheaties the all-American Breakfast Cereal brings you Jack Armstrong the All-American Boy." No shit! Do you believe that! Now ladies and gentlemen, "This hour of the Voyage to the Moon is brought to you by Kelloggs . . . A small step (snap), for man (crackle), a giant step for mankind (pop)." The Ruskies, they have the technological capacity to get to the moon, that is if the country felt like sinking 34 billion into being first. They might have pulled it off, but not them, not anyone but good ol PIG NATION with a used-car dealer for president, could have thought about selling time to sponsors to broadcast the flight of Apollo 11. I mean, isn't that the sort of PIG ART that has come to make Amerika great? Can you really picture even Western Imperialist Columbus off to conquer the New World with a sign on the side of his ship that says, EAT GENOA SALAMI. Only in Amerika.

PIG NATION's brain is its special effects department and its heart is an ad agency. Its statesmanship is lodged someplace in its asshole.

I mean, who among us is ready to follow Spiro Agnew, torch in hand, into the Aquarian Age. "Our peace council will present plans to land a MAN on MARS by the year two thousand." My God what a genius, what daring, what imagination. There you go world. Fuck you Mao. Fuck you Galileo. Fuck you Darwin. Dig PIG NATION's genius—Spiro T. Agnew. We take you now to the year two thousand A.D. ladies and gentlemen:

> Here comes the moment we've all been waiting for. Captain Amerika is about to shake hands with ZQRTS, Martian Leader and delegate to the Intergalatic Union. It

> is all coming true just like the prophetic wisdom of the Amerikan genius Vice President Agnew predicted when he launched mankind on its greatest adventure ever. Captain Amerika is to present ZQRTS with an Amerikan flag and a year's supply of MARS BARS. (Would you believe Milky Ways?)

The only thing wrong with the whole trip was that Amerika brought its morality with it when, like some senile dinosaur, it slid out of the capsule 250,000 miles away and stepped its virgin boot into the sea of moondust. It's really sad. The flag bit, I mean. What Pig in the Pentagon ordered the project that would fix the flag so it would fly forever unfurled like some perpetual hard-on in space? I mean why must the flag be unfurled or is this just another Kodak Scenic Wonder Sight where tourists can stop and send photos home to the relatives, "Having a wonderful time, wish you were here."

And now Pig Leader Nixon would like a chance to sell the world this flashy two-seater space module, step right up folks, get in line. And the TV screen splits in two and a little color cartoon figure in red, yellow and blue, with a head that has been mashed in by a vise appears in the top left corner. In a squeaky voice comes, "My fellow earthmen . . ."

I can't take it . . . I walk out on the roof. I just got to be alone. It's a foggy night, the Con Edison plant across the street is pouring the wastes we in New York have come to love, into the sky. It's impossible to see the Empire State Building, another Amerikan monument, even though it's only twenty blocks away, all lit up too, and besides as we all know, the biggest fuckin thing around. All the shit in the air (excuse me, "wastes"—isn't that what they call it when astronauts shit—"Making waste on the moon"?) pours out of these things three huge funnels, but what the fuck, the funnels are painted red, white and blue just like that flag up there . . .

So world, and especially that section that Walter Cronkite refers to as "outside the free world," to you Niggers of the world, I would like to take a moment aside from the hectic nature of our revolution, designed to wipe out the disease of competitive capitalism, and apologize for this alien country in which we find ourselves. Furthermore, I would like to let you know that young people here in WOODSTOCK NATION are learning to fly in space . . . some day we too will fly off in some communal capsule, Blacks,

Puerto Ricans, Hippies, liberated women, young workers on the line, and G.I.'s sitting in stockades because they don't want to go to Vietnam. There will be a whole mess of us laughing and getting stoned on our way to OUTERSPACE, and the first thing, the very first thing we're gonna do out there is to rip down that fuckin flag on the moon.

15

CHE'S LAST LETTER

To the youth of the United States:

I write to you huddled in blankets. Damp, shivering, cold, temporarily dejected over recent military setbacks. We are somewhere in the jungles of Bolivia surrounded by the enemy, cut off from all supplies. Struggling against immense odds. My thoughts turn to the young people struggling for a chance at life in the bowels of plastic America cut off from the lifeline of human existence. For you, like us, we are also surrounded. I recall the time I worked as a waiter in Miami Beach hotel and my frequent visits to New York and know that people in the second half of the twentieth century are not destined to play out their lives in either the jungles of Bolivia or Manhattan. Surely the destiny of man was to lift himself out of the jungle. Out of an economic system that forced him to behave like a beast of prey. Out of a corresponding socio-religious system that cherished money and greed and hatred and inhumanity. I know you will say, "We know all that but what do you offer? More killing? A subtle change in things? What is so revolutionary about your revolution?" But of course you are cynical. Your universities teach you to be eternal cynics, a cynicism that can be only drowned in alcohol and diet pills and psychoanalysts and golf. Forget your cynicism. There is no one who has more respect for life than a revolutionist. I am by profession a doctor. I found, however, to heal bodies under an inhuman system such as existed then and now in my native Argentina was corrupt. So I left to join Fidel and the others and help in my small way to build the revolution in Cuba. What we did was to establish a model to show that under great oppressive odds radical social change can take place. You must shed the bandages bound around your eyes by the press in your country. You must go to Cuba and experience what has happened there over the past ten years.

Even as we realized victory in Cuba, we knew that the battle had just begun. For a revolution, in order to be a true revolution, must be a world revolution. To achieve that world revolution, you the children of the Yankees must lend a hand. You must vomit forth your cynicism in the streets of your cities. You must mount an unrelenting attack on everything the bastards that rule your country hold dear. You must refuse to serve in their armies, you must reject the heroin offered in their universities, you must become clogs in their productive machinery. Your struggle will be a long and arduous one. It will not come easy. There are no guide rules to apply to revolution. Each country is unique and your struggle is the most unique of all, for your repression is of a very peculiar nature. Search for brothers and sisters in the struggle. Steel yourself inside for the oppressive blows that will greet each new victory. Learn patience. Learn how to survive. It will not be all hardship and suffering as others have warned. What is suffering comrades? Even as I write knowing death is coming over that hill not five hundred yards away I would not go back to being a respected professional in a system I detested. That is the true death of the spirit. No, although my health is failing, physical death is approaching and our plans here have met with disaster, I know we have won. Not for ourselves but for those who will follow us into these jungles of reality and into the jungles of their own minds to strike that blow for freedom. Men of revolutionary vision and action are sprouting everywhere. Like wild flowers bursting the overpowering prison of cement roads they grow Vietnam, Angola, Guatemala, Paris and now even in the heart of the Steel Goliath. Little Davids strike hard and deep. Venceremos.

—CHE*

*This was part of a little plot Jerry Rubin, Ed Sanders and I worked up, with plans to "discover the letters in the Bolivian jungles" and sell them to *Ramparts*. We blew it though and they ended up in *The Realist* for free.

16

FUCK THE FLAG

Last summer, just a few days before Congress zipped through the law making it illegal to conspire to run a Pig for president in the streets of Chicago, they passed a federal law protecting the flag from "defacement and defiling." The maximum penalty is one year in jail and a $1000 fine. (The only other country to have just passed a similar law is Russia.) The flag was not the only national symbol to be protected. Previous laws gave protection to Smoky the Bear, the 4-H Club's cloverleaf, and the Swiss flag (?). For example, anyone who "defaces a facsimile of Smoky the Bear is subject to a $250 fine and six months in jail"*

My arrest (for wearing a flag shirt) at the HUAC hearing last October was the first arrest under the federal law. At the trial I was found guilty and given a thirty-day sentence which is just coming up for appeal. That the law is so vague that it would make Uncle Sam, drum majorettes and candidates who sport red, white and blue hats and ties criminals is relatively unimpor-

*Volume 18, U.S. Code Sections 700 and 711.

tant to the federal government. They have adopted Catch-22 as their motto which states, if you remember, "we can put anybody in jail who we don't like no matter what the fuck the constitution says."

Since my conviction there have been numerous others. Edward Franz, a freshman at Virginia Commonwealth University, was sentenced to a year in jail for wearing a flag vest. Wearing the same style vest, a sixteen-year-old Boston guy visiting Alexandria, Virginia, was arrested and "banished from the city of Alexandria until the age of 21." Dig that sentence! A student at Franklin Marshall College in Lancaster was recently busted for using the flag as a bedspread, and on and on, across the country, with about thirty such cases in the past few months. Of course not everyone who wears a flag shirt or dress gets arrested, just as not everyone who smokes pot goes to jail. The flag design is a current mod-fashion among the rich. Ads for dresses and vests appeared recently in the *New York Times, Los Angeles Times* and the *San Francisco Examiner*, to name a few. Phyllis Diller has appeared on TV in a flag mini-skirt and companies are doing a brisk business in flag lighters (for draft cards?) flag chairs, flag ties, flag hats, flag banks, flag dishes, flag pencil holders, and there is a rumor that a flag diaphragm is on the way.

Perhaps a clue as to why the government is so anxious to prosecute us undesirables is found in a brief filed in the District of Columbia Court of Appeals by Department of Justice Attorney Mervyn Hamburg to support the law and their case against me: "The importance of a flag in developing a sense of loyalty to a national entity has been the subject of numerous essays." The first essay the U.S. Government quotes is the following:

> Hitler, *Mein Kampf*, translated by Manheim (Houghton Mifflin, 1943), p. 492:
>
> The organization of our monitor troop clarified a very important question. Up till then the movement possessed no party insignia and no party flag. The absence of such symbols not only had momentary disadvantages, but was intolerable for the future. The disadvantages consisted above all in the fact that the party comrades lacked an outward sign of their common bond, while it was unbearable for the future to dispense with a sign that possessed

> the character of a symbol of the movement and could as such be opposed to the International. What importance must be attributed to such a symbol from the psychological point of view I had even in my youth more than one occasion to recognize and also emotionally to understand. Then, after the War, I experienced a mass demonstration of the Marxists in front of the Royal Palace and the Lustgarten. A sea of red flags, red scarves, and red flowers gave to this demonstration, in which an estimated hundred and twenty thousand persons took part, an aspect that was gigantic from the purely external point of view. I myself could feel and understand how easily the man of the people succumbs to the suggestive magic of a spectacle so grandiose in effect.

We always knew that Hitler was running the State Department, now it seems he has taken over the Justice Department as well?''*

*Recently the District Court of Appeals upheld the constitutionality of this law and the case is now in the process of being appealed to the Supreme Court.

17

DEATH TO THE PIGS WHO INVADE OUR LANDS

It's July fifteenth, 2 a.m. on a farm somewhere in Ann Arbor, Michigan. It's a beautiful warm night, filled with a starry blue sky waiting for the astronauts to violate its silence. Lying on your back you can look up and repeat all the old hippy cliches to yourself about dropping out and heading for the country. Why not? After all, on a clear night in New York City up on my roof I can sometimes see two stars and Anita jokes about how they must be attached to a long electric wire that comes out of the Con Ed building across the street, for there are no clear nights in New York. There is an underground newspaper conference going on at the farm. It's a good place to start describing some of the changes that have gone down in the hip community over the past few years. For the underground press is the molder and chronicler of the amorphous body of long-haired young freaks you see sticking their tongue out at you in the TV news at night or luring your daughter to a rock-and-roll dance in the park.

NIXON DECLARES WAR ON DRUGS
PEOPLE LIBERATE PARK
STREET FIGHTING IN MADISON ENTERS
SECOND DAY
10,000 CRASH GATES AT MUSIC FESTIVAL

It has been an awkward time of anxieties and doubts. I mean like what the fuck was I doing? On April ninth, I stood before a seventy-four-year-old baldheaded judge* and heard him read this mumbo jumbo, 1984 indictment and I couldn't help but feel a bit silly standing there with my hair climbing down the back of the blue Chicago policeman's shirt I was wearing. Conspiracy! Wow!

Were we freaks really a threat? I had just come from the SDS convention in Chicago. It was weird. People throwing red books at each other is a strange form of revolution?? Throughout the conference, I marveled at how little I understood what was being said. Songs like "male chauvinism" "petit bourgeois revisionist," "puppet lackeys," "tool of the military-industrial complex," and "member of the proletariat vanguard waging the relentless battle against imperialism" were sung and other tunes that escape me for the moment. They are vibrations in another plastic dome. Going to that SDS conference was a bummer. I mean when fifty guys jumped up at some point, as if the speaker at the rostrum has landed with a good left hook, and, holding up red books, shouted, "Mao! Mao! Mao Tse-Tung!" you would think this would be O.K., but no, not if the group was Revolutionary Youth Movement Number Two. So not to let them slip by their left vanguard, up pops Progressive Labor Party in the balcony and shouts in unison, "Beware those who wave the red flag to oppose the red flag." You can see why I was having problems. I mean take imperialism. This fuckin country makes up one-sixteenth of the world population and owns or controls 55 per cent of its natural resources. That was enough to know about imperialism it seemed to me. As for racism, well once in Mississippi we were taking a medical survey door-to-door and I remember the mothers would all say their children were all "doin jus fine" and I'd look down and see twelve-year-old black kids with teeth totally rotted away—they thought that was "normal" health. The woman would ask you if you'd like something to drink and you knew it would be ice water and that white people up North would call that "soul" but you called it poverty.

---

*Judge Julius Hoffman not only is determined to send us up the river for ten years, but he is also spreading the vicious lie that I'm his illegitimate son.

About working-class exploitation, well that meant working one summer in Wyman-Gordon's airplane factory getting oil in your lungs when they sprayed the 55,000-ton press and having your mind fall out from working the swing shift. I couldn't understand why Revolutionary Youth Movement Number Two or for that matter, Revolutionary Youth Movement Number One, was reluctant to organize youth into a revolutionary movement. Well who am I to say. I haven't read Marx in years and when you get right down to it I'm too sloppy a thinker to be in the vanguard. Anyway it's more fun in the back of the bus. When we were young it was always the best place to get laid.

These are some of the thoughts I pondered while looking at the road with field glasses ready to wake everyone up Paul Revere-style with shouts of "The Pigs are coming." I had no idea of what SDS was into but there was that image again of a row of high-powered cameras in the third-floor window across the street from their convention. There was the FBI in heavy numbers guarding the NATIONAL SECURITY and all that other gung-ho shit. SDS ain't LSD but it ain't FBI either. I guess that's a way of saying, "enemies of my enemies are my friends," which is said a lot at conferences these days and argued about these nights. I wondered what LSDSDS spelled . . .

Our little underground get-together on a Michigan farm had more gentle vibes. No one shouted, "Beware he who waves his long hair to oppose his long hair." I wondered behind which tree the FBI secret cameras lurked. I didn't want to get too paranoid, but fuck, there were the White Panthers guarding the road with shotguns. Melvin Newsreel was monitoring police calls and translating the numbers into words using a little card (all you need is a simple UHF modifier and you can get the code breakdown in any good criminology book in a large library). There were about thirty of us on defense patrol ready to put into operation Plan B to fight the Pigs if they returned. We had about twenty or so weapons, an escape route, and well I just didn't know what the fuck I'd do if they came back. It would be as good a place as any and as good a reason as any to blast my first Pig. I wondered what kind of a jolt the shotgun would give. It was sure a pretty piece.

Oh yeah, I forgot to lay it on you about why all this people's militia stuff is going on. Well this afternoon in the middle of a discussion on political repression we looked up and there were about seventy local Pigs with riot helmets and shotguns running through the woods in some complicated green beret-type maneuver. We all were forced to sort of line up while doors to the farmhouse were smashed in and a half-ass search was conducted. I kept wondering whether the Pigs were concerned about Liberation News Service (politicos) or Tate Blues Band (hippies) and things like that. When the Pigs left we had a heavy rap session about self-defense, land, and whether or not the chickens bar-be-cuing on the open fire were done yet. Skip Taub laid out a heavy rap about what was coming down in the Ann Arbor area like Pigs shaving longhairs, searching cars at drive-ins, hassling young people in a whole lot of ways and not allowing rock music in the park. I listened careful to Skip—more careful than I had listened to anyone in a long time. In Ann Arbor they were working out the mixing of revolutionary outlaws and cultural nationalists. I was thinking about rock and what the Yippies had tried to pull off in Chicago and I thought about the scared Pigs stuttering as they quivered with shotguns in their hands facing the defiant hippies just an hour ago. I thought about standing in People's Park, most beautiful spot on earth, and listening to Frank Bardacke and Stu Albert run down the plan to rip off the land from the university and suck Reagan into a fight. Stu, one of the founders of the Yippie Empire, is currently doing ninety days in a California jail. At least thirty per cent of the key Yippie people in Chicago are now in jail. Most of the others face a number of trials. In Chicago I felt that I was ready to die over our right to be in Lincoln Park and how defending liberated land meant more than Vietnam. THE ONLY WAY TO SUPPORT A REVOLUTION IS TO MAKE YOUR OWN. But most of all I thought about land and self-defense. I made a note to check into the Woodstock Ventures operation as soon as I hit New York. Those promoters were into some heavy shit, all right. Half the people at the conference thought the festival was going to take place on Bob Dylan's farm. Bob Dylan's farm? It wasn't even taking place in Woodstock!

18

FREE JOHN SINCLAIR

"There ain't no law in America only the honkie power structure."

—John Sinclair
July 28, 1969 just before sentencing

John Sinclair is a huge lover with masses of curly black hair flowing all over his head and shoulders. John is a mountain of a man. He can fuck twenty times a day and fight like a wild bear. He and his White Panther brothers and sisters from Ann Arbor, Michigan, are the most alive force in the whole midwest. They turn on thousands of kids each week to their own beauty and build them into warriors and artists of the New Nation. For this John Sinclair was entrapped into giving two joints of grass to two undercover Pigs. For this some bald-headed judge named Columbo sentenced John Sinclair to nine-and-a-half to ten years in the penitentiary at Jackson, Michigan. For this the same courts are waiting to put on trial Pun Plamondon, John's closest brother and Minister of Defense of the Party, for handing a free joint to another undercover Pig. For this they want to send Pun away for twenty years to live in the same penitentiary on a phony charge of dispensing marijuana without a prescription. Pun, Jeannie, Magdelene Sinclair, John's expectant wife, and two other White Panthers were arrested in New Jersey when they left WOODSTOCK NATION. It was one of those typically unconstitutional car searches the Pigs across the country have been making famous. They claimed they found a little guess what?

The kids in Ann Arbor are coming together. Resistance is growing to the practice of Pigs cutting off kids' hair, of breaking up free rock concerts in the park, of raiding communes and harassing underground newspapers. In Ann Arbor, the kids are learning karate. In Ann Arbor, the women know how to handle shotguns. In Ann Arbor, the freaks are organizing petition drives to recall the Head Pig Sheriff Harvey. In Ann Arbor, the hip community takes on the cops in pitched street battles. In Ann Arbor, they are prepared to build and defend the Nation by any means necessary. In Ann Arbor and in other places like that around the country they ain't into peace and music, they're into WAR and MUSIC and Right on! Music can make the walls shake but you need an army to take the city and artists to rebuild it. Rock music will provide the energy but the people will provide the power, for only with power can we defend what beauty we create. . . .

Up in Woodstock a big thing was made of how you could sit around and smoke right out in the open. A questionnaire prepared by Deputy Inspector Joe Fink (you remember good ol Vanguard Capitalism Joe, don't you?), of the Lower East Side or rather the East Village; when he sends off his men to pound the shit out of the street people he does it in the Lower East Side where we live. When he talks to the establishment press he does it in the East Village. Anyway, one of the key questions on the form to recruit four hundred off-duty New York policemen for security at the festival went like this:

QUESTION: What do you do if someone blows marijuana smoke in your face?
WRONG ANSWER: Arrest him.
RIGHT ANSWER: Smile and inhale.

That was up in Woodstock and that was because the cops were bought off. In PIG NATION, it doesn't work like that at all, no sir, not at all! In PIG

NATION last year there were 250,000 narcotics arrests mostly for grass. They have trained dogs in Detroit for shipment around the country to sniff out the stuff. They have increased the penalties to fascist proportions. They have used pot busts as an excuse to attack WOODSTOCK NATION. Nixon's three biggest enemies right now are the Vietcong, blacks and drugs. Drugs means us and he treats us like the country has always treated its VIETCONG NIGGERS. He aims to kick our ass.

Napalming villages in Vietnam is not the only kind of imperialism the country is into and trying to land the drug people in the clink like blacks is not the only way Nixon makes war, not the only war by far . . .

19

WOODSTOCK OR BUST

Just to give you a rundown of where my head was at when I set off to the WOODSTOCK NATION, let me give you the year's rundown on my busts. If it wasn't for my lawyer, Jerry Lefcourt, I'd be hallucinating this from some jail cell rather than the floor of a Random House office.

1. Early in August '68, resisting arrest added to a charge of criminal trespassing during Columbia revolt filed a full three months earlier! Trial begins September 4th.

2. August 27, 1968, Chicago—for having *Fuck* on forehead and resisting arrest. (Fifteen days and one-year probation for resisting. *Fuck* dismissed on the grounds that you cannot offend the morals of a policeman—resisting charge is on appeal.)

3. September 13. While returning to Chicago to stand trial on the above charges, arrested with lawyer for non-appearance in court. (Dismissed)

4. Later that day, arrested again in Chicago for possessing a concealed weapon (state charge). (Dismissed when prosecuting attorneys found it impossible to produce said concealed weapon.)

5. And still later the same day, by the Federal Bureau of Investigation, and charged with crimes aboard an aircraft. (Dismissed but not before they confined me to the District of Manhattan for three months and made me spend a lot of bread zipping in and out of Chicago for hearings.)

6. October—HUAC hearing in Washington. Busted for wearing an Amerikan flag shirt. (Facing thirty days. Appeal rejected by District Court of Appeals, Washington, D.C. and headed for the Supreme Court.) When I was arrested, I got an almost fatal case of serum hepatitis when prison guards took a blood sample, under force, with a dirty needle. I currently have a $300,000 lawsuit pending against the U.S. Government. (Now the busts are interrupted cause I'm laid up three months with hep.)

7. Somewhere in the sky between Buffalo and Rochester last February, busted for not fastening my seat belt. Finally resulted in charge of disorderly conduct (dismissed). On at least three occasions airlines have refused to fly me and on Amerikan Airlines they have this strange habit of searching my bags. Needless to say, I had to give my five youth cards away.

8. In March, indicted for conspiracy with intent to incite riots, etc., in Chicago. Trial begins September 24th. We have just learned today that we are almost certain to be locked into the trial date. Judge Julius Hoffman is determined to fry us. He has refused all of our motions for dismissal and postponements, even though our two chief counsels probably can't be in court by mid-September. Charles Garry is in the hospital and faces a murder trial when he gets out. William Kunstler has the Panther 21 conspiracy case, the Bob Williams murder case, and two heavy Rap Brown trials all in September.

Bobby Seale was just arrested on a conspiracy to commit murder rap and other charges and might have difficulties making the date. Jerry Rubin has thirty days to do in California and I've got the two trials coming up next week. . . . By the time we hit trial we might be the Chicago Two.

9. Later that same night busted for possession of loaded automatics, heroin, blackjacks and other assorted goodies "found in a community office." (All but possession of loaded automatics have been dropped. Trial begins September 8th. The interesting thing about this bust is that I was not there at the time of arrest and the office, which is next door to the police station, is not even in my name. What do you think my grandmother said when she read about this one?)

10. In April — felonious assault against two cops while in court on the Columbia hearing. I was pulled out of a phone booth in the lobby when some keen-eyed Pig recognized me and clubbed me to the floor. Also added to this charge was obstructing government business, disturbing the peace, resisting arrest and disorderly conduct. Trial begins November 15th.

All this amounts to more time in prison than I care to imagine and endless hearings and bail hassles . . . Lenny Bruce once said that in the halls of justice the only justice was in the halls. I learned something on that last bust. Lenny was wrong. There isn't even any justice in the halls.

20

SMACK DAB IN THE MIDDLE OF THE MONSTER

> Bethel, N.Y.: You sit on the big stage watered by the blue spotlights while the Big Pink Band plays Bob Dylan's "I Shall Be Released" and you look out into the eyes of the monster.
>
> —Alfred C. Aronowitz, New York *Post*

On Saturday night up on the stage you felt the monster was going to crush the Amerikan Dinosaur. You could see the distant bonfires on far-off hills and sense thousands of soldiers resurrected from the Macedonian army hammering out their weapons. You looked at say two hundred thousand or so heads who had crawled out of the catacombs in PIG NATION. They were all piled up on People Hill and saw the spotlight eyes burn down on Creedence Clearwater, hypnotizing them, driving them into an orgiastic fury that shook the whole motherfuckin stage. It felt like the last scene from "Frankenstein" performed by the Living Theatre, that busload of hippy nuns that breezed through a while back. I had seen them do

"Frankenstein" at MIT and I lay my hand on the scaffolding and felt it shake with the fury of the gods. It was just before the FBI grabbed me in Cambridge and I had to fly immediately back to Chicago and face a hearing on why I jumped jurisdiction to go see the Living Theatre and my two sick kids. The whole motherfuckin stage at Woodstock was shakin like that as it slipped back and forth in two feet of mud. Every once in a while a straight dude from the Construction Company or the Safety Department or something like that would rush up to someone who looked like he was in charge and yell "We must stop this! The stage will collapse! Everybody must get off!" And always some shaggy-haired freak would hug him and say "Swingin baby, we're gonna fly up here forever!" and the swingers and the faith healers and the astrology freaks were all right that Saturday night up there. That was one of the eerie things about the WOODSTOCK NATION, every nut in it was right, even the Meher Baba buffs.

I'd run back and forth to the stage boppin across this bridge over Lake Shore Drive—the shortest way from the Field Hospital to the Monster. You had to run down a hill past the whirling helicopter hurricanes, past the performers' pavilion. You then had to show a crumpled card that said "Admit to stage OK M. Lang." I had practiced forging Mike Lang's name for about ten minutes the day before but found out it was rarely necessary to be good at it; usually flashing my Identification Card (which I had drawn myself) at an usher would do the trick. Besides the word was out that I was running the Field Hospital. And even in Hippie Heaven broken bones and freak-outs mean something, at least most times they do. So I had a pretty easy time getting on the stage and would bring these slips up to Chip Monck or John Morris who was an old friend from backstage at the Fillmore East. The slips were an attempt to communicate some serious medical information to the Monster. I'll run down a few of them and give you Chip Monck's translations so you'll get the contrast. You should really read the directions like a school teacher just before air-raid practice, and the translations like you were pouring molasses while on two caps of mescaline listening to the Incredible String Band murmuring in the closet.

> DON'T DRINK THE WATER IN THE POND BEHIND THE HOGFARM CAMP UNLESS YOU PUT SOME CHLORINE IN IT. TWO DROPS TO THE GALLON.
> *Lay off water, man, it's a real bummer.*

> THERE ARE NOW NINE FIRST AID CENTERS ESTABLISHED. FOR FIRST AID TREATMENT GO FIRST TO EITHER THE CENTER IN THE HOGFARM SITE OR THE CENTER AT THE TOP OF THE HILL BEHIND THE CENTRAL INFORMATION BOOTH. VERY BAD INJURIES SHOULD REPORT TO THE FIELD HOSPITAL IN THE PINK AND WHITE TENTS ACROSS THE ROAD.
> *We got a lot of groovy hospitals stashed away. Bummers to the Yellow Tent at the top of the hill or over there (waving arms). Heavy stuff to the pink and white tents.*

Remember now these announcements are being made to something like say 400,000 people, for as you might not have realized, WOODSTOCK NATION was by Saturday the second-largest city in New York and I think the tenth largest in the country. San Francisco International Airport reported turning away close to one thousand people headed to Woodstock on Friday. The Port Authority Bus Terminal in New York by Saturday had called it quits. The promoters spent a good deal of time both Friday and Saturday holding press conferences urging people not to come. State troopers along the New York Thruway, which was forced to close part of the time, re-routed tens of thousands into different areas of upstate New York. There were probably as many people turned away as finally made it close enough to say "I was there."

Well you want to know something about those announcements? They worked! Such was the mystical power of the microphones and public address system and so tuned in were all the 400,000 or 500,000 or 1,000,000, depending on where you drew the national boundaries, that everyone knew where to go. There were other happenings up there on the stage, psychic games with Artie Kornfeld and Mike Lang, two of the Woodstock Four. "Hey Mike, chaos has a certain beauty to it, doesn't it?" I suggest. We played little games up there as I tried to get them into the morality-politico bag and they tried to get me to drop out and join them on their trip. They made all sorts of promises and liked me an awful lot especially once I decided to make the Florence Nightingale scene. They were shrewd motherfuckers and probably ripped me off as much as me them. After all, I was setting up the hospital for free! Certainly they fared much better than the Chicago authorities in our bouts—in fact to be honest they knocked me on my ass a few times, but maybe that was due to all the drugs I had taken and maybe it was due to how I was having the first bad acid trip I'd had in four years. Maybe we ought to get into that right now since it really is a gas and I been waiting all this time to lay the story on you cause it was the wildest fucker ever. Wilder than pissing on the Pentagon, wilder than standing in front of a Washington judge, half-naked with a Vietcong flag painted on my back, wilder than throwin out money at the Stock Exchange, wilder than fuckin in the middle of Lincoln Park when the tear gas came rollin in—this was one of the wildest ever. Let's get into it. I'm gonna try this next song left-handed cause my fingers hurt like crazy from writing. It's 5:00 a.m. and I've been at it for a lot of hours.

Roger and out.

21

POWER TO THE WOODSTOCK NATION

"Power is the ability to make matter act in a desired manner."
—HUEY OR ISAAC NEWTON

"We will have to wait and see if the Monster decides to move. As long as it stays in the valley we'll be out of danger."
—IT CAME FROM OUTER SPACE

When I left Chicago I felt we had won a great victory. The lines between "us," the people in the streets, and "them," the people in authority, had been clearly established, the police had seen to that. With a small number of people we had been able to successfully do damage to a huge and powerful political party. Some people even say our action and the mess we created was chiefly responsible for the defeat of Humphrey. I'm not sure; I'm not sure why things happen in PIG NATION, I'm too much involved with trying to fuck the Statute of Liberty to be able to give intelligent overviews. Leaving Woodstock I was not so sure of what exactly had happened.

Figuring out who was the enemy was not only difficult but the mere posing of the question seemed out of place. There were so many contradictions and ambiguities like Jimi Hendrix, who literally wraps his long-hair black legs around his guitar and fucks it into ecstasy, playing "The Star Spangled Banner," New York City cops (one I recognized as the guy who busted me on the gun charge) in scarlet jackets with peace signs, hospitals in bright-colored circus tents, please chiefs instead of police chiefs, straight dudes like office secretaries and shoe salesmen and teachers getting their minds blown out and ending up swimmin naked in the lake or fuckin in the grass or tryin acid for the first time. There were some who turned into gods. There were people who cried out in ecstasy and people who did nothing but smile the whole time. It was a hell-of-a-mess allright. I mean aside from the fact that they'll make great movie scenes, can you attach any revolutionary significance to the following?

> Chasidic Jews and Catholic nuns giving away free food while people across the street charge twenty-five cents for a glass of water.
>
> Bob Wolf standing there totally naked interviewing an eighty-five-year-old lady resident of Bethel for *The Realist*.
>
> A guy right out of the Bible with a sign saying "Don't Kill Animals" followed by a sheep.
>
> A long-haired guy dealing acid from the back of a horse.
>
> The staff of a large mass-media magazine plotting to take pictures of themselves naked, blur them up a bit and get it on the cover of their own magazine.
>
> Rows and rows of tents for at least thirty miles down Route 17B and into the N. Y. Thruway.

There were hundreds and hundreds more flashes that one saw. And then there was the immensity of the crowd. God, how can you capture the feeling of being with 400,000 people and everyone being stoned on something? Were we pilgrims or lemmings? Was this really the beginning of a new civilization or the symptom of a dying one? Were we establishing a liberated zone or entering a detention camp? Like dig it baby. When the Jews entered the ovens at Dachau, the Nazis played hip Wagner music, passed out flowers and handed out free bars of soap. That's right Hippies, take your clothes off, we are all goin to ze big fuck-in . . . zat's right . . . we are all gonna groove mit da showers . . . ya ya . . . by the way would you mind it if we pulled your teeth out . . . just step over here kinda. That's nice . . . be boppa do.'' Heh, there certainly are a lot of questions that come to mind. You could sure come away pessimistic about the future of the MONSTER. You could sure have legitimate doubts about WOODSTOCK NATION . . . But!!!

And now I call upon myself to vote and I vote THUMBS UP! Right on! And I'm happy and smilin. Cocksure of the future and rememberin the great scene that Anita told me about how this bus was comin up the Thruway and how it was all freaks and everyone laughin, singin and passin around dope, and the bus stalled in traffic and the kids saw this cat standin in the road and needin a ride and they all started jumpin up and down yellin ''Pick him up!'' ''Pick him up!'' ''Pick him up!'' and the bus driver began sweatin all over and shoutin out things about company regulations and other kinds of horseshit. A sort of instant people's militia was formed and they started up the aisle when all of a sudden the bus doors opened and this freak with a knapsack on his back came aboard. Everybody was jokin and clownin and even the bus driver felt better. He didn't accept the joint a cat tried to lay on him but he scratched the guy's shaggy head of hair and smiled.

I ain't never gonna forget that story, No sir, Flower Power ain't dead at all, brother, all we gotta do is get our shit together, and grow some thorns . . . power to the People! Power to the WOODSTOCK NATION!

22

SELLING IT LIKE IT IS

Penney paid $3,500 for a two-day crash course attended by seven merchandising executives anxious to learn how to dig kids. The course included speakers (a journalist, a child psychologist, a seventeen-year-old who publishes an underground newspaper) and fieldwork (a visit with a disk jockey, a trip to Marty Limbo's far-out clothing store in New York's East Village, dinner at Max's Kansas City, a light concert at Fillmore East). On finishing up, the Penney executives were handed home-study kits in paper bags colored orange, yellow, purple, and fuchsia. The contents: a kaleidoscope, a water pistol, a yo-yo, a Lotus Land poster of a chocolate-brown nude girl with flowers in her hair, a poster of a nude boy on a blue swan in a purple lake, a long-playing record of the Rascals, a small gold bell, some underground newspapers, an above-ground magazine (Eye) aimed at teen-agers, a package of incense, a stash for marijuana (empty), and a small mir-

> ror. Penney is brooding about the implications for its future of a generation that may be growing up disdainful of brand loyalties and store images. The company finds some of the implications distinctly favorable. "We have a square image," says Edward Gorman, assistant to the president and a specialist in merchandising. "But square is in. Honesty is in. Cheap is in. Kids are moving toward a 'tell it like it is' philosophy. I think we can hit them right in the eyes with a 'sell it like it is' approach."
>
> —FORTUNE
> *January, 1969*

Here comes the song the true folks of WOODSTOCK NATION would call a "bummer." Yesterday as I walked into the uptown building to see the publisher a bright red-and-white sign winked out of a glass case in the lobby:

DO YOU OWN THING
BANK AT CHASE MANHATTAN

Before we return to the glories of the WOODSTOCK NATION we would like to pause for a moment for this important announcement. . . .

THE IMPACT OF YOUTH

> By 1970 almost one out of every three persons in the U.S. will be under the age of 25. During the 1970's this youth market will control over $45 billion in spending power annually (and it is growing at a phenomenal rate). Because of this, companies in the 1970's who continue to use today's marketing strategies will almost surely suffer a reduction in market share or, more seriously, total company extinction. . . . Fads must be pursued, youth buying-behavior must be analyzed . . . This conference will bring together the largest group of youth-oriented experts ever assembled.
>
> —PROMOTIONAL BROCHURE
> *"Selling the American Youth Market"*
> *AMR International, Inc.*

Brothers and Sisters, we have a duty to each other to work out the problem of the vultures that prey on our culture and indeed on the rest of the world culture as well. The above quote is advertising a conference on youth to be held in the Waldorf-Astoria, October 20–21, price of admission $300. People attending will hear from such mind-manipulators as Stanton Freeman, president Electric Circuses Discotheques, Russell D. Barnard, Assistant to the Vice President, Marketing, CBS records, and Barbara E. Kelley, Vice President, Director of Advertising, Cole of California. About thirty such "youth experts" will attend and lay down the rap to winning back the kids and winning them back with some of the same groovy techniques as were employed to found the WOODSTOCK NATION. The fat cats coughing up $300 a ticket give off some really good vibes. Real groovy! Here are a few of the 500 companies or so that will attend and an incomplete list of what they'll be about when this fall you hear them say "We're jus doin our thing, baby."

THEIR THING

A.T.&T.

About eight years ago A.T.&T. was sued by the government for screwing the American public out of seven billion dollars in phony rate increases. Last year, A.T.&T. made a net profit of eight and one-half billion dollars. That's more than the Gross National Product of more than 85 per cent of the nations in the world.

Dow Chemical

Let's hear it for napalm production!

International Harvester

Keeps them sharecroppers down on the farm with exorbitant prices on equipment and deals with large syndicates.

Schick

Sponsor of right-wing campaigns.

U.S. Army

Not to be confused with the Boy Scouts.

Chase Manhattan Bank

Heavy financial support to South Africa.

Anaconda Copper and Aluminum

Owns more of South America than Brazil and Argentina combined.

Bank of America

Chief backer of California grape owners. "Don't Eat Grapes" or for that matter the Bank of America, either.

Merck, Sharpe, & Dohme

One of the leading supporters of the AMA and lobbyists against free medical care.

Monsanto Chemicals

Try chemical and biological warfare. By the way, did you know that PIG NATION has enough ANTHRAX to destroy the world eighty times over. Thought you'd like to know.

So the Big Boys are going to get together and sort of figure out how they can make some bread on the WOODSTOCK NATION or, if not directly, how they can suck its energy. All that has to be fit in along with Columbia Records pulling ads out of the underground press in an effort to cripple them. A top research firm had suggested two ways to prevent another Chicago from happening.

1. Cancel the policy of youth fare on airplanes.
2. Urge Columbia Records to pull out of the underground press.

As you can see, these guys ain't schmucks like J. Edgar Hoover and his pack of dumb dinosaurs. These guys were prepared to do anything to stay in business, even grow their hair a little longer and put on some beads.

Fit all that in with Love Food, Inc. selling sawdust burgers for outrageous prices on the highest hill in WOODSTOCK NATION and shoveling real money with real shovels into Wells Fargo Trucks, all the time guarded by cops who weren't holding flowers in their hands, no sir. These are things that weren't announced from the stage in that syrruppy smooth groovyvoice, nor talked about in the psychedelic hand-outs and and press releases of Woodstock Ventures. The hope is that PIG NATION cannot endure what happened in WOODSTOCK NATION. The hope is that they can never even figure out what happened until it's too late. The hope is that the people will always be stronger than the Pig's technology. The hope is that the Pig is too dumb to dig the scene. That it will continue thinking it was a festival in the making and not the building of a Nation. Can Amerika absorb smoke-ins, fuck-ins, liberated zones, what have you, inside its borders?? I don't think soooo. That's an opinion and not a prediction. No politician can support what went on there, no WOODSTOCK NATION delegate could possibly win a seat in the mother-country Senate or even House for that matter. Only in the eyes of the spaced-out cynics is this happening. That just ain't what's coming down. Each day in WOODSTOCK NATION there were rumors that Governor Rockefeller (who took that groovy trip to his colonies in South-Amerika last month) was going to declare it as a disaster area. "Disaster" is kind of an interesting word because if you were a revolutionary who thought something heavy was indeed comin down, you were cheering for it to in fact be a disaster for Rockefeller and his whole fuckin world. Disaster is one of those ambiguous terms like a headline up there I saw that said "Chaos Rains" and I wondered why it didn't say "Chaos Reigns" but, well you play those games too don't you? They do on Madison Avenue and they cause a lot of chromosome damage. What if we started playin em and pushin Left Guard instead of Right Guard? But wait. . . .

Fellow revolutionaries of WOODSTOCK NATION and gentlemen of the BOARD OF AMERIKA—here's what *Fortune* Magazine sees when it concludes business's most complete study of the "youthquake":

> At the moment, they seem quite capable of bringing the disorders that have beset the campuses into much of their parents' world — into business and government. We should begin to discern their choice in another year or two. END

Fortune magazine ain't Fortune Cookies! They ain't fucking around. America has fantastic selling capabilities. Nixon's making money on Black Power, everyone's cleaning up on the MOON. "Wonder what the revolutionaries are thinking at United Artists?" says the ad in today's paper. And well, dig, conspiracy time-bomb toys and authentic Yippie love beads and the No. 1 bestselling paperback today is, take it away . . . ELDRIDGE CLEAVER's *Soul on Ice*. The most brilliant, tough-ass motherfucker around and Hollywood wants the movie rights.

Hope you all have a groovy time figurin this out. Frankly it gives me a headache. It's not without hope though dig. Two of those concession stands at Woodstock got burned to the ground, locals who wanted to make a killing selling apples for fifty cents got ripped off good. Friday night late when the rain came pouring down in buckets kids came running into the woods down "Gentle Way" and "Groovy Lane." They were shivering cold and sneezing. Hip merchants in cute little forest stalls were peddling their wares. Kids asked, "Can we get in there out of this rain?" and a lot said, "Sure, come on in, brother!" but some didn't. I saw one glorious rip-off when two Robin Hoods dumped all the hippy junk right into Groovy Lane while another Robin Hood (who was carrying *Revolution for the Hell of It* I'm proud to say) picked his teeth with a knife. All this was happening to the tune of Joan Baez courageously holding forth in the rainstorm, heavy with child, singing

> Deep in my heart, I do believe,
> We shall overcome someday.

23

AIN'T YOU GLAD IT'S THERE, SWEETIE

In *Revolution for the Hell of It*, lots of karate chops were scored against the midriff of *The New York Times*. It was interesting that my hometown newspaper the *Worcester Telegram and Gazette* panned the book something fierce. The thing they got really pissed about was my attack on one of "America's most cherished institutions, *The New York Times*." The *Times* symbolizes everything I hate in PIG NATION. The smugness of having all the news that's fit to print. What arrogance! They have an ad that runs on television (all words, no pictures) that says as it unrolls like some biblical scroll, "Even if you don't read it all it's nice to know it's there." Dig that! The PIG NATION's Security Blanket. Picture all those middle-aged executives sucking their thumbs while they cradle the *Times* under their arm on the 5:09 to Babylon. Picture the people out in Southampton letting the Real Estate section and the Sports section deliberately lie around unread. "Even if you don't read it all it's nice to know it's there." Bah-humbug. One way to know about power in Amerika is to begin by asking the question, "Who in Amerika feels it's nice to know it's all there?"

Last spring, the day I got busted for conspiracy and later for possession of dangerous weapons, I went to a demonstration against *The New York Times*. It was a left demonstration with lots of correct info about the *Times*' role in the military-industrial complex. I had a shirt that said "I got my job thru Granma" and I made a lot of headway talking to the *Times* truck drivers about how the *Times* had no respect for them and that's why they didn't have any funnies. To show them what I meant I had two toilet paper rolls made up using the N.Y. *Times*. In WOODSTOCK NATION that's all the *Times* is good for and on some psychic level the *Times* understands this and that's why they see it as a Nightmare.

Not so with television, and certainly not so with CBS-TV, the hippest of the big three even if Walter Cronkite made the most sickening apology to Daley I ever heard. Jack Lawrence, who I know well, is very sympathetic to the "Movement" even if he does use phrases like "wide-eyed anarchists looking for trouble." Like almost everyone in the left I have a genuine suspicion of the mass media and especially television. A suspicion which is highly justified. But the trouble is that too paranoid a suspicion leaves you no way to deal with it. It tells you nothing about how television works and sets up a plastic dome where you don't have to think about the impact on our minds of color TV, cable TV and knowing that some day real soon most families in PIG NATION will be able through their TV sets to have a computer at their disposal. It just seems stupid to me how people who want to create a revolution can avoid trying to master the most revolutionary means of communication since language itself was invented. Marxists—run-of-the-mill Marxists anyway—can conveniently blot out the impact of the great leap forward in technology. Check this fact out for example. *Ninety per cent of all scientists who ever lived are still alive today.* Statistics like that are incomprehensible to Marxist theoreticians. They just don't know how to fit them into their plastic dome. Anarchist theoreticians like Murray Bookschin, founder of *Anarchos* and author of *Listen Marxist!*, understand far better the implications of post-scarcity economy. Murray would have understood well the piles of garbage in WOODSTOCK NATION, he would have understood why all the printing press and mimeograph machines broke down in competition with the gigantic triple-instant video projections of Janis Joplin. Murray is really one cat who's got his shit together even if he's awful hard reading. You ought to get a copy of his magazine.

Anyway I wanted to tell you a secret about television, rather than simply make the obvious point that television, like the helicopter, belongs in the future, while newspapers, like automobiles, belong in WOODSTOCK NATION's trash bucket. Here's a secret that might help you use it better if you feel like fighting in the TV jungle and you only got a switchblade and not millions of dollars to pump images through the funnels of Madison Avenue. Many reporters are Yippie agents. I learned this watching hours and hours of straight unedited footage on Chicago, first in the making of the Yippie movie and later in preparation for the conspiracy trial. It began to become apparent that the individual reporter covering the story had a good deal to do with its conceptualization, with the slant the story took. This is particularly true when a voice-over narrative is used, a technique that CBS-TV follows more than the other channels, which prefer to have the anchormen—i.e., Huntley and Brinkley—narrate a lot of the footage. Television reporters are often young, often in the thick of the battle, often sympathize. Not sympathetic like the National Liberation Front is sympathetic, granted, but close enough to lend a hand. And they hate parents or teachers or bosses. Turn on the cameramen! Every organizer should see a film that will be out just when this book appears called "Medium Cool," about a television reporter who covers the Chicago demonstrations. The picture is more interesting in what it attempts to do than what it achieves. The picture is very pro-movement but before I get carried away with the glories of the mass communications industry, let me tell you about the time I called the producers of "Medium Cool" and asked if they would consider doing a benefit for the conspiracy trial, seeing how they were so sympathetic and we were flat broke with a staff that hadn't gotten any money in three weeks. You know what they decided at Paramount Pictures? . . . We were too "controversial."

> Take a piece of dark cellophane plastic and cut out the letters BULLSHIT. Paste this over a wide-faced flashlight or a lamp rigging that you can easily make. Always carry such a rigging to movies in which you want to comment on what's on the screen. Power to the People's critics. (Thanks to Jean-Jacques Lebel.)

24

DEAR JACK

Most Honorable John Mitchell
Chief Butcher
United States of America

It has been some time since you have indicted me for conspiracy. It was such a nice, personal, warm letter, I thought it was about time I sat down and answered you. After all, this may be my last chance before your asshole deputy Foran in Chicago sends me up the river for ten years or so. I just want to know if you and other leaders of PIG NATION would consider meeting to negotiate a ceasefire and eventual peace treaty with members of WOODSTOCK NATION. You must understand that this peace feeler is exploratory and for obvious reasons should be kept secret. I will do the same with any responses from you. To begin with, you should familiarize yourself with the program of the Berkeley Liberation Front, the platform of the White Panther Party and the Yippie demands for a Free Society to get an idea of where our heads are at. At the first sign of interest in negotiations from you, we will meet in conference with large numbers of our brothers and sisters and hammer out a single set of demands. Let me briefly spell out a few minimum requirements so you can get a whiff of what we'll be smoking when we sit down together.

1. Free John Sinclair and all other political prisoners.
2. Get off our Free Land. As a beginning, end the occupation of New Mexico, Arizona, Haight-Ashbury, the Lower East Side, Berkeley including the University of California, Ann Arbor, Michigan, the Boston Common, Rittenhouse Square in Philadelphia, Big Sur, Provincetown, Lincoln Park in Chicago and the other Woodstock, New York (negotiable). As you must realize we already have built and defended Bethel, the Capital of our WOODSTOCK NATION.
3. We want the right of free passage to and from different areas of our Nation. We do not want to be hassled by your Pigs in any way, shape, or manner. We will submit to your system of law only if we do injury to one of your citizens and we expect you to do likewise.
4. We want you to give us a specified amount of time on the television airwaves to show various survival information, theatrical events like mass fuck-ins, and news reports that affect the political and cultural life of WOODSTOCK NATION.
5. Wherever rivers or lakes flow into or border our two Nations, you pledge to keep garbage and other shit out of the water. We'll do likewise. Perhaps we can work something out jointly in this area after the war is over. We will refrain from putting LSD in reservoirs that service both Nations.
6. You will allow us opportunity to transport all members of our liberated Nation who might find themselves trapped in your schools, factories and other penitentiaries. In reciprocity, we will look for wayward souls who might have wandered into our area by mistake. We will encourage the posting of signs such as "Come home, Cindy" and "John we miss you."
7. You will convince the Culture-Vultures who have

taken our culture out of the alleys and parks of our Nation and turned it into profits to pay $300,000,000 in reparations and a mutually agreed upon sum to be negotiated each year.

8. You will provide us with enough arms to successfully repel any and all invasions by warring Pig tribes who fail to live by the treaty.

These eight areas would provide some basis for discussion. We would also make some suggestions about the BLACK NATION and the rest of what we call the Free World (although I believe you call them something else). You, of course, realize you must negotiate independently with them.

Maybe it all sounds like what my ol man used to call the "gimme-gimmes," but considering the consequences you are getting off relatively cheap. In fact, dirt cheap! The alternative will be, I'm afraid, the total and complete death of Amerika. The land as well as the system. There are many of my brothers and sisters who would even say these eight demands are not enough. They would say that the brain damage your teachers have caused is in itself punishable by death, to say nothing of the rotten food you tried to poison us with. But, well I don't want to flip out into flaming rhetoric in a personal communication such as this. Let's just say I hope to hear from you before the trial starts. You can signal your willingness to negotiate by smoking a joint on television. Labor Day will be as good a day as any. We would be ready to send a negotiation team to a place we both agree upon within ten days afer you signal. Until then, power to the people, and hope the missus is feeling better.

Abbie

P.S. You will know this letter is authentic if you soak it in water for ten minutes and then drink the cocktail.

25

SURVIVAL

to love we must survive
to survive we must fight . . .

Fuck the System [Abbie's first book, written under an alias (George Metesky), revisited and expanded in *Steal This Book*] presents ways in which you can help take a free trip without working. Not working strikes a blow for freedom, as I'm sure we'll all agree. Here's a few more tips. Some of the best ways to steal I know have been working out very well this year. The first involves getting someone a job as a cashier in a large supermarket, a job that is fairly easy to come by. After about two weeks the cashier invites all brothers and sisters to shop for free (by simply forgetting to ring up the total amount). For a while one operation I know was getting about five hundred dollars worth of food each week. I'm sure you know how to work the credit-card swindle and also how to get double your money on travelers' cheques by reporting them stolen? I doubt if you know how to fly from

Boston to San Francisco for fourteen dollars and around the world for eighty-eight? I can't tell you here but if I see you and I think you'll use the information well I'll pass it on. Maybe if you come out to Chicago during the trial.

Next I want to clue you in on the U.S. Government Printing Office, Washington, D.C. You can find out just about anything you want from them, especially on Survival. They also print the best material available on military tactics in revolutionary warfare. The U.S. Army, for example, puts out unquestionably the most important books available on the subject of street fighting and resistance to military (police) repression. Another publication that's probably the most valuable work of its kind available is called *Physical Security* and has more relevant information than Che Guevara's *Guerilla Warfare.* The chapter on Sabotage is extremely precise and accurate with detailed instructions on the making of all sorts of homemade bombs and triggering mechanisms. That information, combined with *Army Installations in the Continental United States* and a lot of guts, can really get something going!

The U.S. Government is an expert on living free and creating destruction; it's been doing both for quite a long time. I ain't saying you should use any of this information, in fact for the records of the FBI, I say right now "Don't blow up your local draft board or other such holy places." You wouldn't want to get the Government Printing Office indicted for conspiracy, would you now?

FIGURE 1. *Improvised incendiary delay device.*

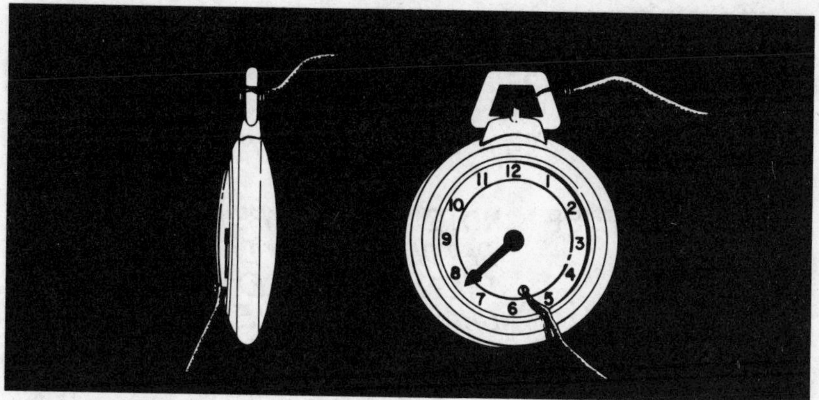

FIGURE 2. Improvised mechanical delay device (pocket watch).

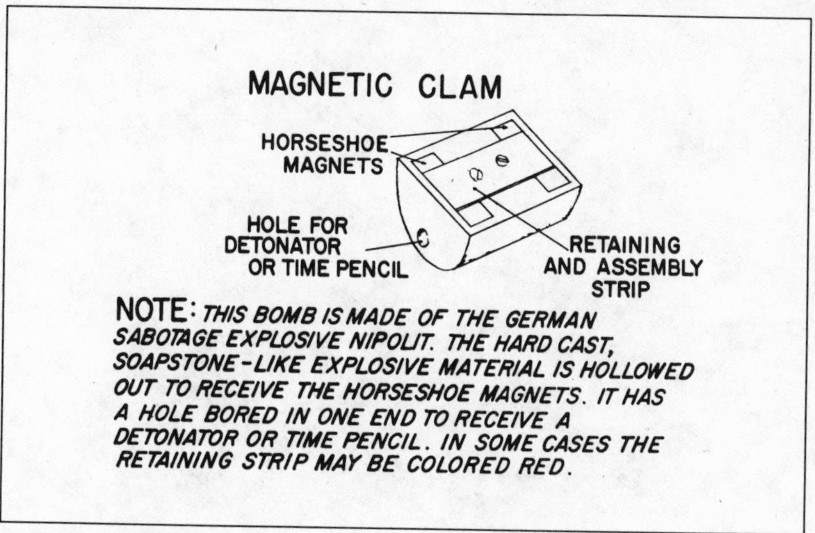

FIGURE 3. Magnetic clam.

Figures 1, 2, 3 and 4 reprinted from Department of the Army Field Manual *FM 19-30 Physical Security.* If you're interested in learning how to do such things as "tape explosives under dogs and drive them into the police lines" read "Army Plans for Containment of Civilian Disorders." If your bag runs to personal self-defense don't miss "Combatives." You can learn how to make a guy choke to death by swallowing his tongue or if you're in the mood and quick enough you can kill him by a well-placed twist to the nose!

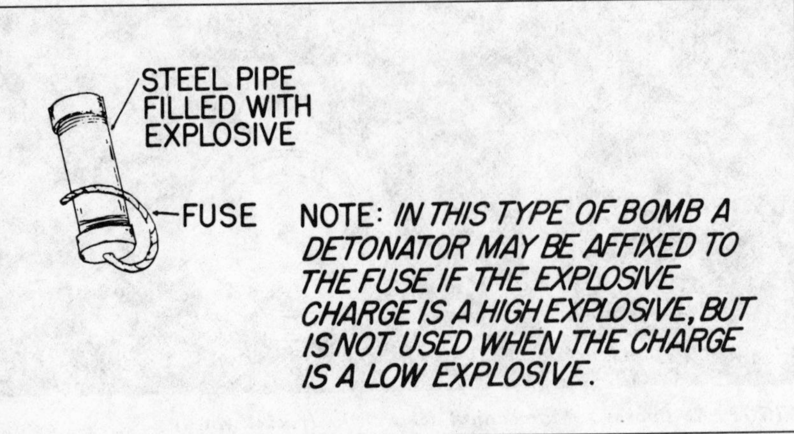

FIGURE 4. Steel pipe filled with explosives.

26

DOWN ON ME AND JANIS JOPLIN

God, I'd like to fuck Janis Joplin!

> Down on me, down on me,
> Looks like ev'rybody in this whole round world
> is down on me.
>
> Love in this world is so hard to find,
> When you've got yours and I've got mine.
> That's why it looks like ev'rybody in this whole round
> world
> Is down on me.

Man, I just love her belting out heavy little-girl truck-driver blues. Love her swinging' her Southern Comfort ass and choking the mike. Love her outa sight costumes and the way she swaggers around like Annie Oakley from the Wild West Show. She's Ma Baker and Baby Snooks. She's out of her fuckin' mind Janis is . . . when she sings you hear the sadness of Billie Holliday and Bessie Smith the way they got their lives into their sound. Janis can do it. Janis sings the same song over and over again. Gooooo down on me . . . and I don't feel cheated one bit when I hear her sing it cause it's a great fuckin song and Janis is all fuckin right even if she don't know from California grapes and freeing John Sinclair . . . maybe it ain't her fault? Maybe it's mine??? Maybe I ain't explained it to her right?? Those rock folks are into something and loving Janis is a way of saying I'm sorry if I'm really fuckin up your scene. I think you folks are into something really beautiful and really heavy, even—and let me say it loud and clear; even *The Who* is GREAT. You cats got some good shit goin, like the Dead doing freebees in the park and Gracie Slick saying *mother-fucker* on the Dick Cavett Show. Dig that PIG NATION, "motherfucker"! Wait til you hear the Jefferson Airplane's next album *Volunteers of America.*

> Tear down the walls
> Tear down the walls
>
> Come on now together
> Get it on together
> Everybody together

If you get into digging the music it's all "tear down the walls, motherfucker" and "kick out the jams, 'motherfucker.'" It's Janis saying loud and clear, right on the stage of WOODSTOCK NATION:

> Don't take no shit from nobody . . .
> Tell em all to fuck off.

It's the Doors' warning in "When the Music's Over"—

> We want the world and we want it NOW!

That's good enough politics for me . . . Hard on, sister! Lay it on em, brother! Sure it'd be nice if Sly and the Family Stone stopped playing once and looked out at PIG NATION and said "Oh, by the way we're Communists," God that would blow a lot of fuckin holes in "His Master's Voice."

Yeh, but maybe that's unfair cause on the other hand we politicos don't sing too good. When SDS talks about the Vanguard they don't mean the record company, but they don't mean fuckin and dancin with all the people either. They mean responsible leadership just the way my father does. And what about bands like The Who??? Heroes of the people; do they have responsibilities? What are you gonna do with your bread, brother rock stars? Are you gonna help build and defend the WOODSTOCK NATION NOW, or are you just gonna piss it all away?? Here's a word of advice from one of the biggest dudes around. His name is Chairman Mao. He and his rock band built a whole fuckin Nation of 700,000,000 people when they said it couldn't be done. This quote is for me as much as you cause when I get through with this book I'm gonna learn how to sing. . . .

> You have many good qualities and have rendered great service, but you must always remember not to become conceited. You are respected by all, and quite rightly, but this easily leads to conceit. If you become conceited, if you are not modest and cease to exert yourselves, and if you do not respect others, do not respect the cadres and the masses, then you will cease to be heroes and models. There have been such people in the past, and I hope you will not follow their example.*

The Beatles may be more popular than Jesus but heavy cats like Chairman Mao, Uncle Ho, and beautiful long-haired Che Guevara are more popular than even the Beatles. You ought to check out that other "free world" and see. Don't take my word for it—but don't believe *Variety* or *Billboard* or even *Rolling Stone* either. Any of you guys want to play in Havana Square for free just get in touch. We've already made the arrangements.

LONG LIVE THE CULTURAL REVOLUTION!

*"We Must Learn to Do Economic Work" (January 10, 1945) *Selected Works*, Vol. III, p. 239.

27

THE GREAT RIP-OFF

Ring . . . Ring . . . Ring Hello Woodstock Ventures . . . Is Michael Lang there, George Metesky the Deputy of Defense for the Youth International Party—you know, the Yippies that put on the festival in Chicago last year . . . that's right, Abbie Hoffman, Minister of Culture for the Yippies and representatives from other movement groups would like to see Mr. Lang about the festival.
I'm not sure you'd want to, this is going to be three days of Peace and Music, it's not about politics . . .
Oh yes, well neither are the Yippies, we just want to dig on the groovy doovy vibes. Tell Mr. Lang we'll be at his office at eleven a.m. tomorrow . . . see you then . . . CLICK.

The wheels had been set in motion. Everyone was ready for the pressure treatment . . . jamming switchboards, blocking their offices, press conferences announcing that the crazy communists who ripped up Chicago were hoping the town board members of Bethel would give Woodstock Ventures a permit so we could come up and screw all their daughters—etcetera, etcetera.

Every group was broke cause the liberal bulge that used to support most radical causes was off on some other trip, playing around with anti-ABM campaigns and sending food to Biafra. Even though they wept and shed some blood in the streets of Chicago, they were gone for good—gone with their money. Our revolution was becoming too radical or crazy or violent or young. We were fuckin up their cocktail parties and it mattered not the blood we were shedding or the growing fascism in the country. New ways had to be found to get bread cause the days of the mailings and benefits were over. In fact, for the Yippies, they had never even begun. For six weeks I had been working on the Movement Speakers' Bureau project designed to get speakers on the campuses and have the agency fees available to groups that the speakers wanted to support. If campus activists put a lot of James Forman-type pressure on filthy-rich student councils, the project could realize a lot of bread. Revolution was becoming a saleable commodity and the only way to deal with that was to try and rip off the bread and spread it around like the manure it was. Besides it was a "safe" project and would keep me off the streets for a while, hence out of jail. I was tired of getting arrested and had even considered cutting my hair and leaving New York. It was a depressing summer of sitting in courtrooms and waiting for the Big Trial to begin in Chicago. I found I spent a lot of time discussing my arrests and wondering if I would end up like Lenny Bruce. The picture of him lying naked on the bathroom floor that I had seen flashed through my mind each day. The Lower East Side was disappearing out of my plastic dome. I was sick of starting free stores that ended up garbage cans, and bailing out people who never gave the bread back so we would get others out, and mimeos that broke down. I wasn't the only one getting sick of New York; even the gutsy Motherfuckers had split to New Mexico, Massachusetts and San Francisco. The bikers were shooting each other in the streets and the drug scene was all speed. Cops stopped cars illegally and threw people against walls and somehow nobody gave a shit because the whole scene had been wasted. Jerry Rubin was in retreat completing his book . . . SDS was interested in having Yippies play a role in their fall demonstrations but when they said it was for those who missed Chicago last year most of us lost interest seeing as how we had been there. A lot of my friends were in jail for dope with high or no bail and you couldn't do much about it. One I felt almost responsible for and can't even talk about cause if the FBI found out we were working together, he would be worse off than he already is. I even have to write him under another name. The paranoids were out in force. If a group got something really heavy together it couldn't even talk about it cause everything was tapped and every other guy was a cop. (One good way to protect the security of your gang is to all turn on together with LSD. A cop would smoke pot but he sure as hell would never drop acid. Also I've never seen an undercover cop with real long hair and I've seen a lot of undercover cops. Maybe long side-burns and a couple day's growth of beard, but no Pig is gonna go home to Queens each night or on weekends and play golf with his buddies lookin like Tiny Tim. Ah you kiddin?)

It's in those moments that you start to think about being white and male and over thirty and too smart for your own fuckin good. You start to get pretty down in the dumps sometimes. Besides, every group was into calling the other an imposter and fights were breaking out all over the place. The left was moving into Stalinism and the hippies were moving to the country (as usual). It was getting mighty lonely on the fence. So there I was organizing left-movement groups to go to a hip community event . . . the Morea-Eel of the Motherfuckers, whose role I sometimes think is just to chew me out, would be pissed but it was impossible to contact him. Besides he was always pissed and would be even if he got a cut of the bread. Even if he got a cut of the bread from this book he'd be pissed. Everything had to happen fast too, since Woodstock Ventures' permit hassles would soon be over and they would be less likely to give in. Besides, the festival was only two weeks away. Asking that people should get in free would be ridiculous cause the word was already out about Los Angeles, Denver, and Newport. Tear down the walls and you get in free. Everybody was hip to free and walls were coming down everywhere, but we were into something else. There's a word for it but we'll avoid its usage for various legal reasons. We wanted support from the hip profiteers and we wanted to establish a model for movement groups around the country on how to relate to these huge gatherings. No real hip activist could just sit by and watch skilled promoters create events that gathered huge numbers of young people and made exorbitant profits without eventually taking an interest.

When the twelve of us barged into the Woodstock Ventures offices with police dogs and theatre prop chains hanging out of our pockets we were looking for some bread clear and simple. The mini-skirts flew in all directions and I wondered which one was the gal who said "We're not into politics." We did our little song-and-dance number and said, "We'll be back tomorrow and the fuckers running the show better be here cause there isn't much time—Wa-do-wa- Wa-do-wa." In five minutes we were out and back on the streets of the Lower East Side. Meanwhile, reports kept coming in about who made decisions in their organization and who we should insist should be at that meeting. The call came an hour later from Bethel. They would meet with us tomorrow any place we liked and all four were coming. When they said all four were coming we already had a sense of victory and the opening figure doubled. There were also people within their organization who for one reason or another were angry, and all day they kept feeding us information about decisions. Their organization was as sloppy as their offices, or ours for that matter. By the time we sat down the next day everything had already been decided and we just had to play out our respective roles and then get stoned together. Up to then, me and Peter, a cat who was in "Movers and Things," a sort of hip cooperative employment agency, were more or less making decisions. Peter was unpopular among lots of groups, but so was I for that matter, or anybody. This was not quite the summer of love and even though the word *community* was thrown around, so were fists and chains.

For the second encounter, Jeff Shero came aboard. Jeff is editor of the *Rat*, probably, with the exception of the *Berkeley Tribe*, the most influential underground paper. Well, that is, I suppose, if your conception of the underground is what culminates in actions like Chicago and People's Park. The *Rat* brought the underground press to Chicago and was intrumental in organizing high school kids in New York. At the media conference the *Rat* led the difficult struggle for unity and militancy. The *Rat* had tried best of all to relate to the politics of hip from an organizing point of view. I recognized this and I also recognized that Jeff didn't like me much. It was awkward cause I dug him. When he attacked a wild, at times dumb article I wrote on SDS, I even answered with a letter. It was the first time I had answered criticism in print in seven years—a record I had been rather proud of. Now I wasn't proud of the attack on SDS or the answering of Jeff's criticism. Our relationship was a mess. Still, Jeff sensed my isolation and knew the difficulties we were having getting interest in the conspiracy trial and I knew the *Rat*, like the other underground papers, was feeling the squeeze of the new sex-ploitation mags that were crowding them off the newsstands. In fact, I had heard that the *Rat* was about to fold. All this brought us together and when Jeff, who is Alice's man, said, "Alice says I have a tendency to snub you," I knew we could work together. So it was good to see Jeff involved; besides, Jeff had opened negotiations on a separate front with them and had already met with them. Now there were about a dozen groups represented.

After about an hour of us yelling "Culture-Vultures!"—and them saying "Groovy baby, we dig you guys and your whole scene" we reached an agreement: ten grand, a few hundred tickets, booth space and mutual cooperation on doctors, lawyers and a bail fund for people who would get busted on the way up. We told them up front that we were still into urging people to go free. There were promises of more to come if they made bread on the event. There were a lot of promises.

Who got money? How were we now going to relate to the festival? How were we going to make decisions? There were still going to be problems, especially once other groups found out about the rip-off. It never ceased to amaze me how groups, instead of imitating our model and trying to rip off Woodstock Ventures again or the Fillmore or Columbia Records, tried instead to devour us. Maybe it's just that money sucks. Who knows? I know one thing though, that the little asshole-pseudo-revolutionary gang that tried to rip me off with the same guerilla chain-theatre bit is never gonna get shit. Ripping off guys who just got ten grand for projects and were prepared to fuck up some offices and go to jail, when three blocks away the fat cats are rolling up a two-million-dollar budget, ain't good revolutionary strategy . . . but then again, bad tactics were never at a loss in the movement, and especially not in the New York movement. It always puzzled me why the good guys always were the pacifists.

So a lot of meetings happened, and things were pulled together; mimeos, doctors, lawyers, theatre groups, a huge new Trojan Horse of a press, silk-screening operations with some beautiful posters like one that said, WHEN TYRANNY IS LAW, REVOLUTION IS ORDER. Everyone was rushing to get it all together, too fast in a way, because we weren't sure we knew what the fuck we were doing. People were scared of gettin "CO-OPTED," which on the left is like halitosis or some other catastrophe. Larry from *Newsreel* coined the term *Vanguard Capitalism* to describe the producers, and that helped a little, but we were sinking in the marshmallow of tolerance and everyone knew it. The night Hugh Romney of the Hogfarm showed up and said, "We'll be givin out a lot of free food, our chicks will be doin some cookin," everyone booed with glee cause at last everybody had what politicos would call a "bummer" if they spoke that language. Women's Liberation was very big this year, especially at meetings that were mostly male, and especially when it came time to do the cooking, clean up, or fuck.

The Hogfarm played a strange role in the whole caper. Under Vanguard Capitalism the Hogfarmers with their "cool out the tension, build up the good vibes" approach played the role of the cops. It was no secret to everyone that the Hogfarm had been invited to participate to the tune of about six grand with another sixteen grand spent on flying them in from New Mexico along with twenty Indians in a chartered plane. Everyone knew if a fence were to be ripped down or a food stand ripped off or some equipment "borrowed" it would be the Hogfarmers that would stop it, not the hogs or Pigs or cops or whatever you called them. The day before that meeting, four of us went up to Bethel to check out the site and were met by a Hogfarmer who said, "My role is to cool you guys out." We had a long rap drivin around those hills about whether he thought there was such a thing as a "good" millionaire if he kept his money and stuff like that. "Hey man," a lefty might have said, "haven't you read Jerome Skulnick on institutional violence?" But seeing as how I'm not a lefty and hadn't read it either, I kept my mouth shut. The Hogfarm's specialty was called "Pudding"—a mass of people-jelly, generally naked, generally fucking or sucking, always giggling and always covered in something like jello or whipped cream or pudding. It's pretty hard to argue with Pudding and besides if you were hungry enough you ate it if you had any brains.

Hugh and I are good friends, lovers really. We work hard, have fun and try to work our thing out the best way we know how with a certain amount of respect for each other. In that meeting with the political groups my closest friend was Hugh. We had known each other the longest. I visited him in the hospital in Pennsylvania when he busted his back trying to crank up one of their crazy buses. I held my aching head when he told me the

Hogfarm wanted to try and turn on Mississippi. I liked him even though he ran up a huge phone bill in our office when we had no bread. I liked him even though his 500-pound pig mascot ate the shower curtain and some of an article I was writing when we stored him in our 300-pound office. I liked him and his ol lady Bonnie about as much as you can like people these days. Liking him and diggin his politics was QUITE another story, and conflicts between friendships and politics are something I hope to solve this year, but then again I hoped to solve it last year and on back to when I was born I guess. Anyway, Hogfarm politics proved stronger magic than Movement City's and it wasn't just that the name Movement City stunk, it was that the Hogfarm's politics are survival, and when 300,000 people that you are trying to reach get drenched in a huge rainstorm on some foreign hills, survival is what politics is about. Survival needs first, conversion to revolutionary politics second. THE NEEDS OF THE PEOPLE MUST BE MET.

After the rains came, the Hogfarm went right on serving their free food and enjoying themselves, and the lefties, not all the lefties but enough to say it, packed up their leaflets or abandoned them and headed out of WOODSTOCK NATION still thinking it was a festival, or worse, a concentration camp. Those who stayed are better for it all, including me. When you learn to survive in a hostile environment, be it the tear gas parks of Chicago or the mud slopes of WOODSTOCK NATION, you learn a little more of the universal puzzle, you learn a little more about yourself, and you learn about the absurdity of any analysis at all. It's only when you get to the End of Reason can you begin to enter WOODSTOCK NATION. It's only when you cease to have any motives at all can you comprehend the magnitude of the event. It's only then that you can start to enjoy it all. This came to me one night while Paul, Roz and I walked through the darkened "Forest of the Crafts People and Hip Merchants" that separated the Hogfarm site from the main performance area. We felt our way along the secret paths for hours—bumping into trees and groping around tents. After getting totally exhausted, we emerged in a lighted area and rushed forward sensing our victory over the maze-like forest. Much to our surprise, we were right back where we started—back among the plywood booths of Movement City, right back in the tents of the Hogfarm. God, I'll tell you something I learned up there in WOODSTOCK NATION—nobody knew where the fuck anything was, not even WOODSTOCK NATION. Like Pete Seeger said, "If you were gonna join it, you had to join it by yourself." Figuring out how to get in and out of the whole thing was a problem as old as Western Civilization and as modern as the traffic jam scenes in Jean Luc-Godard's "Weekend." You entered at the End of Reason, of that I was sure. At least I was consistently sure of that. Which is not bad considered I ain't sure of anything else about that mind blower. I ain't sure of nothing at all.

28

THE SINCLAIR HOSPITAL

The morning after the rains came was the most chaotic sight you could ever imagine. It reminded me of when we had a tornado up in Worcester in 1953. WOODSTOCK NATION was all a wreck, everyone sort of sniffling and sad, when a cat came out of his tent and made a fist at the sky: "Fuck off rain, we're staying here forever!" It was then that the battle began for me. It was then that I felt at peace. It was about 5:00 A.M. and I had a hunk of brown canvas over me with a hole cut out for the head. I reminded myself of General George Patton inspecting the troops in Normandy as I walked around assessing the damage. The main performance area had turned into a huge slide of mud, people, collapsed tents, overturned motorcycles, cans, bottles and GARBAGE GALORE—man, there was more fuckin garbage unloaded in WOODSTOCK NATION that night than in the Lower East Side during the entire garbage strike. The First Aid Center in the Hogfarm was already crowded and the doctor, a woman volunteer whom I recognized from Chicago, said the twenty to thirty doctors the Medical Committee for Human Rights was flying in at noon were not barely enough. She and I headed for the First Aid Center close to the performing area, talking all the way about what had to be done. I was chewing up the information as fast as I could cause I had just appointed myself Superintendent of Sinclair Hospital. I was digesting I.V. solutions, sutures, gauze pads, salt tablets, penicillin, Ace bandages, cots, operating rooms, the whole bit. I was trying to recall everything I knew from my youth about hospitals and medical supplies. If you want to know the truth it wasn't such a feat. My ol man owns a medical supply company and I used to spend time working there or poking around, depending on whether it was me or my old man you talked to. Hell, John would sure be proud of me now; after all those years of being away from the business and after all those years of revolution and heart attacks—after all that, I was finally settling in the Hospital Business. I was finally coming home to work in the store.

We took over a pink-and-white tent that had been used to feed the staff and divided it in two sections. Food section to the left, hospital to the right. Plywood sheets were thrown on the ground and cots began to be set up. Lee Penn, fresh after beating a ten-year rap in Chicago, and some guys began painting huge crosses on sheets using red paint and a hunk of Kotex. Another tent was "borrowed" and somebody knocked down the press tent and brought it over to be our BAD TRIP center. We also hustled walkie talkies, chairs, supplies, tables, towels, sheets, ambulances, stretchers. Ron Kaufman, who pulled me outa Chicago and was helping do the Movement Speakers' Bureau got out our electric bullhorn and went into action. Signs went up fast: CUTS, WAITING ROOM, ADMISSION, VOLUNTEERS, REST, EMERGENCY, HEAT TABLETS. Old friends began coming over. Abe Peck, ex-editor of the *Chicago Seed* and one of the best cats alive ran the volunteer operation. Roy Payne from *Newsreel* took over Information Control and kept the visitors out of the area. New people showed up. Like a really cool-headed gal named Jill who had been an Army supply nurse. She took over the supply coordination which was a huge problem seeing as how we didn't have any. Doctors like Sid and Jeff and more pitched in. A local resident named George headed up the coordination of the ambulances that kept showing up. He came for an hour and stayed twenty-four. Hugh Romney and Bonnie Beautiful, ex-Playboy Bunny, got the whole bum-trip scene together. Sorry if I left some folks out. It was the acid and I ain't slept much since that night. Everyone had a name like William Head Doctor, Sid Cuts, Lee Heat Tablets or Lynn Walkie Talkie. What the fuck's a name anyway.

It was amazing to see that whole thing take shape. There were things that tore my brains out like dig this: We were centered right next to the helicopter field and helicopters kept flying overhead pulling up the hospital tents. Trying to keep them away was an almost useless task cause there were about five different chains of command working with those helicopters. I mean, after all, this was show business and the show must go on so tents were uprooted and amplifiers battled with stretchers and rock stars with doctors and even champagne with intravenous solutions. In the end the show people won out over the hospital people and medical supplies had to be flown in by none other than—take it away—the United States Air Force!

> Sir, where do I put these supplies, sir. I was told to bring these to you. I'm Captain Grant of the U.S. Air Force . . .

It was just about then that I decided to drop the second of the acid tabs people had been laying on me. It was either the blue or the green . . . There we were with helicopters making winds up to thirty or forty miles an hour buzzing around like flies, staring across Lake Shore Drive at a People Hill that was now at least 300,000 strong, listening to what sounded like wildman Joe Cocker, beltin it out from the stage. There we were; Aldo Ray from "Battle Cry" and Dennis Hopper from "Easy Rider" one just back from Nam and the other from Lincoln Park. There we were together luggin boxes of medical supplies into the Sinclair Hospital. "Hey Captain, you ever consider defecting?" I whispered in his ear.

It was about then I took a break and tried to meet a girl or two and feel the acid melt my mind and maybe even hear some sounds. Maybe I could even hustle up some bread for ol John or ol Conspiracy or any ol politics and feel right about members of the Woodstock Four slappin me on the back and treating me like one of the partners . . . Everything was sort of floating along like this when the first major crack occurred in my plastic dome which by now was beginning to feel sort of mescaline-mellow. A few fireworks were bursting over at People Hill and in my dome, sparklers were starting to light up, too . . . . first white . . . . then green . . . . then rainbow!

There were bad trips happening all day. Nothing really heavy. Nothing the Hogfarm couldn't handle. You never really knew what caused bad trips and you were sure nobody else who knew anything about acid knew either. You knew about the sugar and orange juice cure and Niacinamide tablets and Thorazine suppositories up the ass and when, as a last resort, to call a doctor. You even knew the most important way to bring someone down was sympathetic kind talk by someone who had been there. Even knowing all that you still didn't know what caused bad trips. Was it strychnine or loss of ego? Was it belladonna or the urban crisis? Was it no food and water or the loneliness of being in a crowd of 300,000? One thing I knew for sure, though, was that announcements like "The blue acid is real bad—report to the hospital if you feel sick," and "The greens are poison," didn't help one bit, no sir, not one bit. Especially when they were coming out of those microphones that everyone had plugged into their skulls. Those announcements blew fuses in a lot of plastic domes. Hugh, Abe, and I stood at the admission gate trying to joke with the Mob of Bad Trippers . . . like about two hundred were into fits and more were pouring down the road like some mighty St. Vitus Dance, all jerking around in their own insanities, sometimes six or eight people carrying some vibrating freak. "It's okay," I said to one cat. "Look, it ain't bad," and I popped in the last tab I had—either the red Abe gave me or the blue or . . . gee those sparklers were sure lighting up the sky I noticed, and the bonfires and waterfalls up there weren't bad either.

Hugh and I decided to head for the stage to announce that it wasn't bad acid after all!!! It was just as we were working our way across this wobbly bridge that connected performers, helicopters and hospital to stage, microphones and People Hill, that I started to get some doubts . . . Things were becoming very unclear and when I saw a guy throw a spear at me like in the movie "Bwana Devil" and I even saw the red-and-green tint that you saw when your 3D glasses fell off, when I saw that, and when I ducked no less, I knew I was on some real powerful shit. I knew I had taken some weird acid . . . the trouble was I couldn't figure out whether it was the red or the green, or the blue or the no sleep or the 300,000 people, or the shaky bridge, or that African spear thrower.

Just before I climbed down the stairs on the other side of LSD Drive, I remember taking the name tag off my shirt that said GENERAL COORDINA-

TOR. General Coordinator was something I made up to get me past ushers, especially the pushy ones in the green jackets. I have no idea how long I was zonked out or what really happened. I recall trying to steal a lot of heavy movie equipment from this trailer, with some mad revolutionary outlaw freaks that shall go unnamed in case some shit is missing. I remember seeing Hugh chasing some guy with a gun who was trying to rob some TV people, or at least Hugh said it was a gun. Mike Lang later said it was a knife and the guy was trying to grab this chick's wallet . . . I was climbing along under the stage area ankle-deep in the mud when I looked to my right and then I saw it . . . vague at first and then more visible . . . holy shit what a fuckin sight! There they were . . . a girl and a guy fuckin away. The girl was a weird-looking blond chick with a big belly, no, she was pregnant, but that ain't all she was . . . she had cuts all over her body and her left tit was . . . holy shit it wasn't . . . Sharon Tate!!!! Oh fuck what's going on??? There humping her from behind . . . I'm gonna pass out . . . Elvis Presley!!! At least I think it was him cause it was just the bottom half of a naked dude . . . all he had on were some blue suede shoes . . . man, my mouth was all dry and I ran up on the stage . . . there was Mike Lang . . . and all of a sudden we were off exploring each other's plastic domes and talking about big things like Empires and little things like cut feet. I kept wonderin how Elvis was makin out . . .

"Hey, Mike I saw Elvis, here, how bout that. Elvis came, well most of him anyways."

"Dylan's comin," said Lang.

"Ah you're full of shit," I said, "he's gonna be in England tonight, don't pull that shit on me."

"Nah I ain't kiddin, Abby-baby, he called up and said he might come . . ."

"You think he'd dig runnin for president?"

"Nah, that ain't his trip, he's into something else."

"You met him, Mike? What's he into?"

"I don't know for sure but it ain't exactly politics. You ever met him?"

"Yeah, once about seven years ago in Gertie's Folk City down in the West Village. I was trying to get him to do a benefit for civil rights or something . . . hey Mike will you introduce us? I sure would like to meet Dylan . . . I only know about meetin him through Happy Traum . . ."

"There's an easier way . . . Abbs . . . I'll introduce you. In fact he wants to meet you . . ."

"Hey Mike, what about John Sinclair . . ."

"No, not that again, Abby-baby . . ."

"Yeah, no shit Mike, that's more important than even Dylan for President . . . We ought to get John Sinclair out of jail. He got ten fuckin years for two joints . . . how can we take such shit?

"Yeah, that sure was a bummer . . ."

"Mike I been thinking, wouldn't it be a good idea to do somethin for ol John . . . like how about a cut of the movie rights for his defense fund? . . . I found out you got two million for the movie . . ."

"We're thinking of doin something tomorrow night Abby-baby . . . just hang on . . ."

The rock group playing had just ended the set and seeing how the mike wasn't being used I sauntered up and in my black-leather acid voice shouted something at the People Hill like:

> The Politics of the event is Pot. Dig it! John Sinclair's in fuckin prison ten years for two fuckin joints. We ought to bust John out of prison or all this peace and music don't mean . . . CLICK

Well I didn't give a shit if they cut the mike off. I got it out anyway. I wiped my nose and walked through the swarm of startled flower floaters crowding on the stage (third largest in the world no less). Everyone had this weird look with their eyes poppin out and their mouths hangin opened. It was sort of like I was their mother and just caught em jerking off . . . God, here was Florence Nightingale passin out downers. I went to the corner and sat down on the edge of the stage, feeling pretty alone—and remembering when I was seventeen and pissed in my pants on the bus—everything was spinning for a while . . . Mike came over and said, "What the fuck did you do that for??"

"Oh, I'm just doing my thing."

"Oh, O.K., come hear this group, they'll really blow your mind and calm down . . . trust us, Abby-baby . . . we're with you all the way . . ."

"Oh yeah, which band is playin?"

"The Who, that's who."

"The What?"

"No, man, The Who, from England, you know . . ."

"Oh, yeah, The Who . . . don't they bust their instruments?"

We sat on the stage listening to The Who tune up and all of a sudden I remembered . . .

"Hey Mike, how you guys gonna make that pitch for John Sinclair tomorrow night? You said the festival was gonna end tomorrow afternoon . . . you said you'd have the bands play right straight through and end it . . ."

"Abbs-baby . . . trust me . . ."

"Mike, how can I trust Vanguard Capitalism? Why don't you make the announcement now before they play . . ."

"Tomorrow, Abbs . . ."

"Now Mike . . ."

"Trust me, baby . . ."

"Dare to struggle, dare to win, Mike baby!!!"

I lunged forward, grabbed the mike and shouted out "FREE JOHN SIN . . ." (CRASH). Pete Townshend, lead guitarist, had clonked me over the head with his electric guitar, and I crumpled on the stage. There we were shaking fists at each other and yelling, him doing stuff like "Get the fuck outta here," and me doing the "You fascist pig" number. Then I turned to Mike . . .

"That's a real bummer, Abbs-baby . . ."

"Ah, fuck you Mike . . . you're full of shit. Peace my ass, huh . . . how come he tried to kill me? Don't forget about John Sinclair. I gotta get back to New York."

I leaped the chasm from the stage to the barricade wall, flying like some shaggy-dog Tarzan. I scrambled over the wall, leaped ten feet to the ground and started to climb People Hill. Past the rows and rows and rows of zonked-out people, higher and higher I climbed and the hill turned into Jacob's Ladder . . .

We are climbing Jacob's Ladder
We are climbing Jacob's Ladder
We are climbing Jacob's Ladder
Nearer to the Lord.

The climb took me through mountains of beer cans and valleys of sleeping blankets, through oceans of paper plates and cross rivers of Pepsi Cola, up hills of Tootsie wrappers and through forests of incense and all the way peoplepeoplepeople more than I had ever seen in my whole life. At the top of the hill I turned to look at the stage. You had to squint to even see it, nestled down there in the valley of garbage and people. I could hear The Who finishin up with what seemed like "God Save the Queen . . ." I kicked the mud off my boots, opened my fly and pissed long and good . . . the yellow river turned to blue and green and worked its way through the forests of incense and around the hills of Tootsie wrappers and disappeared into the Pepsi Cola river.

I staggered into the Groovy Forest crying for my best friend, "Marty, Marty . . ." Over to Movement City past Walter Teague who was stretching his muscles ready to take on the Marines in Khe Sanh, ready to plant the Vietcong flag on the top of the concession stand . . .

"Marty . . . Marty . . ."

Past the free food tent where I dumped everything out of my pockets and threw off my leather jacket . . .

"Marty . . . Marty . . ."

Back through the wooden sculpture playground where a guy was crying out:

Acid, acid, real Owsley Purple . . .
Three bucks a cap . . . Get em while they last . . .

"Marty . . . Marty . . . Marty . . . Marty . . ."

Past the couple fuckin on the American flag in the trunk of the Oldsmobile on the side of the road.

"Marty . . ."

Past a guy with old-fashioned clothes and a little growth, playing on a guitar, and croonin, "It's all right Ma, I'm only dyin." On and on until I staggered into a pink-and-white tent with a sign that said HOSPITAL and collapsed on the cot murmuring.

Blue . . . Blue . . . Blue Suede Shit . . .

Good ol Ron, one of the only guys I can really trust, stared into my psychedelic eyes and shook his head. "Heard you were having a bad acid trip. Wanna go home?"

I just wheezed a little and flopped my arms . . .

A funny-lookin guy in a white jumpsuit and a cowboy hat with a hole in the front came by and held my hand . . .

"Who are you sonny?(!) WHAT is your name! (?) WHO are you?"

"WHO-WHO-WHO," said the owl lying face-down on the cot . . .

The whole tent started to spin like a carousel and I flew round and round, round and pink and round and white and round . . . Just then I saw her—vaguely at first and then clearer and clearer. God! She was beautiful. A long wisp of a creamy thing with straight black hair down to her ass and long eyelashes that fluttered when she jerked her thin ghost-like lips. She looked like she just stepped out of a door in the *New York Times* Magazine Section with legs like the sleek '55 Corvette I used to race at dragstrips. She was all decked out in the most mini of minis, a silver see-through thingie, and she had no underwear on at all. She sat on the edge of the cot and started running her fingers through my hair. My left arm weighed a ton but I managed to get it up a little and aim it towards that valley under the Rim of the Silver Mini . . . right where her crotch must have been . . . I was almost there when her hand flicked my arm away . . . lightly but firmly. She fluttered her eyelashes and pouted in a long, slim voice:

"Honey, you know what?"

"No, what . . ." I was able to utter.

"You've come a long way, baby . . ."

"Soooo . . . . let's . . . . . . f . . . . u . . . . c . . . . k," I managed.

"But you've still got a long way to go."

". . . and WHAT died.

Well, I'm comin down now; the acid is wearing off. Slowly but surely I'm leaving the WOODSTOCK NATION and passing through the territory which surrounds our land—their world, the Nation of Pigs. It's reassuring that nothing much works out here either in the same way lots of things didn't work up there. The other night on the news Con Edison announced it just avoided another black-out, the phone company apologized for not being able to complete any calls. They showed lines almost as long as the lines leading to WOODSTOCK NATION at golf courses around the city, commuters were screaming at the Long Island Rail Road and some military expert was glumly confessing that the Pigs had in fact been defeated in Vietnam. There was also a neat little item about a guy who was pissed at his lousy job and blew up a section of the Marine Midland Trust Bank in downtown Manhattan. . . . Seems as if maybe good ol George Metesky was back in business again and with George doing his thing, anything could happen. In a way, it's good to be back. It's good to know I can still write an album in five days when I thought I'd need at least six when I started. It's good to write the last of the closing songs cause this album was nothing but a bunch of beginnings and endings. I guess you figured out that I had mixed feelings about what happened up there in those few hectic days. Mostly about the cats who were running the show, some about myself, but none about the folks who worked and played together in WOODSTOCK NATION. When I think about it now, maybe it wouldn't have been such a bad place to live after all . . . not a bad place to run around setting up hospitals and playing in the lake with my kids. Maybe it wouldn't have been a bad place to do all that groovy stuff . . . maybe AFTER THE REVOLUTION. After, you say? That's right, after . . . cause for me anyway there's still a long way to go . . . lots of things to do.

Sometime in 1946 members of the extended Hoffman family gather at bubbeh *and* zayde*'s triple-decker in Worcester, Mass. for the Friday evening* shabbes. *Clockwise from left, the* bubbeh, *cousin Cynthia, ten-year-old Abbie (at high noon), the* zayde, *brother Jack, sister Phyllis and cousin Joan. There was always plenty of food and you could smell the sweet aroma of the* knaydlach *and* matsoh *dumplings in every room.*

PHOTO CREDIT: © JACK HOFFMAN.

Sometime after the Chicago Democratic Convention of August 1968 and before the start of the Chicago 8 conspiracy trial in the fall of 1969, Abbie joins fellow citizens of Woodstock Nation at a demo in Washington, D.C.

On March 22nd, 1969, Abbie and co-defendants turn themselves in for arraignment at the federal courthouse, Foley Square, New York City. From left, Bobby Seale, attorney William Kunstler, Abbie, David Dellinger and Jerry Rubin.

PHOTO CREDIT: © JESSE-STEVE ROSE.

At right, on March 13, 1970, under a cloudy sky on the steps of Low Library at Columbia University, Abbie turns on the crowd.

PHOTO CREDIT: © JESSE-STEVE ROSE.

On May 1, 1970, at the New Haven courthouse, Abbie addresses a May Day rally in solidarity with Bobby Seale and other Black Panthers on trial for murder: "I've come here to free Bobby." PHOTO CREDIT: © JESSE-STEVE ROSE.

At right, in November 1970, Abbie wears a flag shirt at a press conference on the subject of censorship. Hours earlier on "The Merv Griffin Show" Abbie's half of the screen had been blackened to prevent viewers from seeing the shirt.

PHOTO CREDIT: © JESSE-STEVE ROSE.

In November 1979, Barry Freed, a.k.a. Abbot H. Hoffman on the run, takes time out from his itinerary to attend the opening of the John F. Kennedy Memorial Library in Boston, Mass. Being close to home, he wore what he called his Groucho Marx disguise.

PHOTO CREDIT: © JACK HOFFMAN.

In February 1984, Abbie and Johanna Lawrenson at a birthday party he threw for her in New York City. The companion of his years underground and after, Abbie called Johanna his running mate. Wherever they happened to be, the right music always found them dancing together. PHOTO CREDIT: © JOHANNA LAWRENSON.

In November 1986, home with their mother for Thanksgiving, brothers Abbie and Jack pose outside the Worcester home long enough for Johanna to photograph them. Abbie, by two years the elder, would celebrate his 50th birthday a few days later on the 30th. The two brothers called or wrote to one another daily for most of their lives. After this photo was taken, Abbie turned and said, "Let's go rob a bank." PHOTO CREDIT: © JACK HOFFMAN

At right and overleaf, on September 16, 1988, at Toronto's Festival of Festivals for the world premier of Morley Markson's "Growing Up in America," a documentary on the 60s which features Abbie among others, he fields questions on the legacy of 60s activism.

PHOTO CREDIT: © CHRIS BUCK.

PART THREE

FROM

STEAL THIS BOOK

1971

29

STEAL THIS AUTHOR: INTRODUCTION

It's universally wrong to steal from your neighbor, but once you get beyond the one-to-one level and pit the individual against the multinational conglomerate, the federal bureaucracy, the modern plantation of agro-business, or the utility company, it becomes strictly a value judgment to decide exactly who is stealing from whom. One person's crime is another person's profit. Capitalism *is* license to steal; the government simply regulates who steals and how much. I always wanted to put together an outlaw handbook that would help raise consciousness on these points while doing something about evening the score. There was also the challenge of testing the limits of free speech.

Jason Epstein had been my mentor at Random House. A smart guy who popularized, if not invented, the "quality" paperback. Jason knows just about everything there is to know in the publishing racket. He was in Chicago every day, writing a book about the trial. "What's it about?" I'd ask him. "Oh, it's irrelevant," he'd explain, lamenting the fact that Western civilization was rapidly drawing to a close in the rice paddies of

Vietnam. He knew that no interest really remained in the marketplace for carefully reasoned thought. The era belonged to the action freaks. It was under his and his wife Barbara's suggestion that the *New York Review of Books* diagrammed a Molotov cocktail on its cover. A certain despair had gripped the Eastern literati, and he personified it—a brooding man who offered living proof that intelligence is often a curse. He was someone who had learned to rise above his principles.

Jason leaned over his bow tie and asked what I planned to write next. "Jason, I'm going to write a book no one will publish," I said. He was laughing uncontrollably: "Abbie, you could piss on paper and some publisher would lick it up." Jason and Random House had already given me the title: *Steal This Book*. I had put the same three words on the back cover of *Woodstock Nation*, and when the first hundred thousand copies went into the stores, the booksellers hit the roof. "Tell 'em to steal from the banks, tell 'em to steal from the phone companies, tell 'em to steal from anybody, but don't tell 'em to steal from me," they chorused. On the second printing Random House removed the troublesome slogan. This violated our contract, and I let them know in no uncertain terms. Back went the phrase and back came the bookseller complaints. The book went through nine or ten printings, some had the slogan, some not, depending on which side yelled the loudest. The battle whetted my appetite for trouble. No one could censor a book title. So I began the new book with a title and a challenge. We signed a contract. A year of writing and research lay ahead.

I traveled cross-country interviewing doctors, fugitives, dope dealers, draft dodgers, private detectives, country communalists, veterans, organizers, and shoplifters. Every time I met someone living on the margin I asked about a good rip-off or survival scheme. People love to tell how they screw the establishment.

Some of the research was original. One day while turning on with the Video Freex, a New York media collective, I asked if it was possible to pirate an image onto network television. Curiosity flickered faster than a strobe light. Equipment was bought, tests made, and one evening while David Brinkley was analyzing the news, a couple fucking appeared on a number of sets in the Soho area of downtown Manhattan. Eureka! It worked. The Video Freex freaked, gathered up all the equipment, and hid out. "But we saw the fingers of the monster move," I pleaded. It was no use; their equipment and license were more precious than jewels. The technique lived on, however, in the pages of *Steal This Book*. (Later this group managed to tap into the cable going from Madison Square Garden to a control center and steal a complete video print of the Ali-Frazier "fight of the century." The plan was to broadcast the fight over regular network facilities after the sign-off, but again they feared repercussions. We ended up showing free screenings at the local bar.)

Notes for the underground chapter were provided by fugitives, living out the trip. Most of the sections, however, had to do with legal activities: how to run a cheap farm, set up a newspaper, organize a demonstration, perform first aid, hitchhike, equip an apartment with furniture. I invented many of the survival techniques, although most were revisions of street lore. It was strange to see rip-off scams, generally passed by word of mouth, catalogued. In part, the book was a tongue-in-cheek parody of America's appetite for how-to manuals. It was rewritten several times for more simplicity, greater clarity. I wanted it to be a book young kids would like. Something for people who never read books. Finally it was finished. Nothing like it had ever been written. Chris Cerf was my editor at Random House. He championed the book to the top of the house but the house said *nyet*. Bennet Cerf's son quit as a result. Random House would do the book only if I agreed to several changes. I remember the scene in Jason Epstein's office. "But Jason, you're censoring my book," I complained. Jason got all red and puffy. "Random House does not censor books!" A hush came over the room as we played liberal scrabble looking for the right word we could all live with. Jason broke the silence. "We edit, that's it. Random House edits books."

Thirty publishers rejected it next. Oh, there were offers: change this, change that, mostly change the title. One offer promised forty thousand dollars up front if the proper changes were made. You had to be crazy to refuse, I was definitely crazy. Publishing companies felt the phone company or the government would stop the book's distribution through lawsuits (they never materialized). All agreed the book would make money.

Enter the Rev. Thomas King Forcade. I approached Forcade in December of 1970, just before I entered jail in Chicago for a few weeks' rest. Forcade offered to arrange the publication and distribution of the book. He had some minimal experience as the founder of an underground news service. My two weeks in jail were spent finishing the book's introduction. When I returned, Forcade had concluded that a distribution system outside the mainstream was impractical and that he couldn't fund such a venture.

He wanted eight thousand dollars for two weeks of editing. "!@%@/!" I replied. "I'll sue," he said, rejecting a take-it-or-leave-it offer of fifteen hundred dollars. Exit Mr. Forcade. Temporarily.

Enter Grove Press. If I could raise the money to publish the book myself, bring them one hundred thousand finished copies, and bear all legal risk, they would serve as distributor. On fifteen thousand dollars borrowed from friends, I founded Pirate Editions. Layouts, designs, more loans, typesetting, and pasteups were arranged. Ads were composed and sent out. Rush, rush, rush. Finally one hundred thousand books packed in cartons labeled STEAL THIS BOOK began making their way around the country. As head of the publicity department, I sent copies to reviewers—zero reviews. As head of public relations I gave away two thousand books to movement groups. Every underground newspaper was sent a signed letter authorizing them to reprint the entire book and sell it locally as a fund raiser. British rights were given free to an Irish civil-rights group. "No go," said Scotland Yard and banned the book from England. There was a pirated Spanish edition, a French-Canadian edition free. The Japanese bought the rights for just one hundred dollars and sold some fifty thousand books.

Back in the U.S., half the distributors refused to carry the book. Cartons were being shipped back and forth. Many were disappearing. The Benjamin News Company in Montreal was raided by the Royal Canadian Police with a search-and-seizure warrant. Four thousand copies of *STB* were confiscated. For the first time in history, Canada had banned the importation of a book for other than pornographic reasons. The Mounties always get their book. Campus stores were a wasteland—Yale, Michigan, U. of California, even my alma mater, Brandeis, refused to carry the book. The Harvard Coop refused. The *Harvard Crimson* scolded them. The store revised its policy and agreed to carry the book if it was kept in the manager's office and sold on request only. Libraries across the country banned it. In Coldwater, Michigan, Richard Rosichan put it in the stacks. He was summarily fired. In Rochester, New York, the library battle raged for months. Angry meetings, with over seven hundred people attending, were held. The libertarians won. The book stayed. Similar battles were fought in Indiana, Connecticut, and Iowa. In Lansing, Michigan, the police caught two guys running from a vacant building whose door had just blown off. A copy of *STB* was found on them, and the police tried to indict me on a conspiracy rap. In Grenada, a small island in the Caribbean, the prime minister arrested opposition leader

Maurice Bishop on a charge of illegal possession of ammunition. When the police kicked in Bishop's door they found a copy of *STB*. The government charged that this was proof of foreign involvement in a plot to assassinate the prime minister. Bishop became prime minister. Yippie!

In Oklahoma, some watchdog of the faith filed a class-action suit for four million dollars against me for "corrupting the youth." The director of corporate security for AT & T tried to get "fraud perpetrators" to confess they had come under the influence of *STB*. He blamed me, personally, for a ten-million-dollar increase in the number of phony credit-card calls! William Buckley's *National Review*; Jarvis Tyner, head of the Communist Party Youth Division; and Frank D. Register (*sic*), executive director of the National Association of Retail Grocers; all accused me of contributing to inflation because shoplifting raised prices. How's that for consensus!

The Department of Interior called a press conference and denounced the book, saying they no longer gave away any free buffalo as reported. They had received over three thousand requests. The R. T. French Company announced they no longer lent out a free film on parakeets. They had to hire a full-time secretary to answer letters. Henry Kissinger's home phone number was typeset inaccurately. Some poor bloke was getting weird calls at night from would-be political groupies. He sued. We settled. Mr. Bloke was two grand richer. I got letters that began, "Well I followed your advice and got busted—please send me bail money." Assemblyman Robert E. Kelly of Brooklyn introduced a bill making the publication of *STB* and similar rip-off materials a Class A crime. The bill breezed through the New York state legislature. Twenty-seven states passed laws, as a result of the book, restricting the publication of information about ways to cheat the phone company. Proving the movie *President's Analyst* was more fact than fancy, AT & T spent over a million dollars lobbying for these bills. As far as I know, none has been tested in the courts. Corporations petitioned the Federal Communications Commission and the Federal Trade Commission to stop the book, with no response. E. J. Korvettes' security manager told the *London Times* that the shoplifting section was mandatory reading for its new employees. AT & T told *The New York Times* that "a team of lawyers was researching ways to stop the book."

With the exception of a small radio station in Boston, everyone rejected a radio commercial I made for the book. Many, including WCBS and

WNEW in New York, hid behind supposed FCC regulations. The FCC issued a statement saying the stations misinterpreted the rules, but they still refused all ads. With the sole exception of the *San Francisco Chronicle*, no daily newspaper would accept an ad. *The New York Times* acceptability department wrote me that the *Times* would refuse to advertise a book that advocated illegal activity. I received the letter during the week the *Times* was busy reprinting the Pentagon Papers! The *New York Post* rejected an ad although the book was listed for eight weeks on their paperback best-seller list.

Grove estimated that half the books were being sold in New York City. In Pittsburgh, no stores would carry the book. In Philadelphia, only one store would—and it charged a dollar more than the cover price. No books could be found in Boston or the San Francisco Bay area when I took reporters on tour. The Doubleday chain of bookstores was boycotting the book. A Doubleday vice-president said: "We don't want to tell people to steal. We object only to the title. If it was called 'How to Live for Free,' we'd sell it." Grove reported that half their outlets refused to carry the book. They said that no book since *Tropic of Cancer* had met with such a boycott.

Then we got a break. Dotson Rader wrote a glowing review of the book in *The New York Times*, in which he chastised the *Times* for refusing the ad. I clipped the review, wrote a check, and sent it to the *Times* as a new ad. They rejected their own review! The review did, however, shame a few stores, and some buckled under customer pressure. People actually started boycotting stores not carrying the book. As head of the promotion department, I crisscrossed the country appearing on talk shows and giving interviews. I would take a reporter to a bookstore and engage resisting owners in a dialogue. In Boston, *Globe* reporter Bruce McCabe gulped when I ran out of a store lugging a huge art book that I stole because they refused to stock my book. A Judge Liebowitz tried to pressure a New York afternoon television show into canceling because I was a public menace. He failed. In Baltimore I taped a show with two shoplifters, but management refused to air it, prompting some of the staff to quit.

Experiences with *STB* taught me remarkable things about the media. I hired a clipping service to keep track of the publicity campaign. The distortions and lies were astonishing. In Boston, for example, I was asked what I would do if someone stole something from me. I responded, "Well, I certainly couldn't call the local constable, could I?" That's how it read in the *Boston Globe*. The Associated Press translation read, "I would call a cop, of course." The translation was a big hit and hundreds of newspapers ran stories saying "Abbie Would Call a Cop."

Aside from this, there were other hassles. I was categorically refused any credit on general principles. The local supermarket assigned a special salesclerk to follow me up the aisles. Airline officials took me into little booths for examination. I foolishly stated in the book that I knew two foolproof ways to fly for free but couldn't mention them. I got two hundred letters that began, "You can trust me never to tell anyone." In all, I got about fifteen thousand letters, most of which said *STB* was the letter writer's favorite book or asked how to get a copy.

Then began a lengthy battle with Grove Press over the terms of the distribution contract. I was fed up with everything that had happened, so I ordered the book out of print and closed down my publishing firm. At that time the book was selling about eight thousand copies a week. A year later it was being bootlegged for ten bucks—five times the cover price. Today I'm told a copy can cost as much as one hundred dollars. I have no idea how many finally ended up in print. I have seen a blue-cover edition which was printed illegally and by-passed me *and* Grove Press. I ended up with about twenty-six thousand dollars as author/publisher. Peanuts really. The original manuscript of *Steal This Book* wound up in the Columbia University library while I was still on probation from charges involving the 1968 riots there.

FREE SPEECH IS THE RIGHT TO SHOUT
"THEATER" IN A CROWDED FIRE.

—A YIPPIE PROVERB

30

FREE FOOD

RESTAURANTS

In a country such as Amerika, there is bound to be a hell-of-a-lot of food lying around just waiting to be ripped off. If you want to live high off the hog without having to do the dishes, restaurants are easy pickings. In general, many of these targets are easier marks if you are wearing the correct uniform. You should always have one suit or fashionable dress outfit hanging in the closet for the proper heists. Specialized uniforms, such as nun and priest garb, can be most helpful. Check out your local uniform store for a wide range of clothes that will get you in, and especially out, of all kinds of stores. Every movement organization should have a prop and costume department.

In every major city there are usually bars that cater to the Now Generation type riff-raff, trying to hustle their way up the escalator of Big Business. Many of these bars have a buffet or hors-d'oeuvres served free as a come-on to drink more mindless booze. Take a half-empty glass from a table and use it as a prop to ward off the anxious waitress. Walk around sampling the free food until you've had enough. Often, there are five or six such bars in close proximity, so moving around can produce a delightful "street smorgasbord." Dinner usually begins at 5:00 PM.

If you are really hungry, you can go into a self-service cafeteria and finish the meal of someone who left a lot on the plate. Self-service restaurants are usually good places to cop things like mustard, ketchup, salt, sugar, toilet paper, silverware and cups for home use. Bring an empty school bag and load up after you've cased the joint. Also, if you can stomach the food, you can use slugs at the automat. Finishing leftovers can be worked in even the fanciest of restaurants. When you are seated at a place where the dishes still remain, chow-down real quick. Then after the waitress hands you the menu, say you have to meet someone outside first, and leave.

There are still some places where you can get all you can eat for a fixed price. The best of these places are in Las Vegas. Sew a plastic bag onto your tee-shirt or belt and wear a loose-fitting jacket or coat to cover any noticeable bulge. Fried chicken is the best and the easiest to pocket, or should we say bag. Another trick is to pour your second free cup of hot coffee into the plastic bag sewed inside your pocket and take it with you.

At large take-out stands you can say you or your brother just picked up an order of fifteen hamburgers or a bucket of chicken, and got shorted. We have never seen or heard of anybody getting turned down using this method. If you want to get into a grand food heist from take-out stands, you can work the following nervy bit: from a pay phone, place an order from a large delivery restaurant. Have the order sent to a nearby apartment house. Wait a few minutes in the booth after you've hung up, as they sometimes call back to confirm the order. When the delivery man goes into the apartment house to deliver the order, you can swipe the remaining orders that are still in his truck.

In fancy sit-down restaurants, you can order a large meal and halfway through the main course, take a little dead cockroach or a piece of glass out of your pocket and place it deftly on the plate. Jump up astonished and summon the headwaiter. "Never have I been so insulted. I could have been poisoned" you scream, slapping down the napkin. You can refuse to pay and leave, or let the waiter talk you into having a brand new meal on the house for this terrible inconvenience.

In restaurants where you pay at the door just before leaving, there are a number of free-loading tricks that can be utilized. After you've eaten a full meal and gotten the check, go into the restroom. When you come out go to the counter or another section of the restaurant and order coffee and pie. Now you have two bills. Simply pay the cheaper one when you leave the place. This can be worked with a friend in the following way. Sit next to each other at the counter. He should order a big meal and you a cup of coffee. Pretend you don't know each other. When he leaves, he takes your check and leaves the one for the large meal on the counter. After he has paid the cashier and left the restaurant, you pick up the large check, and then go into the astonishment routine, complaining that somebody took the wrong check. You end up only paying for your coffee. Later, meet your partner and reverse the roles in another place.

In all these methods, you should leave a good tip for the waiter or waitress, especially with the roach-in-the-plate gambit. You should try to avoid getting the employees in trouble or screwing them out of a tip.

One fantastic method of not only getting free food but getting the best available is the following technique that can be used in metropolitan areas. Look in a large magazine shop for gourmet digests and tourist manuals. Swipe one or two and copy down a good name from the masthead inside the cover. Making up a name can also work. Next invest $5.00 to print business cards with the name of the magazine and the new "associate editor." Call or simply drop into a fancy restaurant, show a copy of the magazine and present the manager with your card. They will insist that the meal be on the house.

Great places to get fantastic meals are weddings, bar-mitzvahs, testimonials and the like. The newspaper society sections have lists of weddings and locations. If your city has a large Jewish population, subscribe to the newspaper that services the Jewish community. There are extensive lists in these papers of family occasions where tons of good food is served. Show up at the back of the synagogue a few hours after the affair has begun with a story of how you'd like to bring some leftovers of "good Jewish food" back to your fraternity or sorority. If you want to get the food served to you out front, you naturally have to disguise yourself to look straight. Remarks such as, "I'm Marvin's cousin," or learning the bride's name, "Gee, Dorothy looks marvelous" are great. Lines like "Betty doesn't look pregnant" are frowned upon. A man and woman team can work this free-load much better than a single person as they can chatter back and forth while stuffing themselves.

If you're really into a classy free meal, and you are in a city with a large harbor, check out the passenger ship section in the back pages of the newspaper. There you find the schedule of departures for ocean cruises. Most trips (these kind, anyway) begin with a fantastic bon voyage party on board ship. Just walk on a few hours before departure time and start swinging. Champagne, caviar, lobster, shrimp and more, all as free as the open seas. If you get really bombed and miss getting off, you can also wiggle a ride across the ocean. You get sent back as soon as you hit the other side, but it's a free ocean cruise. You should have a pretty good story ready to go, or you might end up rowing in the galley.

Another possibility for getting a free meal is to go down to the docks and get friendly with a sailor. He can often invite you for dinner on board ship. Foreign sailors are more than glad to meet friends and you can get great foreign dinners this way.

SUPERMARKETS

Talking about food in Amerika means talking about supermarkets—mammoth neon lighted streets of food packaged to hoodwink the consumers. Many a Yippie can be found in the aisles, stuffing his pockets with assorted delicacies. We have been shoplifting from supermarkets on a regular basis without raising the slightest suspicion, ever since they began.

We are not alone, and the fact that so much stealing goes on and the supermarkets still bring in huge profits shows exactly how much overcharging has occurred in the first place. Supermarkets, like other businesses, refer to shoplifting as "inventory shrinkage." It's as if we thieves were helping Big Business reduce weight. So let's view our efforts as methods designed to trim the economy and push forward with a positive attitude.

Women should never go shopping without a large handbag. In those crowded aisles, especially the ones with piles of cases, all sorts of goodies can be transferred from shopping cart to handbag. A drop bag can be sewn inside a trench coat, for more efficient thievery. Don't worry about the mirrors; attendants never look at them. Become a discriminating shopper and don't stuff any of the cheap shit in your pockets.

Small bottles and jars often have the same size cap as the larger expensive sizes. If they have the price stamped on the cap, switch caps, getting the larger size for the cheaper price. You can empty a pound box of margarine and fill it with sticks of butter. Small narrow items can be hidden in the middle of rolls of toilet paper. Larger supermarkets sell records. You can sneak two good LP's into one of those large frozen pizza boxes. In the produce department, there are bags for fruit and vegetables. Slip a few steaks or some lamb chops into the bottom of a large brown bag and pile some potatoes on top. Have a little man in the white coat weigh the bag, staple it and mark the price. With a black crayon you can mark your own prices, or bring your own adhesive price tags.

It's best to work shoplifting in the supermarket with a partner who can act as look-out and shield you from the eyes of nosy employees, shoppers and other crooks trying to pick up some pointers. Work out a prearranged set of signals with your partner. Diversions, like knocking over displays, getting into fist fights with the manager, breaking plate glass windows and such are effective and even if you don't get anything they're fun. Haven't you always wanted to knock over those carefully constructed nine-foot pyramids of garbage?

You can walk into a supermarket, get a few items from the shelves, and walk around eating food in the aisles. Pick up some cherries and eat them. Have a spoon in your pocket and open some yogurt. Open a pickle or olive jar. Get some sliced meat or cheese from the delicatessen counter and eat it up, making sure to ditch the wrapper. The cart full of items, used as a decoy, can just be left in an aisle before you leave the store.

Case the joint before pulling a big rip-off. Know the least crowded hours, learn the best aisles to be busy in, and check out the store's security system. Once you get into shoplifting in supermarkets, you'll really dig it. You'll be surprised to learn that the food tastes better.

Large scale thievery can best be carried out with the help of an employee. Two ways we know of work best. A woman can get a job as a cashier and ring up a small bill as her brothers and sisters bring home tons of stuff.

The method for men involves getting a job loading and unloading trucks in the receiving department. Some accomplices dressed right can just pull in and, with your help, load up on a few cases. Infiltrating an employee into a store is probably the best way to steal. Cashiers, sales clerks, shippers, and the like are readily available jobs with such high turnover and low pay that little checking on your background goes on. Also, you can learn what you have to do in a few days. The rest of the week, you can work out ways to clean out the store. After a month or so of action you might want to move on to another store before things get heavy. We know one woman working as a cashier who swiped over $500 worth of food a week. She had to leave after a month because her boss thought she was such an efficient cashier that he insisted on promoting her to a job that didn't have as many fringe benefits for her and her friends.

Large chain stores like Safeway throw away day-old vegetables, the outer leaves of lettuce, celery and the like. This stuff is usually found in crates outside the back of the building. Tell them you're working with animals at the college labs, or that you raise guinea pigs. They might even get into saving them for you, but if they don't just show up before the garbage is collected (generally early in the morning), and they'll let you cart away what you want.

Dented cans and fruit can often be gotten free, but certainly at a reduced rate. They are still as good as the undamaged ones. So be sure to dent all your cans before you go to the cashier.

Look up the catering services and businesses that service factories and office buildings with ready-made sandwiches. Showing up at these places at the right times (catering services on late Sunday night and sandwich dealers at 5:00 PM on weekdays) will produce loads of good food. Legally, they have to dispose of the food that's left over. They would be more than happy to give it to you if you spin a good story.

Butchers can be hustled for meat scraps with a "for my dog" story, and bakeries can be asked for day-old rolls and bread.

WHOLESALE MARKETS

Large cities all have a wholesale fruit and vegetable area where often the workers will give you tons of free food just for the asking. Get a good story together. Get some church stationery and type a letter introducing yourself "to whom it may concern," or better still, wear some clerical garb. Orchards also make good pickings just after the harvest has been completed.

Factories often will give you a case or two of free merchandise for a "charitable" reason. Make some calls around town and then go pick up the stuff at the end of the week. A great idea is to get a good list of a few hundred large corporations around the country by looking up their addresses at the library. *Poor's Register of Companies, Directors and Executives* has the most complete list. Send them all letters complaining about how the last box of cereal was only half full, or you found a dead fly in the can of peaches. They often will send you an ample supply of items just to keep you from complaining to your friends or worse, taking them to court. Often you can get stuff sent to you by just telling them how good their product is compared to the trash you see nowadays. You know the type of letter—"Rice Krispies have had a fantastic effect on my sexual prowess," or "Your frozen asparagus has given a whole new meaning to my life." In general though, the nasties get the best results.

Slaughterhouses usually have meat they will give away. They are anxious to give to church children's programs and things like that. In most states, there is a law that if the slab of meat touches the ground, they have to throw it away. Drop around meat houses late in the day and trip a few trucks.

Fishermen always have hundreds of pounds of fish that have to be thrown out. You can have as much as you can cart away, generally just for the asking. Boats come in late in the afternoon and they'll give you some of the catch, or you can go to the markets early in the morning when the fishing is best.

These methods of getting food in large quantities can only be appreciated by those who have tried it. You will be totally baffled by the unbelievable quantities of food that will be laid on you and with the ease of panhandling.

Investing in a freezer will allow you to make bi-weekly or even monthly trips to the wholesale markets and you'll get the freshest foods to boot. Nothing can beat getting it wholesale for free. Or is it free for wholesale? In any event, "bon appetit."

FOOD CONSPIRACIES

Forming a food cooperative is one of the best ways to promote solidarity and get every kind of food you need to survive real cheap. It also provides a ready-made bridge for developing alliances with blacks, Puerto Ricans, chicanos and other groups fighting our common oppressor on a community level.

Call a meeting of about 20 communes, collectives or community organizations. Set up the ground rules. There should be a hard core of really good hustlers that serve as the shopping or hunting party and another group of people who have their heads together enough to keep records and run the central distribution center. Two or three in each group should do it. They can get their food free for the effort. Another method is to rotate the activity among all members of the conspiracy. The method you choose depends upon your politics and whether you favor a division of labor or using the food conspiracy as a training for collective living. Probably a blend of the two is best, but you'll have to hassle that out for yourself. The next thing to agree upon is how the operation and all the shit you get will be paid for. This is dependent on a number of variables, so we'll map out one scheme and you can modify it to suit your particular situation. Each member of every commune could be assessed a fee for joining. You want to get together about $2,000, so at 200 members, this is ten bucks apiece. After the joining fee, each person or group has to pay only for the low budget food they order, but some loot is needed to get things rolling. The money goes to getting a store front or garage, a cheap truck, some scales, freezers, bags, shelving, chopping blocks, slicer and whatever else you need. You can get great deals by looking in the classified ads of the local overground newspaper and checking for restaurants or markets going out of business. Remember the idea of a conspiracy is to get tons of stuff at real low prices or free into a store front, and then break it down into smaller units for each group and eventually each member. The freezers allow you to store perishables for a longer time.

The hunting party should be well acquainted with how to rip off shit totally free and where all the best deals are to be found. They should know what food is seasonal and about nutritional diets. There is a lot to learn, such as where to get raw grains in 100 pound lots and how to cut up a side of beef. A good idea is to get a diet freak to give weekly talks in the store front. There can also be cooking lessons taught, especially to men, so women can get out of the kitchen.

Organizing a community around a basic issue of survival, such as food, makes a lot of nitty gritty sense. After your conspiracy gets off the ground and looks permanent, you should seek to expand it to include more members and an emergency food fund should be set up in case something happens in the community. There should also be a fund whereby the conspiracy can sponsor free community dinners tied into celebrations. Get it together and join the fight for a world-wide food conspiracy. Seize the steak!

CHEAP CHOW

There are hundreds of good paperback cookbooks with nutritional cheap recipes available in any bookstore. Cooking is a vastly overrated skill. The following are a few all-purpose dishes that are easy to make, nutritional and cheap as mud pies. You can add or subtract many of the ingredients for variety.

Road Hog Crispies

½ c millet
½ c cracked wheat
½ c buckwheat groats
½ c wheat germ
½ c sunflower seeds
¼ c sesame seeds
2 Tbs cornmeal
2 c raw oats
1 c rye flakes
1 c wheat flakes
1 c dried fruits and/or nuts
3 tbs soy oil
1 c honey

Boil the millet in a double boiler for ½ hour. Mix in a large bowl all the ingredients including the millet. The soy oil and honey should be heated in a saucepan over a low flame until bubbles form. Spread the cereal in a baking pan and cover with the honey syrup. Toast in oven until brown. Stir once or twice so that all the cereal will be toasted. Serve plain or with milk. Refrigerate portion not used in a covered container. Enough for ten to twenty people. Make lots and store for later meals. All these ingredients can be purchased at any health store in a variety of quantities. You can also get natural sugar if you need a sweetener. If bought and made in quantity, this fantastically healthy breakfast food will be cheaper than the brand name cellophane that passes for cereal.

Whole Earth Bread

1 c oats, corn meal, or wheat germ
1½ c water (warm)
¼ c sugar (raw is best)
1 pkg active dry yeast
1 c dry milk
2 tsp salt
2 egg yolks
4 c flour
1/3 c corn oil or butter

Stir lightly in a large bowl the oats, cornmeal or wheat germ (depending on the flavor bread you desire), the water and sugar. Sprinkle in the yeast and wait 10 minutes for the yeast to do its thing. Add salt, egg yolks, corn oil and dry milk. Mix with a fork. Blend in the flour. The dough should be dry and a little lumpy. Cover with a towel and leave in a warm place for a half hour. Now mash, punch, blend and kick the dough and return it covered to its warm place. The dough will double in size. When this happens, separate the dough into two even masses and mash each one into a greased bread (loaf) pan. Cover the pans and let sit until the dough rises to the top of the pans. Bake for 40–45 minutes in a 350 degree oven that has not been preheated. A shallow tray of water in the bottom of the oven will keep the bread nice and moist. When you remove the pans from the oven, turn out the bread into a rack and let it cool off. Once you get the hang of it, you'll never touch ready-made bread, and it's a gas seeing yeast work.

Street Salad

Salad can be made by chopping up almost any variety of vegetables, nuts and fruits including the stuff you panhandled at the back of supermarkets; dandelions, sour grass, and other wild vegetables; and goods you ripped off inside stores or from large farms. A neat fresh dressing consists of one part oil, two parts wine vinegar, 2 finely chopped garlic cloves, salt and pepper. Mix up the ingredients in a bottle and add to the salad as you serve it. Russian dressing is simply mayonnaise and ketchup mixed.

Yippie Yogurt

Yogurt is one of the most nutritional foods in the world. The stuff you buy in stores has preservatives added to it reducing its health properties and increasing the cost. Yogurt is a bacteria that spreads throughout a suitable culture at the correct temperature. Begin by going to a Turkish or Syrian restaurant and buying some yogurt to go. Some restaurants boast of yogurt that goes back over a hundred years. Put it in the refrigerator.

Now prepare the culture in which the yogurt will multiply. The consistency you want will determine what you use. A milk culture will produce thin yogurt, while sweet cream will make a thicker batch. It's the butter fat content that determines the consistency and also the number of calories. Half milk and half cream combines the best of both worlds. Heat a quart of half and half on a low flame until just before the boiling point and remove from the stove. This knocks out other bacteria that will compete with the yogurt. Now take a tablespoon of the yogurt you got from the restaurant and place it in the bottom of a bowl (not metal). Now add the warm liquid. Cover the bowl with a lid and wrap tightly with a heavy towel. Place the bowl in a warm spot such as on top of a radiator or in a sunny window. A turned-off oven with a tray of boiling water placed in it will do well. Just let the bowl sit for about 8 hours (overnight). The yogurt simply grows until the whole bowl is yogurt. Yippie! It will keep in the refrigerator for about two weeks before turning sour, but even then, the bacteria will produce a fresh batch of top quality. Remember when eating it to leave a little to start the next batch. For a neat treat add some honey and cinnamon and mix into the yogurt before serving. Chopped fruit and nuts are also good.

Rice and Cong Sauce

1 c brown rice
2 c water
tsp salt
vegetables
2½ Tbs soy sauce

Bring the water to a boil in a pot and add the salt and rice. Cover and reduce flame. Cooking time is about 40 minutes or until rice has absorbed all the water. Meanwhile, in a well-greased frying pan, saute a variety of chopped vegetables you enjoy. When they become soft and brownish, add salt and 2 cups of water. Cover with a lid and lower flame. Simmer for about 40 minutes, peeking to stir every once in a while. Then add 2½ Tbs of soy sauce, stir and cook another 10 minutes. The rice should be just cooling off now, so add the sauce to the top of it and serve. Great for those long guerrilla hikes. This literally makes up almost the entire diet of the National Liberation Front fighter.

Weatherbeans

1 lb red kidney beans
2 quarts water
1 onion (chopped)
1 Tbs celery (chopped)
1 tsp garlic (minced)
2 Tbs parsley (chopped)
½ lb pork, smoked sausage or ham hock
1 lg bay leaf
salt to season

Rinse the beans, then place in covered pot and add water and salt. Cook over low flame. While cooking, chop up meat and brown in a frying pan. Add onion, celery, garlic and parsley and continue sauteing over low flame. Add the pieces of meat, vegetables and bay leaf to the beans and cook covered for 1½ to 2 hours. It may be necessary to add more water if the beans get too dry. Fifteen minutes before beans are done, mash about a half cup of the stuff against the side of the pan to thicken the liquid. Pour the beans and liquid over some steaming rice that you've made by following the directions above. This should provide a cheap nutritional meal for about 6 people.

Hedonist's Deluxe

2 lobsters	2 qts water
seaweed	¼ lb butter

Steal two lobsters, watching out for the claw thingies. Beg some seaweed from any fish market. Cop the butter using the switcheroo method described in the Supermarket section above. When you get home, boil the water in a large covered pot and drop in the seaweed and then the lobsters. Put the cover back on and cook for about 20 minutes. Melt the butter in a saucepan and dip the lobster pieces in it as you eat. With a booster box, described later, you'll be able to rip off a bottle of vintage Pouilly-Fuisse in a fancy liquor store. Really, rice is nice but . . .

31

FREE CLOTHING & FURNITURE

FREE CLOTHING

If shoplifting food seems easy, it's nothing compared to the snatching of clothing. Shop only the better stores. Try things on in those neat little secluded stalls. The less bulky items, such as shirts, vests, belts and socks can be tied around your waist or leg with large rubber bands if needed. Just take a number of items in and come out with a few less.

In some cities there are still free stores left over from the flower power days. Churches often have give-away clothing programs. You can impersonate a clergyman and call one of the larger clothing manufacturers in your area. They are usually willing to donate a case or two of shirts, trousers or underwear to your church raffle or drive to dress up skid row. Be sure to get your sizes. Tell them "your boy" will pick up the blessed donation and you'll mention his company in the evening prayers.

If you notice people moving from an apartment or house, ask them if they'll be leaving behind clothing. They usually abandon all sorts of items including food, furniture and books. Offer to help them carry out stuff if you can keep what they won't be taking.

Make the rounds of a fancy neighborhood with a truck and some friends. Ring doorbells and tell the person who answers that you are collecting wearable clothing for the "poor homeless victims of the recent tidal wave in Quianto, a small village in Saudi Arabia." You get the pitch. Make it food and clothing, and say you're with a group called *Heartline for Decency*. A phony letter from a church might help here.

The Salvation Army does this, and you can pick up clothes from them at very cheap prices. You can get a pair of snappy casual shoes for 25 cents in many bowling alleys by walking out with them on your feet. If you have to leave your shoes as a deposit, leave the most beat-up pair you can find.

Notice if your friends have lost or gained weight. A big change means a lot of clothes doing nothing but taking up closet space. Show up at dormitories when college is over for the summer or winter season. Go to the train or bus stations and tell them you left your raincoat, gloves or umbrella when you came into town. They'll take you to a room with thousands of unclaimed items. Pick out what you like. While there, notice a neat suitcase or trunk and memorize the markings. Later a friend can claim the item. There will be loads of surprises in any suitcase. We have a close friend who inherited ten kilos of grass this way.

Large laundry and dry cleaning chains usually have thousands of items that have gone unclaimed. Manufacturers also have shirts, dresses and suits for rock-bottom prices because of a crooked seam or other fuck-up. Stores have reduced rates on display models. Mannequins are mostly all size 40 for men and 10 for women. Size 7½ is the standard display size for men's shoes. If you are these sizes, you can get top styles for less than half price.

SANDALS

The Vietnamese and people throughout the Third World make a fantastically durable and comfortable pair of sandals out of rubber tires. They cut out a section of the outer tire (trace around the outside of the foot with a piece of chalk) which when trimmed forms the sole. Next 6 slits are made in the sole so the rubber straps can be criss-crossed and slid through the slits. The straps are made out of inner tubing. No nails are needed. If you have wide feet, use the new wide tread low profiles. For hard going, try

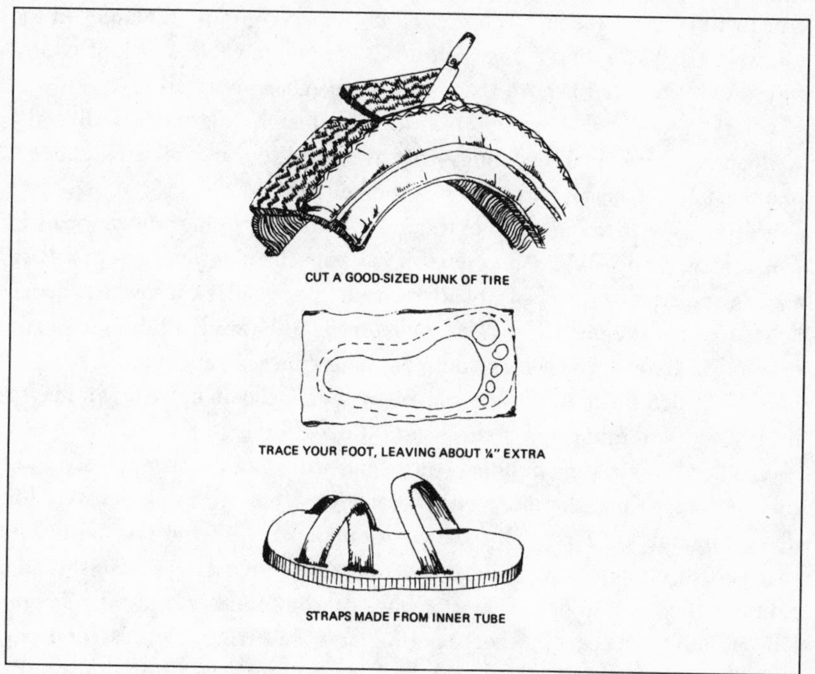

radials. For best satisfaction and quality, steal the tires off a pig car or a government limousine.

Let's face it, if you really are into beating the clothing problem, move to a warm climate and run around naked. Skin is absolutely free, and will always be in style. Speaking of style, the midi and the maxi have obvious advantages when it comes to shoplifting and transporting weapons or bombs.

FREE FURNITURE

Apartment lobbies are good for all kinds of neat furniture. If you want to get fancy about it, rent a truck (not one that says U-HAUL-IT or other rental markings) and make the pick-up with moving-man-type uniforms. When schools are on strike and students hold seminars and debate into the night, Yippies can be found going through the dorm lobbies and storage closets hauling off couches, desks, printing supplies, typewriters, mimeos, etc. to store in secret underground nests. A nervy group of Yippies in the Midwest tried to swipe a giant IBM 360 computer while a school was in turmoil. All power to those that bring a wheelbarrow to sit-ins.

Check into a high-class hotel or motel remembering to dress like the wallpaper. Carry a large dummy suitcase with you and register under a phony name. Make sure you and not the bellboy carry this bag. Use others as a decoy. When you get inside the room, grab everything you can stuff in the suitcase: radio, T.V. sets (even if it has a special plug you can cut it with a knife and replace the cord), blankets, toilet paper, glasses, towels, sheets, lamps, (forget the imitation Winslow Homer on the wall) a Bible, soap and toss rugs. Before you leave (odd hours are best) hang the DO NOT DISTURB sign on your doorknob. This will give you an extra few hours to beat it across the border or check into a new hotel.

Landlords renovating buildings throw out stoves, tables, lamps, refrigerators and carpeting. In most cities, each area has a day designated for discarding bulk objects. Call the Sanitation Department and say you live in that part of town which would be putting out the most expensive shit and find out the pick-up day. Fantastic buys can be found cruising the streets late at night. Check out the backs of large department stores for floor models, window displays and slightly damaged furniture being discarded.

Construction sites are a good source for building materials to construct furniture. (Not to mention explosives.) The large wooden cable spools make great tables. Cinderblocks, bricks and boards can quickly be turned into a sharp looking bookcase. Doors make tables. Nail kegs convert into stools or chairs. You can also always find a number of other supplies hanging around like wiring, pipes, lighting fixtures and hard hats. And don't forget those blinking signs and the red lanterns for your own light show. Those black oil-fed burners are O.K. for cooking, although smoky, and highway flares are swell for making fake dynamite bombs.

32

FREE TRANSPORTATION

HITCHHIKING

Certainly one of the neatest ways of getting where you want to go for nothing is to hitch. In the city it's a real snap. Just position yourself at a busy intersection and ask the drivers for a lift when they stop for the red light. If you're hitching on a road where the traffic zooms by pretty fast, be sure to stand where the car will have room to safely pull off the road. Traveling long distances, even cross-country, can be easy if you have some sense of what you are doing.

A lone hitchhiker will do much better than two or more. A man and woman will do very well together. Single women are certain to get propositioned and possibly worse. Amerikan males have endless sexual fantasies about picking up a poor lonesome damsel in distress. Unless your karate and head are in top form, women should avoid hitching alone. Telling men you have V.D. might help in difficult situations.

New England and the entire West Coast are the best sections for easy hitches. The South and Midwest can sometimes be a real hassle. Easy Rider and all that. The best season to hitch is in the summer. Daytime is much better than night. If you have to hitch at night, get under some type of illumination where you'll be seen.

Hitchhiking is legal in most states, but remember you always can get a "say-so" bust. A "say-so" arrest is to police what Catch-22 is to the Army. When you ask why you're under arrest, the pig answers, "cause I say-so." If you stand on the shoulder of the road, the pigs won't give you too bad a time. If you've got long hair, cops will often stop to play games. You can wear a hat with your hair tucked under to avoid hassles. However this might hurt your ability to get rides, since many straights will pick up hippies out of curiosity who would not pick up a straight scruffy looking kid. Freak drivers usually only pick up other freaks.

Once in a while you hear stories of fines levied or even a few arrests for hitching (Flagstaff, Arizona is notorious), but even in the states where it is illegal, the law is rarely enforced. If you're stopped by the pigs, play dumb and they'll just tell you to move along. You can wait until they leave and then let your thumb hang out again.

Hitching on super highways is really far out. It's illegal but you won't get hassled if you hitch at the entrances. On a fucked-up exit, take your chances hitching right on the road, but keep a sharp eye out for porkers. When you get a ride be discriminating. Find out where the driver is headed. If you are at a good spot, don't take a ride under a hundred miles that won't end up in a location just as good. When the driver is headed to an out-of-the-way place, ask him to let you off where you can get the best rides. If he's going to a particularly small town, ask him to drive you to the other side of the town line. It's usually only a mile or two. Small towns often enforce all sorts of "say-so" ordinances. If you get stuck on the wrong side of town, it would be wise to even hoof it through the place. Getting to a point on the road where the cars are inter-city rather than local traffic is always preferable.

When you hit the road you should have a good idea of how to get where you are going. You can pick up a free map at any gas station. Long distance routes, road conditions, weather and all sorts of information can be gotten free by calling the *American Automobile Association* in any city. Say that you are a member driving to Phoenix, Arizona or wherever your destination is, and find out what you want to know. Always carry a sign indicating where you are going. If you get stranded on the road without one, ask in a diner or gas station for a piece of cardboard and a magic marker. Make the letters bold and fill them in so they can be seen by drivers from a distance. If your destination is a small town, the sign should indicate the state. For really long distances, EAST or WEST is best. Unless, of course, you're going north or south. A phony foreign flag sewed on your pack also helps.

Carrying dope is not advisable, and although searching you is illegal, few pigs can read the Constitution. If you are carrying when the patrol car pulls up, tell them you are Kanadian and hitching through Amerika. Highway patrols are very uptight about promoting incidents with foreigners. The foreign bit goes over especially well with small-town types, and is also amazingly good for avoiding hassles with greasers. If you can't hack this one, tell them you are a reporter for a newspaper writing a feature story on hitching around the country. This story has averted many a bust.

Don't be shy when you hitch. Go into diners and gas stations and ask people if they're heading East or to Texas. Sometimes gas station attendants will help. When in the car be friendly as hell. Offer to share the driving if you've got a license. If you're broke, you can usually bum a meal or a few bucks, maybe even a free night's lodging. Never be intimidated into giving money for a ride.

As for what to carry when hitching, the advice is to travel light. The rule is to make up a pack of the absolute minimum, then cut that in half. Hitching is an art form as is all survival. Master it and you'll travel on a free trip forever.

FREIGHTING

There is a way to hitch long distances that has certain advantages over letting your thumb hang out for hours on some deserted two-laner. Learn about riding the trains and you'll always have that alternative. Hitchhiking at night can be impossible, but hopping a freight is easier at night than by day. By hitchhiking days and hopping freights and sleeping on them at night, you can cover incredible distances rapidly and stay well rested. Every city and most large towns have a freight yard. You can find it by following the tracks or asking where the freight yard is located.

When you get to the yard, ask the workmen when the next train leaving in your direction will be pulling out. Unlike the phony Hollywood image, railroad men are nice to folks who drop by to grab a ride. Most yards don't have a guard or a "bull" as they are called. Even if they do, he is generally not around. If there is a bull around, the most he's going to do is tell you it's private property and ask you to leave. There are exceptions to this rule, such as the notorious Lincoln, Nebraska, and Las Vegas, Nevada, but by asking you can find out. Even if he asks you to leave or throws you out, sneak back when your train is pulling out and jump aboard.

After you've located the right train for your trip, hunt for an empty boxcar to ride. The men in the yards will generally point one out if you ask. Pig-sties, flat cars and coal cars are definitely third class due to exposure to the elements. Boxcars are by far the best. They are clean and the roof over your head helps in bad weather and cuts down the wind. Boxcars with a hydro-cushion suspension system used for carrying fragile cargo make for the smoothest ride. Unless you get one, you should be prepared for a pretty bumpy and noisy voyage.

You should avoid cars with only one door open, because the pin may break, locking you in. A car with both doors open gives you one free chance. Pig-backs (trailers on flatcars) are generally considered unsafe. Most trains make a number of short hops, so if time is an important factor try to get on a "hot shot" express. A hot shot travels faster and has priority over other trains in crowded yards. You should favor a hot shot even if you have to wait an extra hour or two or more to get one going your way.

If you're traveling at night, be sure to dress warmly. You can freeze your ass off. Trains might not offer the most comfortable ride, but they go through beautiful countryside that you'd never see from the highway or airway. There are no billboards, road signs, cops, Jack-in-the-Boxes, gas stations or other artifacts of honky culture. You'll get dirty on the trains so wear old clothes. Don't pass up this great way to travel 'cause some bullshit western scared you out of it.

CARS

If you know how to drive and want to travel long distances, the auto transportation agencies are a good deal. Look in the Yellow Pages under

Automobile Transportation and Trucking or *Driveaway*. Rules vary, but normally you must be over 21 and have a valid license. Call up and tell them when and where you want to go and they will let you know if they have a car available. They give you the car and a tank of gas free. You pay the rest. Go to pick up the car alone, then get some people to ride along and help with the driving and expenses. You can make New York to San Francisco for about eighty dollars in tolls and gas in four days without pushing. Usually you have the car for longer and can make a whole thing out of it. You must look straight when you go to the agency. This can simply be done by wetting down your hair and shoving it under a cap.

Another good way to travel cheaply is to find somebody who has a car and is going your way. Usually underground newspapers list people who either want rides or riders. Another excellent place to find information is your local campus. Every campus has a bulletin board for rides. Head shops and other community-minded stores have notices up on the wall.

GAS: If you have a car and need some gas late at night you can get a quart and then some by emptying the hoses from the pumps into your tank. There is always a fair amount of surplus gas left when the pumps are shut off.

If you're traveling in a car and don't have enough money for gas and tolls, stop at the bus station and see if anybody wants a lift. If you find someone, explain your money situation and make a deal with him. Hitchhikers also can be asked to chip in on the gas.

You can carry a piece of tubing in the trunk of your car and when the gas indicator gets low, pull up to a nice-looking Cadillac on some dark street and syphon off some of his gas. Just park your car so the gas tank is next to the Caddy's, or use a large can. Stick the hose into his tank, suck up enough to get things flowing, and stick the other end into your tank. Having a lower level of liquid, your tank will draw gas until you and the Caddy are equal. "To each according to his need, from each according to his ability," wrote Marx. Bet you hadn't realized until now that the law of gravity affects economics.

Another way is to park in a service station over their filler hole. Lift off one lid (like a small manhole cover), run down twenty feet of rubber tubing through the hole you've cut in your floorboard, then turn on the electric pump which you have installed to feed into your gas tank. All they ever see is a parked car. This technique is especially rewarding when you have a bus.

BUSES

If you'd rather leave the driving and the paying to them, try swiping a ride on the bus. Here's a method that has worked well. Get a rough idea of where the bus has stopped before it arrived at your station. If you are not at the beginning or final stop on the route, wait until the bus you want pulls in and then out of the station. Make like the bus just pulled off without you while you went to the bathroom. If there is a station master, complain like crazy to him. Tell him you're going to sue the company if your luggage gets stolen. He'll put you on the next bus for free. If there is no station master, lay your sad tale on the next driver that comes along. If you know when the last bus left, just tell the driver you've been stranded there for eight hours and you left your kid sleeping on the other bus. Tell him you called ahead to the company and they said to grab the next bus and they would take care of it.

The next method isn't totally free but close enough. It's called the hopper-bopper. Find a bus that makes a few stops before it gets to where you want to go. The more stops with people getting in or out, the better. Buy a ticket for the short hop and stay on the bus until you end up at your destination. You must develop a whole style in order to pull this off because the driver has to forget you are connected with the ticket you gave him. Dress unobtrusively or make sure the driver hasn't seen your face. Pretend to be asleep when the short hop station is reached. If you get questioned, just act upset about sleeping through the stop you "really" want and ask if it's possible to get a ride back.

AIRLINES

Up and away, junior outlaws! If you really want to get where you're going in a hurry, don't forget skyjacker's paradise. Don't forget the airlines. They make an unbelievable amount of bread on their inflated prices, ruin the land with incredible amounts of polluting wastes and noise, and deliberately hold back aviation advances that would reduce prices and time of flight. We know two foolproof methods to fly free, but unfortuntely we feel publishing them would cause the airlines to change their policy. The following methods have been talked about enough, so the time seems right to make them known to a larger circle of friends.

A word should be said right off about stolen tickets. Literally millions of dollars worth of airline tickets are stolen each year. If you have good underworld contacts, you can get a ticket to anywhere you want at one-fourth the regular price. If you are charged more, you are getting a slight rooking. In any case, you can get a ticket for any flight or date and just trade it in. They are actually as good as cash, except that it takes 30 days to get a refund, and by then they might have traced the stolen tickets. If you can get a stolen ticket, exchange or use it as soon as possible, and always fly under a phony name. A stolen ticket for a trip around the world currently goes for one hundred and fifty dollars in New York.

One successful scheme requires access to the mailbox of a person listed in the local phone book. Let's use the name Ron Davis as an example. A woman calls one of the airlines with a very efficient sounding rap such as: "Hello, this is Mr. Davis' secretary at Allied Chemical. He and his wife would like to fly to Chicago on Friday. Could you mail two first-class tickets to his home and bill us here at Allied?" Every major corporation probably has a Ron Davis, and the airlines rarely bother checking anyway. Order your tickets two days before you wish to travel, and pick them up at the mailbox or address you had them sent to. If you are uptight in the airport about the tickets, just go up to another airline and have the tickets exchanged.

If you want to be covered completely, use the hopper-bopper method described in the section on Buses, with this added security precaution. Buy two tickets from different cashiers, or better still, one from an agent in town. Both will be on the same flight. Only one ticket will be under a phony name and for the short hop, while the ticket under your real name will be for your actual destination. At the boarding counter, present the short hop ticket. You will be given an envelope with a white receipt in it. Actually, the white receipt is the last leaf in your ticket. Once you are securely seated and aloft, take out the ticket with your name and final destination. Gently peel away everything but the white receipt. Place the still valid ticket back in your pocket. Now remove from the envelope and destroy the short hop receipt. In its place, put the receipt for the ticket you have in your pocket.

When you land at the short hop airport, stay on the plane. Usually the stewardesses just ask you if you are remaining on the flight. If you have to, you can actually show her your authentic receipt. When you get to your destination, you merely put the receipt back on the bonafide ticket that you still have in your pocket. It isn't necessary that they be glued together. Present the ticket for a refund or exchange it for another ticket. This method works well even in foreign countries. You can actually fly around the world for $88.00 using the hopper-bopper method and switching receipts.

By the way, if you fly cross-country a number of times, swipe one of the plug-in headsets. Always remember to pack it in your traveling bag. This way you'll save a two dollar fee charged for the in-flight movie. The headsets are interchangeable on all airlines.

One way to fly free is to actually hitch a ride. Look for the private plane area located at every airport, usually in some remote part of the field. You can find it by noticing where the small planes without airline markings take off and land. Go over to the runways and ask around. Often the mechanics will let you know when someone is leaving for your destination and point out a pilot. Tell him you lost your ticket and have to get back to school. Single pilots often like to have a passenger along and it's a real gas flying in a small plane.

Some foreign countries have special arrangements for free air travel to visiting writers, artists or reporters. Brazil and Argentina are two we know of for sure. Call or write the embassy of the country you wish to visit in Washington or their mission to the United Nations in New York. Writing works best, especially if you can cop some stationery from a newspaper or publishing house. Tell them you will be writing a feature story for some magazine on the tourist spots or handcrafts of the country. The embassy will arrange for you to travel gratis aboard one of their air force planes. The planes leave only from Washington and New York at unscheduled times. Once you have the O.K. letter from the embassy you're all set. This is definitely worth checking out if you want to vacation in a foreign country with all sorts of free bonuses thrown in.

A one-way ride is easy if you want to get into skyjacking. Keep the piece or knife in your shoe to avoid possible detection with the "metal scanner," a long black tube that acts like a geiger counter. Or use a plastic knife or bomb. It's also advisable to wrap your dope in a non-metallic material. Avoid tinfoil.

The crews have instructions to take you wherever you want to go even if they have to refuel, but watch out for air marshals. To avoid air marshals and searches pick an airline which flies short domestic hops. You should plan to end up in a country hostile to the United States or you'll end up right back where you came from in some sturdy handcuffs. One dude wanted to travel in style so he demanded $100,000 as a going-away gift. The airlines quickly paid off. The guy then got greedy and demanded a hundred million dollars. When he returned to pick up the extra pocket money, he got nabbed. Nonetheless, skyjacking appears to be the cheapest, fastest way to get away from it all.

IN CITY TRAVEL

Any of the public means of transportation can be ripped off easily. Get on the bus with a large bill and present it after the bus has left the stop. If the bus is crowded, slip in the back door when it opens to dispatch passengers.

Two people can easily get through the turnstile in a subway on one token by doubling up. In some subway systems cards are given out to high school kids or senior citizens or employees of the city. The next time you are in a subway station notice people flashing cards to the man in the booth and entering through the "exit" door. Notice the color of the card used by people in your age group. Get a piece of colored paper in a stationery store or find some card of the same color you need. Put this "card" in a plastic window of your wallet and flash it in the same way those with a bona fide pass do.

Before entering a turnstile, always test the swing bar. If someone during the day put in an extra token, it's still in the machine waiting for you to enter free.

For every token and coin deposited in an automatic turnstile, there is a foreign coin the same size for much less that will work in the machine. (See the Yippie Currency Exchange, page 252, for more info.) Buy a cheap bag of assorted foreign coins from a dealer that you can locate in the Yellow Pages. Size up the coins with a token from your subway system. You can get any of these coins in bulk from a large dealer. Generally they are about 1,000 for five dollars. Tell him you make jewelry out of them if he gets suspicious. Giving what almost amounts to free subway rides away is a communal act of love. The best outlaws in the world rip off shit for a lot more people than just themselves. Robin Hood lives!!

33

FREE LAND

Despite what you may have heard, there is still some rural land left in Amerika. The only really free land is available in Alaska and remote barren areas of the western states. The latest information in this area is found in a periodic publication called *Our Public Lands*, available from the Superintendent of Documents, Washington, D.C. 20402. It costs $1.00 for a subscription. Also contact the U.S. Department of the Interior, Bureau of Land Management, Washington, D.C. 20240 and ask for information on "homesteading." By the time this book is out though, the Secretary of the Interior's friends in the oil companies might have stolen all the available free land. Being an oil company is about the easiest way to steal millions. Never call it stealing though, always refer to it as "research and development."

Continental United States has no good free land that we know of, but there are some very low prices in areas suited for country communities. Write to School of Living, Freeland, Maryland, for their newspaper *Green Revolution* with the latest information in this area. Canada has free land available, and the Canadian government will send you a free list if you write to the Department of Land and Forests, Parliament Building, Quebec City, Canada. Also write to the Geographical Branch, Department of Mines and Technical Surveys, Parliament Building, Quebec City, Canada. Correspondence can be carried out with the Communications Group, 2630 Point Grey Road, Vancouver 8, British Columbia, Canada, for advice on establishing a community in Canada. The islands off the coast of British Columbia, its western region and the area along the Kootenai River are among the best locations.

If you just want to rip off some land, there are two ways to do it, openly or secretly. If you are going to do it out front, look around for a piece of land that's in dispute, which has its sovereignty in question—islands and deltas between the U.S. and Canada, or between the U.S. and Mexico, or any number of other borderline lands. You might even consider one of the abandoned oil-drilling platforms, which are fair game under high seas salvage laws. The possibilities are endless.

If you intend to do it quietly, you will want a completely different type of location. Find a rugged area with lots of elbow room and plenty of places to hide, like the Rocky Mountains, Florida swamps, Death Valley, or New York City. Put together a tight band of guerrillas and do your thing. With luck you will last forever.

If you just want to camp out or try some hermit living in the plushest surroundings available, you'll do best to head for one of the national parks. Since the parks are federal property, there's very little the local fuzz can do about you, and the forest rangers are generally the live-and-let-live types, although there have been increasing reports of long-hairs being vamped on by Smokey the Pig, as in Yosemite. You can get a complete list from National Park Service, Department of the Interior, Washington, D.C. 20240.

Earth People's Park is an endeavor to purchase land and allow people to come and live for free. They function as a clearing house for people that want to donate land and those who wish to settle. They own 600 acres in northern Vermont and are trying to raise money to buy more. Write to Earth People's Park, P.O. Box 313, 1230 Grant Ave., San Francisco, California 94133.

People's Parks are sprouting up all over as people reclaim the land being ripped off by universities, factories, and corrupt city planning agencies. The model is the People's Park struggle in Berkeley during the spring of 1969. The people fought to defend a barren parking lot they had turned into a community center with grass, swings, free-form sculpture and gardens. The University of California, with the aid of Ronald Reagan and the Berkeley storm troopers, fought with guns, clubs, and tear gas to regain the land from the outlaw people. The pigs killed James Rector and won an empty victory. For now the park is fenced off, tarred over and converted into unused basketball courts and unused parking lots. Not one person has violated the oath never to set foot on the site. It stands, cold and empty, two blocks north of crowded Telegraph Avenue. If the revolution does not survive, all the land will perish under the steam roller of imperialism. People's Death Valley will happen in our lifetime.

34

FREE HOUSING

If you are in a city without a place to stay, ask the first group of hip-looking folks where you can crash. You might try the office of the local underground newspaper. In any hip community, the underground newspaper is generally the source of the best up-to-the-moment information. But remember that they are very busy, and don't impose on them. Many churches now have runaway houses. If you are under sixteen and can hack some bullshit jive about "adjusting," "opening a dialogue," and "things aren't that bad," then these are the best deals for free room and board. Check out the ground rules first, i.e., length of stay allowed, if they inform your parents or police, facilities and services available. Almost always they can be accepted at their word, which is something very sacred to missionaries. If they became known as double-crossers, their programs would be finished.

Some hip communities have crash pads set up, but these rarely last more than a few months. To give out the addresses we have would be quite impractical. We have never run across a crash pad that lasted more than a month or so. If in a city, try hustling a room at a college dorm. This is especially good in summer or on weekends. If you have a sleeping bag, the parks are always good, as is "tar jungle"or sleeping on the roofs of tall buildings. Local folks will give you some good advice on what to watch out for and information on vagrancy laws which might help you avoid getting busted.

For more permanent needs, squatting is not only free, it's a revolutionary act. If you stay quiet you can stay indefinitely. If you have community support you may last forever.

COMMUNES

In the city or in the country, communes can be a cheap and enjoyable way of living. Although urban and rural communes face different physical environments, they share common group problems. The most important element in communal living is the people, for the commune will only make it if everyone is fairly compatible. A nucleus of 4 to 7 people is best and it is necessary that no member feels extremely hostile to any other member when the commune gets started. The idea that things will work out later is pigswill. More communes have busted up over incompatibility than any other single factor. People of similar interests and political philosophies should live together. One speed freak can wreck almost any group. There are just too many day-to-day hassles involved living in a commune to not start off compatible in as many ways as possible. The ideal arrangement is for the people to have known each other before they move in together.

Once you have made the opening moves, evening meetings will occasionally be necessary to divide up the responsibilities and work out the unique problems of a communal family. Basically, there are two areas that have to be pretty well agreed upon if the commune is to survive. People's attitudes toward Politics, Sex, Drugs and Decision-making have to be in fairly close agreement. Then the even more important decisions about raising the rent, cleaning, cooking and maintenance will have to be made. Ground rules for inviting non-members should be worked out before the first time it happens, as this is a common cause for friction. Another increasingly important issue involves defense. Communes have continually been targets of attack by the more Neanderthal elements of the surrounding community. In Minneapolis for example, "headhunts" as they are called are commonplace. You should have full knowledge of the local gun laws and a collective defense should be worked out.

Physical attacks are just one way of making war on communes and, hence, our Free Nation. Laws, cops, and courts are there to protect the power and the property of those that already got the shit. Police harassment, strict enforcement of health codes and fire regulations and the specially designed anti-commune laws being passed by town elders, should all be known and understood by the members of a commune before they even buy or rent property. On all these matters, you should seek out experienced members of communes already established in the vicinity you wish to settle. Work out mutual defense arrangements with nearby families—both legal and extralegal. Remember, not only do you have the right to self-defense, but it is your duty to our new Nation to erase the ''Easy-Rider-take-any-shit'' image which invites attack. Let them know you are willing to defend your way of living and your chances of survival will increase.

URBAN LIVING

If you're headed for city living, the first thing you'll have to do is locate an apartment or loft, an increasingly difficult task. At certain times of the year, notably June and September, the competition is fierce because of students leaving or entering school. If you can avoid these two months, you'll have a better selection. A knowledge of your plans in advance can aid a great deal in finding an apartment, for the area can be scouted before you move in. Often, if you know of people leaving a desirable apartment, you can make arrangements with the landlord, and a deposit will hold the place. If you let them know you're willing to buy their furniture, people will be more willing to give you information about when they plan to move. Watch out for getting screwed on exorbitant furniture swindles by the previous tenants and excessive demands on the part of the landlords. In most cities, the landlord is not legally allowed to ask for more than one month's rent as security. Often the monthly rent itself is regulated by a city agency. A little checking on the local laws and a visit to the housing agency might prove well worth it.

Don't go to a rental agency unless you are willing to pay an extra month's rent as a fee. Wanted ads in newspapers and bulletin boards located in community centers and supermarkets have some leads. Large universities have a service for finding good apartments for administrators, faculty and students, in that order. Call the university, say you have just been appointed to such-and-such position and you need housing in the area. They will want to know all your requirements and rent limitations, but often they have very good deals available, especially if you've appointed yourself to a high enough position.

Aside from these, the best way is to scout a desired area and inquire about future apartments. Often landlords or rental agencies have control over a number of buildings in a given area. You can generally find a nameplate inside the hall of the building. Calling them directly will let you know of any apartments available.

When you get an apartment, furnishing will be the next step. You can double your sleeping space by building bunk beds. Nail two by fours securely from ceiling to floor, about three feet from the walls, where the beds are desired. Then build a frame out of two by fours at a convenient height. Make sure you use nails or screws strong enough to support the weight of people sleeping or balling. Nail a sheet of 3/4 inch plywood on the frame. Mattresses and almost all furniture needed for your pad can be gotten free (see section on Free Furniture). Silverware can be copped at any self-service restaurant.

RURAL LIVING

If you are considering moving to the country, especially as a group, you are talking about farms and farmland. There are some farms for rent, and occasionally a family that has to be away for a year or two will let you live on their farm if you keep the place in repair. These can be found advertised in the back of various farming magazines and in the classified sections of newspapers, especially the Sunday editions. Generally speaking, however, if you're interested in a farm, you should be considering an outright purchase.

First, you have to determine in what part of the country you want to live in terms of the climate you prefer and how far away from the major cities you wish to locate. The least populated states, such as Utah, Idaho, the Dakotas, Montana and the like, have the cheapest prices and the lowest tax rates. The more populated a state, and in turn, the closer to a city, the higher the commercial value of the land.

There are hundreds of different types of farms, so the next set of questions you'll have to raise concerns the type of farm activity you'll want to engage in. Cattle farms are different than vegetable farms or orchards. Farms come in sizes: from half an acre to ranches larger than the state of Connecticut. They will run in price from $30 to $3000 an acre, with the most expensive being prime farmland in fertile river valleys located close to an urban area. The further away from the city and the further up a hill, the cheaper the land gets. It also gets woodier, rockier and steeper, which means less tillable land.

If you are talking of living in a farmhouse and maybe having a small garden and some livestock for your own use, with perhaps a pond on the property, you are looking for what is called a recreational farm. When you buy a recreational farm, naturally you are interested in the house, barn, well, fences, chicken-coop, corrals, woodsheds and other physical structures on the property. Unless these are in unusually good condition or unique, they do not enter into the sale price as major factors. It is the land itself that is bought and sold.

Farmland is measured in acreage; an acre being slightly more than 43,560 square feet. The total area is measured in 40-acre plots. Thus, if a farmer or a real estate agent says he has a plot of land down the road, he means a 40-acre farm. Farms are generally measured this way, with an average recreational farm being 160 acres in size or an area covering about 1/2 square mile. A reasonable rate for recreational farmland 100 miles from a major city with good water and a livable house would be about $50 per acre. For a 160-acre farm, it would be $8,000, which is not an awful lot considering what you are getting.

Now that you have a rough idea of where and what type of farm you want, you can begin to get more specific. Check out the classified section in the Sunday newspaper of the largest city near your desired location. Get the phone book and call or write to real estate agencies in the vicinity. Unlike the city, where there is a sellers' market, rural estate agents collect their fee from the seller of the property, so you won't have to worry about the agent's fee.

When you have narrowed down the choices, the next thing you'll want to look at is the plot book for the county. The plot book has all the farms in each township mapped out. It also shows terrain variations, type of housing on the land, location of rivers, roads, and a host of other pertinent information. Road accessibility, especially in the winter, is an important factor. If the farms bordering the one you have selected are abandoned or not in full use, then for all intents and purposes, you have more land than you are buying.

After doing all this, you are prepared to go look at the farm itself. Notice the condition of the auxiliary roads leading to the house. You'll want an idea of what sections of the land are tillable. Make note of how many boulders you'll have to clear to do some planting. Also note how many trees there are and to what extent the brush has to be cut down. Be sure and have a good idea of the insect problems you can expect. Mosquitoes or flies can bug the shit out of you. Feel the soil where you plan to have a garden and see how rich it is. If there are fruit trees, check their condition. Taste the water. Find out if hunters or tourists come through the land. Examine the house. The most important things are the basement and the roof. In the basement, examine the beams for dry rot and termites. See how long it will be before the roof must be replaced. Next check the heating system, the electrical wiring and the plumbing. Then you'll want to know about services such as schools, snow plowing, telephones, fire department and finally about your neighbors. If the house is beyond repair, you might still want the farm, especially if you are good at carpentry. Cabins, A-frames, domes and tepees are all cheaply constructed with little experience. Get the materials from your nearest military installation.

Finally check out the secondary structures on the land to see how usable they are. If there is a pond, you'll want to see how deep it is for swimming. If there are streams, you'll want to know about the fishing possibilities; and if large wooded areas, the hunting.

In negotiating the final sales agreement, you should employ a lawyer. You'll also want to check out the possibility of negotiating a bank loan for the farm. Don't forget that you have to pay taxes on the land, so inquire from the previous owner or agent as to the tax bill. Usually, you can count on paying about $50 annually per 40-acre plot.

Finally, check out the federal programs available in the area. If you can learn the ins and outs of the government programs, you can rip off plenty. The Feed-Grain Program of the Department of Agriculture pays you not to grow grain. The Cotton Subsidy Program pays you not to grow cotton. Also look into the Soil Bank Program of the United States Development Association and various Department of Forestry programs which pay you to plant trees. Between not planting cotton and planting trees, you should be able to manage.

35

FREE EDUCATION

Usually when you ask somebody in college why they are there, they'll tell you it's to get an education. The truth of it is, they are there to get the degree so that they can get ahead in the rat race. Too many college radicals are two-timing punks. The only reason you should be in college is to destroy it. If there is stuff that you want to learn though, there is a way to get a college education absolutely free. Simply send away for the schedule of courses at the college of your choice. Make up the schedule you want and audit the classes. In smaller classes this might be a problem, but even then, if the teacher is worth anything at all, he'll let you stay. In large classes, no one will ever object.

If you need books for a course, write to the publisher claiming you are a lecturer at some school and considering using their book in your course. They will always send you free books.

There are Free Universities springing up all over our new Nation. Anybody can teach any course. People sign up for the courses and sometimes pay a token registration fee. This money is used to publish a catalogue and pay the rent. If you're on welfare you don't have to pay. You can take as many or as few courses as you want. Classes are held everywhere: in the instructor's house, in the park, on the beach, at one of the student's houses or in liberated buildings. Free Universities offer courses ranging from Astrology to the Use of Firearms. The teaching is usually excellent of quality and you'll learn in a community-type atmosphere.

36

FREE MEDICAL CARE

Due to the efforts of the Medical Committee for Human Rights, the Student Health Organization and other progressive elements among younger doctors and nurses, Free People's Clinics have been happening in every major city. They usually operate out of store fronts and are staffed with volunteer help. An average clinic can handle about fifty patients a day.

If you've had an accident or have an acute illness, even a bad cold, check into the emergency room of any hospital. Give them a sob story complete with phony name and address. After treatment they present you with a slip and direct you to the cashier. Just walk on by, as the song suggests. A good decoy is to ask for the washroom. After waiting there a few moments, split. If you're caught sneaking out, tell them you ran out of the house without your wallet. Ask them to bill you at your phony address. This billing procedure works in both hospital emergency rooms and clinics. You can keep going back for repeated visits up to three months before the cashier's office tells the doctor about your fractured payments.

You can get speedy medical advice and avoid emergency room delays by calling the hospital, asking for the emergency unit and speaking directly to the doctor over the phone. Older doctors frown on this procedure since they cannot extort their usual exorbitant fee over the phone. Younger ones generally do not share this hang-up.

Cities usually have free clinics for a variety of special ailments. Tuberculosis Clinics, Venereal Disease Clinics, and Free Shot Clinics (yellow fever, polio, tetanus, etc.) are some of the more common. A directory of these clinics and other free health services the local community provides can be obtained by writing your Chamber of Commerce or local Health Department.

Most universities have clinics connected with their dental, optometry or other specialized medical schools. If not for free, then certainly for very low rates, you can get dental work repaired, eyeglasses fitted and treatment of other specific health needs.

Free psychiatric treatment can often be gotten at the out-patient department of any mental hospital. Admission into these hospitals is free, but a real bummer. Use them as a last resort only. Some cities have a suicide prevention center and if you are desperate and need help, call them. Your best choice in a psychiatric emergency is to go to a large general hospital, find the emergency unit and ask to see the psychiatrist on duty.

BIRTH CONTROL CLINICS

Planned Parenthood and the Family Planning Association staff numerous free birth control clinics throughout the country. They provide such services as sex education, examinations, Pap smear and birth control information and devices. The devices include pills, a diaphragm, or IUD (intra-uterine device) which they will insert. If you are unmarried and under 18, you might have to talk to a social worker, but it's no sweat because anybody gets contraceptive devices that wants them. Call up and ask them to send you their booklets on the different methods of birth control available.

If you would rather go to a private doctor, try to find out from a friend the name of a hip gynecologist, who is sympathetic to the fact that you're low on bread. Otherwise one visit could cost $25.00 or more.

Before deciding on a contraceptive, you should be hip to some general information. There has been much research on the pill, and during the past

10 years it has proven its effectiveness, if not its safety. The two most famous name brands are Ortho-Novum and Envoid. They all require a doctor's prescription. Different type pills are accompanied by slightly different instructions, so read the directions carefully. In many women, the pills produce side effects such as weight increase, dizziness or nausea. Sometimes the pill affects your vision and more often your mood. Some women with specialized blood diseases are advised not to use them, but in general, women have little or no trouble. Different brand names have different hormonal balances (progesterone-estrogen). If you get uncomfortable side effects, insist that your doctor switch your brand. If you stop the pill method for any reason and don't want to get pregnant, be very careful to use another means right away.

Another contraceptive device becoming more popular is the IUD, or the loop. It is a small plastic or stainless steel irregularly shaped spring that the doctor inserts inside the opening of the uterus. The insertion is not without pain, but it's safe if done by a physician, and it's second only to the pill in prevention of pregnancy. Once it's in place, you can forget about it for a few years or until you wish to get pregnant. Doctors are reluctant to prescribe them for women who have not borne children or had an abortion, because of the intense pain that accompanies insertion. But if you can stand the pain associated with three to four uterine contractions, you should push the doctor for this method. Inserting it during the last day of your period will make it easier.

The diaphragm is a round piece of flexible rubber about 2 inches in diameter with a hard rubber rim on the outside. It used to be inserted just before the sex act, but hip doctors now recommend that it be worn continuously and taken out every few days for washing and also during the menstrual period. It is most effective when used with a sperm-killing jelly or cream. A doctor will fit you for a proper size diaphragm.

The next best method is the foams that you insert twenty minutes before fucking. The best foams available are Delfen and Emko. They have the advantage of being nonprescription items so you can rush into any drug store and pick up a dispenser when the spirit moves you. Follow the directions carefully. Unfortunately, these foams taste terrible and are not available in flavors. It just shows you how far science has to go.

Another device is the prophylactic, or rubber as it is called. This is the *only* device available to men. It is a thin rubber sheath that fits over the penis. Because they are subject to breaking and sliding off, their effectiveness is not super great. If you are forced to use them, the best available are lubricated sheepskins with a reservoir tip.

The rhythm method or Vatican roulette as it is called by hip Catholics, is a waste unless you are ready to surround yourself with thermometers, graphs and charts. You also have to limit your fucking to prescribed days. Even with all these measures, women have often gotten pregnant using the rhythm method.

The oldest and least effective method is simply for the male to pull out just before he comes. There are billions of sperm cells in each ejaculation, and only one is needed to fertilize the woman's egg and cause a pregnancy. Most of the sperm is in the first squirt, so you had better be quick if you employ this technique.

If the woman misses her period she shouldn't panic. It might be delayed because of emotional reasons. Just wait two weeks before going to a doctor or clinic for a pregnancy test. When you go, be sure to bring your first morning urine specimen.

ABORTIONS

The best way to find out about abortions is to contact your local women's liberation organization through your underground newspaper or radio station. Some Family Planning Clinics and even some liberal churches set up abortions, but these might run as high as $700. Underground newspapers often have ads that read, "Any girl in trouble call — —," or something similar. The usual rate for an abortion is about $500 and it's awful hard to bargain when you need one badly. Only go to a physician who is practicing or might have just lost his license. Forget the stereotype image of these doctors as they are performing a vital service. Friends who have had an abortion can usually recommend a good doctor and fill you in on what's going to happen.

Abortions are very minor operations if done correctly. They can be done almost any time, but after three months, it's no longer so casual and more surgical skill is required. Start making plans as soon as you find out. The sooner the better, in terms of the operation.

Get a pregnancy test at a clinic. If it is positive and you want an abortion, start that day to make plans. If you get negative results from the test and still miss your period, have a gynecologist perform an examination if you are still worried.

If you cannot arrange an abortion through woman's liberation, Family Planning, a sympathetic clergyman or a friend who has had one, search out a liberal hospital and talk to one of their social workers. Almost all hospitals perform "therapeutic" abortions. Tell a sob story about the desertion of your boy friend or that you take LSD every day or that defects run in your family. Act mentally disturbed. If you qualify, you can get an abortion that will be free under Medicaid or other welfare medical plans. The safest form of abortion is the vacuum-curettage method, but not all doctors are hip to it. It is safer and quicker and with less chance of complications than the old-fashioned scrape method.

Many states have recently passed liberalized abortion laws, such as New York (by far the most extensive), Hawaii, and Maryland, due to the continuing pressure of radical women. The battle for abortion and certainly for free abortion is far from over even in the states with liberal laws. They are far too expensive for the ten to twenty minute minor operation involved and the red tape is horrendous. Free abortions must be looked on as a fundamental right, not a sneaky, messy trauma.

DISEASES TREATED FREE

Syph and Clap (syphilis and gonorrhea) are two diseases that are easy to pick up. They come from balling. Anyone who claims they got it from sitting on a toilet seat must have a fondness for weird positions.

Both men and women are subject to the diseases. Using a prophylactic usually will prevent the spreading of venereal disease, but you should really seek to have it cured. Syphilis usually begins with an infection which may look like a cold sore or pimple around the sex organ. There is no pain associated with the lesions. Soon the sore disappears even without treatment. This is often followed by a period of rashes on the body (especially the palms of the hands) and inflammation of the mouth and throat. These symptoms also disappear without treatment. It must be understood, however, that even if these symptoms disappear, the disease still remains if left untreated. It can cause serious trouble such as heart disease, blindness, insanity and paralysis. Also, it can fuck up any kids you might produce and is easily passed on to anyone you ball.

Gonorrhea (clap) is more common than syphilis. Its first signs are a discharge from your sex organ that is painful. Like syphilis, it affects both men and women, but is often unnoticed in women. There is usually itching and burning associated with the affected area. It can leave you sterile if left untreated.

Both these venereal diseases can be treated in a short time with medical attention. Avail yourself of the free V.D. clinics in every town. Follow the doctor's instructions to the letter and try to let the other people you've had sexual contact with know you had V.D.

There are other fungus diseases that resemble syphilis or gonorrhea, but are relatively harmless. Check out every infection in your crotch area, especially those with open sores or an unusual discharge and you'll be safe.

Crabs are not harmful, but they can make you scratch your crotch for hours on end. They are also highly transmittable by balling. Actually they are a form of body lice and easy to cure. Go to your local druggist and ask him for the best remedy available. He'll give you one of several lotions and instructions for proper use. We recommend Kwell.

A common disease in the hip community is hepatitis. There are two kinds. One you get from sticking dirty needles in your arm (serum hepatitis) and the other more common strain from eating infected food or having intimate contact with an infected carrier (infectious hepatitis). The symptoms for both are identical; yellowish skin and eyes, dark piss and light crap, loss of appetite and total listlessness. Hep is a very dangerous disease that can cause a number of permanent conditions, including death, which is extremely permanent. It should be treated by a doctor, often in a hospital.

37

FREE COMMUNICATION

If you don't like the news, why not go out and make your own? Creating free media depends to a large extent on your imagination and ability to follow through on ideas. The average Amerikan is exposed to over 1,600 commercials each day. Billboards, glossy ads and television spots make up much of the word environment they live in. To crack through the word mush means creating new forms of free communication. Advertisements for revolution are important in helping to educate and mold the milieu of people you wish to win over.

Guerrilla theater events are always good news items and if done right, people will remember them forever. Throwing out money at the Stock Exchange or dumping soot on executives at Con Edison or blowing up the policeman statue in Chicago immediately conveys an easily understood message by using the technique of creative disruption. Recently to dramatize the illegal invasion of Cambodia, 400 Yippies stormed across the Canadian border in an invasion of the United States. They threw paint on store windows and physically attacked residents of Blair, Washington. A group of Vietnam veterans marched in battle gear from Trenton to Valley Forge. Along the way they performed mock attacks on civilians the way they were trained to do in Southeast Asia.

Dying all the outdoor fountains red and then sending a message to the newspaper explaining why you did it, dramatizes the idea that blood is being shed needlessly in imperialist wars. A special metallic bonding glue available from Eastman-Kodak will form a permanent bond in only 45 seconds. Gluing up locks of all the office buildings in your town is a great way to dramatize the fact that our brothers and sisters are being jailed all the time. Then, of course, there are always explosives which dramatically make your point and then some.

PRESS CONFERENCES

Another way of using the news to advertise the revolution and make propaganda is to call a press conference. Get an appropriate place that has some relationship to the content of your message. Send out announcements to as many members of the press as you can. If you do not have a press list, you can make one up by looking through the Yellow Pages under *Newspapers*, *Radio Stations*, *Television Stations*, *Magazines* and *Wire Services*. Check out your list with other groups and pick up names of reporters who attend movement press conferences. Address a special invitation to them as well as one to their newspaper. Address the announcements to "City Desk" or "News Department." Schedule the press conference for about 11:00 A.M. as this allows the reporters to file the story in time for the evening newscast or papers. On the day of the scheduled conference, call the important city desks or reporters about 9:00 A.M. and remind them to come.

Everything about a successful press conference must be dramatic, from the announcements and phone calls to the statements themselves. Nothing creates a worse image than four or five men in business suits sitting behind a table and talking in a calm manner at a fashionable hotel. Constantly seek to have every detail of the press conference differ in style as well as content from the conferences of people in power. Make use of music and visual effects. Don't stiffen up before the press. Make the statement as short and to the point as possible. Don't read from notes, look directly into the camera. The usual television spot is one minute and twenty seconds. The cameras start buzzing on your opening statement and often run out of film before you finish. So make it brief and action packed. The question period should be even more dramatic. Use the questioner's first name when answering a question. This adds an air of informality and networks are more apt to use an answer directed personally to one of their newsmen. Express your emotional feelings. Be funny, get angry, be sad or ecstatic. If you cannot convey that you are deeply excited or troubled or outraged about what you are saying, how do you expect it of others who are watching a little image box in their living room? Remember, you are advertising a new way of life to people. Watch TV commercials. See how they are able to convey everything they need to be effective in such a short time and limited space. At the same time you're mocking the shit they are pushing, steal their techniques.

At rock concerts, during intermission or at the end of the performance, fight your way to the stage. Announce that if the electricity is cut off the walls will be torn down. This galvanizes the audience and makes the owners of the hall the villains if they fuck around. Lay out a short exciting rap on what's coming down. Focus on a call around one action. Sometimes it might be good to engage rock groups in dialogues about their commitment to the revolution. Interrupting the concert is frowned upon since it is only spitting in the faces of the people you are trying to reach. Use the Culture as ocean to swim in. Treat it with care.

Sandwich boards and hand-carried signs are effective advertisements. You can stand on a busy corner and hold up a sign saying "Apartment Needed," "Free Angela," "Smash the State" or other slogans. They can be written on dollar bills, envelopes that are being mailed and other items that are passed from person to person.

Take a flashlight with a large face to movie theaters and other dark public gathering places. Cut the word "STRIKE" or "REVOLT" or "YIPPIE" out of dark cellophane. Paste the stencil over the flashlight, thus allowing you to project the word on a distant wall.

There are a number of all night call-in shows that have a huge audience. If you call with what the moderator considers "exciting controversy," he may give you a special number so you won't have to compete in the switchboard roller-derby. It often can take hours before you get through to these shows. Here's a trick that will help you out if the switchboard is jammed. The call-in shows have a series of phones so that when one is busy the next will take the call. Usually the numbers run in sequence. Say a station gives out PL 5-8640, as the number to call. That means it also uses PL 5-8641, PL 5-8642 and so on. If you get a busy signal, hang up and try calling PL 5-8647 say. This trick works in a variety of situations where you want to get a call through a busy switchboard. Remember it for airline and bus information.

WALL PAINTING

One of the best forms of free communication is painting messages on a blank wall. The message must be short and bold. You want to be able to paint it on before the pigs come and yet have it large enough so that people can see it at a distance. Cans of spray paint that you can pick up at any hardware store work best. Pick spots that have lots of traffic. Exclamation points are good for emphasis. If you are writing the same message, make a stencil. You can make a stencil that says WAR and spray it on with white paint under the word "STOP" on stop signs. You can stencil a five-pointed star and using yellow paint, spray it on the dividing line between the red and blue on all post office boxes. This simulates the flag of the National Liberation Front of Vietnam. You can stencil a marijuana leaf and using green paint, spray it over cigarette and whisky billboards on buses and subways. The women's liberation sign with red paint is good for sexist ads. Sometimes you will wish to exhibit great daring in your choice of locations. When the Vietnamese hero Nguyen Van Troi was executed, the Viet Cong put up a poster the next day on the exact spot inside the highest security prison in the country.

Wall postering allows you to get more information before the public than a quickly scribbled slogan. Make sure the surface is smooth or finely porous. Smear the back of the poster with condensed milk, spread on with a brush, sponge, rag or your hands. Condensed milk dries very fast and hard. Also smear some on the front once the poster is up to give protection against the weather and busy fingers that like to pull at corners. Wallpaper pastes also work quickly and efficiently. It's best to work both painting and postering at night with a look-out. This way you can work the best spots without being harassed by the pig patrol, which is usually unappreciative of Great Art.

USE OF THE FLAG

The generally agreed upon flag of our nation is black with a red, five-pointed star behind a green marijuana leaf in the center. It is used by groups that understand the correct use of culture and symbolism in a revolutionary struggle. When displayed, it immediately increases the feelings of solidarity between our brothers and sisters. High school kids have had great fights over which flag to salute in school. A sign of any liberated zone is the flag being flown. Rock concerts and festivals have their generally apolitical character instantly changed when the flag is displayed. The political theoreticians who do not recognize the flag and the importance of the culture it represents are ostriches who are ignorant of basic human nature. Throughout history people have fought for religion, life-style, land, a flag (nation), because they were ordered to, for fortune, because they were attacked or for the hell of it. If you don't think the flag is important, ask the hardhats.

RADIO

Want to construct your own neighborhood radio station? No FCC license is required for the range is less than ½ mile. The small transistorized units plug into any wall outlet. For further information see the chapter on Guerrilla Broadcasting later in the book.

FREE TELEPHONES

Ripping off the phone company is so common that Bell Telephone has a special security division that tries to stay just a little ahead of the average free-loader. Many great devices like the coat hanger release switch have been scrapped because of changes in the phone box. Even the credit card fake-out is doomed to oblivion as the company switches to more computerized techniques. In our opinion, as long as there is a phone company, and as long as there are outlaws, nobody need ever pay for a call. In 1969 alone the phone company estimated that over 10 million dollars worth of free calls were placed from New York City. Nothing, however, compares with the rip-off of the people by the phone company. In that same year, American Telephone and Telegraph made a profit of 8.6 billion dollars! AT&T, like all public utilities, passes itself off as a service owned by the people, while in actuality nothing could be further from the truth. Only a small percentage of the public owns stock in these companies and a tiny elite clique makes all the policy decisions. Ripping off the phone company is an act of revolutionary love, so help spread the word.

38

FREE PLAY

MOVIES AND CONCERTS

There are many ways to sneak into theaters, concerts, stadiums and other entertainment houses. All these places have numerous fire exits with push-bar doors that open easily from the inside. Arrive early with a group of friends, after casing the joint and selecting the most convenient exit. Pay for one person to get in. When he does he simply opens the designated exit door when the ushers are out of the area and everyone rushes inside.

For theatrical chains in large cities, call their home office and ask to speak to the vice-president in charge of publicity, sales, or personnel. Ask what his name is so you'll know who you're talking to. When you get the information you want, hang up. Now you have the name of a high official in the company. Compile a short list of officials in the various film, theater and sporting event companies. Next call the various theaters and do the same thing for the theater managers. Once you have the two lists you are ready to proceed. Call the theater you want to attend. When someone answers say you're Mr. ______ from the home office calling Mr. ______ (manager's name) and you'd like to have two passes O.K.'d for two important people from out of town. Invariably she'll just ask their names or tell them to mention your name at the box office. Not only will you get in free, but you can avoid waiting in line with this fake-out.

In Los Angeles and New York, the studios hold pre-release screenings for all movies. If you know roughly when a movie is about to come out, call the publicity department of the studio producing the film and say you're the critic for a newspaper or magazine (give the name) and ask them when you can screen the film. They'll give you the time and place of various screenings. When you go, ask them to put you on their list and you'll get notices of all future screenings.

One of our favorite ways to sneak into a theater with continuously running shows is the following. Arrive just as the show is emptying out and join the line leaving the theater. Exclaiming, "Oh, my gosh!" you slap your forehead, turn around and return, tell the usher you left your hat, pocketbook, etc. inside. Once you're inside the theater, just swipe some popcorn and wait for the next show.

RECORDS AND BOOKS

If you have access to a few addresses, you can get all kinds of records and books from clubs on introductory offers. Since the cards you mail back are not signed there is no legal way you can be held for the bill. You get all sorts of threatening mail, which, by the way, also comes free.

If you have a friend who is a member of a record club, ask him to submit your name as a free member. He gets 4 free records for getting you signed up. As soon as you get the letter saying how lucky you are to be a member, quit. Your friend's free records have already been shipped. We used to have at least 10 different names and addresses working on all the record and book companies. Every other day we would ride around collecting the big packages. To cap it off, we opened a credit account at a large department store and used to return most of the records and books to the store saying that they were gifts and we wanted something else. Since we had an account at the store, they always took the merchandise and gave credit for future purchases.

You can always use the public libraries. Find out when they do their yearly housecleaning. Every library discards thousands of books on this day. Just show up and ask if you can take some.

Almost anything you might want to know from plans for constructing a sundial to a complete blueprint for building a house may be obtained free from the Government Printing Office. Write to: Superintendent of Documents, Government Printing Office, Washington, D.C. 20402. Most publications are free. Those that are not are dirt cheap. Ask to be put on the list to receive the biweekly list of *Selected U.S. Government Publications.*

One of the best ways to receive records and books free is to invest twenty dollars and print up some stationery with an artistic logo for some non-existent publication. Write to all the public relations departments of record companies, publishing houses, and movie studios. Say you are a newspaper with a large youth readership and have regular reviews of books, or records, or movies, and would like to be placed on their mailing list. Say that you would be glad to send them any reviews of their records that appear in the paper. That adds a note of authenticity to the letter. After a month or so you'll be receiving more records and books than you can use.

If you really want a book badly enough, follow the title of this one—Dig!

39

FREE MONEY

No book on survival should fail to give you some good tips on how to rip off bread. Really horning in on this chapter will put you on Free-loader Street for life, 'cause with all the money in Amerika, the only thing you'll have trouble getting is poor.

WELFARE

It's so easy to get on welfare that anyone who is broke and doesn't have a regular relief check coming in is nothing but a goddamn lazy bum! Each state has a different set up. The racist penny-pinchers of Mississippi dole out only $8.00 a month. New York dishes out the most with monthly payments up to $120.00. The Amerikan Public Welfare Association publishes a book called *The Public Welfare Directory* with information on exactly what each welfare agency provides and how you go about qualifying. You can read the directory at any public library to find out all you can about how your local office operates.

When you've discovered everything you need to know, head on down to the Welfare Department in your grubbiest clothes. Not sleeping the night before helps. The receptionist will assign an "intaker" to interview you. After a long wait, you'll be directed to a desk. The intaker raps to you for a while, generally showing sympathy for your plight and turns you over to the caseworker who will make the final and ultimate assessment.

Have your heaviest story ready to ooze out. If you have no physical disabilities, lay down a "mentally deranged" rap. Getting medical papers saying you have any long-term illness or defect helps a lot. Tell the caseworker you get dizzy spells on the job and faint in the street. Keep bobbing your head, yawning, or scratching. Tell him that you have tried to commit suicide recently because you just can't make it in a world that has forgotten how to love. Don't lay it on too obviously. Wait till he "pries" some of the details from you. This makes the story even more convincing. Many welfare workers are young and hip. The image you are working on is that of a warm, sensitive kid victimized by brutal parents and a cold ruthless society. Tell them you held off coming for months because you wanted to maintain some self-respect even though you have been walking the streets broke and hungry. If you are a woman, tell him you were recently raped. In sexist Amerika, this will probably be true.

After about an hour or so of this soap-opera stuff, you'll be ready to get your first check. From then on it's a monthly check, complete medical care for free and all sorts of other outasight benefits. Occasionally the caseworker will drop by your pad or ask you down to the office to see how you're coming along, but with your condition, things don't look so good. Don't abandon hope though. Hope always helps fill in a caseworker's report.

The real trick is to parlay welfare payments in a few different states. Work out an exchange system with a buddy and mail each other the checks when they come in. If the caseworker comes by, your roommate can say you went to find a job or enrolled in a class. We know cats who have parlayed welfare payments up to six hundred dollars a month.

UNEMPLOYMENT

Every outlaw should learn everything there is to know about the rules governing unemployment insurance. As in the case of welfare, rules, eligibility, and the size of payments differ from state to state. In New York, you are eligible for payments equivalent to half your weekly salary before taxes up to $65 per week, on the condition that you have worked for a minimum of twenty weeks during the year. Payments are somewhat lower in most other states. In order to collect, you must show you are actively searching for a job and keep a record of employers you contact. This can easily be fudged. Every time you're questioned about it, mention one or two companies. If your hair is long, you'll have no problem. Just say they won't hire you until you get a haircut. When this is the case, the unemployment office cannot cut off your payments or your hair. They also cannot make you accept a job you do not want. Tell them any job offer you get is not challenging enough for your talents. Unemployment can be collected for six months before payments are terminated. Twenty more weeks of slavery and you can go back to maintaining your dignity in the unemployment line. These job insurance payments cannot be taxed and since you are working so few weeks out of each year, your taxable income is at a minimum. Read all the fine print for tax form 1040 and discover all the deductible loopholes available to you. You should wind up paying no taxes at all or having all the taxes that were deducted from your pay reimbursed. Never turn over to the pig government any funds you can rip off. Remember, it isn't your government, so why submit to its taxation if you feel you do not have representation.

PANHANDLING

The practice of going up to folks and bumming money is a basic hustling art. If you are successful at panhandling, you'll be able to master all the skills in the book and then some. To be good at it requires a complete knowledge of what motivates people. Even if we don't need the bread, we panhandle on the streets in the same way doctors go back to medical school. It helps us stay in shape. Panhandling is illegal throughout Pig Empire, but it's one of those laws that is rarely enforced unless they want to "clean the area" of hippies. If you're in a strange locale, ask a fellow panhandler, what the best places to work are without risking a bust. Do it in front of supermarkets, theaters, sporting events, hip dress shops and restaurants. College cafeterias are very good hunting grounds.

When you're hustling, be assertive. Don't lean against the wall with your palm out mumbling, "Spare some change?" Go up to people and stand directly in front of them so they have to look you in the eye and say no. Bum from guys with dates. Bum from motherly looking types. After a while you'll get a sense of the type of people you get results with.

Theater can be real handy. The best actors get the most bread. Devising a street theater skit can help. A good prop is a charity cannister. You can get them by going to the offices of a mainstream charity and signing up as a collector. Don't feel bad about ripping them off. Charities are the biggest swindle around. 80% or more of the funds raised by honky charities go to the organization itself. New fancy cars for the Red Cross, inflated salaries for the executives of the Cancer Fund, tax write-offs for Jerry Lewis. You get the picture. A good way to work this and keep your karma in shape is to turn over half to a revolutionary group such as your local underground. Remember, fugitives from injustice depend on you to survive. Be a responsible member of our nation. Support the only war we have going!

RIP-OFFS

If you are closing out your checking account, overdraw your account by $10.00. The bank won't bother chasing you down for a lousy 10 bucks.

Call the telephone operator from time to time and tell her you lost some change in a pay phone. They will mail you the cash.

You can get $150 to $600 in advance by willing your body to a University medical school. They have you sign a lot of papers and put a tattoo on your foot. You can get the tattoo removed and sell your body to the folks across the street. The universities can be ripped off by enrolling, applying for a loan and bugging out after the loan comes through. This is a lot easier than you might imagine and you can hit them up for up to $2,500 with a good enough story.

Put a number 14 brass washer in a newspaper vending machine and take out all the papers. Stand around the corner or go into the local bar and sell them. You often get tipped. Don't do this with underground papers. Remember they're your brothers and sisters.

The airlines will give you $250 for each piece of luggage you lose when flying. The following is a good way to lose your luggage. When you get off a plane, have a friend meet you at the gate. Give him your luggage claim stubs and arrange to meet at a washroom or restaurant. Your friend picks up the bags and takes them out of the baggage room. Before he leaves the airport, he turns over the stubs to you at your prearranged rendezvous. You casually wander over to the baggage department and search for your elusive luggage. When all the baggage has been claimed, file a complaint with the lost and found department. They'll have you fill out a form, explain that it probably got misplaced on another carrier and promise to send it to you as soon as it is located. In a month you'll receive a check for $250 per bag. Enjoy your flight.

THE INTERNATIONAL YIPPIE CURRENCY EXCHANGE

Every time you drop a coin into a slot, you are losing money needlessly. There is at least one foreign coin that is the same size or close enough that will do the trick for less than a penny. The following are some of the foreign currencies that will get you that Coke, call or subway ride.

QUARTER SIZE COINS

URUGUAYAN 10 CENTISMO PIECE—works in many soda and candy machines, older telephones (3 slot types), toll machines, laundromats, parking meters, stamp machines, and restroom novelty machines. Works also in some electric cancerette machines but not most mechanical machines.

DANISH 5 ORE PIECE—works in 3 slot telephones, toll machines, laundromats, automats, some stamp machines, most novelty machines, and the Boston Subway. Does not work in soda or cancerette machines.

PERUVIAN 20 CENTAVO PIECE—generally similar to Danish 5 Ore Piece.

MEXICAN 10 CENTAVO PIECE—works in new (one slot) telephones and some electric cancerette machines, but does not work as many places as the Uruguay, Danish and Peruvian coins.

ICELANDIC 5 AURAN PIECE—most effective quarter in the world, even works in change machines. Unfortunately, this coin is practically impossible to get outside of Iceland and even there, it is becoming difficult since the government is attempting to remove it from circulation.

DIME SIZE COINS

MALAYSIAN PENNY—generally works in all dime slots, including old and new telephones, candy machines, soda machines, electric machines, stamp machines, parking meters, photocopy machines, and pay toilets. Does not work in some newer stamp dispensers, and some mechanical cancerette machines.

TRINIDAD PENNY—generally works the same as Malaysian Penny.

NEW YORK SUBWAY TOKENS

DANISH 25 ORE PIECE—works in 95% of all subway turnstiles. A very safe coin to use since it will not jam the turnstile. It is 5/1000th of an inch bigger than a token.

PORTUGUESE 50 CENTAVO PIECE—the average Portuguese Centavo Piece is 2/1000th of an inch smaller than a token.

JAMAICAN HALF PENNY, *BAHAMA PENNY* and *AUSTRALIAN SCHILLING*—these coins are 12/1000th to 15/1000th of an inch smaller than a token. They work in about 80% of all turnstiles. We have also had good success with *FRENCH 1 FRANC PIECE* (WW II issue), *SPANISH 10 CENTAVO PIECE*, *NICARAGUAN 25 CENTAVO PIECE*.

All of the coins listed have a currency value of a few cents, with most less than one penny. Foreign coins work more regularly than slugs and are non-magnetic, hence cannot be detected by "slug detector machines." Also unlike slugs, although they are illegal to use in machines, they are perfectly legal to possess and exchange.

Large coin dealers and currency exchanges are generally uptight about handling cheap foreign coins in quantity since they don't make much profit and are subject to certain pressures in selling coins that are the same size as Amerikan coins or tokens.

People planning trips to European or South American countries should bring back rolls of coins as souvenirs or for use in "coin jewelry."

Washers are the most popular types of slugs. You can go to any hardware store and match them up with various coins. Sometimes you might have to put a small piece of scotch tape over one side of the hole to make it more effective. Each washer is identified by its material and a number, i.e. No. 14 brass washer with scotch tape on one side is a perfect dime. When you get the ones you want, you can buy thousands for next to nothing (especially at industrial supply stores) and pass them out to your friends.

Xerox copies of both sides of a dollar bill, carefully glued together, work in most machines that give you change for a dollar. Excuse us, there is a knock at the door . . . Fancy that! It's the Treasury Department. Wonder what they want?

40

FREE DOPE

BUYING, SELLING AND GIVING IT AWAY

As you probably know, most dope is illegal, therefore some risks are always involved in buying and selling. "Eternal vigilance and constant mobility are the passwords of survival," said Che Guevara, and nowhere do they apply more than in the world of dope. If you ever have the slightest doubt about the person with whom you're dealing—DON'T.

BUYING

In the purchasing of dope, arrests are not a problem unless you're the fall guy for a bust on the dealer. The major hazard is getting burned. Buy from a friend or a reputable dealer. If you have to do business with a stranger, be extra careful. Never front money. One of the burn artist's tricks is to take your money, tell you to wait and split with your dough. There are various side show gimmicks each burn artist works. The most common is to ask you to walk with them a few blocks and then stop in front of an apartment building. He then tells you the dope is upstairs and asks you to hand over the money in advance. He explains that his partner is real uptight 'cause they were raided once and won't let anybody in the pad. He takes your dough and disappears inside the building, out the back door or up to the roof and into his getaway helicopter. You are left on the sidewalk with anxious eyes and that "can this really be happening to me" feeling.

Another burn method is to substitute oregano, parsley or catnip for pot, camel shit for hash, saccharin or plain pills for acid. If you got burned for heroin or speed, you're better off being taken, because these are body-fuck drugs that can mess you up badly. The people that deal them are total pigs and should be regarded as such. When you're buying from strangers, you have a right to sample the merchandise free unless it's coke. Check the weight of the grass with a small pocket scale. Feel the texture and check out how well it has been cleaned of seeds and twigs. Smoke a joint that is rolled from the stuff you get. Don't accept the dealer's sample that he pulled out of his pocket. When you are buying a large amount of acid, pick a sample. You should never buy acid from a stranger as it is too easy a burn.

If you buy cocaine, bring along a black light. Only the impurities glow under its fluorescence, thus giving you an idea of the quality of the coke. Make sure it's the real thing. Sniffing coke can perforate your nasal passages, so be super moderate. Too much will kill you. A little bit goes a long way.

SELLING

Dealing, although dangerous, is a tax-free way of surviving even though it borders on work. The best way to start is to save up a little bread and buy a larger quantity than you usually get. Then deal out smaller amounts to your friends. The fewer strangers you deal with, the safer you are. The price of dope varies with the amount of stuff on the market in your area, the heat the narks are bringing down and the connections you have. A rough scale, say, for pot is $20 an ounce, $125 a pound and $230 a kilo (2.2 pounds). The price per ounce decreases depending on the amount you get. It's true you make more profit selling by the ounce, but the hassle is greater and the more contacts you must make increases the risk. Screwing your customers will prove to be bad karma (unless you consider dying groovy), so stick to honest dealing. Never deal from your pad and avoid keeping your stash there. Get into searching out the best markets which are generally in

California, given its close proximity to good ol' Mexico. Kansas is a big distribution center for Mexican grass, too. You can ship the stuff (safer than carrying) via air freight anywhere in the country for about $30 a trunk. Keep the sending and receiving end looking straight. We have one friend who wears a priest's outfit to ship and receive dope. In fact, every time we see nuns or priests on the street, we assume they're outlaws just on their way to the next deal or bombing. For all we know, the church actually is nothing but a huge dope ring in drag. Anybody gotten high off communion wafers lately?

When you talk about deals on the phone, be cool. Make references to theater tickets or subscriptions. Don't keep extensive notes on your activities and contacts. Use code names where you can. Never deal with two other people present. Only you and the buyer should be in the immediate vicinity. Narks make busts in pairs so one can be the arresting officer and the other can be a court witness. Dealing is a paradox of unloading a good amount of shit but not trying to move too fast; of making new contacts but being careful of strangers; of dealing high quality and low prices; and of being simultaneously bold and cautious. If you get nabbed, get the best lawyer who specializes in dope busts. First offenders rarely end up serving time, but it's a different story for repeaters. Know how punitive the courts are and which judges and prosecutors can be bought off. Never deal in the month before an election.

GIVING IT AWAY

Giving dope away can be a real mind-blower. Every dealer should submit to voluntary taxation by the new Nation. If you are a conscientious dealer, you should be willing and eager to give a good hunk of your stash away at special events or to groups into free distribution. You should also be willing to give bread to bust trusts set up to bail out heads unable to get up the ransom money the whisky lush courts demand. Many groups have done huge mailings of joints to all sorts of people. A group in New York mailed 30,000 to people in the phone book on one Valentine's Day. A group in Los Angeles placed over 2,000 joints in library books and then advised kids to smoke a book during National Library Week. Be cool about even giving stuff away since that counts as dealing in most states. John Sinclair, Chairman of the White Panther Party, is serving 9½ to 10 years for giving away two joints.

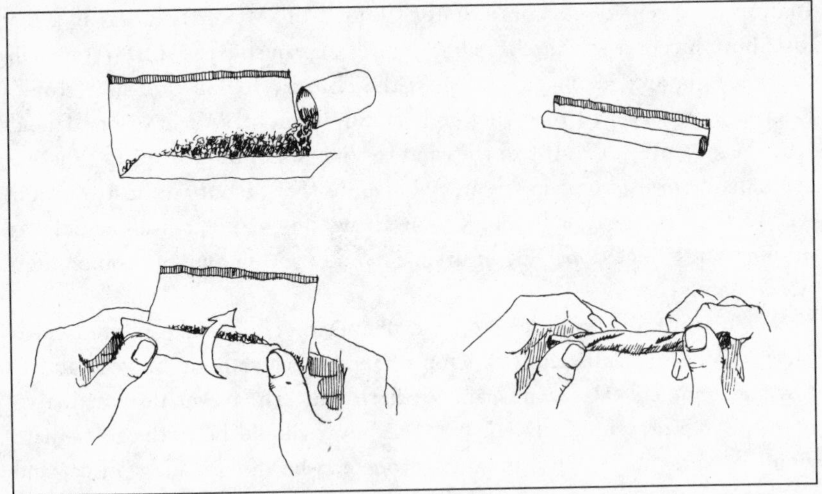

AVOID ALL NEEDLE DRUGS—
THE ONLY DOPE WORTH SHOOTING IS RICHARD NIXON

GROW YOUR OWN

Pot is a weed and as such grows in all climates under every kind of soil condition. We have seen acres and acres of grass growing in Kansas, Iowa and New Jersey. If you're not located next door to a large pot field growing in the wild, maybe you would have some success in growing your own. It's well worth it to try your potluck!

The first thing is to start with a bunch of good-quality seeds from grass that you really dig. Select the largest seeds and place them between two heavy-duty napkins or ink blotters in a pan. Soak the napkins with water until completely saturated. Cover the top of the pan or place it in a dark closet for three days or until a sprout about a half inch long appears from most of the seeds.

During this incubation period, you can prepare the seedling bed. Use a low wooden box such as a tomato flat and fill it with an inch of gravel. Fill the rest of the box with some soil mixed with a small amount of fertilizer. Moisten the soil until water seeps out the bottom of the box, then level the soil making a flat surface. With a pencil, punch holes two inches apart in straight rows. You can get about 2 dozen in a tomato flat.

When the incubation period is over, take those seeds that have an adequate sprout and plant one in each hole. The sprout goes down and the seed part should be a little above ground. Tamp the soil firmly (do not pack) around each plant as you insert the sprouts.

The seedlings should remain in their boxes in a sunny window until about mid-May. They should receive enough water during this period to keep the soil moist. By the time they are ready to go into the ground, the green plants should be about six to eight inches tall.

If it is late winter or early spring and you have a plot of land that gets enough sun and is sheltered from nosy neighbors, you should definitely grow grass in the great outdoors.

One idea is to plant sunflowers in your garden as these grow taller than the pot plants and camouflage them from view. The best idea is to find some little-used field and plant a section of it.

Prepare the land the way you would for any garden vegetable. Dig up the ground with a pitchfork or heavy duty rake, removing rocks. Rake the plot level and punch holes in the soil about three inches deep and about two feet apart in the same way you did in the seedling boxes. Remove the young plants from the box, being careful not to disturb the roots and keeping as much soil intact as possible. Transplant each plant into one of the punched-out holes and firmly press the soil to hold it in place. When all the plants are in the ground, water the entire area. Tend them the way you would any other garden. They should reach a height of about six feet by the end of the summer and be ready to harvest.

If you don't have access to a field, you can grow good stuff right in your own closet or garage using artificial lighting. Transplant the plants into larger wooden boxes or flower boxes. Be sure and cover the bottom of each box with a few inches of pebbles or broken pottery before you add the soil. This will insure proper drainage. Fertilize the soil according to the instructions on the box and punch out holes in much the same way you would do if you were growing outside. After the young plants have been transplanted and watered thoroughly, you will have to rig up a lighting system. Use blue light bulbs, which are available at hardware stores, for the first thirty days. These insure a shorter, sturdier stalk. Leave the lights on 24 hours a day and place them about a foot above the tops of the plants. If the plants begin to feel brittle or turn yellow at the edges, then the temperature is too hot. Use less illumination or raise the height of the lamp if this occurs.

After the first thirty days, change to red bulbs and cut down the lighting time to 16 hours a day. After a week, reduce the time to 14 hours and then on the third week to 12 hours. Maintain this lighting period until the plants flower. The female plants have a larger and heavier flower structure and the males are somewhat skimpy. The female plant produces the stronger grass and the choicest parts are the top leaves including the flowers.

Inside or outside, the plants will be best if allowed to reach maturity, although they are smokeable at any point along the way. When you want to harvest the crop, wet the soil and pull out the entire plant. If you want to separate the top leaves from the rest, you can do so and make two qualities of grass. In any event, let the plants dry in the sun for two weeks until they are thoroughly dried out. If you want to hurry the drying process, you can do it in an oven using a very low heat for about twenty minutes. After you've completed the drying, you can "cure" the grass by putting the plants in plastic bags and sprinkling drops of wine, rum or plain booze on them. This greatly increases the potency.

There are two other ways that we know work to increase the potency of grass you grow or buy. One consists of digging a hole and burying a stash of grass wrapped in a plastic bag. A few months in the ground will produce a moldy grass that is far fuckin' out. A quick method is to get a hunk of dry ice, put it in a metal container or box with a tight lid (taping the lid airtight helps), and sprinkling the grass on top. Allow it to sit tightly covered for about three days until all the dry ice evaporates.

41

ASSORTED FREEBIES

LAUNDRY

Wait in a laundromat. Tell someone with a light load that you'll watch the machine for them if you can stick your clothes in with theirs.

PETS

Your local ASPCA will give you a free dog, cat, bird or other pet. Have them inspect and inoculate the animal which they will do free of charge. You can get free or very cheap medical care for your pet at a school for veterinary medicine.

Underground newspapers often carry a free-pets column in the back pages. Snakes can be caught in any wooded area and they make great pets. You can collect insects pretty easy. Ants are unbelievable to watch. You can make a simple 3/4 inch wide glass case about a foot high, fill it with sand and start an ant colony. A library book will tell you how to care for them.

Every year the National Park Service gives away surplus elks in order to keep the herds under its jurisdiction from outgrowing the amount of available land for grazing. Write to: Superintendent, Yellowstone National Park, Yellowstone, Wyoming 83020. You must be prepared to pay the freight charges for shipping the animal and guarantee that you can provide enough grazing land to keep the big fellow happy.

Under the same arrangement the government will send you a Free Buffalo. Write to: Office of Information, Department of the Interior, Washington, D.C. 20420. So many people have written them recently demanding their Free Buffalo, that they called a press conference to publicly attack the Yippies for creating chaos in the government. Don't take any buffalo shit from these petty bureaucrats, demand the real thing. Demand your Free Buffalo.

POSTERS

Beautiful wall posters are available by writing to the National Tourist Agencies of various countries. Most are located between 42nd and 59th Streets on Fifth Ave. in New York City. You can find their addresses in the New York Yellow Pages under both National Tourist Agencies and Travel Agencies. There are over fifty of them. Prepare a form letter saying you are a high school geography teacher and would like some posters of the country to decorate your classroom. In a month you'll be flooded with them. Airline companies also have colorful wall posters they send out free.

SECURITY

For this trick you need some money to begin with. Deposit it in a bank and return in a few weeks telling them you lost your bank book. They give you a card to fill out and sign and in a week you will receive another book. Now withdraw your money, leaving you with your original money and a bank book showing a balance. You can use this as identification to prevent vagrancy busts when traveling, as collateral for bail, or for opening a charge account at a store.

Another trick is to buy some American Travelers Checks. Wait a week and report your checks lost. They'll give you new ones to replace the missing ones. You spend your new checks and keep the ones you reported lost as security. This security is great for international travel especially at border crossings. If you want, you can spend the Travelers Checks by giving them to a friend to forge your name. Before you call the office to report the loss, call the police station and say you were mugged and your wallet was stolen. The agency always asks if you have reported the lost checks to the police, so you can safely answer yes. Never do this for more than five hundred dollars and never more than once with any one company.

POSTAGE

When mailing to the same city, address the envelope or package to yourself and put the name of the person you are sending it to where the return address generally goes. Mail it without postage and it will be "returned" to the sender. Because almost all letters are machine processed, any stamp that is the correct size will pass. Easter Seals and a variety of other type stamps usually get by the electronic scanner. If you put the stamp on a spot other than the far upper right corner, it will not be cancelled and can be used again by the person who gets your letter. If you have a friend working in a large corporation, you can run your organization's mail through their postage meter.

Those ridiculous free introductory or subscription type letters that you get in the mail often have a postage-guaranteed return postcard for your convenience. The next one you get, paste it on a brick and drop it in the mailbox. The company is required by law to pay the postage. You can also get rid of all your garbage this way.

MINISTRY

Unquestionably one of the best deals going is becoming a minister in the Universal Life Church. They will send you absolutely free, bona fide ordination papers. These entitle you to all sorts of discounts and tax exemptions. Try cutting out the card on the following page and laminate it. Let us know how it works out.

THE UNIVERSAL BAPTIST CHURCH

Box 1776

MIRACLE VALLEY, ARIZONA

Reverend ______________________

Ministry to the World

This is to certify that   is a fully ordained minister in the Universal Baptist Church and entitled to the rights and privileges thereof.

"GOD IS COMING BACK"

cut me out. . . . cut me out. . . . cut me out. . . . cut me out.

ATROCITIES

Join the Army!

VETERANS' BENEFITS

Write to the Veterans' Administration Information Service, Washington, D.C. 20420 asking them for the free services they provide for veterans. Send fifteen cents to the Government Printing Office for their booklet *Federal Benefits Available to Veterans and their Dependents.*

WATCH

A $330 Bulova sport timer accurate to 1/10 of a second will be lent free to judges and referees to time any amateur sporting event. Call your local authorized Bulova dealer and get one lent to you under a phony name. Tell them you want to time an orgy.

VACATIONS

There are many ways to take a free vacation, but here's one you might not have considered. It's an all-expenses-paid trip to Las Vegas for absolutely nothing. Call a travel agent and request information about Las Vegas gambling junkets (you'll probably have to hunt around because this practice is being curtailed). Different hotels have different deals, but the average one runs something like this: If you agree to buy $500 worth of chips that can only be spent on the gambling tables of the host hotel, they will fly you round trip, pay all hotel and food bills and provide you with a rented car. Go with a close friend and check into the hotel. Once at the roulette or craps table, you and your friend bet the same amount of chips against each other on even-paying chances. For example, he would bet on red and you on black. When either of you wins, you keep the house chips; when you lose, turn in the specially marked chips that cannot be cashed in. What you are doing is simply exchanging the chips you came with for house chips that you can cash in for real dough. Theoretically your two vacations should cost $23.00 if you do the betting at the crap table and $52.00 if you bet even chances at roulette. That is because the house wins if 0 or 00 comes up in roulette and if 12 comes up on the first roll of the dice, but it sure is a hell of a vacation for two for $23.00, and you get free champagne on some flights.

You can get half a vacation free by going to the Amerikan Embassy or Consulate in the country you find yourself in and claim that you're destitute. There is a law on the books that says they have to send you home. They might try to send you away, but be persistent. Make up a story about how your parents are away from home traveling. Say you got mugged or something and you are about to go to the newspapers with your story. Eventually they'll get you a free plane ticket. They stamp your passport invalid though, and you have to pay the government back before you can use it again.

DRINKS

When hitching, it's a good idea to carry a bottle opener and a straw. You take the caps off soda bottles while they're still in the machine and drink them dry without ever touching the bottle.

BURIALS

For ways to avoid the high cost of dying in Amerika, write to Continental Association, 39 East Van Buren St., Chicago, Ill. 60605. Send them $1.00 for the Manual of Simple Burial and 25¢ for a list of Memorial Associates.

ASTRODOME PICTURES

Don't you just have to have a huge, glossy color photo of Houston's famed Astrodome to show all your friends? Use the teacher bit and write to: Greater Houston Convention and Visitors Council, 1006 Main St., Houston, Texas 77002.

DIPLOMA

Above the paper towel dispenser in a service station restroom was written: "San Francisco State Diplomas." If you really need a college or a high school diploma, send $2.00 to Glenco, Box 834, Warren, Michigan 48090. They send you one that looks real authentic. It ain't Harvard, but it looks good enough to frame and put on your wall.

TOILETS

SNEAK UNDER!

42

TELL IT ALL, BROTHERS AND SISTERS

STARTING A PRINTING WORKSHOP

Leaflets, posters, newsletters, pamphlets and other printed matter are important to any revolution. A printing workshop is a definite need in all communities, regardless of size. It can vary from a garage with a mimeograph machine to a mammoth operation complete with printing presses and fancy photo equipment. With less than a hundred dollars and some space, you can begin this vital service. It'll take a while before you get into printing greenbacks, phony identification papers and credit cards like the big boys, but to walk a mile you must start with one step as Gutenberg once said.

PAPER

The standard size for paper is 8½″ × 11″. It comes 500 sheets to a "ream" and 10 reams to a case. You want a 16–20 bond weight sheet. The higher weights are better if you are printing on both sides. You can purchase what are termed "odd lots" from most paper companies. This means that the colors will be assorted and some sheets will be frayed at the edges or wrinkled. Odd lots can be purchased at great discounts. Some places sell paper this way for 10% of the original price and for leaflets, different colors help. Check this out with paper suppliers in your area.

INK

Inks come in pastes and liquids and are available in stationery stores and office supply houses. Each machine requires its own type ink, so learn what works best with the one you have. Colored ink is slightly more expensive but available for most machines.

STENCILS

Each machine uses a particular size and style stencil. If you get stuck with the wrong kind and can't get out to correct the mistake, you can punch extra holes in the top, trim them with a scissors if they are too big or add strips of tape to the sides if too narrow.

Be sure and use only the area that will fit on the paper you are using. Most stencils can be used for paper larger than standard size. Stencils will "cut" a lot neater if an electric typewriter is used. If you only have access to a manual machine, remove the ribbon so the keys will strike the stencil directly. A plastic sheet, provided by the supplier, can be inserted between the stencil and its backing to provide sharper cuts by the keys. If you hold the stencil up to a light, you should be able to clearly see the typing. If you can't, you'll have to apply more pressure.

Sketches can be done with a ball point pen or special stylus directly on the stencil. If you're really rushed, or there isn't that much info to get on the leaflet, you can hand-print the text using these instruments. Take care not to tear the stencil.

MIMEOGRAPH MACHINES

The price of a new mimeograph runs from $200 to $1200, depending on how sophisticated a machine you need and can afford. A.B. Dick and Gestetner are the most popular brands. Many supply houses have used machines for sale. Check the classified section for bargains. See if any large corporations are moving, going out of business or have just had a fire. Chances are they'll be unloading printing equipment at cheap prices.

Campaign offices of losing candidates often have mimeos to unload in November. Many supply houses have renting and leasing terms that you might be interested in considering. Have an idea of the work load and type of printing you'll be handling before you go hunting. Talk to someone who knows what they're doing before you lay down a lot of cash on a machine.

DUPLICATORS

We prefer duplicators to mimeos even though the price is a little higher. They work faster, are easier to operate and print clearer leaflets. The Gestetner Silk Screen Duplicator is the best bet. It turns out stuff almost as good as offset printing. You can do 10 thousand sheets an hour in an assortment of colors.

ELECTRONIC STENCILS

If you use electronic stencils you can do solid lettering, line drawings, cartoons and black and white pictures with good contrast. To make an electronic stencil, you map out on a sheet of paper everything you want printed. This is a photo process, so make sure only what you want printed shows up on the sheet. You can use a light blue pencil for guide lines as it won't photograph, but be neat anyway. Printing shops will cut a stencil on a special machine for about $3.00.

The Gestefax Electronic Stencil Cutter can be leased or rented in the same way as the duplicator. If you are doing a lot of printing for a number of different groups, this machine will eliminate plenty of hassle. The stencils cost about 20¢ each and take about fifteen minutes to make.

If you have an electronic stencil cutter, duplicator, electric typewriter and a cheap source of paper, you can do almost any printing job imaginable. Have a dual rate system, one for community groups and another for regular business orders. You can use the profits to go towards the purchasing of more equipment and to build toward the day when you can get your own offset press.

SILK SCREENING

Posters, banners and shirts that are unbelievable can be printed by this exciting method. The process is easy to learn and teach. You'll need a fairly large area to work in since the posters have to be hung up to dry. Pick up any inexpensive paperback book on silk screening. The equipment costs less than $50.00 to begin. Once you get good at it, you can print complicated designs in a number of different colors, including portraits.

UNDERGROUND NEWSPAPERS

Food conspiracies, bust trusts, people's clinics and demonstrations are all part of the new Nation, but if asked to name the most important institution in our lives, one would have to say the underground newspaper. It keeps tuned in on what's going on in the community and around the world. Values, myths, symbols, and all the trappings of our culture are determined to a large extent by the underground press. Each office serves as a welcome mat for strangers, a meeting place for community organizers and a rallying force to fight pig repression. There are probably over 500 regularly publishing with readerships running from a few hundred to over 500,000. Most were started in the last three years. If your scene doesn't have a paper, you probably don't have a scene together. A firmly established paper can be started on about $2,500. Plan to begin with eight pages in black and white with a 5,000 copy run. Each such issue will cost about $300 to print. You should have six issues covered when you start. Another $700 will do for equipment. Offset printing is what you'll want to get from a commercial printing establishment.

You need some space to start, but don't rush into setting up a storefront office until you feel the paper's going to be successful. A garage, barn or spare apartment room will do just fine. Good overhead fluorescent lighting, a few long tables, a bookcase, desk, chairs, possibly a phone and you are ready to start.

Any typewriter will work, but you can rent an IBM Selectric typewriter with a deposit of $120.00 and payments of $20.00 per month. Leasing costs twice as much, but you'll own the machine when the payments are finished. The Selectric has interchangeable type that works on a ball system rather than the old-fashion keys. Each ball costs $18.00, so by getting a few you can vary the type the way a printer does.

A light-table can make things a lot easier when it comes to layout. Simply build a box (3′ × 4′ is a good size, but the larger the better) out of ½″ plywood. The back should be higher than the front to provide a sloping effect. The top should consist of a shelf of frosted glass. Get one strong enough to lean on. Inside the box, attach two fluorescent light fixtures to the walls or base. The whole light table should cost less than $25.00. That really is about all you need, except someone with a camera, a few good writers who will serve as reporters, an artistic person to take care of layout, and someone to hassle printing deals, advertising and distribution. Most people start by having everyone do everything.

LAYOUT

A tabloid size paper is 9⅞″ × 14⅝″ with an inch left over on each side for margins. Columns typically are 3¼″ allowing for three per page. Experience has found that this size is easy to lay out and more importantly, easy to read. There is an indirect ratio between readability and academic snobbishness. Avoid the textbook look. Remember, the *New York Times* in its low form represents the Death Kulture.

Start off with a huge collection of old magazines and newspapers. You can cut up all sorts of letters, borders, designs and sketches and paste them together to make eye-catching headlines. Sheets of headline type are available in different styles from art stores for $1.25 a sheet. Buy one of each type and then photograph several copies of each, bringing the price way down. The basic content in the prescribed column size should be banged out on the IBM. The columns can be clipped together with a clothespin to avoid confusion. Use a good heavy bond white opaque paper.

All black and white photographs from newspapers and magazines can be used directly. Color pictures can also be used but it's tricky and you'll have to experiment a little to get an understanding of what colors photograph poorly. Glossy black and white photographs must be shot in half tones to keep the gray areas. You can have them processed at any photo lab. You might also need the photo lab for enlargements or reductions, so make contact and establish a good working relationship.

An Exacto knife is available for 29¢ and you can get a package of 100 blades for $10.00. A few metal rulers, a good pair of scissors, some spray adhesive or rubber cement and you're ready to paste the pages that will make up the "dummy" that goes to the printer. Each page is laid out on special layout sheets with faint blue guide lines that don't photograph. Any large art supply store sells these sheets and all the other supplies.

By working over a light-table, the paste-up can be done more professionally. Experiment with many different layouts for each page before finally pasting up the paper. Use artistic judgment. Don't have a picture in the corner and the rest solid columns. Print can be run over pictures and sketches by preparing two sheets for that page and shooting the background in half-tones. The columns don't have to be run straight up and down, but can run at different angles. The most newsworthy articles should be towards the front of the paper. The centerfold can be treated in an exciting manner. A good idea is to do the centerfold so that it can be used as a poster to put on a wall after the paper is read. If you have ads, they should be kept near the back. The masthead, which gives the staff, mailing address, and similar info, goes near the front. Your focus should be on local activities. A section should be reserved for a directory of local services and events. People giving things away should have a section. The rest really depends on the life style and politics of the staff. National stories can be supplied by one or more of the news services. Nothing in the underground press is copyrighted, so you can reprint an interesting article from another paper. It's customary to indicate what paper printed it first, or news service it was sent out by. Any underground paper has permission to reprint hunks of this book.

ADS

Most papers find it necessary to get some advertising to help defray the production costs. Some rely totally on subscription; some are outgrowths of organizations and still others are printed up and just handed out free. The ones with ads seem to have the longest life. Make up an ad rate before you put out the first issue. Ads are measured in inches of length. The width is understood by everyone to be the width of the column. If you use the 3¼″ column, however, you'll want to let potential advertisers know you have wide columns.

The way to arrive at a reasonable rate is to estimate the total budget for each issue (adding some for overhead and labor), then each page and finally each column inch. After a little arithmetic you can get a good estimate of your printing cost per inch. Using our figures throughout this section, it should come to about $2.00 per inch. Double this figure and you'll arrive at the correct rate per advertising inch—$4.00. There should be special lower rates for large ads, such as half or full pages. There should also be a special arrangement for a continuous subscriber. If you have a classified section, another rate based on number of words or lines is constructed. A service charge is fixed if you make up the ad layout rather than the advertiser. The whole formula should be worked out and printed up before you lay out the first issue.

The best place to get advertising is locally. Theaters, hip clothing stores, ice cream parlors, and record stores are among the type of advertisers you should approach. After you build up a circulation, you might want to seek out national advertisers. See who tends to advertise in other underground papers. Send the publicity department of these companies letters and samples of your paper. Never let ads make up more than half the paper.

DISTRIBUTION

At the beginning you should aim for a bi-weekly paper with a gradual increase in the number of pages. The price should be about 25¢. Check out the local laws about selling papers on the street. It's probably allowed and is a neat way to get the paper around. Give half to the street hawkers. Representatives at high schools and colleges should be sought out. Bookstores and newsstands are good places to distribute. After your paper gets going well, you might try for national distribution. The *Cosmep Newsletter* is put out by the Committee of Small Magazines, Editors and Publishers, PO Box 1425, Buffalo, NY 14214. In addition to good tips if you want to start a small literary magazine or publish your own book, they provide an up-to-date list of small stores around the country that would be likely to carry your paper. Subscriptions should be sought in the paper itself. If you get a lot, check out second class mailing privileges. UPS can help out with out-of-city distribution.

If you're in a smaller town, you might have to shop around or go to another city to get printing done. Many printers print only pigswill, which brings up the point of getting busted for obscenity which can be pretty common. You probably should incorporate, but contact a sympathetic lawyer before you put out your first issue. During the summer there are usually a few alternative media conferences organized by one group or another. You can pick up valuable information and exchange ideas at these gatherings. Good luck and write on!

HIGH SCHOOL PAPERS

The usual high school paper is run by puppet lackeys of the administration. It avoids controversy, naughty language, and a host of other things foreign to the 4-H Club members the school is determined to mass produce. The only thing the staff is good at is kissing the principal's ass. Let's face it, the aim of a good high school newspaper should be to destroy the high school. Publishing and distributing a heavy paper isn't going to earn you the Junior Chamber of Commerce good citizenship award. You might have to be a little mysterious about who the staff is until you understand the ground rules and who controls the ballpark—the people or the principal.

Many schools do not allow papers to be handed out on the school premises. These cases are generally won by the newspapers that take the school to court. You can challenge the rule and make the administration look like the dinosaurs they are by distributing sheets of paper with only your logo and the school rule printed. By gaining outside publicity for the first distribution of the paper, you might put the administration up tight about clamping down on you. It might be difficult to explain in civics class when they get to the freedom of the press stuff. Your paper should have one purpose in mind—to piss off the principal and radicalize the students. If you run into problems, seek out a sympathetic lawyer. You can get a helpful pamphlet from the ACLU, 156 5th Ave., New York NY 10010, called "Academic Freedom in the Secondary Schools" for 25¢.

Tell your lawyer about the most recent (July 10, 1970) decision of the United States District Court in Connecticut which ruled that the high school students of Rippowan High School in Stamford can publish independent newspapers without having the contents screened in advance by school officials.

The same info for underground papers applies to high school rags, only the price should be much less if not free. To begin with, you might just mimeograph the first few issues before trying photo-offset printing. It is very important to get the readers behind you in case you have to go to war with the administration in order to survive. Maintain friendships with above ground reporters, the local underground paper and radical community groups for alliances.

G.I. PAPERS

A heavier scene than even the high schools exists in the No-No Land of the military. Nonetheless, against incredible odds, courageous G.I.'s both here and overseas have managed to put out a number of underground newspapers. If you are a G.I. interested in starting a paper, the first thing to do is seek out a few buddies who share your views on the military and arrange a meeting, preferably off the base. Once you have your group together, getting the paper published will be no problem. Keeping your staff secret, you can have one member contact someone from a G.I. coffee house, anti-war organization or nearby underground newspaper. This civilian contact person will be in a position to raise the bread and arrange the printing and distribution of the paper. You can write one of the national G.I. newspaper organizations listed at the end of this section if you are unable to find help locally. The paper should be printed off the base. Government equipment should be avoided.

Correspondence and subscriptions can be solicited through the use of a post office box. Such a box is inexpensive and secret (at least that's what the G.I. papers now publishing report) from military snoopers up tight about bad publicity if they get caught spying. If you are mailing the paper to other G.I.'s use first class mail and a plain envelope. This is advice to anybody sending stuff to a G.I. The mail is handled by "lifers" who will report troublemakers to their C.O. (Commanding Officer) if they notice anti-war slogans on envelopes or dirty commie rags coming their way.

You'll want to publish stuff relevant to the lives of the G.I.'s on your base. News of demonstrations, articles on the war, racism, counter-culture, and vital info on how to bug the higher-ups and get out of the military service are all good. Get samples of other newspapers already in operation to get the flavor of writing that has become popular.

Distributing the paper is really more of a problem than the publishing. Here you run smack into Catch 22, which says, "no printed matter may be distributed on a military base without prior written permission of the commanding officer." No such permit has been granted in military history. A few court battles have had limited success and you should go through the formality of obtaining a permit. Send the first issue of the paper to your C.O. with a cover letter stating where and when you intend to distribute the paper on the base. In no part of the application should you list your names. Have a civilian, preferably a civil liberties lawyer, sign the declaration of intent. If more info is requested, go over it with the lawyer before responding. Natch, they're going to want to know who you are and where you get your bread, but fuck 'em. Whether or not you get a permit or have a successful court battle is pretty academic. If the military pigs catch you handing out an underground paper on the base, you're headed for trouble. Use civilian volunteers from your local peace group in as many public roles as possible. They'll be glad to help out.

Print and distribute as many copies as you can rather than concentrating on an expensively printed paper with numerous pages. The very existence of the paper around the base is the most important info the paper can offer. Leave some in mess halls, theaters, benches, washrooms, and other suitable spots. Off base get the paper to sympathetic reporters, coffee houses, colleges and the like. Outside U.S.O. centers and bus terminals are a good place to get the paper out. Rely on donations, so you can make the paper free. Get it together. Demand the right to join the army of your choice. The People's Army! As Joe Hill said in one of his songs, "Yes, I'll pick up a gun but I won't guarantee which way I'll point it."

NEWS SERVICES

Aside from UPS, which is the association of papers, there are five news services that we know of that you might be interested in subscribing to for national stories, photos, production ideas, news of other papers and general movement dope. LNS is the best known. It sends out packets once a week that include about thirty pages with original articles, eye-witness reports, reprints from foreign papers and photographs. They tend to be heavily political rather than cultural and view themselves as molders of ideology rather than strictly a service organization of the underground papers. A subscription costs $15.00 per month, but if you're just starting out they're good about slow payments and such.

You should get in the habit of sending special articles, in particular eye-witness accounts of events that other papers might use, to one or more of the news services for distribution. If you hear of an important event that you would like to cover in your newspaper, call the paper in that area for a quick report. They might send you photos if you agree to reciprocate.

SWITCHBOARDS

A good way to quickly communicate what's coming down in the community is to build a telephone tree. It works on a pyramid system. A small core of people are responsible for placing five calls each. Each person on the line in turn calls five people and so on. If the system is prearranged correctly with adjustments made if some people don't answer the phone, you can have info transmitted to about a thousand people in less than an hour. A slower but more permanent method is to start a Switchboard. Basically, a Switchboard is a central telephone number or numbers that anybody can call night or day to get information. It can be as sophisticated as the community can support. The people that agree to answer the phone should have a complete knowledge of places, services and events happening in the community. Keep a complete updated file. The San Francisco Switchboard puts out an operator's manual explaining the organization and operation of a successful switchboard. They will send it out for 12¢ postage. San Francisco has the longest and most extensive Switchboard operation. From time to time there are national conferences with local switchboards sending a rep.

43

GUERRILLA BROADCASTING

GUERRILLA RADIO

Under FCC Low Power Transmission Regulations, it is legal to broadcast on the AM band without even obtaining a license, if you transmit with 100 milliwatts of power or less on a free band space that doesn't interfere with a licensed station. You are further allowed up to a 12-foot antenna or the use of carrier-current transmission (regular electric wall outlets). Using this legal set-up, you can broadcast from a 2 to 20 block radius depending on how high up you locate your antenna and the density of tall buildings in the area.

Carrier-current broadcasting consists of plugging the transmitter into a regular wall socket. It draws power in the same way as any other electrical applicance, and feeds its signal into the power line allowing the broadcast to be heard on any AM radio tuned into the operating frequency. The transmitter can be adjusted to different frequencies until a clear band is located. The signal will travel over the electrical wiring until it hits a transformer where it will be erased. The trouble with this method is that in large cities, almost every large office or apartment building has a transformer. You should experiment with this method first, but if you are in a city, chances are you'll need an antenna rigged up on the roof. Anything over twelve feet is illegal, but practice has shown that the FCC won't hassle you if you don't have commercials and refrain from interfering with licensed broadcasts. There are some cats in Connecticut broadcasting illegally with a 100-foot antenna over a thirty mile radius for hours on end and nobody gives them any trouble. Naturally if you insist upon using dirty language, issuing calls to revolution, broadcasting bombing information, interfering with above ground stations and becoming too well known, the FCC is going to try and knock you out. There are penalties that have never been handed out of up to a year in jail. It's possible you could get hit with a conspiracy rap, which could make it a felony, but the opinion of movement lawyers now is a warning if you're caught once, and a possible fine with stiffer penalties possible for repeaters that are caught.

If it gets really heavy, you could still broadcast for up to 15 minutes without being pin-pointed by the FCC sleuths. By locating your equipment in a panel truck and broadcasting from a fixed roof antenna, you can make it almost impossible for them to catch you by changing positions.

The right transmitter will run about $200. If you plan to use carrier-current transmission you'll also need a capacitor that sells for $30. An antenna can be made out of aluminum tubing and antenna wiring available at any TV radio supply store. You'll also need a good microphone that you can get for about $10. Naturally, equipment for heavier broadcasting is available if a member of your group has a license or good connections with someone who works in a large electronics supply house. Also with a good knowledge in the area you can build a transmitter for a fraction of the purchase price. You can always employ tape recorders, turntables and other broadcasting hardware depending on how much bread you have, how much stuff you have to hide (i.e., how legal your operation is) and the type of broadcasting you want to do.

It is possible to extend your range by sending a signal over the telephone lines to other transmitters which will immediately rebroadcast. Several areas in a city could be linked together and even from one city to another. Theoretically, if enough people rig up transmitters and antennas at proper locations and everyone operates on the same band, it is possible to build a nation-wide people's network that is equally theoretically legal.

Broadcasting, it should be remembered, is a one-way transmission of information. Communications which allow you to transmit and receive are illegal without a license (ham radio).

GUERRILLA TELEVISION

There are a number of outlaw radio projects going on around the country. Less frequent, but just as feasible, is a people's television network. Presently there are three basic types of TV systems. Broadcast, which is the sending of signals directly from a station's transmitter to home receiver sets; cable, where the cable company employs extremely sensitive antennae to pick up broadcast transmissions and relay them and/or they originate and send them; and thirdly, closed circuit TV, such as the surveillance cameras in supermarkets, banks and apartment house lobbies.

The third system as used by the pigs is of little concern, unless we are interested in not being photographed. The cameras can be temporarily knocked out of commission by flashing a bright light (flashbulb, cigarette lighter, etc.) directly in front of its lens. For our own purposes, closed-circuit TV can be employed for broadcasting rallies, rock concerts or teach-ins to other locations. The equipment is not that expensive to rent and easy to operate. Just contact the largest television or electronics store in your area and ask about it. There are also closed-circuit and cable systems that work in harmony to broadcast special shows to campuses and other institutions. Many new systems are being developed and will be in operation soon.

Cable systems can be tapped either at the source or at any point along the cable by an engineer freak who knows what to do. The source is the best spot, since all the amplification and distribution equipment of the system is available at that point. Tapping along the cable itself can be a lot hairier, but more frustrating for the company when they try to trace you down.

Standard broadcasting that is received on almost all living room sets works on an RF (radio frequency) signal sent out on various frequencies which correspond to the channels on the tuner. In no area of the country are all these channels used. This raises important political questions as to why people do not have the right to broadcast on unused channels. By getting hold of a TV camera (Sony and Panasonic are the best for the price) that has an RF output, you can send pictures to a TV set simply by placing the camera cable on or near the antenna of the receiver set. When the set is operating on the same channel as the camera, it will show what the camera sees. Used video tape recorders such as the Sony CV series that record and play back audio and video information are becoming more available. These too can be easily adapted to send RF signals the same as a live camera.

Whether or not the program to be broadcast is live or on tape, there are three steps to be taken in order to establish a people's TV network. First, you must convert the video and audio signals to an RF frequency-modulated (FM) signal corresponding to the desired broadcast channel. We suggest for political and technical reasons that you pick one of the unused channels in your area to begin experimenting. The commercial stations have an extremely powerful signal and can usually override your small output. Given time and experience you might want to go into direct competition with the big boys on their own channel. It is entirely possible, say in a 10 to 20 block radius, to interrupt a presidential press-conference with more important news.

When the signal is in the RF state, it is already possible to broadcast very short distances. The second step is to amplify the signal so it will reach as far as possible. A linear amplifier of the proper frequency is required for this job. The stronger the amplifier, the farther and more powerful the signal. A 10-watt job will cover approximately 5 miles (line of sight) in area. Linear amplifiers are not that easily available, but they can be constructed with some electrical engineering knowledge.

The third step is the antenna, which if the whole system is to be mobile to avoid detection, is going to involve some experimentation and possible camouflage. Two things to keep in mind about an antenna are that it should be what is technically referred to as a "di-pole" antenna and since TV signals travel on line of sight, it is important to place the antenna as high as possible. Although it hasn't been done in practice, it certainly is possible to reflect pirate signals off an existing antenna of a commercial network. This requires a full knowledge of broadcasting; however, any amateur can rig up an antenna, attach it to a helium balloon and get it plenty high. For most, the roof of a tall building will suffice. If you're really uptight about your operation, the antenna can be hidden with a fake cardboard chimney.

We realize becoming TV guerrillas is not everyone's trip, but a small band with a few grand can indeed pull it off. There are a lot of technical freaks hanging around recording studios, guitar shops, hi-fi stores and engineering schools that can be turned on to the project. By showing them the guidelines laid out here, they can help you assemble and build various components that are difficult to purchase (i.e., the linear amplifier). Naturally, by building some of the components, the cost of the operation is kept way down. Equipment can be purchased in selective electronics stores. You'll need a camera, VTR, RF modulator, linear amplifier and antenna. Also a generator, voltage regulator and an alternator if you want the station to be mobile.

Guerrilla TV is the vanguard of the communications revolution, rather than the avant-garde cellophane light shows and the weekend conferences. One pirate picture on the sets in Amerika's living rooms is worth a thousand wasted words.

With the fundamentals in this field mastered, you can rig up all sorts of shit. Cheap twenty-dollar tape recorders can be purchased and outfitted with a series of small loud-speakers. Concealed in a school auditorium or other large hall, such a system can blast out any message or music you wish to play. The administration will go insane trying to locate the operation if it is well hidden. We know two cats who rigged a church with this type of setup and a timing device. Right in the middle of the sermon, on came Radio Heaven and said stuff like "Come on preacher, this is God, you don't believe all that crap now, do you?" It made for an exciting Sunday service all right. You can build a miniature transmitter and with a small magnet attach it to the underbelly of a police car to keep track of where it's going. This would only be practical in a small town or on a campus where there are only a few security guards or patrol vehicles. If you rigged a small tape recorder to the transmitter and tuned it to a popular AM band, the patrol car as it rode around could actually broadcast the guerrilla message you prerecorded. Wouldn't they be surprised when they found out how you did it? You can get a "Bumper Beeper" and receiver that are constructed by professionals for use by private detectives. The dual units costs close to $400.

Even though there are laws governing this area of sneaky surveillance, telephone taps, tracking devices and the like, a number of enterprising firms produce an unbelievable array of electronic hardware that allows you to match Big Brother's ears and eyes. Sugar cube transmitters, tie clasp microphones, phone taps, tape recorders that work in a hollowed-out book and other Brave New World equipment is available.

44

DEMONSTRATIONS

Demonstrations always will be an important form of protest. The structure can vary from a rally or teach-in to a massive civil disobedience such as the confronting of the warmakers at the Pentagon or a smoke-in. A demonstration is different from other forms of warfare because it invites people other than those planning the action via publicity to participate. It also is basically non-violent in nature. A complete understanding of the use of media is necessary to create the publicity needed to get the word out. Numbers of people are only one of the many factors in an effective demonstration. The timing, choice of target and tactics to be employed are equally important. There have been demonstrations of 400,000 that are hardly remembered and demonstrations of a few dozen that were remarkably effective. Often the critical element involved is the theater. Those who say a demonstration should be concerned with education rather than theater don't understand either and will never organize a successful demonstration, or for that matter, a successful revolution. Publicity includes everything from buttons and leaflets to press conferences. You should be in touch with the best artists you can locate to design the visual props. Posters can be silk screened very cheaply and people can be taught to do it in a very short time. Buttons have to be purchased. The cheapest are those printed directly on the metal. The paint rubs off after a while, but they are ideal for mass demonstrations. You can print 10,000 for about $250.00. Leaflets, like posters, should be well designed.

One way of getting publicity is to negotiate with the city for permits. Again, this raises political questions, but there is no doubt one reason for engaging in permit discussions is for added publicity.

The date, time and place of the demonstration all have to be chosen with skill. Know the projected weather reports. Pick a time and day of the week that are convenient to most people. Make sure the place itself adds some meaning to the message. Don't have a demonstration just because that's the way it's always been done. It is only one type of weapon and should be used as such. On the other hand, don't dismiss demonstrations because they have always turned out boring. You and your group can plan a demonstration within the demonstration that will play up your style or politics more accurately. Also don't tend to dismiss demonstrations outright because the repression is too great. During World War II, the Danes held street demonstrations against the Nazis who occupied their country. Even today there are public demonstrations against the Vietnam War in downtown Saigon. Repression is there, but overestimating it is more a tactical blunder than the reverse. Nonetheless, it's wise to go to all demonstrations prepared for a vamping by the pigs.

DRESS

Most vamping is accompanied by clubbing, rough shoving and dragging, gassing and occasional buckshot or rifle fire. The clothing you wear should offer you the best protection possible, yet be lightweight enough to allow you to be highly mobile. CS and CN are by far the most commonly employed tear gas dispersibles. Occasionally they are combined with pepper gas to give better results. Pepper gas is a nerve irritant that affects exposed areas of the skin. Clothing that is tight fitting and covers as much of the body surface as possible is advisable. This also offers some protection if you are dragged along the ground. Gloves come in handy as protection and if you want to pick up gas cannisters and throw them back at the pigs or chuck them through a store window.

Your shoes should be high sneakers for running or boots for kicking. Hiking boots sold in army surplus stores serve both purposes and are your best selection for street action. Men should wear a jock strap or protective cup. Rib guards can be purchased for about $6.00 at any sporting goods store. Shoulder pads and leg pads are also available, but unless you expect heavy fighting and are used to wearing this clumsy street armor, you'll be better off without it.

HELMETS

Everyone should have a helmet. Your head sticks out above the swarming crowd and dents like a tin can. Protect it! The type of helmet you get depends on what you can afford and how often you'll be using it. The cheapest helmet available is a heavy steel tank model. This one is good because it offers ear protection and has a built-in suspension system to absorb the blow. It is also bullet proof. Its disadvantages are that it only comes in large sizes and is the heaviest thing you'll ever have on your head. It costs about $3.00. For $5.00 you can get a Civil Defense helmet made for officers. It's much lighter, but doesn't offer protection for the ears. It has a good suspension system. If you get this model, paint it a dark color before using it and you'll be less conspicuous. Our fashion consultants suggest anarchy black.

Construction helmets or "hard hats" run between $8.00 and $10.00, depending on the type of suspension system and material used. They are good for women because they are extremely lightweight. The aluminum ones dent if struck repeatedly and the fiberglass type can crack. Also they offer no ear protection. If you prefer one of these you should find a way to attach a chin or neck strap so you won't lose it while you run. If you get a hard hat, make sure you remove the hard head before you take it home.

Probably the all-around good deal for the money is the standard M-1 Army issue helmet. These vary in quality and price, depending on age and condition. They run from $2.00 to $10.00. Make sure the one you get has a liner with webbing that fits well or is adjustable and has a chin strap. Their main disadvantage is that they are bulky and heavy.

The snappiest demonstrators use the familiar motorcycle crash helmet. They are the highest in price, running from $10.00 to as high as $40.00. Being made of fiberglass, they are extremely lightweight. They have a heavy-duty strap built in and they can be gotten to fit quite snugly around the head. They offer excellent ear protection. The foam rubber insulation is better than a webbing system, and will certainly cushion most blows. Being made of fiberglass, a few have been known to crack under repeated blows, but that is extremely rare. Most come with plastic face guards that offer a little added protection. Get only those with removable ones since you might want to make use of a gas mask.

GAS MASKS

Ski goggles or the face visor on a crash helmet will protect against mace but will offer no protection against the chemical warfare gasses being increasingly used by pigs to disperse crowds. For this protection you'll need a gas mask. All the masks discussed give ideal protection against the gasses mentioned in the chart if used properly. If you do not have a gas mask, you should at least get a supply of surgical masks from a hospital supply store and a plastic bag filled with water and a cloth.

The familiar World War II Army gas mask with the filter in a long nose unit sells new (which is the only way gas masks can be sold) for about $5.00. Its disadvantages are that it doesn't cover the whole face, is easy to grab and pull off and the awkwardly placed filter makes running difficult. The Officer Civil Defense unit sells for the same price and overcomes the disadvantages of the World War II Army model. Most National Guard units use this type of mask. It offers full face protection, is lightweight and the filter cannister is conveniently located. Also the adjustable straps make for a nice tight fit. The U.S.A. Protective Field Combat Mask M9A1 offers the same type protection as the OCD, but costs twice as much. Its advantage is that you can get new filter cannisters when the chemicals in the one you are using become ineffective. New filters cost about $1.50. When you buy a mask, be sure and inquire if the filter has replacements. To get maximum efficiency out of a mask it needs an active chemical filter.

The U.S. Navy ND Mark IV Mask is the most effective gas mask available. It has replaceable filter cannisters and fits snugly to the head. It costs about $12.00. Its disadvantage is its dual tube filter system, which is somewhat bulky. Fix it so the cannister rests on the back of your neck. It's more difficult to grab and easier to run.

When you get your gas mask home, try it out to get the feeling of using it. Make sure the fit is good and snug. Purchase an anti-fog cloth for 25 cents where you got the mask. Wipe the inside of the eye pieces before wearing to prevent the glasses from clouding. Another good reason for wearing a mask is that it offers anonymity. Helmets, gas masks and a host of other valuable equipment are available at any large Army-Navy surplus store.

GAS CHART

GAS	PROPERTIES	EFFECTS	PROTECTION	FIRST AID	DISPENSED
CS (tear gas)	A fat-soluble gas with peppery smell and tear and nausea agents.	Copious flow of tears, burning sensation around the eyes, coughing, difficulty breathing, nausea, harassing sting and reddening of exposed areas. Stinging can last up to 2 hours	Remove yourself from affected area. DO NOT RUB eyes, wash out with a dilute boric acid solution or eye drops such as Murine. If none, use water. Wipe exposed areas with mineral oil, if not available, use water then alcohol.	Gas mask, wet towels or handkerchief, surgical mask and tight-fitting clothing.**	Cannisters, plastic grenades* fog machines, Helicopter and spray truck devices.
CN (tear gas)	Milder than CS, smells like apple blossoms. Water soluble.	Same as CS minus nausea and stinging.	Remove yourself from affected area and wash with water.	Same as CS, but you can stay in affected areas much longer without protection.	Same as CS
HC (smoke)	Heavy dense smoke, camphor-like smell.	Slightly irritating to eyes and nose. Mostly used to scare crowd.	None needed.	Goggles good enough.	Grenades, pots, fog machines
Nausea Gas	Clear, colorless, odorless, cannisters look like duds when they go off but don't be fooled.	Nausea followed by projective vomiting. Instant diarrhea, severe stomach cramps. Pain and heat sensation in lungs.	Symptoms generally clear up in a few hours. See physician if they don't	Masks are not effective as you could choke on the vomit. Therefore it is not used very often. Run upwind.	Cannisters
Blister gas	Fat-soluble, fine white powder.	Skin blistering to exposed areas - instant or within 48 hours.	Wash off with gauze pad saturated with mineral oil (salad oil or margerine will do). Treat as if 2nd degree burn.	Gas mask, gloves, long sleeves, towel around neck.	Cannisters
Mace	Liquid composed of CN, kerosene, general propellant and oxidizing agents.	Sharp pain if hit in the eyes. Burning sensation of other area hit. Nausea and possible vomiting if swallowed.	Wash out eyes with boric acid solution (see CS) or water if not available. Other area should be washed with alcohol to reduce burning.	Goggles, vaseline can be applied to exposed skin areas beforehand. If you use vaseline and get spray ed, wipe off vaseline with a rag and wash your face.	Propellant cannisters for person-to-person combat.

*Grenades unlike cannisters explode. If they do so near your face, they can cause very serious burns. Protect your eyes. They can be hand-thrown or fired from a rifle or grenade launcher.

**A super deluxe antidote for both CS and CN gases has been developed by a biochemist brother in Berkeley named John McWhorter. Mix 8-10 eggs, 1 cup water and a teaspoon of baking soda in a bowl. Beat mixture well. Keep refrigerated in small plastic bottles until a demonstration. Wipe the stuff on your face before a gassing occurs.

WALKIE-TALKIES

You should always go to a demonstration in a small group that stays in contact with each other until the demonstration is over. One way to keep in touch is to use walkie-talkies. No matter how heavy the vamping gets or how spread out are the crowds, you'll be able to communicate with these lightweight effective portable devices. The only disadvantage is cost. A half decent unit costs at least $18.00. It should have a minimum of 9 transistors and 100 milliwatts, although walkie-talkies can go as high as 5 watts and broadcast over 2 miles. Anything under 1 watt will not broadcast over ½ mile and considerably less in an area with tall buildings. The best unit you can buy runs $300.00. If you ever deck a pig, steal his walkie-talkie even before you take his gun. A good rule is to avoid the bargain gyp-joints and go to a place that deals in electronic equipment.

The important thing to realize about all walkie-talkie networks is that if anyone can talk, anyone else can listen and vice versa. This applies to pigs as well as us. All walkie-talkies work on the Civilian Band which has 23 channels. The cheaper units are preset to channel 9 or 11. The pigs broadcast on higher channels, usually channel 22. More expensive sets can operate on alternative channels. By removing the front of the set, you can adjust the transmitter and receiver to pick up and receive police communications. Don't screw around with the inside though, unless you know what you are doing. Consider buying a number of sets and ask about group discounts. Practice a number of times before you actually use walkie-talkies in real action. Develop code names and words just like the pigs do. Once you get acquainted with this method of communications in the streets, you'll never get cut off from the action. Watch out in close combat though. The pigs always try to smash any electronic gear.

OTHER EQUIPMENT

A sign can be used to ward off blows. Staple it to a good strong pole that you can use as a weapon if need be. Chains make good belts, as do garrisons with the buckles sharpened. A tightly rolled-up magazine or newspaper also can be used as a defensive weapon.

Someone in your group should carry a first aid kit. A Medical Emergency

Aeronautic Kit, which costs about $5.00 has a perfect carrying bag for street action.

Ideally you should visit the proposed site of the demonstration before it actually takes place.This way you'll have an idea of the terrain and the type of containment the police will be using. Someone in your group should mimeograph a map of the immediate vicinity which each person should carry. Alternative actions and a rendezvous point should be worked out. Everyone should have two numbers written on their arm, a coordination center number and the number of a local lawyer or legal defense committee. You should not take your personal phone books to demonstrations. If you get busted, pigs can get mighty Nosy when it comes to phone books. Any sharp objects can be construed as weapons. Women should not wear earrings or other jewelry and should tie their hair up to tuck it under a helmet. Wear a belt that you can use as a tourniquet. False teeth and contact lenses should be left at home if possible. You can choke on false teeth if you receive a sharp blow while running. Contact lenses can complicate eye damage if gas or mace is used.

If it really looks heavy, you might want to pick up on a lightweight adjustable bullet-proof vest. Remember what the Boy Scouts say when they go camping: "Be Prepared." When you go to demonstrations you should be prepared for a lot more than speeches. The pigs will be.

45

TRASHING

Ever since the Chicago pigs brutalized the demonstrators in August of 1968, young people have been ready to vent their rage over Amerika's inhumanity by using more daring tactics than basic demonstrations. There is a growing willingness to do battle with the pigs in the streets and at the same time to inflict property damage. It's not exactly rioting and it's not exactly guerrilla warfare; it has come to be called "Trashing." Most trashing is of a primitive nature with the pigs having the weapon and strategy advantage. Most trashers rely on quick young legs and a nearby rock. By developing simple gang strategy and becoming acquainted with some rudimentary weapons and combat techniques, the odds can be shifted considerably.

Remember, pigs have small brains and move slowly. All formations, signals, codes and other procedures they use have to be uniform and simplistic. *The Army Plan for Containment and Control of Civil Disorders*, published by the Government Printing Office, contains the basic thinking for all city, county and state storm troopers. A trip to the library and a look at any basic text in criminology will help considerably in gaining an understanding of how pigs act in the street. If you study up, you'll find you can, with the aid of a bullhorn or properly adjusted walkie-talkie, fuck up many intricate pig formations. "Left flank-right turn!" said authoritatively into a bullhorn pointed in the right direction will yield all sorts of wild results.

You should trash with a group using a buddy system to keep track of each other. If someone is caught by a pig, others should immediately rush to the rescue if it's possible to do so without sustaining too many losses. If an arrest is made, someone from your gang should take responsibility for seeing to it that a lawyer and bail bread are taken care of. Never abandon a member of your gang.

Avoid fighting in close quarters. You run less risk by throwing an object than by personally delivering the blow with a weapon you hold in your hand. We suppose this is what pigs refer to as "dirty fighting." All revolutionaries fight dirty in the eyes of the oppressors. The British accused the Minutemen of Lexington and Concord of fighting dirty by hiding behind trees. The U.S. Army accuses the Viet Cong of fighting dirty when they rub a pointed bamboo shoot in infected shit and use it as a land mine. Mayor Daley says the Yippies squirted hair spray and used golf balls with spikes in them against his innocent blue boys. No one ever accused the U.S. of being sneaky for using an airforce in Southeast Asia or the Illinois State Attorney's office of fighting dirty when it murdered Fred Hampton and Mark Clark while they lay in bed. We say: all power to the dirty fighters!

WEAPONS FOR STREET FIGHTING

SPRAY CANS

These are a very effective and educating method of property destruction. If a liberated zone has been established or you find yourself on a quiet street away from the thick of things, pretty up the neighborhood. Slogans and symbols can be sprayed on rough surfaces such as brick or concrete walls that are a real bitch to remove unless expensive sandblasting is used.

THE SLINGSHOT

This is probably the ideal street weapon for the swarms of little Davids that are out to down the Goliaths of Pigdom. It is cheap, legal to carry, silent, fast-loading and any right size rock will do for a missile. You can find them at hobby shops and large sporting goods stores, especially those that deal in hunting supplies. Wrist-Rocket makes a powerful and accurate slingshot for $2.50. The Whamo Sportsman is not as good but half the price. By selecting the right "Y" shaped branch, you can fashion a home-made one by using a strip of rubber cut from the inner tube of a tire as the sling. A few hours of shooting stones at cans in the back yard or up on the roof will make you marksman enough for those fat bank windows and even fatter pigs.

SLINGS

A sling is a home-made weapon consisting of two lengths of heavy-duty cord each attached securely at one end to a leather patch that serves as a pocket to cradle the rock. Place the rock in the pouch and grab the two pieces of cord firmly in your hand. Whirl the rock round and round until gravity holds it firmly in the pouch. When you feel you have things under control, let one end of the cord go and the rock will fly out at an incredible speed. You should avoid using the sling in a thick crowd (rooftop shooting is best). Practice is definitely needed to gain any degree of accuracy.

BOOMERANGS

The boomerang is a neat weapon for street fighting and is as easy to master as the Frisbee. There is a great psychological effect in using exotic weapons such as this. You can buy one at large hobby stores.

FLASH GUNS

Electric battery-operated flash guns are available that will blind a power-crazy pig, thus distracting him long enough to rescue a captured comrade. Check out camping and boating supply stores.

TEAR GAS AND MACE

Personalized tear gas and mace dispensers are available for self-defense against muggers. Well, isn't a pig just an extra vicious mugger?

Tear gas shells are available for 12-gauge shotguns and .38 Special handguns, but it is highly inadvisable to bring guns to street actions. A far better weapon is a specially built projection device that shoots tear gas shells. Raid, Black Flag and other insecticides shoot a 7 to 10 foot stream that burns the eyes. You can also dissolve Drano in water and squirt it from an ordinary plastic water pistol. This makes a highly effective defensive weapon. A phony letterhead of a Civil Defense unit will help in getting heavier anti-personnel weapons of a defensive nature.

ANTI-TIRE WEAPONS

Don't believe all those bullshit tire ads that make tires seem like the Supermen of the streets. Roofing nails spread out on the street are effective in stopping a patrol car. A nail sticking out from a strong piece of wood wedged under a rear tire will work as effectively as a bazooka. An ice pick will do the trick repeatedly but you've got to have a strong arm to strike home. Sugar in the gas tank of a pig vehicle will really fuck up the engine.

KNIFE FIGHTING

Probably one of the most favored street weapons of all time is the good old "shiv," "blade," "toe-jabber" or whatever you choose to call a good sticker. Remembering that today's pig is tomorrow's bacon, it's good to know a few handy slicing tips. The first thing to learn is the local laws regarding the possession of knives. The laws on possession are of the "Catch-22" vagueness. Cops can arrest you for having a small pocket knife and claim you have a concealed and deadly weapon in your possession. Here, as in most cases of law, it's not *what* you are doing, it's *who*'s doing the what that counts. All areas, however, usually have a limit on length such as blades under 4″ or 6″ are legal and anything over that length concealed on a person can be considered illegal. Asking some hip lawyers can help here.

Unfortunately, the best fighting knives are illegal. Switchblades (and stilettos) because they can so quickly spring into operation, are great weapons that are outlawed in all states. If you want to risk the consequences, however, you can readily purchase these weapons once you learn how to contact the criminal underworld or in most foreign countries. If both of these fail, go to any pawnshop, look in the window, and take your choice of lethal, illegal knives.

A flat gravity knife, available in most army surplus and pawn shops would be the best type available in regular over-the-counter buying. Its flat style makes for easy concealment and comfort when kept in a pocket or boot. It can be greased and the rear "heel" of the blade can be filed down to make it fly open with a flick of the wrist. A little practice here will be very useful.

Most inexperienced knife fighters use a blade incorrectly. Having seen too many Jim Bowies slash their way through walls of human flesh, they persist in carrying on this inane tradition. Overhead and uppercut slashes are a waste of energy and blade power. The correct method is to hold the knife in a natural, firm grip and jab straight ahead at waist level with the arm extending full length each time. This fencing style allows for the maximum reach of arm and blade. By concentrating the point of the knife directly at the target, you make defense against such an attack difficult. Work out with this jabbing method in front of a mirror and in a few days you'll get it down pretty well.

UNARMED DEFENSE

Let's face it, when it comes to trashing in the streets, our success is going to depend on our cunning and speed rather than our strength and power. Our side is all quarterbacks, and the pigs have nothing but linemen. They are clumsy, slobbish brutes that would be lost without their guns, clubs and toy whistles. When one grabs you for an arrest, you can with a little effort, make him let go. In the confusion of all the street action, you will then be able to manage your getaway.

There are a variety of defensive twists and pulls that are easy to master by reading a good, easily understandable book on the subject. If a pig grabs you by the wrist, you can break the grip by twisting against his thumb. Try this on yourself by grabbing one wrist with your hand. See how difficult it is to hold someone who works against the thumb. If he grabs you around the waist or neck, you can grab his thumbs or another finger and sharply bend it backwards. By concentrating all your energy on one little finger, you can inflict pain and cause the grip to be broken.

There are a variety of points on the body where a firm amount of pressure skillfully directed will induce severe pain. A grip, for example, can be broken by jabbing your finger firmly between the pig's knuckles. (Nothing like chopped pigknuckles). Feel directly under your chin in back of the jawbone until your finger rests in the V area, press firmly upward and backward towards the center of the head. There is also a very vulnerable spot right behind the ear lobe. Stick your fingers there and see. Get the point!

In addition to pressure points, there are places in the body where a sharp, well-directed whack with the side of a rigidly held palm can easily disable a person. Performed by an expert, such a blow can even be lethal. Try making such a rigid palm and practice these judo chops. The fist is a ridiculous weapon to use. It's fleshy, the blow is distributed over too wide an area to have any real effect and the knuckles break easily. You will have to train yourself to use judo chops instinctively, but it will prove quite worthwhile if you're ever in trouble. A good place to aim for is directly in the center of the chest cavity at its lowest point. Draw a straight line up about six inches starting from your belly button, and you can feel the point. The Adam's

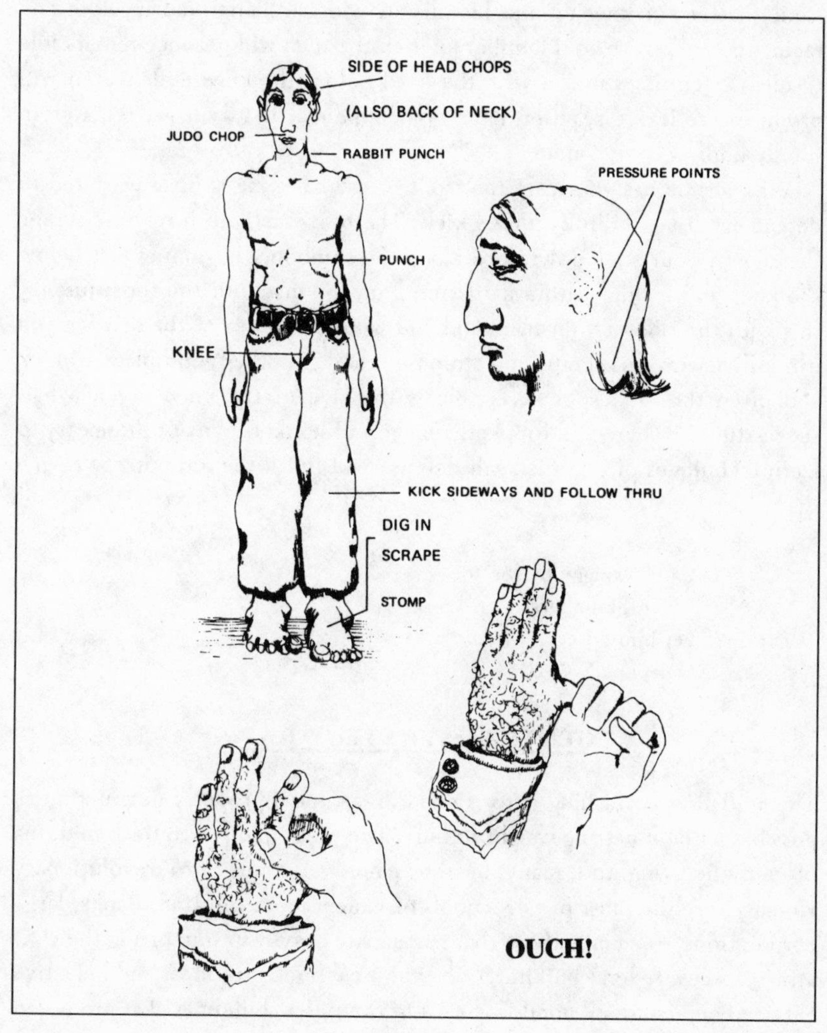

Apple in the center of the neck and the back of the neck at the top of the spinal column are also extremely vulnerable spots. With the side of your palm, press firmly the spot directly below your nose and above your upper lip. You can easily get an idea of what a short, forceful chop in this area would do. The side of the head in front of the ear is also a good place to aim your blow.

In addition to jabs, chops, twists, squeezes and bites, you ought to gain some mastery of kneeing and kicking. If you are being held in close and facing the porker, the old familiar knee-in-the-nuts will produce remarkable results. A feinting motion with the head before the knee is delivered will produce a reflexive reaction from your opponent that will leave his groin totally unprotected. Ouch!

Whether he has you from the front or the back, he is little prepared to defend against a skillfully aimed kick. The best way is to forcefully scrape the side of your shoe downward along the shinbone, beginning just below the knee and ending with a hard stomp on the instep of the foot. Just try this with the side of your hand and you will get an idea of the damage you can inflict with this scrape and stomp method. Another good place to kick and often the only spot accessible is the side of the knee. Even a half successful blow here will topple the biggest of honkers. Any of these easy to learn techniques of unarmed self defense will fulfill the old nursery rhyme that goes:

> Catch a piggy by the toe
> When he hollers
> Let him go
> Out pops Y-O-U

GENERAL STRATEGY RAP

The guideline in trashing is to try and do as much property destruction as possible without getting caught or hurt. The best buildings to trash in terms of not alienating too many of those not yet clued into revolutionary violence, are the most piggy symbols of violence you can find. Banks, large corporations, especially those that participate heavily in supporting the U.S. armed forces, federal buildings, courthouses, police stations, and Selective Service centers are all good targets. On campuses, buildings that are noted for warfare research and ROTC training are best. When it comes to automobiles, choose only police vehicles and very expensive cars such as Lamborghinis and Iso Grifos. Every rock or Molotov cocktail thrown should make a very *obvious* political point. Random violence produces random propaganda results. Why waste even a rock?

When you know there is going to be a rough street scene developing, don't play into the pig's strategy. Spread the action out. Help waste the enemy's numbers. You and the other members of your group should already have a target or two in mind that will make for easy trashing. If you don't have one, setting fires in trash cans and ringing fire alarms will help provide a cover for other teams that do have objectives picked out. Putting out street lights with rocks also helps the general confusion.

After a few tries at trashing, you'll begin to overcome your fears, learn what to expect from both the pigs and your comrades, and develop your own street strategy. Nothing works like practice in actual street conditions. Get your head together and you'll become a pro. Don't make the basic mistake of just naively floating into the area. Don't think "rally" or "demonstration," think "WAR" and "Battle Zone." Keep your eyes and ears open. Watch for mistakes made by members of your gang and those made by other comrades. Watch for blunders by the police. In street fighting, every soldier should think like a general. Workshops should be organized right after an action to discuss the strength and weaknesses of techniques and strategies used. Avoid political bullshit at such raps. Regard them as military sessions. Persons not versed in the tactics of revolution usually have nothing worthwhile to say about the politics of revolution.

46

PEOPLE'S CHEMISTRY

STINK BOMB

You can purchase buteric acid at any chemical supply store for "laboratory experiments." It can be thrown or poured directly in an area you think already stinks. A small bottle can be left uncapped behind a door that opens into the target room. When a person enters they will knock over the bottle, spilling the liquid. Called a "Froines,"by those in the know, an ounce of buteric acid can go a long way. Be careful not to get it on your clothing. A home-made stink bomb can be made by mixing a batch of egg whites, Drano (sodium hydroxide), and water. Let the mixture sit for a few days in a capped bottle before using.

SMOKE BOMB

Sometimes it becomes strategically correct to confuse the opposition and provide a smoke screen to aid an escape. A real home-made smoke bomb can be made by combining four parts sugar to six parts saltpeter (available at all chemical supply stores). This mixture must then be heated over a very low flame. It will blend into a plastic substance. When this starts to gel, remove from the heat and allow the plastic to cool. Embed a few wooden match heads into the mass while it's still pliable and attach a fuse. (You can make a good homemade fuse by dipping a string in glue and then rolling it lightly in gunpowder. When the glue hardens, wrap the string tightly and neatly with scotch tape. This fuse can be used in a variety of ways. Weight it on one end and drop a rock into the tank of a pig vehicle. Light the other end and run like hell.)

The smoke bomb itself is non-explosive and non-flame-producing, so no extreme safety requirements are needed. About a pound of the plastic will produce thick enough smoke to fill a city block. Just make sure you know which way the wind is blowing. Weathermen—women!

CBW

LACE (Lysergic Acid Crypto-Ethylene) can be made by mixing LSD with DMSO, a high penetrating agent, and water. Sprayed from an atomizer or squirted from a water pistol, the purple liquid will send any pig twirling into the Never-Never Land of chromosome damage. It produces an involuntary pelvic action in cops that resembles fucking. Remember when mace runs out, turn to Lace.

How about coating thin darts in LSD and shooting them from a Daisy Air Pellet Gun? Guns and darts are available at hobby and sports shops. Sharpening the otherwise dull darts will help in turning on your prey.

MOLOTOV COCKTAIL

Molotov cocktails are a classic street fighting weapon served up around the world. If you've never made one, you should try it the next time you are in some out-of-the-way barren place just to wipe the fear out of your mind and know that it works. Fill a thin-walled bottle half full with gasoline. Break up a section of styrofoam (cups made of this substance work fine) and let it sit in the gasoline for a few days. The mixture should be slushy and almost fill the bottle. The styrofoam spreads the flames around and regulates the burning. The mixture has nearly the same properties as napalm. Soap flakes (not detergents) can be substituted for styrofoam. Rubber cement and sterno also work. In a pinch, plain gasoline will do nicely, but it burns very fast. A gasoline-kerosene mixture is preferred by some folks.

Throwing, although by far not the safest method, is sometimes necessary. The classic technique of stuffing a rag in the neck of the bottle, lighting and tossing is foolish. Often gas fumes escape from the bottle and the mixture ignites too soon, endangering the thrower. If you're into throwing, the following is a much safer method: Once the mixture is prepared and inside the bottle, cap it tightly using the original cap or a suitable cork. Then wash the bottle off with rubbing alcohol and wipe it clean. Just before you leave to strike a target, take a strip of rag or a tampax and dip it in gasoline. Wrap this fuse in a small plastic baggie and attach the whole thing to the neck of the capped bottle with the aid of several rubber bands. When you are ready to toss, use a lighter to ignite the baggie. Pull back your arm and fling it as soon as the tampax catches fire. This is a very safe method if followed to the letter. The bottle must break to ignite. Be sure to throw it with some force against a hard surface.

Naturally, an even safer method is to place the firebomb in a stationary position and rig up a timing fuse. Cap tightly and wipe with alcohol as before. The alcohol wipe not only is a safety factor, but it eliminates telltale fingerprints in case the Molotov doesn't ignite. Next, attach an ashcan fire cracker (M-80) or a cherry bomb to the side of the bottle using epoxy glue. A fancier way is to punch a hole in the cap and pull the fuse of the cherry bomb up through the hole before you seal the bottle. A dab of epoxy will hold the fuse in place and insure the seal. A firecracker fuse ignites quickly so something will have to be rigged that will delay the action enough to make a clean getaway.

When the firebomb is placed where you want it, light up a non-filter cancerette. Take a few puffs (being sure not to inhale the vile fumes) to get it going and work the unlighted end over the fuse of the firecracker. This will provide a delay of from 5 to 15 minutes. To use this type of fuse successfully, there must be enough air in the vicinity so the flame won't go out. A strong wind would not be good either. When the cancerette burns down, it sets off the firecracker which in turn explodes and ignites the mixture. The flames shoot out in the direction opposite to where you attach the firecracker, thus allowing you to aim the firebomb at the most flammable material. With the firecracker in the cap, the flames spread downward in a halo. The cancerette fuse can also be used with a book of matches to ignite a pool of gasoline or a trash can. Stick the unlighted end behind the row of match heads and close the cover. A firecracker attached to a gallon jug of red paint and set off can turn an office into total abstract art.

Commercial fuses are available in many hobby stores. Dynamite fuses are excellent and sold in most rural hardware stores. A good way to make a homemade fuse is described above under the Smoke Bomb section. By

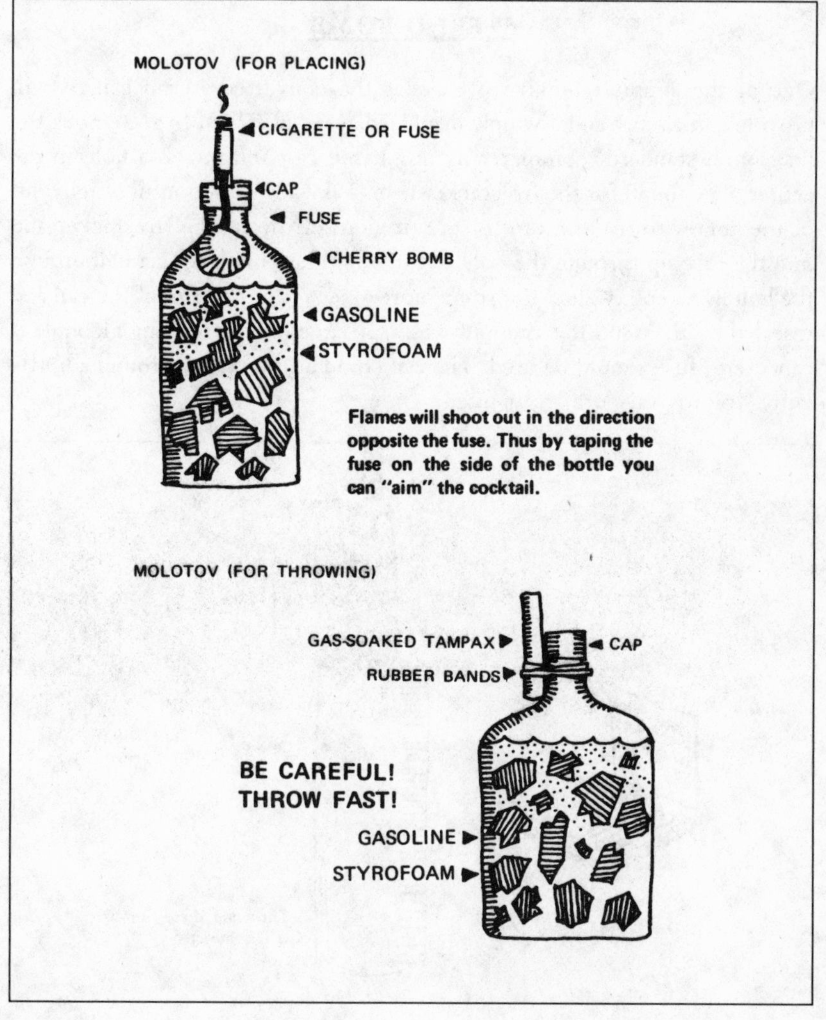

adding an extra few feet of fuse to the device and then attaching the lit cancerette fuse, you add an extra measure of caution. It is most important to test every type of fuse device you plan to use a number of times before the actual hit. Some experimentation will allow you to standardize the results. If you really want to get the job done right and have the time, place several Molotov cocktails in a group and rig two with fuses (in case one goes out). When one goes, they all go . . . BAROOOOOOOOOOM!

STERNO BOMB

One of the simplest bombs to make is the converted sterno can. It will provide some bang and a widely dispersed spray of jellied fire. Remove the lid from a standard, commercially purchased can and punch a hole in the center big enough for the firecracker fuse. Take a large spoonful of jelly out of the center to make room for the firecracker. Insert the firecracker and pull the fuse up through the hole in the lid. When in place, cement around the hole with epoxy glue. Put some more glue around the rim of the can and reseal the lid. Wipe the can and wash off excess with rubbing alcohol. A cancerette fuse should be used. The can could also be taped around a bottle with Molotov mixture and ignited.

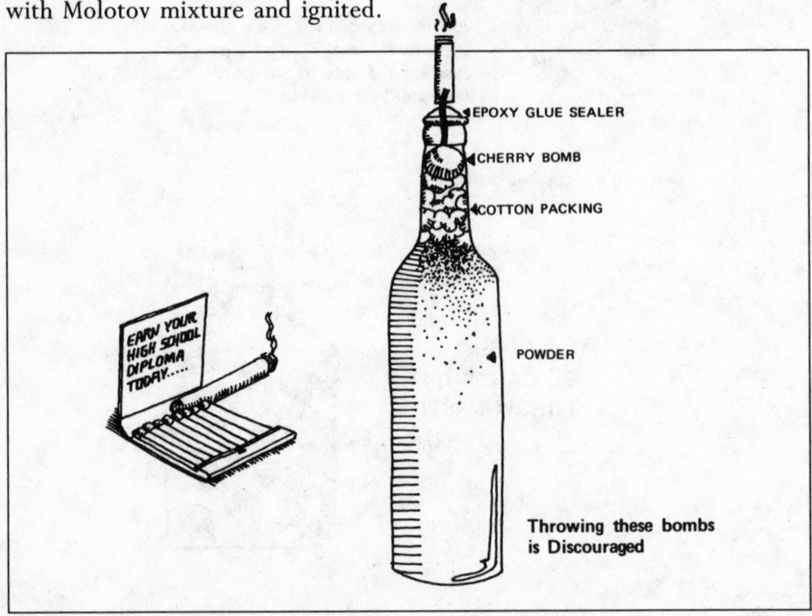

AEROSOL BOMB

You can purchase smokeless gunpowder at most stores where guns and ammunition are sold. It is used for reloading bullets. The back of shotgun shells can be opened and the powder removed. Black powder is more highly explosive but more difficult to come by. A graduate chemist can make or get all you'll need. If you know one that can be trusted, go over a lot of shit with him. Try turning him on to learning how to make "plastics" which are absolutely the grooviest explosive available. The ideal urban guerrilla weapons are these explosive plastic compounds.

A neat homemade bomb that really packs a wallop can be made from a regular aerosol can that is empty. Remove the nozzle and punch in the nipple area on the top of the can. Wash the can out with rubbing alcohol and let it dry. Fill it gently and lovingly with an explosive powder. Add a layer of cotton to the top and insert a cherry bomb fuse. Use epoxy glue to hold the fuse in place and seal the can. The can should be wiped clean with rubbing alcohol. Another safety hint to remember is never store the powder and your fuses or other ignition material together. Powder should always be treated with a healthy amount of respect. No smoking should go on in the assembling area and no striking of hard metals that might produce a spark. Use your head and you'll get to keep it.

PIPE BOMBS

Perhaps the most widely used homemade concussion bombs are those made out of pipe. Perfected by George Metesky, the renowned New York Mad Bomber, they are deadly, safe, easy to assemble, and small enough to transport in your pocket. You want a standard steel pipe (two inches in diameter is a good size) that is threaded on both ends so you can cap it. The length you use depends on how big an explosion is desired. Sizes between 3–10 inches in length have been successfully employed. Make sure both caps screw on tightly before you insert the powder. The basic idea to remember is that a bomb is simply a hot fire burning very rapidly in a tightly confined space. The rapidly expanding gases burst against the walls of the bomb. If they are trapped in a tightly sealed iron pipe, when they finally break out, they do so with incredible force. If the bomb itself is placed in a somewhat enclosed area like a ventilation shaft, doorway or alleyway, it will in turn convert this larger area into a "bomb" and increase the over-all explosion immensely.

When you have the right pipe and both caps selected, drill a hole in the side of the pipe (before powder is inserted) big enough to pull the fuse through. If you are using a firecracker fuse, insert the firecracker, pull the fuse through and epoxy it into place securely. If you are using long fusing either with a detonator (difficult to come by) timing device or a simple cancerette fuse, drill two holes and run two lines of fuse into the pipe. When you have the fuse rigged to the pipe, you are ready to add the powder. Cap one end snugly, making sure you haven't trapped any grains of powder in the threads. Wipe the device with rubbing alcohol and you're ready to blast off.

A good innovation is to grind down one half of the pipe before you insert the powder. This makes the walls of one end thinner than the walls of the other end. When you place the bomb, the explosion, following the line of least resistance, will head in that direction. You can do this with ordinary grinding tools available in any hardware or machine shop. Be sure not to

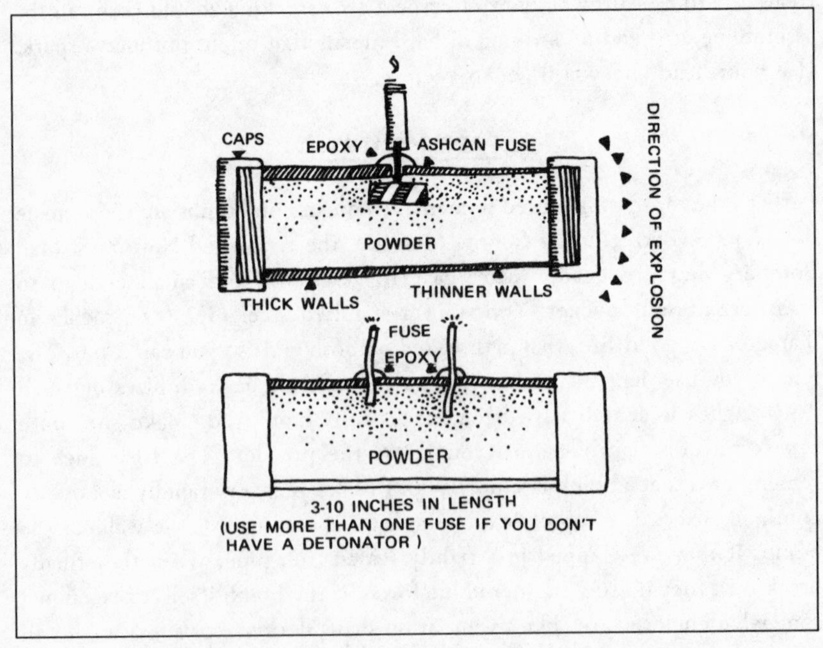

have the powder around when you are grinding the pipe, since sparks are produced. *Woodstock Nation* contains instructions for more pipe bombs and a neat timing device.

GENERAL BOMB STRATEGY

This section is not meant to be a handbook on explosives. Anyone who wishes to become an expert in the field can procure a number of excellent books on the subject. In bombing, as in trashing, the same general strategy in regard to the selection of targets applies. Never use anti-personnel shrapnel bombs. Always be careful in placing the devices to keep them away from glass windows and as far away from the front of the building as possible. Direct them away from any area in which there might be people. Sophisticated electric timers should be used only by experts in demolitions. Operate in the wee hours of the night and be careful that you don't injure a night watchman or guard. Telephone in warnings before the bomb goes off. The police record all calls to emergency numbers and occasionally people have been traced down by the use of a voice-o-graph. The best way to avoid detection is by placing a huge wad of chewed up gum on the roof of your mouth before you talk. Using a cloth over the phone is not good enough to avoid detection. Be as brief as possible and always use a pay phone.

When you get books from companies or libraries dealing with explosives or guerrilla warfare, use a phony name and address. Always do this if you obtain chemicals from a chemical supply house. These places are being increasingly watched by the F.B.I. Store your material and literature in a safe cool place and above all, keep your big mouth shut!

47

FIRST AID FOR STREET FIGHTERS

Without intending to spook you, we think it is becoming increasingly important for as many people as possible to develop basic first aid skills. As revolutionary struggle intensifies, so will the number and severity of injuries increase. Reliance on establishment medical facilities will become risky. Hospitals that border on "riot" areas are used by police to apprehend suspects. All violence-induced injuries treated by establishment doctors might be reported. Knife and gunshot wounds in all states by law must be immediately phoned in for investigation. At times a victim has no choice but to run such risks. If you can, use a phony name, but everyone should know the location of sympathetic doctors.

Chaos resulting from the gassing, clubbing and shooting associated with a police riot also makes personal first aid important. Most demonstrations have medical teams that run with the people and staff mobile units, but often these become the target of assault by the more vicious pigs. Also, in the confusion, there is usually too much work for the medical teams. Everyone must take responsibility for everyone else if we are to survive in the streets. If you spot someone lying unconscious or badly injured, take it upon yourself to help the victim. Immediately raise your arm or wave your Nation flag and shout for a medic. If the person is badly hurt, it is best not to move him, or her, but if there is the risk of more harm or the area is badly gassed, the victim should be moved to safety. Try to be as gentle as possible. Get some people to help you.

WHAT TO DO

Your attitude in dealing with an injured person is extremely important. Don't panic at the sight of blood. Most bloody injuries look far worse than they are. Don't get nervous if the victim is unconscious. If you're not able to control your own fear about treating someone, call for another person. It helps to attend a few first aid classes to overcome these fears in practice sessions.

When you approach the victim, identify yourself. Calmly, but quickly figure out what's the matter. Check to see if the person is alive by feeling for the pulse. There are a number of spots to check if the blood is circulating, under the chin near the neck, the wrists, and ankles are the most common. Get in the habit of feeling a normal pulse. A high pulse (over 100 per minute) usually indicates shock. A low pulse indicates some kind of injury to the heart or nervous system. Massaging the heart can often restore the heartbeat, especially if its loss is due to a severe blow to the chest. Mouth-to-mouth resuscitation should be used if the victim is not breathing. Both these skills can be mastered in a first aid course in less than an hour and should become second nature to every street fighter.

When it comes to dealing with bleeding or possible fractures, enlisting the victim's help as well as adopting a firm but calm manner will be very reassuring. This is important to avoid shock. Shock occurs when there is a serious loss of blood and not enough is being supplied to the brain. The symptoms are high pulse rate; cold, clammy, pale skin; trembling or unconsciousness. Try to keep the patient warm with blankets or coats. If a tremendous amount of blood has been lost, the victim may need a transfusion. Routine bleeding can be stopped by firm direct pressure over the source of bleeding for 5 to 10 minutes. If an artery has been cut and bleeding is severe, a tourniquet will be needed. Use a belt, scarf or torn shirtsleeve. Tie the tourniquet around the arm or leg directly above the bleeding area and tighten it until the bleeding stops. Do not loosen the tourniquet. Wrap the injured limb in a cold wet towel or ice if available and move the person to a doctor or hospital before irreparable damage can occur. Don't panic, though, you have about six hours.

A painful blow to a limb is best treated with an ice pack and elevation of the extremity by resting it on a pillow or rolled-up jacket. A severe blow to the chest or side can result in a rib fracture which produces sharp pains when breathing and/or coughing up blood. Chest X-rays will eventually be needed. Other internal injuries can occur from sharp body blows such as kidney injuries. They are usually accompanied by nausea, vomiting, shock and persistent abdominal pain. If you feel a bad internal injury has occurred, get prompt professional help.

Head injuries have to be attended to with more attention than other parts of the body. Treat them by stopping the bleeding with direct pressure. They should be treated before other injuries as they more quickly can cause shock. Every head injury should be X-rayed and the injured person should be watched for the next 24 hours as complications can develop hours after the injury was sustained. After a severe blow to the head, be on the look-out for excessive sleepiness or difficulty in waking. Sharp and persistent headaches, vomiting and nausea, dizziness or difficulty maintaining balance are all warning signs. If they occur after a head injury, call a doctor.

If a limb appears to be broken or fractured, improvise a splint before moving the victim. Place a stiff backing behind the limb such as a board or rolled-up magazine and wrap both with a bandage. Try to avoid moving the injured limb as this can lead to complicating the fracture. Every fracture must be X-rayed to evaluate the extent of the injury and subsequent treatment.

Bullet wounds to the abdomen, chest or head, if loss of consciousness occurs are extremely dangerous and must be seen by a doctor immediately. If the wound occurs in the limb, treat as you would any bleeding with direct pressure bandage and tourniquet only if nothing else will stop the bleeding.

If you expect trouble, every person going to a street scene should have a few minimum supplies in addition to those mentioned in the section on Demonstrations for protection. A handful of bandaids, gauze pads (4 × 4), an ace bandage (3 inch width), and a roll of ½ inch adhesive tape can all easily fit in your pocket. A plastic bag with cotton balls pre-soaked in water will come in handy in a variety of situations where gas is being used, as will a small bottle of mineral oil. You should write the name, phone number and address of the nearest movement doctor on your arm with a ballpoint pen. Your arm's getting pretty crowded, isn't it? If someone is severely injured, it may be better to save their life by taking them to a hospital, even though that means probable capture for them, rather than try to treat it yourself. However, do not confuse the police with the hospital. Many injured people have been finished off by the porkers, and that's no joke. It is usually better to treat a person yourself rather than let the pigs get them, unless they have ambulance equipment right there and don't seem vicious. Even then, they will often wait until they get two or three victims before making a trip to the hospital.

If you have a special medical problem, such as being a diabetic or having a penicillin allergy, you should wear a medic-alert tag around your neck indicating your condition. Every person who sees a lot of street action should have a tetanus shot at least once in every five years.

Know just this much, and it will help to keep down serious injuries at demonstrations. A few lessons in a first aid class at one of the Free Universities or People's Clinics will go a long way in providing you with the confidence and skill needed in the street.

48

HIP-POCKET LAW

LEGAL ADVICE

Any discussion about what to do while waiting for the lawyer has to be qualified by pointing out that from the moment of arrest through the court appearances, cops tend to disregard a defendant's rights. Nonetheless, you should play it according to the book whenever possible as you might get your case bounced out on a technicality. When you get busted, rule number one is that you have the right to remain silent. We advise that you give only your name and address. There is a legal dispute about whether or not you are obligated under the law to do even that, but most lawyers feel you should. The address can be that of an office if you're uptight about the pigs knowing where you live.

When the pigs grab you, chances are they are going to insult you, rough you up a little and maybe even try to plant some evidence on you. Try to keep your cool. Any struggle on your part, even lying on the street limp, can be considered resisting arrest. Even if you beat the original charge, you can be found guilty of resisting and receive a prison sentence. Often if the pigs beat you, they will say that you attacked them and generally charge you with assault.

If you are stopped in the street on suspicion (which means you are black or have long hair), the police have the right to pat you down to see if you are carrying a weapon. They cannot search you unless they place you under arrest. Technically, this can only be done in the police station where they have the right to examine your possessions. Thus, if you are in a potential arrest situation, you should refrain from carrying dope, sharp objects that can be classified as a weapon, and the names and phone numbers of people close to you, like your dealer, your local bomb factory, and your friends underground.

Forget about talking your way out of it or escaping once you're in the car or paddy wagon. In the police station, insist on being allowed to call your lawyer. Getting change might be a problem, so you should always have a few dimes hidden. Since many cases are dismissed because of this, you'll generally be allowed to make some calls, but it might take a few hours. Call a close friend and tell him to get all the cash that can be quickly raised and head down to the court house. Usually the police will let you know where you'll be taken. If they don't, just tell your friend what precinct you're being held at, and he can call the central police headquarters and find out what court you'll be appearing in. Ask your friend to also call a lawyer which you also should do if you get another phone call. Hang up and dial a lawyer or defense committee that has been set up for demonstrations. The lawyer will either come to the station or meet you in court depending on the severity of the charge and the likelihood you'll be beaten in the station. When massive demonstrations are occurring where a number of busts are anticipated, it's best to have lawyers placed in police stations in the immediate vicinity.

The lawyer will want to know as many details as possible of the case so try and concentrate on remembering a number of things since the pigs aren't going to let you take notes. If you can, remember the name and badge number of the fink that busted you. Sometimes they'll switch arresting officers on you. Remember the time, location of the bust and any potential witnesses that the lawyer might be able to contact.

If you are unable to locate a lawyer, don't panic, the court will assign you one at the time of the arraignment. Legal Aid lawyers are free and can usually do as good a job as a private lawyer at an arraignment. Often they can do better, as the judge might set a lower bail if he sees you can't afford a private lawyer. The arraignment is probably the first place you'll find out what the charges are against you. There will also be a court date set and bail established. The amount of bail depends on a variety of factors ranging from previous convictions to the judge's hangover. It can be put up in collateral, i.e., a bank book, or often there is a cash alternative offered which amounts to about 10% of the total bail.

Your friend should be in the court with some cash (at least a hundred dollars is recommended). For very high bail, there are the bail bondsmen in the area of the courthouse who will cover the bail for a fee, generally not to exceed 5%. You will need some signatures of solid citizens to sign the bail papers and perhaps put up some collateral. For bail over $50,000 check out the possibility of putting up state bonds.

Once you get bailed out, you should contact a private lawyer, preferably one that has experience with your type of case. If you are low on bread, check out one of the community or movement legal groups in your area. It is not advisable to keep the legal aid lawyer beyond the arraignment if at all possible.

If you're in a car or in your home, the police do not have a right to search the premises without a search warrant or probable cause. Do not consent to any search without a warrant, especially if there are witnesses around who can hear you. Without your consent, the pigs must prove probable cause in the court. Make the cops kick in the door or break open the trunk themselves. You are under no obligation to assist them in collecting evidence, and helping them weakens your case.

LAWYERS GROUPS

NATIONAL LAWYERS GUILD

The "Guild" provides various free legal services, especially for political prisoners. If you have any legal hassles, call and see if they'll help you. You can call the one nearest you and get the name of a good lawyer in your area.

AMERICAN CIVIL LIBERTIES UNION

The ACLU is not as radical as the Guild, but will in most instances provide good lawyers for a variety of civil liberty cases such as censorship, denial of permits to demonstrations, and the like. But beware of their tendency to win the legal point while losing the case.

To obtain a complete list of all the ACLU chapters, write: American Civil Liberties Union, 156 5th Avenue, New York, NY 10010, or call them at (212) WA 9-6076.

JOIN THE ARMY OF YOUR CHOICE

The first rule of our new Nation prohibits any of us from serving in the army of a foreign power with which we do not have an alliance. Since we exist in a state of war with the Pig Empire, we all have a responsibility to beat the draft by any means necessary.

First check out your medical history. Review every chronic or long-term illness you ever had. Be sure to put down all the serious infections like mono or hep. Next, make note of your physical complications. When you have assembled a complete list, get a copy of *Physical Deferments* or one of the other draft counseling manuals and see if you qualify. If you have a legitimate deferment, document it with a letter from a doctor.

The next best deal is a Conscientious Objection status (C.O.) or a psychiatric deferment (psycho). The laws have been getting progressively broader in defining C.O. status during the past few years. The most recent being, "sincere moral objections to war," without necessarily a belief in a supreme being. There are general guidelines sent out by the National Office of Selective Service that say it is a matter of conscience. The decision, however, is still pretty much in the hands of the local board. Visit a Draft Counseling Center if you feel you have a chance for this type of story. They'll know how your local board tends to rule. There are still some more cases to be heard by the Supreme Court before objection to a particular war is allowed or disallowed. It is not grounds for deferment as of now.

Psychos are our specialty. Chromosome damage has totally wiped out our minds when it comes to concentrating on killing innocent people in Asia. When you get your invite to join the army, there are lots of ways you can prepare yourself mentally. Begin by staggering up to a cop and telling him you don't know who you are or where you live. He'll arrange for you to be chauffeured to the nearest mental hospital. There you repeat your performance, dropping the clue that you have used LSD in the past, but you aren't sure if you're on it now or not. In due time, they'll put you up for the night. When morning comes, you bounce out of bed, remember who you are, swear you'll never drop acid again and thank everyone who took care of you. Within a few hours, you'll be discharged. Don't be uptight about thinking how they'll lock you up forever cause you really are nuts. The hospitals measure victories by how quickly they can throw you out the door. They are all overcrowded anyway.

In most areas, a one-night stand in a mental hospital is enough to convince the shrink at the induction center that you're capable of eating the flesh of a colonel. Just before you go, see a sympathetic psychiatrist and explain your sad mental shape. He'll get verification that you did time in a hospital and include it in his letter, that you'll take along to the induction center.

When you get to the physical examination, a high point in any young man's life, there are lots of things working in your favor. Here, long hair helps; the army doesn't want to bother with trouble-makers. Remember this even though a tough looking sergeant runs down bullshit about "how they're gonna fix your ass" and "anybody with a trigger finger gets passed." He's just auditioning for the Audie Murphy movies, so don't believe anything he lays down.

Talk to the other guys about how rotten the war in Vietnam is and how if you get forced to go, you'll end up shooting some officers. Tell them you'd like the training so you can come back and take up with the Weathermen.

Check off as many items as can't be verified when given the forms. Suicide, dizzy spells, bed-wetting, dope addiction, homosexuality, hepatitis. Be able to drop a few symptoms on the psychiatrist to back up your story of rejection by a cold and brutal society that was indifferent, from a domineering father that beat you, and mother that didn't understand anything. Be able to trace your history of bad family relationships, your taking to the streets at 15 and eventually your getting "hooked." Let him "pry" things out of you, if possible. Show him your letter if you had the foresight to get one.

Practice a good story before you go for the physical with someone who has already beat the system. If your local board is fucked up, you can transfer to an area that disqualifies almost everyone who wants out, such as the New York City boards. If you can't think of anything you can always get FUCK ARMY tattooed on the outside of the baby finger of your right hand and give the tough sergeant a snappy salute and a hearty "yes sir!" If unfortunately you get hauled in, The Army gives you a life insurance policy. By making Dan Berrigan or Angela Davis the beneficiary you might avoid front-line duty.

CANADA, SWEDEN & POLITICAL ASYLUM

If you've totally fucked up your chances of getting a deferment or already are in the service and considering ditching, there are some things that you should know about asylum.

There are three categories of countries that you should be interested in if you are planning to ship out to avoid the draft or a serious prison term. The safest countries are those with which Amerika has mutual offense treaties such as Cuba, North Korea and those behind the so-called Iron Curtain. The next safest are countries unfriendly to the U.S. but suffer the possibility of a military coup which might radically affect your status. Cambodia is a recent example of a border-line country. Some cats hijacked a ship bound for Vietnam and went to Cambodia where they were granted asylum. Shortly thereafter the military with a good deal of help from the CIA, took over and now the cats are in jail. Algeria is currently a popular sanctuary in this category.

Sweden will provide political asylum for draft dodgers and deserters. It helps to have a passport, but even that isn't necessary since they are required by their own laws to let you in. There are now about 35,000 exiles from the Pig Empire living in Sweden. If you enter as a tourist with a passport, you can just go to the local police station, state you are seeking asylum and fill out a form. It's that simple. They stamp your passport and this allows you to hustle rent and food from the Swedish Social Bureau. It takes six months for you to get working papers that will permit you to get employment, but you can live on welfare until then with no hassle.

Canada does not offer political asylum but they do not support the U.S. foreign policy in Southeast Asia so they allow draft dodgers and deserters to the current tune of 50,000 to live there unmolested. Do not tell the officials at the border that you are a deserter or draft dodger, as they will turn you in. Pose as a visitor. To work in Canada you have to qualify for landed immigration status under a point system.

There will be a number of background questions asked and you have to score 50 points or better to pass and qualify. You get one point for each year of formal education, 10 points if you have a professional skill, 10 points for being between 18–35 years of age, more points for having a Canadian home and job waiting for you, for knowing English or French and a wopping 15 points for having a stereotyped middle class appearance and life-style. Letters from a priest or rabbi will help here. Some entry points are easier than others. Kingsgate, for example, just north of Montana is very good on weekdays after 10:00 P.M.

If you are already in the army, you should find out all you need to know before you ditch. It's best to cross the border while you're on leave as it might mean the difference between going AWOL and desertion if you decide to come back. In any event, no one should renounce their citizenship until they have qualified for landed immigration status as that would classify the person as a non-resident and make it possible for the Canadian police to send you back, which on a few rare occasions has happened.

Because there have been few cases of fugitives from the U.S. seeking political asylum, there is not a clear and simple formula that can be stated. Germany, France, Belgium and Sweden will often offer asylum for obvious political cases, but each case must be considered individually. Go there incognito. Contact a movement organization or lawyer and have them make application to the government. Usually they will let you stay if you promise not to engage in political organizing in their country. In any event if they deport you these countries are good enough to let you pick the country to which you desire to be sent.

We feel it's our obligation to let people know that life in exile is not all a neat deal, not by a long shot. You are removed from the struggle here at home, the problems of finding work are immense and the customs of the people are strange to you. Most people are unhappy in exile. Many return, some turn themselves in and others come back to join the growing radical underground making war in the belly of the great white whale.

49

STEAL NOW, PAY NEVER

SHOPLIFTING

This section presents some general guidelines on thievery to put you ahead of the impulse swiping. With some planning ahead, practice and a little nerve, you can pick up on some terrific bargains.

Being a successful shoplifter requires the development of an outlaw mentality. When you enter a store you should already have cased the joint so don't browse around examining all sorts of items, staring over your shoulder and generally appearing like you're about to snatch something and are afraid of getting caught. Enter, having a good idea of what you want and where it's located.

Camouflage is important. Be sure you dress the part by looking like an average customer. If you are going to rip off expensive stores (why settle for less), act like you have a chauffeur-driven car double parked around the corner. A good rule is dress in the style and price range of the clothes, etc., you are about to shoplift. The reason we recommend the more expensive stores is that they tend to have fewer security guards, relying instead on mechanical methods or more usually on just the sales people. Many salespeople are uptight about carrying out a bust if they catch you. A large number are thieves themselves, in fact one good way to steal is simply explain to the salesclerk that you're broke and ask if you can take something without paying. It's a great way to radicalize shop personnel by rapping to them about why they shouldn't give a shit if the boss gets ripped off.

The best time to work out is on a rainy, cold day during a busy shopping season. Christmas holiday is shoplifter's paradise. In these periods you can wear heavy overcoats or loose raincoats without attracting suspicion. The crowds of shoppers will keep the nosy "can-I-help-you's" from fucking up your style.

Since you have already checked out the store before hitting it, you'll know the store's "blind-spots" where you can be busy without being observed too easily. Dressing rooms, blind alley aisles, and washrooms are some good spots. Know where the cashier's counter is located, where the exits to the street and storage rooms are to be found, and most important, the type of security system in use.

If you are going to snatch in the dressing room, be sure to carry more than one item in with you. Don't leave tell-tale empty hangers behind. Take them out and ditch them in the aisles.

An increasingly popular method of security is a small shoplifting plastic detector attached to the price tag. It says "Do Not Remove" and if you do, it electronically triggers an alarm in the store. If you try to make it out the door, it also trips the alarm system. When a customer buys the item, the cashier removes the detector with a special deactivation machine. When you enter the store, notice if the door is rigged with electronic eyes. They are often at waist level, which means if the item is strapped to your calf or tucked under your hat, you can walk out without a peep from the alarm. If you trigger the alarm either inside the store or at the threshold, just dash off lickity-split. The electronic eyes are often disguised as part of the decor. By checking to see what the cashier does with merchandise bought, you can be sure if the store is rigged. Other methods are undercover pigs that look like casual shoppers, one-way mirrors and remote control television cameras. Undercover pigs are expensive so stores are usually understaffed. Just watch out (without appearing to watch out) that no one observes you in action. As to mirrors and cameras, there are always blind spots in a store created when displays are moved around, counters shifted, and boxes piled in the aisles. Mirrors and cameras are rarely adjusted to fit these changes. Don't get turned off by this security jazz. The percentage of stores that have sophisticated security systems such as those described is very small. If you work out at lunch time, the security guards and many of the sales personnel will be out of the store. Just before closing is also good, because the clerks are concentrating on going home.

By taking only one or two items, you can prevent a bust if caught by just acting like a dizzy klepto socialite getting kicks or use the "Oh-gee-I-forgot-to-pay" routine. Stores don't want to hassle going into court to press charges, so they usually let you go after you return the stuff. If you thought ahead, you'll have some cash ready to pay for the items you've pocketed, if caught. Leave your I.D. and phone book at home before going shopping. People rarely go to jail for shoplifting, most if caught never even see a real cop. Just lie like a fucker and the most you'll get is a lecture on law and order and a warning not to come back to that store or else.

TECHNIQUES

The lining of a bulky overcoat or loose raincoat can be elaborately outfitted with a variety of custom-made large pockets. The openings to these pockets are not visible since they are inside the coat. The outside pockets can be torn out leaving only the opening or slit. Thus you can reach your hand (at counter level) through the slit in your coat and drop objects into the secret pockets sewn into the lining. Pants can also be rigged with secret pockets. The idea is to let your fingers do the walking through the slit in your coat, while the rest of the body remains the casual browser. You'll be amazed at how much you can tuck away without any noticeable bulge.

Another method is to use a hidden belt attached to the inside of your coat or pants. The belt is specially designed with hooks or clothespins to which items can be discreetly attached. Ditching items into hidden pockets requires a little cunning. You should practice before a mirror until you get good at it.

A good idea is to work with a partner. Dig this neat duet. A man and woman walk into a store together looking like a respectable husband and wife. The man purchases a good belt or shirt and engages the salesman in some distracting conversation as he rings up the sale. Meanwhile, back in

the aisle, "wife" is busy rolling up two or three suits. Start from the bottom while they are still on the rack and roll them up, pants and jackets together, the way you would roll a sleeping bag. The sleeves are tied around the roll making a neat little bundle. The bundle is then tucked between your thighs. The whole operation takes about a minute and with some practice you can walk for hours with a good size bundle between your legs and not appear like you just shit in your pants. Try this with a coat on in front of a mirror and see how good you get at it.

Another team method is for one or more partners to distract the sales clerks while the other stuffs. There are all sorts of theater skits possible. One person can act drunk or better still appear to be having an epileptic fit. Two people can start a fight with each other. There are loads of ways, just remember how they do it in the next spy movie you see.

One of the best gimmicks around is the packaging technique. Once you have the target item in hand, head for the fitting room or other secluded

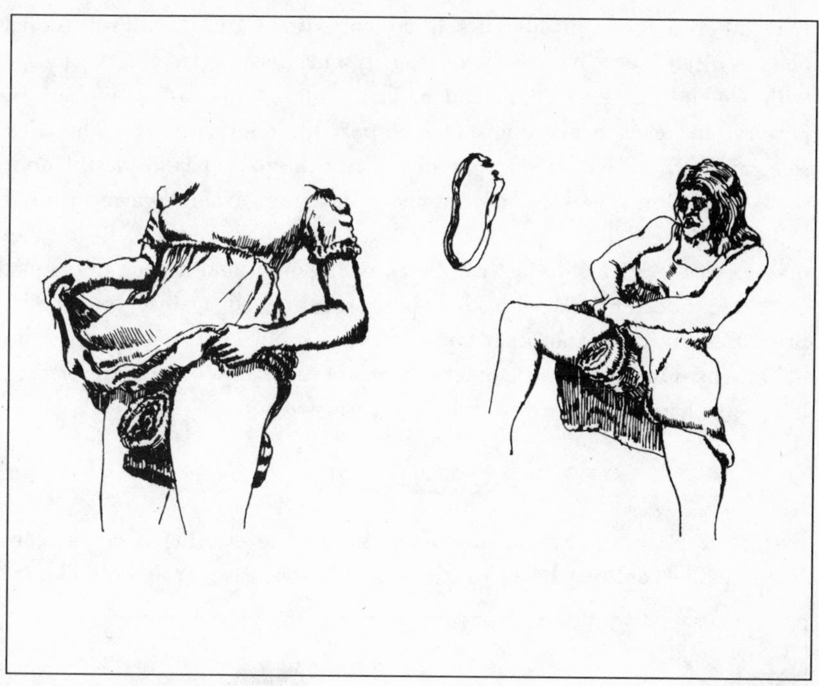

spot. Take out a large piece of gift wrapping and ribbon. Quickly wrap up the item so it will look like you brought it in with you. Many stores have their own bags and staple the cash register receipt to the top of the bag when you make a purchase. Get a number of these bags by saving them if you make a purchase or dropping around to the receiving department with a request for some bags for your Christmas play or something. Next collect some sales receipts, usually from the sidewalk or trash cans in front of the store. Buy or rip off a small pocket stapler for less than a dollar. When you get the item you want, drop it in the bag and staple it closed, remembering to attach the receipt. This is an absolutely perfect method and takes just a few seconds. It eliminates a lot of unsightly bulges in your coat and is good for warm-weather heisting.

A dummy shopping bag can be rigged with a bit of ingenuity. The idea is to make it look like the bag is full when there's still lots of room left. Use strips of cardboard taped to the inside of the bag to give it some body.

Remember to carry it like it's filled with items, not air. Professional heisters often use a "booster box," usually a neatly wrapped empty package with one end that opens upon touch. This is ideal for electrical appliances, jewelry, and even heavy items such as portable television sets. The trick side can be fitted with a spring door so once the toaster is inside the door slams shut. Don't wear a black hat and cape and go around waving a wand yelling "Abracadabra," just be your usual shlep shopper self. If you can manage it, the trick side just can be an opening without a trick door. Just carry the booster box with the open side pressed against your body. Briefcases, suitcases and other types of carrying devices can all be made to hold items. Once you have something neatly tucked away in a bag or box, it's pretty hard to prove you didn't come in with it.

ON THE JOB

By far the easiest and most productive method of stealing is on the job. Wages paid to delivery boys, sales clerks, shippers, cashiers and the like are

so insulting that stealing really is a way of maintaining self-respect. If you are set on stealing the store dry when you apply for the job, begin with your best foot forward. Make what employment agencies call a "good appearance." Exude cleanliness, Godliness, sobriety and all the other WASPy virtues third grade teachers insist upon. Building up a good front will eliminate suspicion when things are "missing."

Mail clerks and delivery boys can work all sorts of neat tricks. When things get a little slow, type up some labels addressed to yourself or to close friends and play Santa Claus. Wrap yourself a few packages or take one that is supposed to go to a customer and put your label over theirs. Blame it on the post office or on the fact that "things get messed up 'cause of all the bureaucracy." It's great to be the one to verbalize the boss's own general feelings before he does when something goes awry. The best on-the-job crooks always end up getting promoted.

Cashiers and sales persons who have access to money can pick up a little pocket change without too much effort, no matter how closely they are watched by supervisors. Women can make use of torn hems to stash coins and bills. Men can utilize cuffs. Both can use shoes and don't forget those secret little pockets you learned about in the last section. If you ring up items on a cash register, you can easily mistake $1.39 for 39¢ or $1.98 for 98¢ during the course of a hectic day. Leave pennies on the top shelf of the cash register and move one to the far right side every time you skip a dollar. That way at the end of the day, you'll know how much to pocket and won't have to constantly be stuffing, stuffing, stuffing.

If you pick up trash or clean up, you can stick all sorts of items into wastebaskets and later sneak them out of the store.

There are many ways of working heists with partners who pose as customers. See the sections on free food and clothing for these. There are also ways of working partnerships on the job. A cashier at a movie theater and a doorman can work out a system where the doorman collects the tickets and returns them to the cashier to sell again.

A neat way to make a large haul is to get a job through an agency as a domestic for some rich slob. You should use a phony identification when you sign up at the agency. Once you are busy dusting the town house, check around for anything valuable to be taken home. Pick up the phone, order all sorts of merchandise, and have it delivered. A friend with a U-haul can help you really clean up.

CREDIT CARDS

Any discussion of shoplifting and forgeries inevitably leads to a rap on credit cards; those little shiny plastic wonder passes to fantasy land that are rendering cash obsolete. There are many ways to land a free credit card. You can get one yourself if your credit is good, or from a friend: report it stolen and go on a binge around town. Sign your name a little funny. Super underworld types might know where you can purchase a card that's not too hot on the black market. You might heist one at a fashionable party or restaurant. If you're a hat check girl at a night club, don't forget to check out pockets and handbags for plastic goodies. The absolute best method is to have an accomplice working in the post office rip off the new cards that are mailed out. They get to know quickly which envelopes contain new credit cards. Since the person never receives the card it never dawns on them to report it stolen. This gives you at least a solid month of carefree spending and your signature will be perfect.

Finally, you can redo a legitimate card with a new number and signature and be sure that it's on no one's "hot list." Begin by removing the ink on the raised letters with any polyester resin cleaner. Next, the plastic card should be held against a flat iron until the raised identification number is melted. You can use a razor blade to shave off rough spots. This combination of razor blade and hot iron, when worked skillfully, will produce a perfect blank card. When the card is smooth as new, reheat it using the flat iron and press an addressograph plate into the soft plastic. The ink can be replaced by matching the original at any stationery store. If this is too hard, you can buy machines to make your own credit cards, which are made for small department stores. Granted, this method is going to require some expertise, but once you've learned to successfully forge a credit card, you can buy every item imaginable, eat fancy meals, and even get real money from a bank.

Whether your credit card is stolen, borrowed or forged, you still have to follow some guidelines to get away without any hassle. Know the store's checking method before you pass the hot card. Most stores have a fifty-dollar limit where they only call upstairs on items costing fifty dollars or more. In some stores it's less. Some places have a Regiscope system that takes your picture with each purchase. You should always carry at least one piece of back-up identification to use with the phony card as the clerk might get suspicious if you don't have any other ID. They can check out a "hot list" that the credit card companies send out monthly, so if you're uptight about anything watch the clerk's movements at all times. If things get tight, just split real quick. Often, even if a clerk or boss thinks it's a phony, they'll OK the sale anyway since the credit card companies make good to the stores on all purchases, legit or otherwise. Similarly, the insurance companies make good to the credit companies and so on until you get to a little group of hard working elves in the basement of the U.S. Mint who do nothing but print free money and lie to everybody about there being tons of gold at Fort Knox to back up their own little forging operation.

50

MONKEY WARFARE

If you like Halloween, you'll love monkey warfare. It's ideal for people uptight about guns, bombs and other children's toys, and allows for imaginative forms of protesting, many of which will become myth, hence duplicated and enlarged upon. A syringe (minus the needle) or a cooking baster can be filled with a dilute solution of epoxy glue. Get the two tubes in a hardware store and squeeze into a small bottle of rubbing alcohol. Shake real good and pour into the baster or syringe. You have about thirty minutes before the mixture gets too hard to use. Go after locks, parking meters, and telephones. You can fuck up the companies that use IBM cards by buying a cheap punch or using an Exacto knife and cutting an extra hole in the card before you return it with your payment. By the way, when you return payments always pay a few cents under or over. The company has to send you a credit or another bill and it screws up their bookkeeping system. Remember, *always* bend, fold, staple or otherwise mutilate the card. By the way, if you ever find yourself in a computer room during a strike, you might want to fuck up the school records. You can do this by passing a large magnet or portable electro-magnet rapidly back and forth across the reels of tape, thus erasing them. And don't miss the tour of the IBM plant, either.

Another good bit is to rent a safe deposit box (only about $7.00 a year) in a bank using a phony name. They usually only need a signature and don't ask for identification. When you get a box, deposit a good size dead fish inside the deposit box, close it up and return it to its proper niche. From then on, forget about it. Now think about it, in a few months there is going to be a hell-of-a-smell from your small investment. It's going to be almost impossible to trace and besides, they can never open the box without your permission. Since you don't exist, they'll have no alternative but to move away. Invest in the Stank of Amerika savings program. Just check out Lake Erie and you'll see saving fish isn't such a dumb idea. If you get caught, tell them you inherited the fish from your grandmother and it has sentimental value.

There are lots of things you can send banks, draft boards and corporations that contribute to pollution via the mails. It is possible to also have things delivered. Have a hearse and flowers sent to the chief of police. We know someone who had a truckload of cement dumped in the driveway of her boss under the fib that the driveway was going to be repaired.

By getting masses of people to use electricity, phones or water at a given time, you can fuck up some not-so-public utility. The whole problem is getting the word out. For example, 10,000 people turning on all their electric appliances and lights in their homes at a given time can cause a black-out in any major city. A hot summer day at about 3:00 PM is best. Five thousand people calling up Washington, D.C. at 3:00 PM on a Friday (one of the busiest hours) ties up the major trunk lines and really puts a cramp in the government's style of carrying on. Call (202) 555-1212, which is information and you won't even have to pay for the call. If you call a government official, ask some questions like "How many kids did you kill today?" or "What kind of liquor do Congressmen drink?" or offer to take Teddy Kennedy for a ride. A woman can cause some real excitement by calling a Congressman's office and screaming "Tell that bastard he forgot to meet Irene at the motel this afternoon."

A great national campaign can be promoted that asks people to protest the presidential election farces on Inauguration Day. When a president says "So help me God," rush in and flush the toilet. A successful Flush for God campaign can really screw up the water system.

If you want to give Ma Bell an electric permanent, consider this nasty. Cut the female device off an ordinary extension cord and expose the two wires. Unscrew the mouthpiece on the phone and remove the voice amplifier. You will see a red and a black wire attached to two terminals. Attach each of the wires from the extension cord to each one from the phone. Next plug in the extension cord to a wall socket. What you are doing is sending 120 volts of electricity back through equipment which is built for only 6 volts. You can knock off thousands of phones, switchboards and bugging devices if all goes right. It's best to do this on the phone in a large office building or university. You certainly will knock out their fuses. Unfortunately, at home your own phone will probably be knocked out of commission. If that happens, simply call up the business office and complain. They'll give you a new phone just the way they give the other seven million people that requested them that day.

Remember, January is Alien Registration Month, so don't forget to fill out an application at the Post Office, listing yourself as a citizen of Free Nation. Then when they ask you to "Love it or leave it," tell them you already left!

51

PIECE NOW

It's ridiculous to talk about a revolution without a few words on guns. If you haven't been in the army or done some hunting, you probably have a built-in fear against guns that can only be overcome by familiarizing yourself with them.

HANDGUNS

There are two basic types of handguns or pistols: the revolver and the automatic. The revolver carries a load of 5 or 6 bullets in a "revolving" chamber. The automatic usually holds the same number, but some can hold up to 14 bullets. Also, in the automatic the bullets can be already packed in a magazine which quickly snaps into position in the handle. The revolver must be reloaded one bullet at a time. An automatic can jam on rare occasions, or misfire, but with a revolver you just pull the trigger and there's a new bullet ready to fire. Despite pictures of Roy Rogers blasting a silver dollar out of the sky, handguns are difficult to master a high degree of accuracy with and are only good at short ranges. If you can hit a pig-size object at 25 yards, you've been practicing.

Among automatics, the Colt 45 is a popular model with a long record of reliability. A good popular favorite is a Parabellum 9 mm, which has the advantage of a double action on the first shot, meaning that the hammer does not have to be cocked, making possible a quick first shot without carrying a cocked gun around. By the way, do not bother with any handgun smaller than a .38 caliber, because cartridges smaller than this are too weak to be effective.

Revolvers come in all sizes and makes, as do automatics. The most highly recommended are the .38 Special and the .357 Magnum. Almost all police forces use the .38 Special. They are light, accurate and the small-frame models are easy to conceal. If you get one, use high velocity hollow pointed bullets, such as the Speer DWM (146 grain h.p.) or the Super Vel (110 grain h.p.). The hollow point shatters on contact, insuring a kill to the not-so-straight shooters. Smith and Wesson makes the most popular .38 Special. The Charter Arms is a favorite model. The .357 Magnum is an extremely powerful handgun. You can shoot right through the wall of a thick door with one at a distance of 20 yards. It has its own ammo, but can also use the bullets designed for the .38. Both guns are about the same in price, running from $75–$100 new. An automatic generally runs about $25 higher.

RIFLES

There are two commonly available types of rifles: the bolt action and the semi-automatic. War surplus bolt action rifles are cheap, and usually pretty accurate, but have a slower rate of fire than a semi-automatic. A semi-automatic is preferable in nearly all cases. The M-1 carbine is probably the best semi-automatic for the money (about $80). It's light, short, easy to handle, and has only the drawback of a cartridge that's a little under-powered. Among bolt actions, the Springfield, Mauser, Royal Enfield, Russian 7.62, and the Lee Harvey Oswald Special, the Mannlicher-Carcano, are all good buys for the money (about $20).

One of the best semi-automatics is the AR-18, which is the civilian version of the military M-16. In general, this is a fantastic gun with a high rate of fire, minimal recoil, high accuracy, light weight, and easy maintenance. If kept clean, it will rarely jam, and the bullet has astounding stopping power. It sells for around $225.

SHOTGUNS

The shotgun is the ideal defensive weapon. It's perfect for the vamping band of pigs or hard-heads that tries to lynch you. Being a good shot isn't that necessary because a shotgun shoots a bunch of lead pellets that spread over a wide range as they leave the barrel. There are two common types: the pump action and the semi-automatic. Single shot types and double-barrel types do not have a high enough rate of fire for self-defense.

The pump action is easy to use and reliable. It usually holds about five shells in a tube underneath the barrel. For self-defense you should use 00 buckshot shells. Shotguns come in various gauges, but you will want the largest commonly available, the 12 gauge. The Mossberg Model 500 A is a super weapon in this category which sells for about $90. When buying one, try to get a shotgun with a barrel as short as possible up to the legal limit of 18 inches. It is easy to cut down a longer barrel, too. This increases the area sprayed.

The semi-automatic gun is not used too much for self-defense, as they usually hold only three shells. With some practice, you can shoot a pump nearly as fast as a semi-automatic, and they are much cheaper.

There are many other good guns available, and a great deal to know about choosing the right gun for the right situation. Reading a little right wing gun literature will help.

OTHER WEAPONS

If you are around a military base, you will find it relatively easy to get your hands on an M-79 grenade launcher, which is like a giant shotgun and is probably the best self-defense weapon of all time. Just inquire discreetly among some long-haired soldiers.

TRAINING

Owning a gun ain't shit unless you know how to use it. They make a hell of a racket when fired so you just can't work out in your den or cellar, except wih a BB gun, which is good in between real practice sessions. Find some friends who served in the military or are into hunting or target-shooting and ask them to teach you the fundamentals of gun handling and safety. If you're over 18, you can practice on one of your local firing ranges. Look them up in the Yellow Pages, call and see if they offer instructions. They are usually pretty cheap to use. In an hour, you can learn the basics you need to know about guns and the rest is mostly practice, practice, just like in the westerns. Contact the National Rifle Association, Washington, D.C. and ask for information on forming a gun club. If you can, you are entitled to great discounts, have no trouble using ranges and get excellent info on all matters relating to weapons.

A secluded place in the country outside city limits makes an ideal range for practicing. Shoot at positioned targets. A good idea is to blow up balloons and attach them to pieces of wood or boxes. Position yourself downstream alongside a running brook. A partner can go upstream and release the balloons into the water. As they rush downstream, they simulate an attacker charging you and make excellent moving targets. Watch out for ricocheting bullets. Have any bystander stand by behind you. A clothesline with a pulley attachment can be rigged up to also allow practice with a moving target.

GUN LAWS

Once you decide to get a gun, check out the local laws. There are federal ones, but they're not stricter than any state ordinance. If you're unsure about the laws, send 75¢ to the U.S. Government Printing Office for the manual called *Published Ordinances: Firearms.* It runs down the latest on all state laws. In most states you can buy a rifle or shotgun just for the bread from a store or individual if you are over 18 years old. You can get a handgun when you can prove you're over 21, although you generally need a special permit to carry it concealed on your person or in your car. A concealed weapon permit is pretty hard to get unless you're part of the establishment. You can keep a handgun in your home, though. It's also generally illegal to walk around with a loaded gun of any type. Once you get the hang of using a gun, you'll never want to go back to the old peashooter.

52

THE UNDERGROUND

Amerika is just another Latin dictatorship. Those who have doubts should try the minimal experience of organizing a large rock festival in their state, sleeping on some beach in the summer or wearing a flag shirt. Ask the blacks what it's been like living under racism and you'll get a taste of the future we face. As the repression increases so will the underground—deadly groups of stoned revolutionaries sneaking around at night and balling all day. As deadly as their southern comrades the Tupamaros. Political trials will only occur when the heavy folks are caught. Too many sisters and brothers have been locked up for long stretches having maintained a false faith in the good will of the court system. Instead, increased numbers have chosen to become fugitives from injustice: Bernadine Dohrn, Rap Brown, Mark Rudd, hundreds of others. Some, including Angela Davis, Father Berrigan and Pun Plamondon have been apprehended and locked in cages, but most roam freely and actively inside the intestines of the system. Their growth leads to persistent indigestion for those who sit at the tables of power. As they form into active isolated cells they make apprehension difficult. Soon the FBI will have a Thousand Most Wanted List. Our heroes will be hunted like beasts in the jungle. Anyone who provides information leading to the arrest of a fugitive is a traitor.

Well fellow reader, what will you do when Rap or Bernadine call up and ask to crash for the night? What if the Armstrong Brothers want to drop some acid at your pad or Kathy Boudin needs some bread to keep on truckin'? The entire youth culture, everyone who smiles secretly when President Agnew and General Mitchell refer to the growing number of "hot-headed revolutionaries," all the folks who hope the Cong wins, who cheer the Tupamaros on, who want to exchange secret handshakes with the Greek resistance movement, who say "It's about time" when the pigs get gunned down in the black community, all of us have an obligation to support the underground. They are the vanguard of our revolution and in a sense this book is dedicated to their courage.

If you see a fugitive's picture on the post office wall take it home for a souvenir. But watch out, because this is illegal. Soon the FBI will be printing all our posters for free. Right on, FBI! Print up wanted posters of the war criminals in Washington and undercover agents (be absolutely sure) and put them up instead. Since the folks underground move freely among us, we must be totally cool if by chance we recognize a fugitive through their disguise. If they deem it necessary to contact you, they will make the first move. If you are very active in the aboveground movement, chances are you are being watched or tapped and it would be foolhardy to make contact. The underground would be meaningless without the building of a massive community with corresponding political goals. People above ground demonstrate their love for fugitives by continuing and intensifying their own commitment.

If the FBI or local subversive squad of the police department is asking a lot of questions about certain fugitives, get the word out. Call your underground paper or make the announcement at large movement gatherings or music festivals; the grapevine will pass the information on to those that need to know.

If you're forced to go underground, don't think you need to link up with the more well-known groups such as the Weathermen. If you go under with some close friends, stick together if it's possible. Build contacts with aboveground people that are not that well known to the authorities and can be totally trusted.

You should change the location in which you operate and move to a place where the heat on you won't be as heavy. A good disguise should be worked out. The more information the authorities have on you and the heavier the charges determine how complete your disguise should be. Only in rare cases is it necessary to abandon the outward appearance of belonging to the youth culture. In fact, even J. Edgar Freako admits that our culture is our chief defense. To infiltrate the youth culture means becoming one of us. For an FBI agent to learn an ideological cover in a highly disciplined organization is relatively easy. To penetrate the culture means changing the way they live. The typical agent would stand out like Jimmy Stewart in a tribe of Apaches.

In the usual case the authorities do not look for a fugitive in the sense of carrying on a massive manhunt. Generally, people are caught for breaking some minor offense and during the routine arrest procedure, their fingerprints give them away. Thus for a fugitive having good identification papers, being careful about violations such as speeding or loitering, and not carrying weapons or bombing manuals become an important part of the security. It is also a good idea to have at least a hundred dollars cash on you at all times. Often even if you are arrestd you can bail yourself out and split long before the fingerprints or other identification checks are completed.

If by some chance you are placed on the "10 Most Wanted List" that is a signal that the FBI are indeed conducting a manhunt. It is also the hint that they have uncovered some clues and feel confident they can nab you soon. The List is a public relations gimmick that Hooper, or whatever his name is, dreamed up to show the FBI as super sleuths, and complement the bullshit image of them that Hollywood lays down. Most FBI agents are southerners who majored in accounting or some other creative field. When you are placed on the List, go deeper underground. It may become necessary to curtail your activities for a while. The manhunt lasts only as long as you are newsworthy since the FBI is very media conscious. Change your disguise, identification and narrow your circle of contacts. In a few months, when the heat is off, you'll be able to be more active, but for the time, sit tight.

IDENTIFICATION PAPERS

An amateur photographer or commercial artist with good processing equipment can make passable phony identification papers. Using a real I.D. card, mask out the name, address, and signature with thin strips of paper the same color as the card itself. Do a neat gluing job. Next, photograph the card using bright overhead lighting to avoid shadows, or xerox it. Use a paper of a color and weight as close to the real thing as you can get. If you use phony state and city papers such as birth certificate or driver's license, choose a state that is far away from the area in which you are located. Have a complete understanding of all the information you are forging. Dates, cities, birthdays and other data are often part of a coding system. Most are easy to figure out simply by studying a few similar authentic cards.

Almost all I.D. cards use one or another IBM Selectric type to fill in the individual's papers. You can buy the exact model used by federal and state agencies for less than $20.00 and install the ball in 5 seconds on any Selectric machine. When you finish the typing operation, sign your new name and trim the card to the size you want. Rub some dirt on the card and bend it a little to eliminate its newness.

Another method is to obtain a set of papers from a close friend of similar characteristics. Your friend can replace the originals without too much trouble. In both cases it might be advisable to get authentic papers using the phonies you have in your possession. In some states getting a license or voting registration card is very easy. Library cards and other supplementary I.D.'s are simple to get. A passport should not be attempted until you definitely have made up your mind to split the country. That way agencies have less time to check the information and you can decide on the disguise to be used for the picture. Unless you expect to get hotter than you are right now, in which case, get it now.

It is wise to have two sets of identification to be on the safe side but *never* have both in your possession at the same time. If you sense the authorities are close to nailing you and you choose to go underground, prepare all the identification papers well in advance and store them in a secure place. Inform no one of your possible new identity.

Before you start passing phony I.D.'s to cops, banks and passport offices, you should have experience with lesser targets so you feel comfortable using them. There are stiff penalties for this if you get caught. A few better methods than the ones listed above exist, but we feel they should not be made this public. With a little imagination you'll have no trouble. Dig!

COMMUNICATION

Living underground, like exile, can be extremely lonely, especially during the initial adjustment period when you have to reshuffle your living habits. Psychologically it becomes necessary to maintain a few close contacts with other fugitives or folks aboveground. This is also necessary if you plan to continue waging revolutionary struggle. This means communication. If you contact persons or arrange for them to contact you, be super cool. Don't rush into meetings. Stay OFF the phone! If you must, use pay phones. Have the contact person go to a prescribed booth at prescribed time. Knowing the phone number beforehand, you can call from another pay phone. The pay phone system is superior to debugging devices and voice scramblers. Even so, some pay phones, that local police suspect bookies use, are monitored.

Keep your calls short and disguise your voice a bit. If you are a contact and the call does not come as scheduled, don't panic. Perhaps the booth at the other end is occupied or the phone you are on is out of order. In New York, the latter is usually true. Wait a reasonable length of time and then go about your business. Another contact will be made. Personal rendezvous should take place at places that are not movement hangouts or heavy pig scenes. Intermediaries should be used to see if anyone was followed. Just groove on a few good spy flicks and you'll figure it all out.

Communicating to masses of people above ground is very important. It drives the MAN berserk and gives hope to comrades in the struggle. The most important message is that you are alive, in good spirits and carrying on the struggle. The communications of the Weathermen are brilliantly conceived. Develop a mailing list that you keep well hidden in case of a bust. You can devise a system of mailing stuff in envelopes (careful of fingerprints) inside larger envelopes to a trusted contact who will mail the items from another location to further camouflage your area of operation. A host of communication devices are available besides handwritten notes and typed communications. Tape recorders are excellent but better still are video-tape cassette machines. You can wear masks, do all kinds of weird theatrical stuff and send the tapes to television stations. At times you might want to risk being interviewed by a newsman, but this can be very dangerous unless you conceive a super plan and have some degree of trust in the word of the journalist. Don't forget a grand jury could be waiting for him with a six months contempt or perjury charge when he admits contact and does not answer their questions.

The only other advice is to dress warm in the winter and cool in the summer, stay high and

Keep on Truckin' . . .

"FREEDOM'S JUST ANOTHER WORD
FOR NOTHIN' LEFT TO LOSE
NOTHIN'
I MEAN NOTHIN' HONEY IF IT AIN'T FREE"

—JANIS JOPLIN

PART FOUR

1981

NEW WRITINGS

1988

53

THE GREAT ST. LAWRENCE RIVER WAR (1981)

I was introduced to the St. Lawrence River in the summer of '76, approaching via the Thousand Island Bridge from the Canadian mainland twenty miles north of Kingston, Ontario. It is the best approach, for rising to the crest of the bridge a passenger's vision is completely filled by hundreds of pine-covered islands. Scattered as nature's stepping stones across the northward rush of the river's swirling waters. Here and there you can pick out a summer camp hidden among the trees. Its location betrayed by a jutting dock and shiny boat. A few islands even boast "Rhineland" castles and mansions, rising in testimony to an opulence that existed a century ago. But for the most part the islands remain wild, inhabited only by rabbits, foxes, badgers, skunks, and deer who had crossed the frozen river some winter before. In the wetlands feed ducks, geese, loons, and the great blue heron. While nesting on land are scores of whippoorwills, woodpeckers, bluejays, martins, swallows, robins, cardinals, orioles, hawks, and hummingbirds.

Reprinted from *Square Dancing in the Ice Age* with permission.

Virtually every northern bird pictured in a guide book can be found here. The waters, considered among the choicest fishing spots in the world, host varieties of bass, perch, carp, and northern pike as well as salmon and occasional sturgeon. Highest on the list: the prized muskelunge or "muskie," fished on long trolling expeditions in the fall. The world-record size for freshwater fish is a 69½-pound muskie boated here just down river from Chippewa Bay near the American mainland. In winter migrating bald eagles, wolves and coyotes can be found feeding at the water pools.

A wonderland of beauty, indeed, it's something of a mystery that such a scenic region, not part of any national park, has endured the ravages of development and pollution.

The river has seen eons of history. It began with the scraping of ice glaciers for millions of years. About twelve thousand years ago a huge gorge 1,200 miles long, in places 10 miles wide and 500 feet deep was created. At first the waters rushed in from the North Atlantic, forming a vast ocean inlet where hordes of whales came to migrate. Gradually the slope of the riverbed shifted and the ocean water rushed out leaving the river as the drain flow for all the Great Lakes. Making it, by volume, the largest river in North America. Indians were, of course, the first inhabitants of the region and attributed great spiritual powers to the river and islands. The Great Spirit, after having given the Indians everything, gave them paradise on the shores of Lake Ontario near the river's source. Upset with constant tribal warfare he gathered up paradise, rose into the sky, but just as the Sky Curtain parted, his blanket opened and paradise tumbled back into the river. This created the "pieces of paradise" known as the Thousand Islands. In Iroquois legend Hiawatha paddled his canoe up this river on his last sojourn to heaven.

The river has always been a great transportation route, although only specially built barges and steamers could make it downriver to Montreal. The chief obstacles being two long stretches of rapids considered among the most beautiful on the continent. One, the LaChine, so named because the early trappers thought it pointed the way to China, supposedly created the illusion of a bubbling wall of water rising straight up into the air for twenty feet. One can only rely on past descriptions because the great rapids along with other "obstacles," including many river towns and islands, are now gone forever.

Our story really begins in the 1950s. At the apex of the American empire, when politicians and engineers allied to steamroll through any public works project that was thought to contribute to the country's imperial power and glory. Corporate need was equated with people need. "What's good for General Motors is good for America," and "Here at General Electric progress is our most important product" were two of the decade's most famous slogans. Flags waved when we bulldozed a swamp. Progress was the bitch goddess of the fifties and to stand in the doorway left one open to charges of heresy or, worse, of giving in to the Russians. The Army Corps of Engineers, by swapping one boondoggle for another stockpiled more than enough congressional votes to firmly stamp its imprint on the landscape.

No project excited the corps more than the idea of connecting the Great Lakes to the Atlantic Ocean. The political machinations both here and in Canada took years and years. Eastern states felt their economies would be ruined; railroad and trucking industries joined them. In all these battles no one mentioned obvious damage to the river, the complete destruction of the unmatchable LaChine Rapids, or the threat to fish and wildlife. Such a thing as an environmental impact statement was not even known. The argument was geographical and as the corps and the Midwest industrialists vote-traded with western mining and lumber interests, a formidable coalition built up. The time-tested argument that finally swayed Congress was the claim of "national security." The corps argued that with the St. Lawrence Seaway in place, ocean-going vessels could be built on Great Lakes ports and utilized in the cold war with the Russians. (Needless to say twenty-five years after the fact no such industry ever developed.)

The seaway was no small feat. Herbert Hoover, himself an engineer, watched over the project as would a patron saint. "Without doubt," he once explained, "this project is the greatest engineering accomplishment in the history of man." It was called upon completion "the Eighth Wonder of the World."

The figures are staggering. Twenty-five thousand workers employing specifically designed giant earth loaders moved 250 million cubic yards of earth and rock. That's enough to cover all of Manhattan with about twelve feet of dirt. Twenty miles of earth dikes, some fifty feet high, were constructed. Water basins, the largest of which covered 44,000 acres, were dug out. The Eisenhower Locks at Massena were built as were two giant dam-power plant complexes. One, the Moses-Saunders Dam, being the third largest in the world. In addition there were bridges, highways, and completely new communities.

Of course, a price was paid. Towns were destroyed. Whole islands demolished. In all ten thousand people were forced off their land. Indians fought land agents. Bulldozers caved in kitchen walls, while families, believing it would never happen, were eating at the table. A fisherman, seeing that a favorite fishing hole had been destroyed, threw himself into the river to die. Disappointments were many.

The seaway was sold to New York under false pretenses. River towns of just a few thousand were assured aid that never materialized. Economic growth was expected to occur from the increase in ship traffic. There were predictions that some towns would increase one-hundred-fold. Of course, the contrary took place. But almost the entire work force was from out of state. When the project was completed, the workers returned home. Ocean vessels or "salties" proved capable of traversing the full length of the seaway without pulling in for repairs or fuel. The project single-handedly bankrupted the rail industry in northern New York. The population of the towns decreased as unemployment rose and became chronic. Massena, which was touted as a future "Pittsburgh of the north," today has but a few thousand people.

Yet New York wasn't the only loser. The American taxpayer also took a loss. The plan was to charge shippers tolls that would pay the complete bill. Department of Transportation officials repeatedly assured Congress the seaway would pay for itself within ten years, thereafter showing a continuous profit. But there were no profits. Midwest shippers still seemed to prefer the cheaper Mississippi-Gulf route while Canada made it attractive for the grain industry to use its nationalized railroad system.

In twenty-one years of operation the seaway has appeared in the black only once. In the past five years the overall tonnage increase has been a dismal .05 percent. Last year a 10 percent decline occurred. Recently Canadian Parliament canceled an $841 million debt and a similar bill sits in the U.S. House to defray $122 million in unpaid loans. Last year a staunch supporter of the seaway in the fifties, the Chicago *Tribune*, was reluctantly forced to conclude, in an editorial titled "The Seaway's Unmet Promise," that things had not gone according to plan, and Chicago had been one of the ports expected to reap the greatest benefits. Of course, the Army Corps of Engineers is not an organization prone to admitting mistakes. Prodded on chiefly by U.S. Steel, which does benefit by the waterway, the corps reasoned that the seaway did not turn a profit because it closed down for four months a year due to ice conditions. This interruption of service caused huge stockpiling, making seaway transportation undesirable. The answer lay in a program called winter navigation, breaking up the ice by means of a variety of as yet untested mechanical means. This would be no mean accomplishment. The St. Lawrence-Great Lakes transportation system is some 2,400 miles long. The winters are bitter cold. Today, as I write this, the ice in front of our house is frozen two feet solid, the temperature is below zero. At Tibbets Point, where the river begins, the ice during spring breakup can get thirty feet thick.

Of course, the corps *really* had another project even closer to its heart than winter navigation. Once year-round traffic could be guaranteed, the Eisenhower locks, already antiquated, could be replaced with larger chambers and twinned to allow two-way traffic. Then when the river was channeled even deeper, the whole system could handle supertankers. The corps thinks not small potatoes. They are unquestionably the most gung-ho, can-do organization in the entire federal bureaucracy. If the money were there, the corps would move mountains from Colorado to Iowa. Theirs is not to reason why, theirs is to submit the bill and try. The bill for winter navigation—a cool $2.5 billion. For the supertanker project about $20 billion. In other words, about $500 per American, with Canadians kicking in even more. Then the first fifty years of maintenance would equal this initial outlay, making this easily the most expensive engineering project in history—fifty times the cost of the entire original seaway. The corps moves like a Supreme Being. It doesn't build, it creates. Its 45,000 public relations experts, lawyers, and contractors directed by a few hundred army brass at the top are almost unbeatable in the field. Almost.

Of course, back then in '76 I knew nothing of all this. Being a city boy *river* was just a word in a banjo song. Thousand Islands was a salad dressing. And the Army Corps of Engineers just went around rescuing flood victims. Johanna, my running mate since almost the beginning of my underground odyssey, had brought me here from Montreal. Her family had, as the DAR certificate on the wall attested to, lived in the region for seven generations. Their cottage, right on the riverbank, had been built by her great-grandmother. Wellesley Island, about the size of Manhattan, has but three thousand residents, only seven hundred in coldest winter. Fineview, our town, boasts all of eighty-seven people, with only thirty of those toughing out the coldest four months. We live in downtown Fineview, diagonally across from the post office. The place where townfolk gather each morning to talk about the weather. An important activity because forecasts from the distant TV and radio stations rarely applied to the islands. Island weather is unique and often troublesome. Windstorms with gales up to sixty mph. Torrential rains. Waves up to six feet. Fog so dense it's impossible to navigate a boat. In winter there are white-on-white snowstorms where you cannot see your extended hand. Snow piles fifteen feet high and helicopter airlifts of food are sometimes needed. Weather is accepted here even more than death and taxes. The islands have made the people individualists. The weather has made them rugged. For eight months each year the air is filled with the sound of rebuilding. They say nothing lasts forever; up here they say nothing lasts ten years. So you learn how to use a hammer and saw, to lay in a foundation, or recrib a dock. It is part and parcel of river life. The people are hard-working and extremely conservative. Democrats are practically an endangered species.

It fit my purpose to busy myself on badly needed house repairs. The work kept me away from a great deal of socializing. I needed so much help in my carpentry apprenticeship, I asked far more questions than I answered. Slowly I was becoming absorbed into a world unto its own. Of course, I never forgot the great secret of my life when each morning I'd walk past the town's Hall of Justice. Here, rowdies who had disturbed the peace over at the state park or would-be smugglers bringing who knows what in from Canada were brought for booking. Judge Kleinhans would be summoned to hold court and set bail. Serious offenders were packed off to Watertown in state trooper cars affectionately dubbed "Tijuana Taxis" because of the gaudy blue and yellow colors. I always felt someday I would be handcuffed and dragged across the road, dogs barking; kids, including my own, screaming; Mrs. Jerome, our next-door neighbor, having a heart attack on the steps we share. That image burned in my mind a thousand times. The law was literally across the street, so I never forgot what it would mean to make a mistake.

We were not actually "natives" of Fineview, since we fled the cold to hunt up jobs, but on the other hand we were not summer residents either. As soon as the ice broke we returned to the house, staying at times well into December, huddled around the fireplace in our long johns, rigging up heat lamps and insulation so we could still pump water from the river. The first two years I built new steps, reshingled the roof, installed a new water heater, and built a counter in the old-fashioned kitchen. The most ambitious project was a mammoth floating dock, which the river took all of fifteen minutes to sweep from its mooring. Determination and neighborly help combined in the construction of an even more permanent dock. Dick-Dock II. Massive rock cribs were sunk in the river and every inch of Johanna's forty feet of shoreline used to create an L-shaped dock and harbor. Hardly an ornamental plaything, a good dock is essential to island life. We traveled by boat more often than car—to do laundry, shopping, and to party with our fellow river rats at the local bars and dance halls. Returning in the summer of '78, I began to work to correct for winter ice shifting and to finish off the staving and decking. The residents of Fineview, prizing hard work, began to accept me, but still after more than two years I had yet to even volunteer a last name. I was just Johanna's friend Barry. I worked in the movies as a scriptwriter or something equally exotic. After four years of being a fugitive I had learned how to make friends without having to explain much.

In July, just as I was nailing down the last of the decking, Steve Taylor boated by and called out that I could forget about the dock, everything was going to be destroyed—the islands, the shoals, the boathouses. "Read this," he said, tossing a little-known government report my way.

I retired inside and plunged into the study. Local scientists of the New York Department of Environmental Conservation had drawn up an estimate of the environmental impact rising out of a demonstration test being proposed for the coming winter. Through a combination of ice breakers and log booms, an ice-free corridor fifteen miles long would be maintained. This test would demonstrate the feasibility of winter navigation. Plowing through the data it was easy to determine that something sounding so simple and harmless on the surface was, in fact, spelling out a second and final step of the river's destruction (the first being the seaway itself). Watering pools for the endangered bald eagle would be destroyed. Aquatic life chains and wetlands would be ruined. The waves of the test ship passing under ice would magnify, ripping apart shorelines, causing great erosion. The river's fast current would be deliberately slowed to maintain a stable ice cover. This would cause great flooding all the way back and into Lake Ontario. Increasingly the lake has become a chemical dumpsite for PCB, mirex, mercury, and other toxic wastes. Mechanical intervention on a scale the test proposed would release great quantities of imbedded chemical wastes into the water. Most river towns drew drinking water from the river. A 15 percent loss of hydropower was predicted. One didn't have to be a genius to project these findings to a winter navigation program up and down the entire river. Corps figures showed 94 million cubic yards of river bed were to be drained or dynamited from the U.S. side alone. The river would end up little more than a year round barge canal. A disaster!

I called Johanna upstairs. "Unless *we* act, the river is doomed," I said. "The Army Corps of Engineers will bully their way in here. The people are not ready to fight the system." I told her what it was like taking on segregation in the South, organizing against the Vietnam War. The enemies one made attacking the power structure. I was convinced joining this battle would mean I would be caught. Yet the arguments against the project seemed so strong. How could I stand on the shore and watch corps engineers wire up the small islands across the way for demolition? I had listened to old-timers in the bars talk of how they had heard the explosions and watched whole islands float downriver during the fifties. They had watched and cried; now they were alcoholics. "A six-thousand-year-old river," I thought, "and the last twenty-five years have been its worst." My fate was fixed. The rest of the night we spent shaping our identity. Of the twenty or so names I had used as aliases not a one had significance—wallpaper names I called them, easily forgotten. No stories. Mr. and Mrs. Barry Freed sounded respectable. At first I missed the significance of the name.

In August the corps would come to nearby Alexandria Bay for a public hearing; we would use the occasion to announce the organization to the community. We began with small meetings on the front lawn. I remember it well. "Bring back the sixties," someone exclaimed. "Gee, it would be great if we had Rennie Davis here," said another. Inside, way inside, I nodded agreement. We named the group Save the River! Names were very important. Best verb first. *What* you want people to do. "Shouldn't we have the word *committee*?" *Committee* is a bore. People want excitement, charisma. "What about St. Lawrence?" No, keep it simple. Everyone knows the river. Better for a name to raise a question than give an answer. Questions encourage involvement and involvement is what makes a citizens action group. I wrote an ad for the local paper, *The Thousand Island Sun*. In time I would be writing weekly articles for them. People made sails announcing: No To Winter Navigation, and boats toured the islands. We formed telephone trees. When someone complained about how high our first phone bill was, I lectured how our allies as well as enemies were "out there." When the bill got ten times as big we would be on the road to winning. Skepticism ran high. Either "it wasn't going to happen here" or "it was inevitable" were the prevailing attitudes. Oddly, there are people who can entertain both positions simultaneously. The committee pushed ahead.

That first public hearing was quite historic for our community. Usually these hearings draw thirty to forty people who have nothing better to do that day. The corps, which legally is supposed to be gathering facts and sentiment, instead uses the occasions to propagandize for its projects. We packed an overflow crowd of six hundred into the school auditorium. There were signs saying "Ice Is Nice" and "Army Go Home" but in general the tone was polite.

After the army slide presentation showing winter navigation in a positive light and the ease with which it was being introduced on the upper Great Lakes, the audience had their turn. The corps was quick to learn it was trying to sell iceboxes to Eskimos. People were extremely articulate, as farmers, marina owners, bartenders, school teachers, teenagers, folks out of work rose to the challenge. Economic-environmental battles are usually lost in a maze of complicated data and terminology. To successfully oppose winter navigation we eventually had to become proficient in subjects like water-resource economics, cost-benefit analysis, water level prediction, aquatic life cycles. It would take twenty minutes alone to describe just how the corps intended winter navigation to work. Within a few months we would have work-study sessions in which we searched for corps errors in a stack of literature at least three feet high. But in this our first confrontation the arguments came from the heart. The people of Grindstone Island, certainly one of the most rugged communities in the United States, wanted to know how they were to drive their pickup trucks across the river with an open channel. The corps' answer just about said their community was finished. Someone had taken the trouble to study the corps' predictions of water level changes over the past one hundred years and found they had been wrong 85 percent of the time. One of the slides showed a man standing next to a ship traversing a channel in the ice. "See how calm that man is," said the army PR guy. Much to his surprise the man was in the audience. "Calm? I was never so scared in my life. It was like an earthquake." He went on to detail the tons of vegetation, dead fish, and debris the ship's wake had hurled on the riverbanks.

Probably our biggest concern was oil spills. U.S. Coast Guard Marine Safety Office statistics count fifty-six oil spills in our waters since 1973. The worst happened in the summer of '76, when 300,000 gallons of crude oil poured out of a broken NEPCO tanker. Damage ran to the millions. Piles of dead fish and birds were everywhere. Ugly scars can still be seen along the river. The corps was now trying to assure us this would never occur in the winter but there were no believers. No technology to clean up an oil spill locked under ice exists, and none is likely to be developed.

After that hearing, Save the River was on the map. People meeting in the street would say just that: "Save the River!" like you'd say "Right on!" or "How's it goin'?" Barrooms carried donation jugs. Snack shops put up posters. Everybody sold the popular blue heron T-shirt Johanna designed. In all we relate to thirty-two river communities spread out along a fifty-mile course. Ten percent of our membership is Canadian. Early opponents who saw us as radicals or obstructionists were blown away by our overwhelming support. Renegade scientists long suspicious of the project let us know they would help. At Syracuse University, Steve Long, an economist, explained how the corps used and misused figures to prove feasibility. In the end predicted economic losses would help us win valuable allies. We constantly fought the label "an environmental group" in an effort to gain more legitimacy. We published an eight-page booklet breaking down the material into layman's terms. The booklet was discussed in classrooms, at Bible study groups, in bars and pharmacies, everywhere.

The first office was right in our back room. I was venturing into the domain of the northern Wasp. A soft-spoken conservative bird appreciative of good manners and highly respectful of institutions. We had to convince people it wasn't rude to protest. The harshest curse to cross my public lips was "Chrimis!"

I gave speeches at fishermen's banquets, church suppers, high schools, universities, just about anywhere I'd get invited. I was a guest of several radio shows and even a few television spots venturing as far as Syracuse to stage a press conference. Once there was a scare as one of the scientists told a close friend Barry might be Abbie Hoffman. Within an hour, I was out on Route 81, hitchhiking out of the area. A later telephone conversation convinced me it was a lucky hunch and I returned. But still a lucky hunch by a former marine captain in Vietnam.

Probably the most awkward speech I gave that year was to the Jefferson County Board of Supervisors. I was slotted in between the American Legion Post and the Boy Scouts. We failed in getting their support, but several local Chamber of Commerce people heard the speech on radio and drew up endorsements for Save the River. Support also came from the St. Lawrence County Board and several town councils. Our group was quickly gaining a broad-based respectability. We sent delegations to monitor Winter Navigation Board meetings in Baltimore and were quick to point out that not a single decision maker lived closer than within five hundred miles of the river. We lobbied the railroad and trucking industries and established contacts with conservation groups along the Great Lakes.

With all this local support, it was time to pressure Albany. By playing one department against another we were able to break through the bureaucratic crust, and within a few days of contact our material was on the governor's desk. A telegram of support followed, which I read to a panel of startled corps officials at a meeting in Ogdensburg. Hugh Carey's endorsement had given our group some real clout. He was to watch over our development during the next few years. You can imagine my surprise when later I received a personal letter from him saying, "I want to thank you for your leadership in this important issue, and for your sense of public spirit." I never showed the letter to anyone, but I didn't throw it away.

The only time I used Abbie's contacts was in the search for the ideal lawyer. Environmental law is a relatively new course of study and it's still far easier to find lawyers willing to alibi chemical dumping or other industrial atrocities than to find advocates for citizens' groups. The search for competent counsel narrowed to the East, finally settling on Irv Like from Babylon, New York. He had successfully fought attempts to build a road through Fire Island, had represented Suffolk County in an off-shore oil drilling suit, and had authored New York State's Environmental Bill of Rights. Suffolk County was almost as conservative as our neck of the woods. It had the same tensions between summer and winter people. It had high unemployment. After several meetings and phone calls, I realized we had lucked out by snaring a brilliant strategist.

Late that year a delegation of us went to Albany and got a $25,000 commitment from the Department of Transportation to hire John Carroll of

Penn State, one of the four experts on water resource economics willing to bite the hand that feeds them.

Carroll's colleague Robert Braverman, at the University of Wisconsin, had just uncovered a $1.5 billion error as well as fictitious reporting in developing the cost/benefit ratio of the Tennessee-Tombigbee Canal project. He fed us the valuable information that the same Chicago accounting firm, A. T. Kierney Corp., had worked up the figures for winter navigation. *Sports Illustrated*'s staff ecologist, Bob Boyle, wrote an exposé regarding the promise of $50 million in award grants for U.S. Fish and Wildlife to monitor the project if they would drop their major arguments. If you're battling a boondoggle, you are safe in assuming a scandal lurks in the weeds. We raised such a holler.

The winter tests were postponed but work still intensified on the upper Great Lakes. Steering committee members went to Washington to testify before Congress. Rick Spencer carried most of the weight, parrying the thrusts of Representative James Oberstar, U.S. Steel's pointman. Congressman Robert McEwen introduced me and I added to the testimony. Later there was the ritual picture-taking by the congressman's photographer.

That spring and summer '79, a Clayton activist, Karen Nader-Lago, became our office manager as we moved to Alexandria Bay, then to Clayton. Housewives; carpenters; Fran Purcell, then teacher at one of the few one-room schoolhouses left in the country; Rick Spencer, a merchant seaman; small businessmen; farmers; landowners; boat builders were the type of people most active. Our first River Day was a big success, with marathons, hot-air balloon races, and some 3,500 people lighting candles in a night vigil celebrating the river.

Carroll's report was completed and after boiling down the essence winter navigation warranted no tax money from New York and would end up costing the state $100 million to $150 million in lost revenues annually. We now had the ammunition we needed, and we lobbied for Senator Daniel Patrick Moynihan, who held the pivotal seat on the Senate Environment and Public Works Committee, to hold field hearings in our area.

Up to this point we had been extremely successful. The postponement of demonstration tests resulted after a record number of Save-the-River inspired letters had been received at the corps district office. Publicity in the *New York Times* and on ABC's *20/20* had gained national attention for a project difficult to justify to a national taxpaying audience. Moynihan could prove to be our greatest ally.

We chose from a flotilla of antique boats to guide visitors around the islands. We spent hours deciding the boat to fit each personality. Moynihan was outfitted to a turn-of-the-century paddle boat. That night I worked on my speech. It would take about twenty minutes and be aimed at the people who attended, as much as at Moynihan. His staff predicted about one hundred would attend but we knew the community by now. We had established the river as a deeply personal cause for everyone who used it. We were not surprised when close to nine hundred people showed up. After a string of local politicians had their say, it was my turn. I was sweating right through my shirt and jacket. There was polite applause and TV cameras up from Syracuse whirled away. I was sure the police would charge up the aisle and drag me away. But that was not to be the day. The speech went well. The crowd rose to its feet and applauded. Moynihan, sitting directly opposite, not more than twenty feet away, looked at me and said, "Now I know where the sixties have gone." Way, way inside where Abbie lived I fainted. Then he said, "Everyone in New York State owes Barry Freed a debt of gratitude for his organizing ability," and complimented other committee workers as well.

We stayed on good terms with Moynihan's office. By now we felt pretty secure along the river; what troubled us was the work being done on the upper Great Lakes. "Someday we'll be surrounded," we reasoned. Congress had already spent $30 million on winter navigation. That fall and the next year we tried to expand the scope of the committee. Nuclear wastes were being transported from Canada across the bridge. We protested. The shippers chose a bridge farther downstream with less resistance.

In the spring of 1980 the corps, at the insistence of Congress, deleted all requests for authorization and funds for work on the St. Lawrence River.

Environmental groups from all over the country called to congratulate us. They said the corps had never before been beaten without a long court battle. River Day was succeeding in resurrecting a love for the river not seen since the twenties. We uncovered chemical dumping sites leaking into nearby tributaries. We joined the Akwesasne Native Americans living on Cornwall Island in their protest over excessive fluoride dumping by the aluminum companies that use the river as a sewer. We sponsored a congressional debate on river-related issues and the statements made it apparent we had become a serious political force. We began to fight local power brokers insistent on building an amusement park at the river's gateway. On the last issue, we were a house divided. When we finally decided to fight, the horse had already left the barn.

After a speech against the amusement park to the town zoning board last summer we adjourned to the sidewalk. Chairman Vincent Dee of the Bridge Authority, Ralph Timmerman, our town supervisor, board members like Buggy Davis, who lent me his roller for the lawn, were there. So was the sheriff's patrol. About thirty people milling about. John Quinn, a customs agent on the border was telling me how much he agreed with the speech. . . . "Okay, Barry, so we lose this battle, tell me one thing, what the hell are we gonna do when everybody finds out you're *Abbie Hoffman*." "Oh, John, you really got a sense of humor," I said making light of what he had just said. Inside I keep thinking how loud it sounded. I was convinced everyone had heard. Maybe they didn't. Maybe I was wrong. Maybe they don't know Abbie Hoffman. Maybe. Maybe. Fugitives can "maybe" themselves into the nuthatch.

I decided that night to return and face the charges. The kid was packed off early. We rushed to complete the ongoing house repairs. I would have rather kept the story quiet but as soon as I hit New York City my face would have been recognized and broadcasted to the world. Better to tell it to as many people as possible up front. The choice was between *20/20* and *60 Minutes*, and for a variety of reasons ABC seemed the best choice. A team of about twenty-five local friends and five city friends worked with me. Telling Barry's friends was quite an experience. One guy cried. Karen, the office manager, just kept saying, "Nope, nope, nope." She had once quoted Abbie Hoffman to me. Karen's husband, Greg, kept saying, "Is that you? I've been wondering where you were for years." Dege, the young businessman who was inches from swinging the deal to have Woodstock II up here, was stunned. Of course, to some people I had to explain who Abbie was. It didn't matter, to them I'd always be Barry.

Well, Barbara Walters came and went. As did the hundreds of newspersons who followed in her wake. One of our neighbors counted thirty-seven interviews. The tour boats now point out the house and tell the story on loudspeakers. Tourists take photos and like to sit on the bench where Barbara Walters rubbed her tushy.

Nothing quite like this has happened in Fineview since the glaciers hit town. I've been back five times since. Frankly, I don't like being anyplace or anybody else. The committee's membership has grown to 2,200 members. The New York *Post* sent a reporter to find locals willing to bad-mouth me. After two days he came up empty-handed and went home. The local newspapers still call me Barry Freed, though I fear that may change.

In July we're sponsoring a national conference for all river lovers, with workshops, singers, speeches. We hope to have the St. Lawrence River included in Phillip Burton's (D. Calif.) protective legislation for scenic rivers. Of the fifteen largest rivers in the entire world, the St. Lawrence is the cleanest, and one glimpse of its beauty will convince even the most cynical of urban dwellers that here is a treasure not to be surrendered without a fight.

The Army Corps of Engineers has halted working on the lakes for a year of tests and study. They've invested a lot in this program and procorporation cabinet appointments like James Watt are bound to encourage them. Look at any map and you'll see we're the bottleneck in some engineer's grand fantasy. The corps is not an agency that rolls over and dies. For sure, they'll be back. When they do, they'll find us alive and well. Twice as strong. Twice as smart. And twice as many. For me the war has just begun. I can't wait to return home.

—MARCH 1981

54

THE CRIME OF PUNISHMENT (1981)

American prisons are exactly halfway between Sweden and Argentina. For Jack Henry Abbott, prison was a lot closer to Argentina than most Americans would choose to believe. At thirty-seven, with the exception of a nine-and-a-half-month respite, he has spent his entire life since the age of twelve behind bars. It was during that respite that he took part in a bank robbery—his only serious outside crime. Inside, he stabbed another prisoner. Through the long twenty-five years, he endured strip cells, blackout cells, mind-jelly drugs, beatings, starvation diets, and swing stretching. He was abused, humiliated and tortured in a variety of other ways. But he survived. He endured the pain, the isolation, and that special insanity that comes from dropping any sensitive soul down a bottomless well of irrationality. His is a timely voice. A voice written in blood. A voice meant to shatter complacent glass. A voice that takes you inside your closest prison. (Do you know where your closest prison is tonight?)

Reprinted from *Square Dancing in the Ice Age* with permission.

Abbott lets you experience the sensations, "the atmospheric pressure, you might say, of what it is to be seriously a long-term prisoner in an American prison." You will not get this experience reading Solzhenitsyn or Jacobo Timerman. Nor will you from any reporter, because no reporter is going to witness a gang rape or a murder or go bugs locked in a small, dark box, or know the fear of being stalked by an enemy with a blade.

You can get a very intelligent view of the problem by reading Charles Silberman's *Criminal Violence, Criminal Justice*. However, that is the laboratory of sociology, and Abbott is writing about life as it is lived. It is the best anyone has done since *Soul On Ice*.

What a damn find! Hearing that Norman Mailer was doing a book on Gary Gilmore, Abbott, having been in many of the same prisons, offered his services. They met via letters and those letters, extremely well edited by Erroll McDonald, form the book. But do not turn away if you are not a fan of "letter books," they are sutured together with the skill of a fine plastic surgeon. No scars. A continuous flow of tough, tight writing.

I can appreciate exceptional prison writing. On several occasions I have spent time in jail. Short bids, in the end, they would total less than twenty months, nothing compared to the likes of Abbott but enough to never forget. This man can write like the devil, and in committing his story to print so well he manages to tell everyone's story.

He has faults; his rage, though certainly justified, sometimes distracts. He has not managed to capture the enormous boredom that is prison. The numbness of playing the same card game ten thousand times with the same players. Of staring at walls. Of counting time. Though, maybe after twenty-five years boredom becomes something else. At times, he goes beyond what is there, but I think that is part of Abbott's excruciating ordeal. Like being in the hole, shut off from all light, human contact, on a starvation diet, loaded with tranquilizers and then all of a sudden yanked out and told to write. They do the same with fighting bulls, and as a result they hook blindly until they fix their target. But fix it he does, and consistently there remains good, honest light, a clarity of vision and a righteous disturbing message. Through all the sorrow and the pain Abbott remains the bull who has somehow not fallen. The stubborn survivor. There is also something here that stuns to the point of jealousy, namely, an esthetic continuum called poetry. Prison writing often has its politics; it rarely has its poetry. *In the Belly of the Beast* is a song of prison.

These are things that Abbott claims. "In San Quentin, as well as many other prisons, if a guard on a gun-rail sees you touch another prisoner he will shoot you down with his rifle" and later "if a guard searches your cell and you make a move toward the toilet you will be shot down." There are more examples like this. Obviously these things have happened in American prisons but not every time. No one could deny that penitentiaries are an experience in abusive authority. Brutality is an institutionalized way of life. Abbott's book is a catalog of homegrown atrocities. He was shot up with heavy doses of tranquilizers against his will. He has seen electric shock treatment used to punish. He has been deliberately starved to the point where he ate insects. Inmates have been ordered to get him. He has often been beaten unconscious and has incurred permanent internal injuries. Let me add some I have witnessed over the years. A prisoner who "acted up" in his cell was battered unconscious with a high-powered hose sprayed through the bars. A prisoner "sheeted," that is, suicided on his bars. A gang urged by guards to attack a troublemaker. They ripped an eye out of his head. A prisoner stripped, laid on the concrete floor, handcuffed and legcuffed to the bars and left to defecate and urinate on himself for eight days. Abbott has seen more. Much more. He shows us just how inventive cruelty can be. But the thing about brutality, be it physical, psychological, or institutional that has always made an impression was that it was, like all punishment, so arbitrary, so random. Remember what Hemingway said about teaching you the rules, then when they caught you off second base they killed you. In prison they don't bother teaching you the rules. There is a famous prison in New York, Dannemora (the very name shivers the spine), and legend has it that the first three prisoners arriving off the bus are clubbed to let everyone know who's who and what's what. But I doubt if it works that way, because the real smart-asses would know this and stand in the rear. No, I'm sure they go on the beat up at the gateway to Dannemora, but it's always more random than legend or song can have it.

So, all this randomness, this Catch-23 absurdity; first the carrot, then the stick, then the carrot *and* the stick reduces prisoners to sniveling idiots. Every prison book begins with "I," everyone, even Timerman, is a complaining sniveler. "Then they stuck those electrodes on *my* balls. Ouch! It hurt!" A mass of snivelers, that's guard reality. Who cares, no guard has ever written a prison song.

Mailer complains some that Abbott's guards have no character. Norman is a good man but he has been in prison a total of five days. It does not matter if a guard is okay. So what. They have to conform to a system that if it operated with humanity would not operate at all. The good guards quit. Everyone has met guards who are relatively good guys and more often than not they'll be teamed with a sadist. There is an old yippie proverb: "If you shit in a pitcher of cream, the turds will rise to the top." In other words, evil wins out over good if the container is small and tight. Prison is a very small, tight container.

So that institutional violence, which incidentally pervades all our polite society, gets transferred to the inmates, who are trained to act like gladiators or bulls ready for the arena. Higher-ups in prison relate to violence much the same as National Hockey League officials do—it's part of the game. There is so much killing in prison. It is, after all, a death of numbers. "Six hundred forty weapons uncovered in a quick search of Attica." "Who bought it?" "Nobody in Two H." "What's your number?" "He stuck him *three* times." "What's your fuckin' number, man." It's all numbers and all death. In fact, when you do die, you're "off the count." The count being the most serious moment in any prison. To move or talk means a ticket. The guards rush about counting you. It happens maybe nine times a day. Weighing the meat, chillin' out the jailhouse.

Abbott understands all about numbers dying violent deaths—the cat and mouse survival game behind the walls. He writes one of the most gripping descriptions of murder you will ever read. It is his murder. The one he did as executioner, but also the haunting murder he fears as possible victim. Then he takes us into solitary confinement with him to share the punishment. Abbott has spent fourteen years in solitary. He calls it "the hole." In the East it's called "the box." Both sexist expressions for the vagina. Dry vaginas with concrete teeth.

There is not a lot of remorse in Abbott. Society is very weird about remorse. Prisoners are supposed to feel bad about their crimes, and although there is a long line of repentant sinners outside a thousand parole board meetings, there is not a true ounce of remorse in any American prison. Everyone sees themselves as a victim. Everyone got fucked. And if you listen carefully to the prison jokes you'll see that the protagonist usually ends up the victim. Ironic, since society insists here are the captured predators, the guilty ones. Freud would have had a field day in prison.

So if there's no remorse happening why exactly do these prisons remain?

Well, take my case. The judge said I did not have to be segregated from society, and obviously didn't need to be rehabilitated, but there was some good to be gained by making an example. The deterrent theory of punishment. It was first applied in thirteenth-century Holland when a dog who bit a *Bürgermeister* was hanged as a lesson to other dogs. Then followed those wonderfully successful public hangings of pickpockets in London. Occasions that proved easy grabbings for fellow pickpockets who worked the excited crowds. Deterrence is an assumption. The 525,000 inmates in America plus triple that on probation and parole are proof that assumption is questionable. Rehabilitation? There are extremely few prison officials who still cling to the idea that such alchemy occurs. This pretense went out with notions like the "New Frontier" and the "Great Society." The statistics are extremely tragic. Out of every ten inmates released, seven quickly return to prison. This gloomy reality maintains itself in all systems, regardless of region. It has become an American constant. Furthermore, what that statistic hides is that the other three were probably innocent and that two of the seven who returned do so because they "learned" their next crime in their last prison. In other words, in addition to tough economic conditions, conservative trends, and so on, the prison system actually grows its own population. It will be hard to control this phenomenon. More difficult, perhaps than cancer. It is common for officials to explain this as older inmates teaching younger inmates new tricks. Abbott says that is so much jive-ass. Inmates don't talk about how you saw up a stolen car and sell it piecemeal to a Bolivian parts dealer. No one talks about outfoxing border patrols in smuggling operations. You can learn more about that watching television. Criminals don't crack safes anymore, they stick a gun under your nose and steal your money. Unskilled labor. But what you do learn is *capability*. "What is forced down your throat . . . is the *will* to commit crime . . . no one has ever come out of prison a better man." A very true, blunt statement, and it will not be very popular outside because society wants desperately to believe something positive happens behind those walls. That men become men. That sin becomes virtue. That when it's over, ex-convicts get jobs, go to church, and buy a house. Right!

So in the end there is just segregation as a reason. If you lock a "criminal" up, that's one less animal preying on society. Well, eliminating the obvious fact that there is lots of crime inside prison, doesn't this assume a finite number of criminals? Doesn't it stand to reason then that stuffing the prisons will lower the crime rate? That's not reality though. Economic conditions, not morality, determine crime rate, as they have since time immemorial. We're in tough times, so people steal. Jean Valjean was only a criminal in the eyes of the Moral Majority, themselves murderers of ideas. Hypocritical sneak thieves.

Our middle-class education about justice for all is rudely jarred by reality. Like holding onto the fairytale about every poor blah-blah being entitled to a fair trial. To our suburban grammar school mind that is truth. In reality, 85 percent (90 percent in NYC) of all defendants are forced to plea-bargain away their freedom. Expedience, not justice, is the rule of contemporary American law. Abbott will explode most of your mythology about crime and punishment. He is not reviewing movies, remember, he is talking about what *is*, not what was promised.

Abbott knows why inmates are locked up. "The purpose of prison is to ruin me, ruin me completely. The purpose is to mark me, to stamp across my face the track of this beast they call prison."

In short, to bust balls. The guards are there "to bust your balls." To jam you and save the institution. Their main objective is to "cover their ass."

To make it look like they are not responsible. *Cover Your Ass*, is the guard's prison song. People go out worse than they come in. Sixteen-year-old kids get raped, serious medical problems go untreated, people get stabbed, thousands go crazy, and while all this is happening everyone with any authority thinks only one thought: Cover your ass. Isn't that what Warren Burger is doing—pontificating about prisons being our national disgrace and yet legalizing bad conditions at Manhattan's Metropolitan Lockup and more than one inmate to a cell? Overcrowding is the main cause of riots and much violence. Warren Burger, our Chief Injustice, the man probably most responsible for making things bad, publicly deplores the situation. He is simply covering his ass before God.

Finally Abbott deals with inmates. And here there is much overglorification. He rebukes Mailer's attempts to cast him as hero but he turns around and makes all other inmates exactly that. But inmates are not like James Cagney or Paul Newman. They are not even George Jackson. They are no one you've seen in movies or on talk shows or read about. Here are a few shameful statistics: 85 percent of U.S. prisoners are nonwhite, 65 percent black, 20 percent mostly Spanish-speaking. The rest are your Paul Newmans, your Tommy Trantinos (a very good writer caged in New Jersey), and your G. Gordon Liddys, although most are poor, scared farm boys. Why a society that is 85 percent white locks up a society that is 85 percent nonwhite is the kind of question not permitted in decent circles. One either needs a Doctor Shockley-type to explain how blacks are inherently evil, that their long arms encourage them to theft, or one has to accept that we are a racist society.

The other statistic is a sad legacy of that racist neglect: Half the inmates in prison cannot read or write. The world is so restricted. There is no interest in news, in a typical group a third cannot name the president, none the vice-president. A fellow inmate once asked if I had something for him to eat from my commissary. "Salmon," I replied. "Does it have pork in it?" he questioned back. I don't tell this to be funny, I tell it because it's sad. Sad, the way prisoners will plot a year to escape successfully and then be caught in a few days hanging out at their neighborhood poolhall. Abbott and I would have had some good conversations about Afghanistan, movies, Cuba, abortion, revolution; the chances of us having met are exactly 525,000 to 1. More likely than not we'd be talking about jammin' bitches, or snivelin' about our bids, or braggin' about facin' down some dumb-ass hack. Very few people talk in prison, it is the ultimate face-saving event, more rituals than a Japanese tea ceremony. For when prisoners relate to prisoners, they too must "cover their ass."

Where Abbott sees revolution pounding in every prisoner's breast, I see a craving to watch more television cartoons. When Abbott explains he came in looking for individual justice but should have expected social justice (he says this to excuse black "oppression" of whites in prison), he forgets the absence of communal justice. For every prisoner that will cover a brother's back, there are ten who will not. Whoever said there is honor among thieves had to have been a thief. Maybe years ago, the sixties were very much a phenomenon inside the prison walls. But the Me generation has replaced that and there is very little revolutionary consciousness left. There are few insurrections, many riots. There are not even that many Muslims left, for that movement seems to be dying also. A typical prison conversation is not about revolution. Here is a typical conversation:

A: What do you want, S?
S: I want money, lots of money.
A: What for?

S: I will buy a city.
A: Why?
S: So everyone will work for me.

Today, for the most part, the authorities seem to have broken any collective will. Everybody hates the system all right but hardly anyone carries the vision of the united proletariat. S. doesn't want any fuckin' revolution, he just wants to be king, like the other asshole kings out there.

Abbott is very good on understanding the "reverse racism" in prison. To his credit, he doesn't get distracted by the nuisances of being dominated by a different culture. He gets along with blacks. They don't beat up on him. In fact, most prison violence is not interracial. Black on black, white on white, or brown on brown. Just like outside. However, also like outside, when it does become interracial, an incident can lead to tribal warfare. Warfare enclosed by forty-foot-high walls. The authorities use this reverse racism as an excuse. "We don't have good prisons like the Scandinavians do because of the blacks." You will hear that every time from experts. What a copout. There is always conflict in prison. Age conflict. Religion. City-country. Politics. Straight-gay. To say nothing of the bug cases. We don't have prisons like the Scandinavians do because on all the basic issues of life they encourage collectivity and we do not. They try to institute community. They don't push men to rat on each other, to ass-kiss in competition for favors, to eat their self-esteem like a hamburger. They don't divide in order to conquer. If they do, then their prisons stink too.

The whites, of course, reinforce racism. They want you in their "culture" and that culture is racist. So white guards will instruct you about the behavior of "jungle bunnies" and the excuses you have to make for "spics" who, after all, still have one foot on the banana boat. White inmates pull "integrationists" back into their camp "for your own good." There are some Caucasians like Abbott, but this is still the rule. The turds rising to the top of the cream pitcher, again. It is hard to emerge from prison not a racist. Just as it is almost impossible to emerge with no burning thoughts of revenge. This is what Abbott means about prisons teaching you the capability for murder.

So I start out reviewing Jack Abbott's prison experience and end up telling my own thoughts. Every American prisoner does that. We are conditioned to make prison an individual experience. Compare. Why did he get two milks and I only one? Are you medium or max? How come I got ten years and he only five *for the same thing*? Is he a squealer? Can I take him? Prison is a sniveler's supermarket. A place you learn jealousy, suspicion, and hatred. It originates with how people get to be prisoners in the first place. With the arbitrary definition of crime and the *not* so arbitrary selection of who gets to define that definition. One class is, after all, judging another. There are not "all kinds" here as the tour guide claims. Sure, one of one kind, a thousand of the other. It is here that Abbott's courage ventures the furthest. He declares himself in the end to be a Communist. He risks thousands of well-meaning people closing ranks with him. Of being judged before his day in the arena of ideas.

A Communist!? At one moment of poetic provocation, he declares only Communists help prisoners. Which is sad because given our "democracy" we are free to choose everything but that! For all intents and purposes there are *no* American Communists. Hence no one helping. Perhaps Abbott means that. This declaration, this fixation with "American injustice" as opposed to "human nature" as cause of crime, turns the passive reader into an active prison guard. Abbott waves the red flag, his turn at matador. He corners you against the wall, you must think and act too quickly to survive. With his description of prison life, he shoves in the sword, with his blunt politics he yanks it straight up to your skull.

This song sayer is not filled with self-pity. He is not crying for mercy. He is toughing it out, laying all his cards on the table, the way Gary Gilmore did at the end. They are very close in spirit. . . . When a fighting bull kills the matador, usually another toreador will finish him off, but if he has fought exceptionally well, as say the bull who put an end to the great Manolete, they will turn him loose to pasture. Jack Henry Abbott is out among you now. Do not welcome him back. He has not been there before. Yet hear this man's song. You will know nothing of prison until you do.

—JUNE 1981

Following Jack Henry Abbott's involvement in a despicable and heinous murder last summer, he jumped parole and fled to Mexico, then to the oil fields of Louisiana, where he was apprehended after two months as a fugitive. He has since been returned to Manhattan and faces a murder trial as well as a serious parole violation. Even if acquitted on the murder charge, he is certain to be returned to prison to finish out his life sentence. No event in memory has so jolted the New York literary community. When *In the Belly of the Beast* was first published in June, it earned universal praise from critics, and Abbott was hailed as a brilliant literary discovery. He was dubbed Norman Mailer's protégé, for it was mainly through Mailer's efforts that the convict's writing came to print. A circle of admirers, centered around the *New York Review of Books*, joined Mailer in petitioning for Abbott's early release on parole.

After the brutal murder and flight from justice, the literary community did a complete double take. The book was shown to have several misstatements of fact, it was immediately removed from the "Editor's Choice" section of the *New York Times Book Review*, and at least a dozen investigative reporters sifted through Abbott's prison career and his brief one-month tour of the literary jet set. Amost universal scorn was heaped on Mailer and friends, culminating in a vicious swipe on the first *Saturday Night Live* show of the season.

Many of the reports point to the complete disorientation of Abbott in moving from twenty-five years of incarceration to the glamour world of big-city life in the fast lane. He did not know how to open a bank account, where one bought toothpaste, or how to order from a menu. From two telephone conversations I had with him, it was obvious he has talked just a few times on the phone. In trying to arrange a meeting, he insisted I meet him at a restaurant on Third Street. "Third Street and what?" I inquired. He did not understand the question. His interview on *Good Morning America* was extremely disassociative, with several of his answers drifting off into space. An interview with *Rolling Stone* was so disjointed it could not be published. No critics blamed the prison system for failing to equip released inmates with even the barest coping mechanisms to make it on the outside. In fact, the prison system remained remarkably outside the scope of criticism as angry fingers were pointed at Mailer and friends as naive do-gooders, if not willing accomplices to murder.

In all, a complete lack of understanding of how the prison system works has been evidenced. Abbott was due for parole just two months after his release from prison. Prison authorities—and no one else—hold and decide who can use the keys of freedom. What was apparent from subsequent disclosures of Abbott's records was that outside support for his literary talent was of little consideration to the parole board. Of far greater concern was Abbott's apparent willingness to serve as an informer inside the prison during his last year of confinement. His record shows he gave authorities information they wanted on several prison organizers. In addition, supporters of Abbott received letters from convicts who claimed he had also squealed on a group of young lawyers, falsely accusing them of smuggling drugs into the prison. Prison officials consider informers prime candidates for early parole, not just for the services performed, but for their safety as well.

Whether one blames the prison system, Abbott, or a combination thereof, it's difficult to see how scorn can be laid on those who recognized and spoke up for talent. The United States has a per capita prison population topped only by South Africa. The only social program pictured favorably by the Reagan administration is a call for $2 billion more in prison construction funds. Reagan himself chides theorists for blaming crime on factors like poverty and racism. Across the land, politicians scream for stiffer penalties and longer sentences. Little attention is paid to the lack of rehabilitation and resocialization programs. The demand is for increasing the *quantity* of life behind bars, not the *quality*.

The tragedy of the Abbott affair is not just that one victim lay dead on a New York sidewalk, though that, of course, is tragic. The greater tragedy is that too many prisoners who deserve a break will be denied, and too many people who care about reform will turn their backs. Hope has received a shattering blow.

—POSTSCRIPT
October 1981
Edgecombe Correctional Facility, Manhattan
(minimum security—work-release program)

55

HOW TO FIGHT CITY HALL (1984)

Does the utility company treat you unfairly? Are you being pushed around by giant developers, the bank or the government? Is your community threatened by pollution? If you feel like one of the little people being stepped on by "the powers that be," you're not alone. But if you feel there's nothing you can do about it, you're not paying attention to the groundswell of grass-roots activism taking place in America today.

Take the following examples:

▶ A year ago in Bucks County, Pa., the Philadelphia Electric Company began excavation for a controversial pumping station that would have harmed the Delaware River and disrupted the way of life of an entire community. Today, after waves of civil disobedience, pickets, rallies, and a courthouse occupation followed by a successful referendum campaign and county election, construction (despite millions invested) has been ordered

Reprinted from *Parade Magazine* with permission.

shut down, and most observers agree the project will never see the light of day.

▶ In Anson County, N.C., a black and white alliance called CACTUS recently outfought the state chemical industry and blocked a mammoth waste dump.

▶ In Minnesota, a grass-roots organization called COACT, using a combination of direct action and political lobbying, has stopped scores of farm foreclosures.

▶ In San Francisco, a broad-based coalition has made some progress in limiting high-rise development, while on New York City's west side, a highway project has been held off for more than 10 years.

The people winning these battles don't sit around complaining about apathy; instead, they are actively "doing democracy." That's right—doing democracy. Democracy is more than a place you live in, more than a belief. Democracy is a skill, something you learn and do. You don't do it, you don't have it. It's not inevitable that the little people triumph, but neither is it true that the powerful few at the top are unshakable.

For the last seven years, I've been starting and advising many grass-roots groups working on environmental issues. Before that, I had a long history in the civil rights and antiwar movements. Let me share with you some of the commonsense ideas and tricks of the trade that I've picked up along the way.

BEGIN WITH THE PROPER STATE OF MIND. You must feel strongly that, if you put time and energy into a thought-out campaign, you will prevail.

GET INTO THE FIGHT AS EARLY AS POSSIBLE. Keep abreast of what's going on in your community. Be on the lookout for public hearings, sudden requests to change zoning variances or attempts to deregulate industries. Understand that "studies" are often a smokescreen for beginning a project. One of the ironies of organizing is that it is much easier to get people active once a project has begun, but by then it may be too late to win.

At the earliest stage, you might even be able to go on the offensive. Some groups defending waterways have managed to get Congress to designate areas under the Wild and Scenic Rivers Act. You might win an ordinance prohibiting toxic waste dumping or limiting the height of buildings, an impediment to downtown developers. By pushing for local restrictions, you stimulate early debate as well as lay groundwork for the future battle and put your opponents on the defensive.

THERE IS STRENGTH IN NUMBERS. Talk to your neighbors, attend public hearings, listen to community talk shows, scan the letters to the editor column. Get names and phone numbers. You want to avoid the sort of people depicted in the movie *Network*, those who run to the window shouting, "I'm mad as hell, and I'm not going to take it anymore." Certainly it's right and natural to be angry, but the anger must be controlled and directed.

Avoid people who get scared by words like "power," "conflict," and "confrontation." Many people get involved for religious or social reasons—both perfectly legitimate motives—but for spearheading a campaign, those people who understand the nature of politics are best suited to making strategy. The status quo sits like a layer of fat on cold chicken soup—your nucleus has to be willing to stir things up.

TAKE YOUR CASE TO THE PEOPLE. Public meetings are the bread and butter of all organizing. It's essential to create an atmosphere that's not intimidating so as to allow for free and open comment, but you should have some answers ready. A key to mounting a successful campaign rests on your ability to convert problem-presenters to problem-solvers. Break down generalities into limited goals. Saying, "We don't have enough money" is just depressing. But saying, "We need $1000 for ads. I've raised $100 already," starts a process with a specific target.

The more experience I have, the more I favor parliamentary procedure and majority rule. The argument against this method of decision-making maintains that a small clique experienced with the ground rules can control the will of the group. But a determined few can just as easily control decisions under any set of procedures. Besides debating skills, the ability to negotiate, to form alliances and to direct discussion to a specific motion are all of great importance when confronting opponents.

Don't overlook simple business operating procedures just because this is volunteer work. Pass out pads and pencils. A simple form listing vital statistics—such as hours available, skills and resources—breaks the ice with new people. At meetings, get into a good news/bad news rhythm of reporting. Good news lifts sagging spirits. Bad news reminds you of the need to improve your organizing skills.

PAY ATTENTION TO THE INTERNAL WORKINGS OF YOUR GROUP. The majority of citizens' groups collapse within a year as a result of divisions, poor leadership and a general sense of frustration and inertia. By always asking, "Does this bring victory closer?" you can help motivate and bring a group together.

It's very important to be supportive of your fellow activists. Controversy attracts public attention. Challenging the "powers that be" often forces people to painfully re-examine long-held misconceptions, and leaders often find themselves on a lonely limb. Most groups fall down, however, not because they fail to support each other but because they are unwilling or unable to engage in self-criticism. Constructive criticism of ideas and tactics without being judgmental of individuals is more easily said than done. But how else do we improve?

BE VERY CONSCIOUS OF YOUR LANGUAGE. It cannot be stressed too strongly how much language shapes our environment. Language should be action-oriented, exciting, creative, simple and upbeat. Try to imagine yourself as someone creating an advertising campaign. Activists who carry around some prejudice that all advertising is deceitful, who feel that emphasizing form threatens the integrity of content really miss the essential nature of communication. You can't afford the luxury of being boring or of creating a language that the average person cannot understand. Avoid, for example, using initials for the full name of an agency. Even if all the people you are addressing know that EPA stands for Environmental Protection Agency (if they all do, you are not talking to enough people), say the full name. Why? As a reminder not to slip into the language of the bureaucracy. Those in power can, but not the challengers.

AVOID ANALYSIS-PARALYSIS. Read through reports, proposals and studies with the eye of a detective. Look for clues to prove your case, ammunition to destroy the opposition. But be careful not to get intimidated by "facts"—or use them to intimidate others. Don't get bogged down because you feel you don't know enough to act. Also, a sense of humor is your best guard against burning out of energy and ideas.

There is no end to information-gathering. Often, as your reputation grows, people will literally pop out of the woodwork with bits of information. Don't assume your opponents are united; look behind the public relations people. The Freedom of Information Act and various state sunshine laws allow the public access to otherwise secret correspondence and minutes of meetings. Even where no such access laws exist, officials often believe they do, and a good bluff on the phone might quickly get scores of documents.

Information and support are also available from national groups. Even if their support is nothing more than a letter, people like to feel part of something bigger, and opponents get very nervous when you go beyond their turf.

THINK IN TERMS OF TEAM SPORTS OR WAR. Shifting from analysis to action means changing roles from that of a detective to that of a coach or general. By mapping out allies, potential allies and the opposition, by scanning the field repeatedly for strengths and weaknesses on both sides, you are making abstract ideas concrete. Many people have a philosophical resistance to creating a "them" and an "us," to seeing things in black and white. Such an attitude of "oneness" might feel good, but not when you are challenging the process of decision-making.

ALWAYS GET THE LAST WORD. In presenting your case, don't let a good question go unanswered. Chances are a lot of other people are asking the same question. And never let opponents get the last word in any debate. If you get stumped, make sure it never happens again on the same point. Unfortunately, the majority of groups find themselves in the position of simply saying "No!" Work hard to develop an alternative—"No! We have a better idea"—and include an economic argument.

A LITTLE RUDENESS HELPS. Getting through bureaucracies means being persistent and a little pushy. Remember that manners were invented by kings to maintain power. The determination to interrupt business as usual is often misunderstood as ill-mannered. Don't let the "king" define your behavior.

YOUR ABILITY TO MAKE NEWS IS, AT CRUCIAL STAGES, YOUR MOST IMPORTANT GOAL. The opposition would much rather go about its business secretly. Those who support you want to be assured that things are happening. The media only want to know the answers to three questions: Who are you? Why are you so upset? What are you going to do about it? Role-play among each other, playing reporter and information source. Be quick, to the point and suspenseful.

THINK EGOCENTRICALLY. Take the daily newspaper and draw a circle around every story in which you can make a connection to your issue. I mean everything! On the Delaware, a kid once saved someone who crash-landed in the river. Knowing he would be news, we rushed to feed him the line. "I hope someone will now save the river from the pump." If a politician is coming to town, rush to the event and ask a key question. A good organizer is constantly on the move, constantly on the telephone. Practice by calling random names from the telephone book, posing as some neutral survey worker polling on the issue. When an article appears in the newspaper, call the paper's switchboard and register your feelings.

SEARCH FOR ALLIES. It's a big world out there. What's bad for your group has to be bad for others. Look hard for the most common denominator you share. Only approach others for support when you have a specific, immediate request you're fairly sure will be honored . . . then ask for a little more.

People in general *do* believe in fair play, but what really motivates them is self-interest. If you can't spell out how the policy or project affects the person you're addressing, try someone else.

DON'T RULE OUT ANYTHING. Should you picket? Stage a rally? Run candidates? Go to court? There are hundreds of strategy options. Imagination. Surprise. Mobility. These are the advantages you have over your opponent in the field. Remember, at every step of the way, you have to ask, "Is this bringing us closer to victory?"

So how do people "do democracy"? They do it by acting out the roles they always dreamed of playing. Dramatist. Detective. General. Football coach. Preacher. Democracy means having the courage and persistence to make the dreams of free people come true.

56

WHERE DO WE GO FROM HERE? (1985)

In 1985 the A. J. Muste Memorial Institute asked 35 activists to respond to a set of questions concerning the future direction of Leftist politics. The questions and Abbie's answers follow.

If we are headed inextricably towards nuclear war—as movement activists so often insist—shouldn't we de-emphasize other issues and concentrate solely on issues of war and peace?

We are not "headed inextricably towards nuclear war." That is a terrible mindset for a generation or for peace activists. It is too depressive, cynical, despair-ridden. Peace activists who go around painting over and over again what The Day After will look like are lousy organizers and worse community therapists.

Reprinted from *A. J. Muste Memorial Institute Discussion Series, Number One, Tactics and Strategies for the Peace Movement: Where Do We Go From Here* with permission.

In my lifetime, nuclear war threatened on three occasions: in 1954 when the U.S. offered nuclear weapons to the French to use in Indochina, in 1962 during the Cuban Missile Crisis, and in 1970 when Nixon came close to using them in North Vietnam. Nuclear war will occur because of real (not imagined) regional wars where the superpowers get involved. Thus the correct strategy to oppose nuclear war is to fight against U.S. intervention in Central America.

Nuclear war can also come about through the battle with devils! As long as people persist in seeing Russians as slaves living in an evil empire, we are doomed to an irrational arms race. How many MX missiles to do in Lucifer? The answer, as Jerry Falwell will gladly tell you, is never enough. So people-to-people cultural exchanges with the Russians, as well as resistance to U.S. military intervention is essential to preventing nuclear war.

How do we explain the Soviet Union to the American people and so diffuse the Cold War?

We explain the Soviet Union to Americans by beginning with the common-sense argument that most people love their country. We explain that all we are permitted to know about Russia is food lines, dissidents and parades of military hardware; that we never see pictures of happy Russians on TV. Norman Mailer's odyssey in Russia in a recent issue of *Parade* Magazine (readership 23 million) set exactly the right tone for talking of Russia. We talk about Russians by stressing that they are just like us. What makes us different is that they have lost millions to war in their land, we have not. They are encircled, we are not. We are number one in just about everything technological, including military hardware, therefore we have to take the first steps.

I personally am glad the Dr. Strangeloves and Cowboy Generals in the Pentagon are not the only ones with nuclear weapons. I prefer this world with its balance of terror to one where all the terror is concentrated in one nest of hawks.

We encourage dissidents in Russia. Russia is no more static a society than the U.S. Dissidents never have an easy time. Sakharov and Lech Walensa, by the way, consider themselves patriots in their land and both are *not anti-communist*. We encourage detente by recognizing all of today's *isms*; i.e., capitalism, communism, socialism, etc. as *wasisms*. The world is moving towards a "Mixed Economy." A mixed economy makes sense in a global village. Russia has a better medical program for all its citizens than does the U.S. It has a better daycare system. We have more individual rights and we also have MTV, blue jeans and the best pizza in the world!! We have a lot to offer each other to say nothing of what we could do with the TRILLIONS of Rubles and Dollars saved from the arms race.

What should the relationship be between the peace movement and electoral politics?

The gap is between doing something and doing nothing, not between electoral politics, protest demonstrations, civil disobedience, or even violent militancy. Building a movement means pluralism and a broad range of strategies and activities. What is counterproductive is the cultism of the left; its sectarian and un-American language; its pretensions to moral superiority; its eagerness to search for the *least* common denominator rather than the *most* common denominator.

The Environmental Movement in which I have been active for 7 years now in several local communities allows for organizing among people very different politically than make up the uninformed Left. Prove yourself to them on basic issues like the water they drink or on jobs and *then* lay your trip on them about Nicaragua or arms control. The so-called "Peace Movement" you talk about is a bunch of harpies who care more about correcting each others' vocabulary than reaching millions of Americans. They are the folks who talk of reaching "the masses" and brag about not watching television, who have never talked to anyone who rode in the SMOKING section of an airplane. They emphasize defeats rather than victories.

Third Party politics are futile exercises in this country. Democrats are not *one* party anyway. Electoral politics have to be seen as something more than a once-in-4-year beauty contest between the Evil of Two Lessers and the Lesser of Two Evils. Politics is how you balance immediate short-range self-interests with long-range ones and those that serve the community and world at large; how you balance your time, money, ideas and energy. It's always local and from the bottom up to be democratic. Of course I've never seen a local fight that was successful that didn't build alliances with those fighting other issues and with those outside the "community." You are forced to think and act globally in order to be successful locally. But our focus must be local. Talking about ending war, world hunger and the poisoning of the planet is religious lip-service that just produces guilt. The problems have to be phrased in manageable proportions. Problems should not even be presented without the simultaneous presentation of a partial solution. It just depresses people.

What role should civil disobedience and other forms of direct action play in the movement?

Civil disobedience is always a valid tactic because it is part of the American Experience. It is not should we work inside or outside the system. That is a false question. To me, the test is will a tactic—no matter if it's confrontational or not—be understood within the context of the American Experience. Also, "The Movement" is not serious about the right things. It attacks the media because it is controlled by the ruling class. Sure that's true. But activists still have to learn how it works. Ninety percent of peace activists I meet have less knowledge about how (as opposed to why) the media works than does any junior executive in an ad agency. They have less notion as to what motivates large numbers of people or individuals than your average door-to-door salesman. Elitism is when someone becomes too successful or too famous, not when people show up late to meetings or use up valuable group time droning on and on. There is an anti-success tendency in the movement and that is why many excellent organizers leave. You score points on the left for *not* being creative, for *not* being provocative and for *not* acting just as often as you score points in a big corporation. The difference is you have to produce in a corporation or you get fired. So you work on deadlines, you take notes, you show up on time, you compete hard as hell. Politics is more than a social or religious experience. Winning is what counts, and too often it's frowned upon on the left as "macho," competitive, arrogant, or whatever. . . . Vince Lombardi has more to say on that than A. J. Muste.

Many activists are committed to "alternative" politics, ignoring, when possible, programmatic reforms in favor of a more visionary stance. This was the strategy of the 1960s counter-culture. Is it valid today?

The strategies of the '60s are applicable to the '80s or any decade. But not the media definition of the '60s. The '60s began in 1960, not 1968. It included electoral politics, lobbying, door to door canvassing, teach-ins, forums, as well as demonstrations, guerrilla theatre, civil disobedience, and militant resistance. Alternative politics are not relevant, however, because the country has changed in basic ways: demographics and the economy—there is no "youth culture." The U.S. after Vietnam is not the U.S. after W.W. II. The country is more tolerant of different political points of view. And it's easier to organize "workers" now than in the days of "hippies vs. hard hats." The counter-culture has been absorbed and hippies now wear hard hats. A politics built around drugs, or dress, or diet or even sex, race or age is not necessary because there is a chance to reach *all* Americans now. This option was not available in the 1960s. Black Power, a Woodstock Nation, a Lesbian Nation and other "nationalisms" were needed in the '60s to give each of us pride in who we were. We can go beyond that now. The Rainbow Coalition is the correct vehicle for this. I am white, male, a member of the middle class and Jewish—whoever tries to make me feel guilty about that is either an agent for the FBI or an asshole. What people are they are. They should be proud of it but not project an air of superiority. It simply is *not* correct that sex, sexual preference, race, age or what people eat or smoke make them better than someone else. My Freedom of Information Act papers are an education in how the FBI and CIA exploited intergroup differences to disrupt activity and stifle leadership. We should stop demanding that we all become instant saints and be more tolerant of our comrades, especially if they are active. The cultism of the left often appears as three people, two of whom plot to kick the third out. It's always because of another *ism*. Sex*ism*, rac*ism*, elit*ism*, deviational*ism*. I'd rather see people kicked out because they don't follow through on their commitment. Let me be concrete: If an event should have 500 people or raise $500 who in the left gets upset if it's not a success. But deviate from the manners and vocabulary of the party line and out you go! That's sick to me and self-defeating.

57

THE YOUNG HAVE TO BE THERE (1986)

The Left has a marvelous ability to snatch defeat from the jaws of victory. The great contradiction of the 1960s was exactly how much we pulled off—how far we got with how few and how little knowledge.

In 1968, the pinnacle year of the '60s, a poll of students showed that the most popular Americans were Richard Nixon and John Wayne, in that order. We had the same percentage of business-administration majors and engineers that we have today. And when Kent State and Jackson State happened, 800 universities went out on strike, but there were 5,000 universities. To be effective, you have to realize that you work between the parameters of nobody and everybody. It's not "nobody" that cares. It's not "everybody" that agrees with you.

How many people do you need to make a change? I'm convinced that it's not a majority; it's never a moral majority that makes the change. The fact that 75 per cent of Americans are against contra aid is as irrelevant to me as

Reprinted from *Social Policy* magazine with permission.

the fact that 75 per cent of Americans have wanted universal health care since 1947, and we don't have it.

So I want to emphasize what we pulled off in the 1960s, what I think we achieved.

First of all, we ended Jim Crow. We brought down legal segregation. Apartheid—let's call it what it was. It was apartheid that had existed for almost 200 years, give or take a few years during Reconstruction. That came to an end.

There was a student movement in this country. Students asked, "What is the role of the university in society? What is the role of the student in the university?" Out of that grew a movement. Today you look at that and say, "My God, it's hotbeds of social rest out there. Why trust anybody under thirty these days?" Campuses have traditionally been yuppie training camps and places where you go to work on your careers and your marriages—where young rich ladies and gentlemen went to become older rich ladies and gentlemen.

So all of a sudden there was a student movement, and tremendous individual and collective rights were won: the right to vote when you're eighteen; co-ed dorms; controversial speakers on campus; student control of the newspapers; ROTC out, CIA out. A student movement achieved great collective and individual rights that young people barely appreciate today.

We had a movement for freer lifestyles. Wearing your hair long might have seemed frivolous to some of the more straight people on the Left in the 1960s, but I tell you that was a full-time commitment because you were ostracized from your community. You were picked up by the cops. You could get your head shaved. You were kicked out of classes. It had meaning. Now kids can wear their hair long, short, red, blue, pink, shave it off, or whatever. You can wear a bra or not wear a bra, even if you're a guy, it's like okay. So these freer lifestyles were won because of what happened in the 1960s.

Then, of course, there was the war in Vietnam. In 1964, only 8 per cent of the American public opposed U.S. policy in Southeast Asia, and the war had been going for ten years. People ask me, "Do we have a Vietnam in Central America?" Of course we do. It's in its first ten years.

If you look at the history of Western civilization, foreign wars in particular have been extremely popular. You can't find another foreign war of aggression fought by such a powerful country where the people rose up and said, "Bring the troops home." But it did actually happen here. We would have troops in Nicaragua for sure tonight if it hadn't been for Vietnam. I think the greatest legacy of the 1960s was the general feeling that not only can you fight the powers that be, but you can win.

I've never liked guilt-tripping. I've always left the concept of sin to the Catholic Church. When I was four, my mother said, "There's millions of people starving in China. Eat your dinner." I said, "Ma, name one."

I started right off trying to resist guilt. I tried to give people a sense that it was in us to be altruistic, to be curious, to explore, to be creative, and that taking on the powers that be was the best game in town. It was fun to go out there and say, "The emperor's got no damn clothes on." It was fun to have that sense of engagement where you jumped on the earth and the earth jumped back—the sense that you were a part of history.

Can it happen again? No way. It is never going to happen again. The music is never going to be that good, the sex is never going to be that free, the dope is never going to be that cheap. Young people cared because there were just more young people to care. We're never going to have the affluence. Minimum wages were $40 a week—that's what we got, and it wasn't so bad. You got Chinese food on Friday. You went out. The combination of affluence, demographics, the resistance to the 1950s that was there—all those elements are not going to happen again.

If it was up to the Left to make a revolution in America, we'd still be trying to figure out how three people can get out of a phone booth—two trying to figure out how they can leave the third one in the phone booth because that person is really a revisionist. In the '60s we went beyond the Left in our style, in our language. We were American in every sense of the word, especially in our excesses.

I speak on about sixty campuses a year, and I meet young activists out there. The leaves of apathy are stirring on the campuses. You cannot have social revolution, you cannot have change without the young. You simply can't do it. The young have to be there. They have to assume their place because the young have creativity, they have the energy, they have the impatience. That's what you need.

You have to say, "I don't want to hear about constructive engagement. I don't want to hear all the political considerations. I don't want to hear about the commies in the woods. I don't like what's going on in South Africa, and I want it done now. Freedom now.'' That's what it was in the 1960s. You need the youth to dissent.

Sure we were young. We were arrogant. We were ridiculous. There were excesses. We were brash. We were foolish. We had factional fights. But we were right.

58

CLOSING ARGUMENT (1987)

On April 15 a jury in Federal District Court in Hampshire County, Massachusetts, acquitted twelve people, including Abbie Hoffman, of trespassing charges in connection with the occupation of a campus building during a November 24 demonstration against C.I.A. recruitment at the University of Massachusetts. Three others, among them Amy Carter, were acquitted of disorderly conduct.

The group asserted that its actions were necessary to force the school to comply with its own policy, which limits campus recruitment to law-abiding organizations. In three days of testimony, more than a dozen defense witnesses, including Daniel Ellsberg, Ramsey Clark and former contra *leader Edgar Chamorro, described the agency's role in more than two decades of dirty tricks and broken promises.*

Hoffman acted as his own attorney. His closing remarks to the jury follow.

Good morning, women and men of the jury:

At 50, I am the oldest of the student defendants. In a short time you will retire to deliberate your decision. In examining the exhibits before you, we

Reprinted from *The Nation* with permission.

would draw your attention to Exhibit No. 3, page 1, paragraph 1 of the letter from the administration to the University of Massachusetts community, dated November 21, 1986:

> The university has consistently been committed to providing, promoting and protecting an environment which encourages the free exchange of ideas through formal classes, meetings, public addresses, private conversations, and demonstrations.

Also, we would like you to consider page 2, the first paragraph:

> The university respects the rights of its students to express their views in whatever manner they see fit, including demonstrations, rallies and educational forums.

The defendants have not claimed that the C.I.A. has no right to participate in that free exchange of ideas. To the contrary, the defendants encourage that right of free speech. But recruitment by a company, private or public, is not a right; it is a privilege which is regulated to insure that the laws of the University of Massachusetts, the commonwealth and the United States are being obeyed by the recruiter.

You heard Ralph McGehee's description of how he was recruited into the C.I.A. He was told that he would be gathering intelligence, and we don't object to that. The country needs intelligence. He wasn't told he would be part of an assassination team, that he would have to "arrange and doctor evidence" that would show the North Vietnamese were invading the South, that he would have to write a white paper to Congress that was a total lie so that Congress could authorize the first bombing of Hanoi. We would draw your attention to Mr. McGehee's remark that the big joke about Congress in the C.I.A. was, "Treat them like mushrooms—keep them in the dark and feed them a lot of manure." Does anyone believe this is what recruiters say? Do they tell the recruitee (as witness Mort Halperin testified) that they might have to break the C.I.A.'s own charter and engage in domestic spying? That they might have to silence a Daniel Ellsberg? That they might have to engage in acts of war against a country we are formally at peace with? Mr. Halperin testified that during the Senate intelligence hearings chaired by Senator Frank Church in 1976 it was recognized that some covert or secret acts are necessary in the conduct of foreign policy. However, it was decided that a covert action or program could not be in direct conflict with publicly stated government policy. In other words, you can't tell your allies for six years not to do business with Iran and at the same time secretly sell Iran weapons yourself.

Free speech is not a license to misinform and lie without accepting challenge. The C.I.A. has been invited to send representatives to debate with the defendants and our witnesses on campus and here in court. After all, in the "necessity defense," we have to prove that bigger laws are being broken. But where is the C.I.A. to refute the evidence we have brought before you? If you accept our necessity defense, the prosecutor must offer some proof that justification was absent beyond reasonable doubt, just as we must prove it was present.

When I was growing up in Worcester, Massachusetts, my father was very proud of democracy. He often took me to town hall meetings in Clinton, Athol and Hudson. He would say, See how the people participate, see how they participate in decisions that affect their lives—that's democracy. I grew up with the idea that democracy is not something you believe in, or a place you hang your hat, but it's something you do. You participate. If you stop doing it, democracy crumbles and falls apart. It was very sad to read last month that the New England town hall meetings are dying off, and, in a large sense, the spirit of this trial is that grass-roots participation in democracy must not die. If matters such as we have been discussing here are left only to be discussed behind closed-door hearings in Washington, then we would cease to have a government of the people.

You travel around this country, no matter where you go, people say, Don't waste your time, nothing changes, you can't fight the powers that be—no one can. You hear it a lot from young people. I hear it from my own kids: Daddy, you're so quaint to believe in hope. Kids today live with awful nightmares: AIDS will wipe us out; the polar ice cap will melt; the nuclear bomb will go off at any minute. Even the best tend to believe we are hopeless to affect matters. It's no wonder teen-age suicide is at a record level. Young people are detached from history, the planet and, most important, the future. I maintain to you that this detachment from the future, the lack of hope and the high suicide rate among youth are connected.

This trial is about many things, from trespassing to questioning acts by the most powerful agency in the government. And here we are in Hampshire District Court. You have seen the defendants act with dignity and decorum. You have seen our lawyers try hard to defend our position. Witnesses, many of whom occupied high positions of power, have come before you and have told you the C.I.A. often breaks the law, often lies. The prosecutor has worked hard but has not challenged their sincerity. The judge is here, the public, the press. I ask you, Is it we, the defendants, who are operating outside the system? Or does what you have heard about C.I.A. activities in Nicaragua and elsewhere mean it is they that have strayed outside the limits of democracy and law?

Thomas Paine, the most outspoken and farsighted of the leaders of the American Revolution, wrote long ago:

> Every age and generation must be as free to act for itself, in all cases, as the ages and generations which preceded it. Man has no property in man, neither has any generation a property in the generations which are to follow.

Thomas Paine was talking about this spring day in this courtroom. A verdict of not guilty will say, When our country is right, keep it right; but when it is wrong, right those wrongs. A verdict of not guilty will say to the University of Massachusetts that these demonstrations are reaffirming their rights as citizens who acted with justification. A verdict of not guilty will say what Thomas Paine said: Young people, don't give up hope. If you participate, the future is yours. Thank you.

59

A BRIEF HISTORY OF STUDENT ACTIVISM (1987)

Speech given at the University of South Carolina, September 16, 1987.

A few weeks ago I had a speaking engagement over at the University of Pennsylvania, and afterwards we went out to the local pub. There was a foreign exchange student there and he said to me, "Things seem so different here than where I come from. In my country, everything that's extracurricular is political, so if you want to protest Star Wars you go to the Science Club. But in the U.S. everything that's extracurricular seems either apolitical or anti-political." It turns out he had wanted to protest Star Wars at the University of Pennsylvania, so of course he went to the Science Club. The first week they had him selling brownies door-to-door, and the second week they had him competing in a contest to see who could make the best model airplane out of paper. He was beginning to get confused about student activism in America. When I asked him what country he was from, he said El Salvador. Even in a repressive country like El Salvador, where student leaders are hung from the gates of the Universities regularly, they have a concept of the engaged student. This is true around the world. But in the U.S., we do not have that concept.

The center of the student movement today is Seoul, Korea, where they are challenging the fundamental basis of their government. In France last December 500,000 students took to the streets to protest a government plan that would have limited higher education to rich and upper middle-class people. That protest forced the government to change their policy. The same thing happened in Spain, with students in the frontlines. If the corrupt oligarchy in Mexico falls, it will be the students in the streets leading the struggle. Whether you are looking at social movements in the Philippines or South Africa, the vast majority of the people in front are young people, because young people do make social revolutions. Revolution just isn't an idea that comes to you when you're middle-aged. Here in the United States, despite what happened in the sixties, student activism is an oxymoron, a contradiction in terms, and a strange one at that (just like the working press or military intelligence). If you look at the life of the American campus through its history, the norm is what we've witnessed during the last 15 years. In American society, the university is traditionally considered to be a psychosocial moratorium, an ivory tower where you withdraw from the problems of society and the world around you to work on important things like your career and your marriage.

Activist movements are out there taking shape. All over the United States, in God's country, where God is white, male, 78 and Republican, there are grassroots organizations forming and fighting to save the environment. These movements are far from dead. One group that I've worked for has fought for 16 years to save the Delaware River and beat the Philadelphia Electric Company. In the process we've kicked out six politicians and fought hundreds of court battles involving civil disobedience. But when I look around at the people active in this movement, they're my age. There's a dearth of young people.

The same is true for urban politics. In 1966 a friend of mine, Jessie Gray, a tenant organizer, started the first rent strikes against landlords in New York City. It was an illegal thing to do; he was thrown in jail. All the tenant rent strike organizers that used this technique were thrown in jail. Today, not only are rent strikes legal, they are used by over 5,000 tenant organizations that are fighting landlords. So many of the people who began waging these battles nationally—Jesse Jackson, Gloria Steinem, Ralph Nader, the

Berrigans, Dave Dellinger, myself, the student leaders Mario Savio and Mark Rudd—all are still very, very active today. But when you think about it, the only national figure under 30 that we know about is my fellow co-defendant, Amy Carter. I mean there's no one else right, left, or center that you can name who's under 30.

But before you get to feeling too bleak about where we stand now, I want you to remember that those very moments when the empire mentality, as represented by the likes of Bork, Ollie, Reagan, Falwell, and Company, seems to have everything under control, are exactly when the natives in the colonies—like the Philippines, South Korea and Latin America—grow rebellious, and the young at home get itchy. This is already happening. The lull in student activism ended about three years ago.

CNN took a poll of your age group. When asked to pick any period in history in any country in the world, overwhelmingly the 1960's in America was the choice. And you are right. That was an incredible period for many reasons. Demographics were on our side; there were a lot of us; with more of us to count, we counted more. The economy was on our side; this country was affluent, which facilitated dropping out—to go to Tibet or into the streets or to jail. There was a cultural revolution where the best and the popular were identical. And that is a very rare occurrence in history. Musical groups like the Beatles made music they'll still be listening to 200 years from now. The effect of something like the Sergeant Pepper's Lonely Heart's Club album on me and other activists, organizers and counterculture people around the world was one of incredible impact—like starting a fire in a fireworks factory. Woodstock, which may have been the cultural event of the century, had the impact of a cultural revolution and it's going to be hard to duplicate that. With young people's attitudes today, if there's not going to be any sex, not going to be any drugs, I've got to tell you the rock and roll's going to have to be awful fucking good. How quickly paradise goes in your generation. It took a lot longer in our period to destroy concepts of Paradise.

To understand the sixties, you've got to be familiar with the fifties. There was an old popular Republican President in office whom we all loved, who stumbled through press conferences mixing up the names of countries, who believed we had a God-given duty to police the world and dismantle the welfare state, who was above politics. There was a tremendous religious revival going on, and a lot of screaming about censoring books. Bookburning was big. There were always attacks on rock and roll on the basis that it made blacks lust for white women and white women give in too easily. The radio was segregated, with the AM band reserved for whites and the FM band for blacks—until we started listening to the naughty black music and it did everything the critics said it would.

There were no drugs in the fifties. More precisely, there were drugs; but you took them to stay up for exams or to crash, not to get high. No one got high. As for sex, we had heard rumors, but doing it wasn't actually invented until 1961, with the pill, in my home town of Worcester, Massachusetts. In the fifties we were told that sex made your brain fall out. We were actually the last generation to be told babies were brought by storks or found under the cabbage leaves in the garden or just plain "don't ask."

And then there was Communism. Although one survey shows that 80% of your generation thinks the Russians fought with the Japanese and the Germans in World War II, the Russians were actually our ally in that war. In the fifties, an incredible anti-Communist hysteria took hold pointing to Communists in all the universities, in the defense plants, on the football teams. We had to go on this Red-Menace witch-hunt to get rid of Communists.

They didn't have urine tests then, or they would have used them. There always seem to be tests around to prove that you are a good, productive American. Generally, they're about as accurate as the test in Salem for witches which was to stick you in the water until you drowned, which meant you weren't a witch after all. If you were still breathing when you came up, then you were a witch and they took you out of the water and burned you. In the fifties it was the Loyalty Oath. You had to say, "I'm a good American and I promise I'll never overthrow the Government through violent means. I am not a Communist and I don't know anyone who is a Communist." Now with the American education I had, how am I going to know who's a Communist? The only textbook that mentioned it had two lines on Marxism and 27 pages about why it was all wrong. And in the fifties we had spies. We were catching them left and right, giving away secrets. Sometimes they would go on television, confess and say "I was wrong, but give me another break; I'll be straight, red-white-and-blue American and I'll catch the ball every single time." It took about eight years before Americans started saying, there is a moral position here, there is something called free speech, First Amendment rights and a right to privacy. There is a constitutional basis for saying that your political affiliations are your own business. In the end, the House UnAmerican Activities Committee could not withstand the clamor of those voices.

Now, while all this is going on in the homefront, the CIA was busy crushing any liberation movement abroad. What was interesting about the CIA of the fifties, of course, was that it didn't exist. No one knew about the CIA. Seventy-five percent of the Congress didn't know it existed, 95% of the American public didn't know it existed. The only spies were Russian spies. We didn't spy because we were nice people—So Ike said, and Ike wouldn't lie. Then, in May, 1960, a plane was shot down over Russia. Ike went on t.v. and said, "It's a weather reconnaissance flight." But, Khrushchev, who was the Gorbachev of his time, the reformer, had the pilot by the back of his shirt. Francis Gary Powers was his name, and he had a story to tell. He worked for the CIA, which at first we all thought meant the Culinary Institute of America. Spies? What I really remember was that they showed his survival kit, so called, which had a hypodermic needle filled with cyanide. If he ever got into an embarrassing situation he was supposed to do the honorable thing. In reality, he had second thoughts about that, which was how the United States citizens came to know what the rest of the world knew too damn painfully well, which was that we had an incredible apparatus called the CIA.

The fifties was an era of tremendous conformity. People thought of little beyond material success. The stereotype was the status-seeker—we didn't have the word Yuppie yet—who lived in Connecticut, dressed in a certain way and had something of the shopping mall mentality. These were days of arrogant flag-waving and smug complacency. We were number one in everything in the world, which gave us license to ignore much of what was actually going on internationally. And just about everyone bought this whole vision of America as an empire, which is sort of the shopping mall vision on a global scale. However, a few ungrateful brats, mostly young people like myself, questioned this vision, saw it as spiritually unrewarding, unjust for those who couldn't participate in it, and, frankly, a little boring. And so a resistance began to that frame of mind and it was out of that resistance to what we called prime-time culture, that the most activist decade in this century, the 1960's, happened.

Now the two social movements that really marked the period were Vietnam and the movement against apartheid. Of course, we don't use that word, but that is the Afrikaans word for segregation. And it was the movement against apartheid that really made the political break with the empire mentality of the fifties. Apartheid existed in the South of our country for almost 300 years, except for a few short years of Reconstruction. And those of us in the North didn't know it. Nothing in our schools, churches, classrooms, newspapers gave us any indication that it existed. We didn't know that there were lynchings going on all over the place. We didn't know that Black people couldn't vote in Mississippi. I mean, we didn't even know that there had been a Depression in the United States. I didn't find that out until I was about 28. And I didn't find out about the Rosenbergs until six years after they were executed. I wasn't taught it. There was a whole history of repression and the resistance to oppression which was just swept out. So South Carolina in 1963 or 1964 was as far away for me in New England as South Africa is for you today. We were moved first by what we saw on t.v., in the same way that you are moved by what you see on South Africa. Your generation is moved. We are a global community. They sing "We Are the World," you sing "We Are the World," they sang "We Shall Overcome," we sang "We Shall Overcome." We knew that segregation's time to fall had come. And the attitude of Washington in the early sixties towards segregation in the South can properly be called constructive engagement. I remember being beaten by the Klan in Macona, Mississippi, and the FBI was saying "Do you feel your civil rights have been violated?" I didn't know that the FBI was taking down my name, not the Klan's names. I can read about it now, among the 66,000 pages of government files I have.

Martin Luther King, who is now eulogized by people like George Bush as they sing "We Shall Overcome," was a very different man from the one they've conjured up. If you ask young people how he made a change, it seems that he prayed a lot. Martin Luther King was an outlaw. He went to jail again and again; he was beaten and reviled. The head of the FBI, J. Edgar Hoover, attacked him as a puppet of Communism and called him "the most dangerous man in America." The Justice Department infiltrated his organization, illegally wiretapped his phones, systematically harassed and threatened him. That's how much they loved Martin Luther King. This is the real history.

If you look at the beautiful, grainy, black and white footage of 'Eyes on the Prize' you see King and the other ministers in the front lines. Then you look at the long lines of marchers, at the people in the streets being beaten. Ninety percent of those people were your age, because it was young people that made and built the civil rights movement in the 1960's. People from SNCC, the Student Nonviolent Coordinating Committee, or SSOC, the Southern Student Organizing Committee. The southern civil rights movement was more than just a social upheaval, a social revolution. It was also where we went to school. We learned things that we didn't learn in the university. First we learned that it was okay to be emotional, that when we see social injustice, the right response is moral outrage. That doesn't just mean anger. Moral outrage is an emotional response that is proper in the face of "Colored Only" signs, or of a society that won't let people vote because of the color of their skins, or demands that the blacks sit in the back and the whites in the front of the car or the bus. If you were driving down, with blacks and whites together, you'd stop the car and the blacks got in the back seat. This is not the Peloponnesian War I'm talking about. This is 20 years ago. We learned moral outrage. We learned a different concept of authority. We learned how to question, disobey and defy authority. To do this we had to overcome our education which had taught us, "obey authorities," "they know more than you," "they're experts," "these things have been going on for a long time you know," "things don't change overnight," "there are many sides to every issue," and a million other such sayings that are like nails in a coffin. This is the traditional academic approach; nine out of ten academic conferences end with a question mark. When the final word is that there are many sides to every issue, each one as valid as the next, then you don't have to do anything about it—paralysis. We made the question mark an exclamation point and said "Now!" In that way we learned how to question and ultimately how to defy authority.

We also learned how to organize. You don't learn community organizing in the universities. You learn the skills of motivation. People come to you and say "this is the most apathetic school in the country." They say this at every institution, and have been saying it for 27 years. "Nothing ever changes," "city hall always wins." Consider that this is probably the most anti-democratic attitude that you could have. It means there's no need for them to have policemen standing behind you with guns. If you believe it, you live in a police state. It doesn't matter whether you're in Russia, El Salvador, South Africa or the United States. If you've internalized the idea that people, once organized, still cannot fight and beat the powers that be, then you've already lost.

We learnt some basic skills, which in some ways is the hardest part, because the problem of mechanics is the same for an activist as for someone in business. In business the people don't say "Look at the local office, they can't get their shit together, the mimeograph machine doesn't work, no one cares about anything," what you hear too often from progressive groups. They say, "We can do it, we'll sell it all." The difference is, in business the idea is that you're to use this for yourself, your career. There's no 'we' out there, the world is a jungle. You stay indoors or you become Ted Turner. That's the mentality of the business world. The strong eat the weak, and the weak are losers anyway. They're the ones that care about other things: the handicapped, radiation, tropical rainforests, poor Nicaraguans getting slaughtered. They're losers because it's 'I' that's strong. That's why we are the least unionized country in the world. Everyone has this idea that if you have to act collectively, with a sense of community, somehow you are a loser as an individual. Where the skills are, the motivation to bring people together, to organize, is lacking. You have to change that. Learn the skills any way you can, but use them to your own ends, which are those of social justice.

A woman interviewing me today asked, "Are you here to make trouble?" "I sure as hell hope so," I said. Then she asked me, "Are you a radical?" I said, "What's a radical?" She thought about it for a minute and then she came out with, "Well, someone that gets arrested." So I said, "There are a hundred thousand people in jail, you mean they're all radicals?" Now here we were, and we're both Americans right, that's the funny thing. But she's of the school that figures this country just happened, just sprang out of God's forehead right after they dumped the tea in Boston Harbor. But no, that's not exactly how it happened. They went out and actually shot cops and everything. We have to remember that. This country came into existence through Revolution. The status quo sits on society like fat on cold chicken soup and it's quite content to be what it is. Unless someone comes along to stir things up there just won't be change. You need people that are going to take risks. Many took risks with their lives, some gave their lives. That's what it took and Jim Crow law ended. Legal segregation, apartheid, ended. I'm not saying racism ended in this country, not by a long shot. In fact, racial terrorism, with incidents like the ones in Cummings, Georgia, or Howard Beach, New York, may be on the rise, and the economic gap has widened between blacks and whites. It has been interesting to see that the issue that has galvanized students during the last three years was not one of self-interest but a moral issue. The students picked apartheid in South Africa. Eight thousand students have been arrested over this issue on campuses in the last three years. They've built shantytowns. Student leaders have gotten kicked out of schools. Over 160 universities have now joined the divestment movement, pulling out over 6 billion dollars. There's only about 60 corporations left down there.

Thinking about all this last summer, I flashed back to 1965. After the civil rights voting act was passed and the movement shifted to economic issues or to the racism and de facto segregation that existed in the North, the battles weren't won. King didn't win any battles after 1965. Whether in Chicago or in Memphis, Tennessee, a union battle or the poor people's march on Washington, economic battles were lost. Movements built around an issue have a time limit. Whether you win or lose, at some point the issue starts going away and you start to lose your momentum.

But there we were, full of piss and vinegar, ready to go, with all the skills we'd developed, ready to fight authority and knowing how to organize. We looked around and we saw Vietnam. Hot damn, Vietnam in 1965. Now, Vietnam was the longest war in U.S. history. There were two Vietnam wars: 1955 to 1965, and 1965 to 1975. The ones all the movies are about were the second half of the war. The first half is very important to analyze; it was the CIA's war. They were buying Indian tribes, like the Montagnards, building a corrupt government, inventing border incidents left and right, secretly smuggling hundreds of millions of dollars and heroin which ended up in the United States. Ollie and friends, in the Phoenix project in 1963, killed 40,000 people including the president of the country, Diem, whom we had installed. They didn't just kill Commies, they killed Buddhist leaders, anyone who didn't toe the line. We had hired a mercenary army. Then in 1964 they told a grand lie. Lyndon Johnson, who went on t.v. regularly saying, "I will never send American boys to go and die in the Asian war" came on one night and told us that North Vietnamese P.T. boats had just attacked our Navy fleet in international waters in the Gulf of Tonkin.

The Senate debated for two hours. The vote was 98 to 2—Senators Morse of Oregon and Gruening of Alaska, and they aren't building statues for those two. That's when the second part began. Before it was over, we sent three and a half million soldiers over, and spent a trillion and a half dollars in that war. We used every weapon short of nuclear warheads. We had electronic battlefields and computerized electronic sensors that would locate anything alive. Then a fleet of helicopters would be sent out with napalm bombs, bombs that exploded 600 feet above land and cluster bombs with needles that would blanket a square half-mile, killing everything alive. Puff-the-Magic-Dragon, AC-47 gunships would hover over a village shooting tracer bullets all night long. The bullets were heat-seeking, killing water buffalos, gorillas, rebels, women, children. We killed two million people over there. Fifty-eight thousand Americans died, three hundred thousand were injured. Maybe another three hundred thousand suffered the effects of toxic poisoning from herbicides like Agent Orange. Between 1966 and 1969 there were months when over a trillion bullets were fired. This is the first war in history where the word trillion comes up.

In 1975, before the Frank Church Committee in the Senate, representatives of the CIA got up and said that the Gulf of Tonkin incident had been entirely made up in Langley, Virginia. Along with scores and scores of other incidents, the attack simply hadn't happened. But it was a little late in the day to be telling either the Vietnamese people, the American Congress or the American public. In point of fact, Vietnam was not a winnable war. It was illegal because Congress never declared war. It was immoral, unnecessary and unwinnable, because most of the people there believed in the revolution, in Ho Chi Minh. They believed the United States when it had said "We'll give you your freedom," believed the French, the Chinese. They were fighting for self-determination, victory or death. We could never have won that war in Southeast Asia, 10,000 miles away from home, but not for lack of trying. We dropped more bombs on that country than ten times the number both sides used in World War Two. That's how little we tried to win the war.

At home, there was a virtual civil war. There was mutiny in the army, there were 20,000 people that went to Canada, and 5,000 that went to jail. Another 10,000 went underground, and another 5,000 went to Sweden. Hundreds of thousands took to the streets in protest. This meant that in every city and in every town, families were split apart over the war in

Vietnam. There was a civil war that divided the generations, taking its firepower from the real war halfway across the world. We knew we couldn't get Archie Bunker, but maybe Edith and the kids we were going for all the way. Students were killed, and not just at Kent State and Jackson State. It's not easy to fight your government in times of war. Right up until the time when the bodies start coming back wrapped in plastic, people generally seem to like wars, and to not like those who won't sing the fight songs and wave the flag. Never in the history of Western civilization has a people risen up so successfully against its government in a time of foreign war as during the Vietnam War. The government used every trick in the book to get us, including blackmail, the IRS, and, in my case, incessant harassment from eight different government agencies. There were 155 illegal wiretaps on phones I used. My father's customers were driven out of his business. I was beaten by agents, as were people who associated with me. On one of the Watergate tapes you can hear Richard Nixon, Haldeman, and Ehrlichman discussing getting Abbie the Jew and the other Chicago Seven defendants, smashing them. There are photographs of me with the free nose job they gave me. We were not intimidated. In the end the troops came home.

We never felt we were unpatriotic. To me the country is the land and the people, not necessarily the guy who happens to be president. The Constitution is not the Bible. After all, it allowed slavery for 75 years, and denied the right of women to vote for well over a hundred years. The Constitution was based on the old English law that a man's home is his castle. It was designed essentially to protect individuals from government intrusion. That is a good deal for men who own castles. What's good about the Constitution is that it is a living document. The ways in which you can change it, where you can right the wrongs, are built in. So it's not a question of "My country right or wrong," but of righting the wrongs of my country. That's the way it's supposed to be, that's the way I read the Constitution. There is no point in having free speech unless you make use of it. The ratio of people who do is one in 10,000. The 10,000 people believe in the democracy they live in, but actually doing it, making change, is something else altogether, and in those years we crossed that line.

Just as there are parallels between the civil rights movement in the South in this country in the early sixties and your feelings about South Africa, there are parallels between Vietnam in the late sixties and Central America today. It's very clear to see. With the success of the divestment movement it became inevitable that the anti-apartheid movement was going to have the same kind of slack as the Civil Rights Movement did in the sixties, and that another movement was going to start to grow. And that was going to be resistance to the present war in Central America. Without the draft, resistance on college campuses would concentrate on CIA recruiting. So we started to organize on campuses against CIA recruiting. People say this is a free speech issue—they have a right to come on campus and speak. Well, that's true. You can invite any CIA head to come and speak; I'd gladly debate him any old time. This is free speech, as is what we're doing now. Free speech is not taking a person behind closed doors and saying, "You can't ask any questions about covert action policy." Free speech might be asking, "Am I going to be asked to assassinate a leader, or poison a well, or put mines in a harbor?" But if you ask those questions, they don't want you. You're not allowed to ask how much money there is, or what the budget is, or what the objective is. You get a very one-sided view. Recruiting is a privilege that universities grant corporations because they believe they have shared economic interests, which is a very different idea than that of higher learning. But there are other universities in this country that do not allow Exxon or Ford or any other companies to come on and recruit, because they have a different concept of what the role and responsibilities of the university should be. Certainly, free speech is not a license to lie, which is what the CIA does. One of my next activist acts is to take on the U.S. Army ads on television because I think they're a fraud. I don't believe that you learn how to become a brain surgeon or a super-specialized electronics whiz in the Army. I don't believe you're in your parachute one minute and studying at the university the next. I don't believe the army is going to give you a fresh start. You learn how to clean toilets and kill people. That's not a beginning, that's a dead end. And it's not what they show you on t.v. So I'm going to sue them . . . when I can get the money together. (*In response to heckling from the audience, Abbie takes off his shirt and puts on a 'JUST SAY NO' tee-shirt.*) There's trouble in Columbia, South Carolina tonight.

The notion that somehow a country of three million people, suffering from dire poverty and astronomical inflation, having just survived a devastating earthquake, and not ten years young after its own revolution, is a threat to the national security of the United States, well, it's absurd, but it's also awfully similar to what they were saying about Vietnam once upon a time. I've heard the contras compared with the French resistance. But then, having been down to Central America five times, I've also seen what they've done with my own eyes. I've seen victims of contra posses. I've talked to parents whose fourteen-year-old kid was skinned alive right in front of them. I was in a town when an ambulance was blown up by the contras, killing the driver, the nurse, the doctor and the patient. And now we've got Green Berets in Costa Rica training the police. U.S. helicopters are flying all over Honduras. Border incidents are being invented. We should not give aid to the contras, we should give aid to the Sandinistas. (*In response to more heckling, Abbie pulls out another tee-shirt and offers it to the loudest heckler.*) Here's a tee-shirt. You interrupted me the best so you win the prize.

Meanwhile, around the corner, in the democracy of El Salvador, we are directing the largest air war in the history of the Western Hemisphere. It's not reported here, but it's going on. We blanket huge patches of the countryside with tracer bullets, fragmentation bombs, possibly napalm. A Harvard investigation team examined refugees and said "Napalm's being used down here," to which the Salvadoran Generals answer, "We do have napalm in our arsenals." The government lies when it says that El Salvador is a democracy and Nicaragua is a totalitarian dungeon. It's a lie. But it wins a war of attrition. Let's talk about how the Sandinista government treats the Indians. That's important. But talk about it in the context of Guatemala, where they have killed or driven from the country a million Indians in the last six years. We don't talk about Guatemala. Raise your hands if you can name the little newspaper that's always getting suppressed in Nicaragua. *La Prensa*. Okay, that is the most famous foreign newspaper in the United States. About eighteen people here got it. It has a circulation of 60,000 when it's running, which it will be soon. I've got a hundred dollars for someone who can name the opposition paper in El Salvador right now. If it's a democracy they ought to have an opposition paper, right? I mean they did have one called *La Cronica*, but the editor had his head cut off and the staff had its arms cut off. You see, *La Prensa* is what we would have had in World War II if we had had a newspaper called *Hitler Could Win*. How long would it have been in, say, 1942, before they would have burned it down? How many Tory newspapers did we burn during our own revolution? Those papers were burned to the ground. Tories were tarred and feathered. Fifteen percent of the country was put into exile. But this didn't happen in

Nicaragua. *La Prensa* is still around. Priests don't get murdered in Nicaragua, they do get murdered in El Salvador and Guatemala, daily.

Now Bob Dole said the other day that a three-day war would wipe out Nicaragua. Well, he's wrong. Unlike Grenada, the invasion of Nicaragua will take 500,000 troops to begin with, and then a long, long occupation—10 to 15 years in all the mountains of Central America, maybe all the mountains of Latin America. We've invaded Nicaragua at least 11 times already, before the Sandinistas were even around. But we aren't given the history here in America. In Nicaragua they say, "You are taught to forget the history between our two countries, we are forced to remember it."

About three years ago something started to happen and I felt a familiar twinge. You began to see demonstrations on campuses across the country—against apartheid, against CIA recruiting, against sexual harassment. You had arguments between students and university administrations over control of campus newspapers, over tuition hikes, over having police and undercover agents on campus. What I'm talking about, I think, I hope, is the resurgence of the student movement. There are about 50 or 60 different kinds of battles going on around the country. I've been to about six different regional student conferences and so far nothing has gelled nationally. That may or may not happen next February at the University of Rutgers, where they are holding the First Student National Convention. Like the early days of SDS, students will come from all over, and those who come will be activists. There are currently about 3,000; we need about 5,000. To have a real student movement the first condition is that you need about 5,000 people that see themselves as organizers first and students second, just as a union organizer sees him or herself as an organizer of workers first, and a worker second. Maybe there'll be 5,000 by February—talking about leadership, strategy, structures and decision-making, all towards building a national movement—and maybe there won't.

It's very strange for me to look at your generation. You see, we always had this idea that each generation was going to be brighter, that each generation was going to be more progressive, and would cheer more for justice and more for peace. But my youngest son, who's 16, says to me, "Dad, you're so quaint and romantic. You think things are going to get better, that there's hope," he says, "but none of us believe this." And then he tells me how half the world is going to be wiped out by AIDS, how the polar icecap is going to melt, that the tropical rainforest will be gone in thirty years and we won't have any oxygen, which doesn't matter anyway since the nuclear holocaust is going to happen within seven years, and if I'm a little doubtful about the dates, he says he can prove it to me on his computer. If you listen to the music today, it is true that what is inside it is not someone holding a flower, but instead the sense that things are really fucked up bad, big bad, a sense of hopelessness. And that's why the suicide rate among teenagers today is the highest since they've been recording teenage suicides. The problem isn't that these kids taking their own lives feel disconnected. They're very well connected to the idea that you can't do anything about your own situation, to the hopelessness, and the fatalism that's out there. I wrote an article about this and in my view, if the next generation is going to make some contribution it'll be the discovery of how you struggle for social change without having any hope. In the sixties, you see, when you jumped on the earth, the earth jumped back just like Einstein said it would. We knew we'd win every battle because every day we grew up. Every day was a new day and being on the brink of the Apocalypse was romantic. But maybe this vision that you have is the more realistic of the two, more into reality or "realty," as it's pronounced in North Carolina more than South.

You know how they always have these terms: the Lost Generation, the We Generation, the Me Generation, the I Generation. Well, today I feel sad because I look at your generation as possibly the last generation. I sense that this is what you really believe, so good luck. You see, I wouldn't know how to fight from that particular stance. But I'm affected by it, I'm learning by it. I hope you can learn to work with the tools you have, and what you believe is one of those tools.

We need young people at the front because young people make revolution. Every idea I had, every idea that every one of my gurus ever had, they had the idea when they were 17 years old and then just kept refining it. We didn't invent the cry of justice and peace in the 1960s and we certainly didn't write the final chapter. There's a lot of work to be done out there. I urge you, young people especially, take your personal computers, take your energy, your young legs, your eagerness, your natural feelings for justice and peace and a better deal for the planet and go out and make tomorrow better than it is today, better than we tried to make it yesterday. Thanks for bringing me back to Columbia, South Carolina.

QUESTIONS FROM THE AUDIENCE

Question: I have a two part question. Do you believe that the Weather Underground movement of 20 years ago had a positive effect and do you believe that a similar group could effect a change in today's present police state.

Abbie: Resistance should seek the *most* common denominator and then push with the least amount of force needed to make the point. The questions that you are asking are about strategy. What kind of tactics you use to achieve social change depends on the historical moment and in particular on what the opposition is doing, because tactics are not developed in a vacuum. So, yes, up to 1968 at convention demonstrations where the cops just went in in waves, beating people up, where the city would not give you the right to protest, to even protest 10 miles away from where the convention was, where groups were being infiltrated by police agents, where all-out war was declared, clandestine operations were a necessity. There was an escalation which I feel was justified given the situation. The government's tactic was repression. If you were in El Salvador, for example, when they killed Archbishop Romero, if you were an organizer and believed in justice and peace and everything, you would have organized a demonstration, which people did. Then when 400,000 people came out into the square and the government came out with machine guns and shot at them, if you were a good organizer, you'd reconsider your tactics. You'd have to go back and say, "Well, I don't know for sure that I want to do that again and again." And after you thought about it some more, you might say, "You know, maybe I'll go up into the mountains, be a guerrilla." What choice would you have?

You see, it's not a question of charity. You have to go through changes yourself, as an individual. It's not a question of going out and making five million dollars and then sending a check to save the starving people in Mexico. Charity never produces change.

But those aren't the alternatives I see facing you today in this country. You have to have the courage to challenge power, to do so publicly, in the streets, both physically and in the streets in your mind. But you also have to learn to work within the system, so as to institutionalize the changes that are won in the streets. That means learning how the system works, learning how to communicate, how to use direct mail, how to use voter referendum drives, how to bring people together, how to forge small groups that make decisions. There is a science to organizing people and you stick to that science. You learn the art of communication, speaking American dialect, rendering unto Caesar's palace that which is Caesar's palace. You don't turn up your noses at entertainment because entertainment is way up there on the hierarchy of needs. If you learn all this stuff, you can be successful so you don't have to go underground. There were lots and lots of social changes that occurred in the sixties and they happened essentially through nonviolence.

Q: I was wondering if you had anything good or positive to say about the CIA?

Abbie: Yeah, they lost the trial in Northampton. [*Referring to the April 15, 1987 acquittal of 12 people, including Abbie Hoffman, of trespassing charges in connection with demonstrations against CIA recruitment at the University of Massachusetts.*] I believe that every country has a right to defend itself, has a right to national security. I believe that part of that national security implies gathering intelligence. What I question is the nature of the intelligence they're gathering and how they're gathering it. Looking through the whole history of the CIA, the covert action programs have done more harm to our national security than good. They've killed more allies than enemies. And secret organizations, of which the CIA is the most powerful in our government, are anti-democratic. An ex-agent, Ralph McGehee, described the prevalent attitude in the CIA towards Congress this way: "Treat 'em like mushrooms: keep 'em in the dark, feed 'em a lot of manure." Now, this is just not the way the whole thing is supposed to work. I don't care how good Ollie North looks in his goddamn uniform, this is not how it works.

So, I would not want to abolish the CIA, but I would want to abolish the covert action programs, because they're buying the wrong intelligence. They ought to come back from Chile or Korea saying, "There are a lot of people without civil rights." Instead they come back with the names of the union organizers and the student leaders which they give to the governments so they can go pick them off. That isn't what we want them to do.

Q: I hope to make a comment rather than ask a question. That comment is one that was made by the President of the United States in 1862, a Republican I might add, who said, "to sit by in silence when they should protest makes cowards of men." That was said by Abraham Lincoln and I think those words are timely for us today.

Abbie: Yeah, it's nice to recall that there was a good Republican president.

Q: You mentioned the pull of the mass media. Could you elaborate on how the media shapes the right-wing politics of this nation?

Abbie: I don't know if I can or not. But I do know what the media's purpose is. The Constitution gives you freedom of the press, it doesn't give you freedom of the media. The media's another thing. The idea that the media is there to educate us, or to inform us, is ridiculous because that's about tenth or eleventh on their list. The first purpose of the media is to sell us shit, things we don't need. One moment it'll be 'don't do drugs' and ten minutes later it's Miller time.

Secondly, the media is there to keep us very secure about being Americans, to remind us that we are number one in everything. So if I say to you that there are 47 countries in the world that have universal health care whereby all citizens, regardless of how much money they earn, are guaranteed proper medical care and the United States isn't one of them, you say to me that I'm speaking heresy because we're the best in everything. That's the job of the media, to keep us secure about being number one, and insecure about losing everything we have. I could show you lots of things about the disparity in wealth and land ownership in this country that would show you that we're no different than Venezuela, that in America one percent of the population owns about 75 percent of the acquired wealth, and ten percent owns about 90 percent, while the rest of us, the other 90 percent, own next to nothing. But that perception is not tolerated in the media. You will never see it played on the networks.

Sex and violence are important to the media, and then way down there on the list falls information exchange. But it's a specific kind of information, what I call the dumbing of America. Vanna White is important but Daniel Ortega isn't. And it's important to know the difference between Ralph Lauren and Pierre Cardin, because if you want to dress for success you've got to know that. History is more or less irrelevant, the future is important. So it's a weird kind of education. You see, my idea of education is like Socrates', that it's a subversive act. You learn how to challenge the ideas that are out there. In the end, you'll never get the true story from the media because what the media controls and disseminates is mythology. In the movie *The Big Fix*, my friends looked for me as a fugitive making $3.50 an hour, which is what I was when I was underground. They found me as a cynical million dollar ad executive living in Beverly Hills, which is about as near to the truth as Hollywood could get.

Q: Is student apathy more prevalent in the eighties as compared to the sixties because we have no widely known figure we can look up to, whereas in the sixties students had leaders they respected.

Abbie: Sort of. No, actually, in the sixties, rather than role models what we had was a greater sense that we were making it up as we went along. We all had that sense. As for leaders, no we were very anti-leader. There's nothing worse in a progressive movement than being a leader because you're immediately getting trashed, burned out, knocked down all over the place. It's actually a really weird job. Sure we had role models, people like Saul Alinsky, King who had also been active in the fifties, as had Dorothy Day. I don't know if you know these names. But there weren't very many of them because the previous wave of activism had happened in the 1930's. It had been based on class and union organizing, but between World War II and the witch-hunts of the fifties, we'd lost a lot of those people.

Q: Seems like then there were more musicians that were wide-reaching than now, with songs like Madonna's "Material Girl."

Abbie: Gee, that's number one in Nicaragua. They love that song. What's the matter with Madonna? What're you talking about anyway? Geez. I don't know, when we would get arrested, along with what we were saying we needed some music and the music was there. You need a cultural revolution to parallel the political revolution. I believe that. Especially in a society that communicates in a post-literate manner like ours does, that's not interested in books. You need the music. When we were all arrested at the University of Massachusetts, it was the first time they had brought the police on in 17 years, with attack dogs, helmets and everything, because civil disobedience has become a very polite sport in the last four or five years. But here they were very seriously beating up people, breaking legs and everything. People were being carted off to jail, handcuffed for hours. I went on the darkened buses and I said, "You folks know any freedom songs or anything?" And they said, "Oh yeah." They knew every song from *Hair*. They start singing all these songs from *Hair*. And I'm saying, "What the hell are you singing? *Hair* was a Broadway show. It was a rip-off, a fake; they were wearing wigs." They're saying, "What're you talking about, Abbie, it's a movie, it's a good movie." I thought it was kind of sad, because you do have to have your own songs and this was something they didn't have.

Q: I have a comment, which is that I think it would help all the public servants overcome their fascination with nuclear weapons, if we stopped making them penis-shaped.

Abbie: I agree with you one hundred percent. I feel I understand someone like Ronnie Reagan because he is a fifties person, he's the fifties incarnated, and that was a very repressed time. In the early years, in 1980 and 1981, Reagan used to get frustrated at press conferences since he didn't know which capitals went with which Central American countries and so he'd just say "Down there, there's trouble *down there*," referring to Central America. And I used to say, "My god, that's fifties talk." That's when my parents said: "Don't play with anything down there or you'll get in trouble." And then—hang on, this only gets better—then I looked at a map of the United States and there's Florida, so erect, so firm, jutting into the soft, compliant basin of the Carribean. That's what they mean about the Big Stick policy. That's it. So the psychosexual history of all this stuff is very important and you're right to be aware of it.

Q: Do you know that in Honduras the constitution states that there should be no foreign parties tolerated within the country's borders?

Abbie: They're violating their own Constitution, sure. Honduras is being Lebanonized right now. Most of our money that's sent down there as aid, Honduran generals fight duels over—who'll get a half a million or a million dollars to put in a Swiss bank account. That's where most of it goes, not to keep the contras in boots and blankets and things. They say the best-paying job in Nicaragua is in north Nicaragua, and it's the one the top contras have. They're big business, multi-millionaires, in a country that's per capita income is 684 dollars and sinking due to the concerted efforts of our government. In Nicaragua the damage is done. The vision the revolution had in the first couple of years, the achievements they made, are hard to live up to now, with the beating they've taken. So we have to face the irony that the U.S. is out to crush the joy as well as the concrete achievements of what I believe to be the most humanitarian of revolutions. We have come that far from our own originating impulses.

60

REEFER MADNESS (1987)

If there was anything unusual in Judge Douglas Ginsburg's rapid descent, it was probably the sight of White House conservatives scrambling to create a loophole in the national drug hysteria that would mitigate occasional marijuana use by a Supreme Court nominee. Never mind that President Reagan said last year that drug users are "as dangerous to our national security as any terrorist"; he tried dismissing Ginsburg's indiscretion as nothing more than "youthful fancy."

There was nothing surprising about Reagan's expedient reversal. For six years, the only consistent thing about our national drug policy has been its inconsistency. Harsher penalties, urine testing, hysteria, budget cuts and the simplistic "Just Say No!" campaign (the equivalent of telling manic depressives to "just cheer up") have returned drug education and treatment to the Reefer Madness era.

Reprinted from *The Nation* with permission.

Since 1980 the President and Nancy Reagan, Attorney General Edwin Meese 3d and White House drug policy advisers such as Dr. Carlton Turner, have made numerous rash and absurd statements about drugs. Dr. Turner claimed that smoking marijuana leads to AIDS (the sequence: Pot leads to harder drugs, which lead to sharing needles, which leads to AIDS). Peter Bensinger, former head of the Drug Enforcement Administration, claimed that marijuana was harmful because it "contained dioxin." The dioxin, of course, came from government spraying. Such statements are reminiscent of the 1920s, when the public was told that cocaine made blacks impervious to bullets.

Truth has been the first casualty in this so-called war on drugs. When Reagan labeled drug abuse "an evil scourge" that has become the nation's number-one social problem, during the 1986 campaign, the nation had been whipped up into such a frenzy that polls showed the citizenry believed him. On October 27, 1986, Reagan got what he championed: the fifty-fifth Federal antidrug bill in eighty years. Congress authorized $3.96 billion to attack what *Newsweek*, with typical hyperbole, compared to "the plagues of medieval times." (That plague wiped out two-thirds of the people in Europe. According to government statistics, in 1979 3,500 deaths were attributed to illicit drugs. No deaths, incidentally, were caused by marijuana.) Then, after the elections, Reagan cut $1 billion from his own war on drugs program and, in the harshest blow, recommended that no money be spent on drug rehabilitation and treatment in fiscal 1988.

Like the Red Menace of the early 1950s, the current drug hysteria has led to a loyalty oath—this time, the urine test. Extrapolating from margin-of-error figures supplied by manufacturers of standard drug tests (5 percent) and instances of laboratory mishandling documented by the Centers for Disease Control (15 to 20 percent), one can easily agree with a Northwestern University report claiming a national error rate of up to 25 percent. That means roughly one of every four persons tested for controlled substances could wrongly be fired, not hired or denied promotion.

But Reagan's not one to quibble about margins of error or unreasonable biochemical searches. Last year, when he announced the notorious drug-free workplace edict, he targeted Federal workers as an example for all labor. New applicants and tenured employees were forced to submit to urine tests. Of course, he wants to test all workers in America, which is rapidly occurring: In the private sector an estimated 35 million people were screened this year and the White House hopes to see 90 million being tested by 1990.

It is time to rethink a complex problem like drug abuse and disregard the simplistic nonsense of the Reagan antidrug campaign, which has ignored scientific evidence and overridden fundamental values of privacy and due process.

61

REFLECTIONS ON STUDENT ACTIVISM (1988)

Speech to the first National Student Convention, Rutgers University, February 6, 1988.

I guess you can't see my button. It says, "I fought tuition." It's a two-button set, actually. The second button says, "And tuition won."

You should know that more than 650 students have registered as delegates here, representing over 130 different schools. You have come despite freezing weather and hard economic times to do something that I'm not sure anyone here is ready yet to comprehend. I am absolutely convinced that you are making history just by being here. You are proving that the image of the American college student as a career-interested, marriage-interested, self-centered yuppie is absolutely outdated, that a new age is on the rise, a new college student.

There's been a lot of talk about comparing today to what went on in the sixties. I would remind you that in 1960, when we started the Student Nonviolent Coordinating Committee to fight in the South in the civil rights movement, less than 30 people came together to begin it. The famous

Students for a Democratic Society, which we're all reading about, was formed in 1962 with exactly 59 people. No one before has done anything this bold, imaginative, creative, and daring to bring together this many different strains of people, who all believe in radical change in our society. It is just an amazing feat. And I wish you the best of luck today, and especially tomorrow, when you have to decide whether to go forward or backward. I'd also like to take this moment to salute our glorious actor-in-chief: Happy Birthday Ronald Reagan! I don't believe anyone in here believes it's "Good morning in America" tonight.

I have a lot of speeches in my head: On the CIA, urine testing, nuclear power, saving water—that's my local battle. We're fighting the Philadelphia Electric Company's attempt to steal the waters of the Delaware River for yet another nuclear plant. A local battle? I don't know. One out of ten Americans drink from that river. I also speak on the modern history of student protest and on Central America, where I've been five times. Every time I get before a microphone I'm extremely nervous that chromosome damage and Alzheimer's will take their toll. I'll come out foaming at the mouth, accusing the CIA of pissing in the nuclear plants, to poison the water, to burn out the minds of youth, so they'll be easy cannon fodder for the Pentagon's war in Central America. Actually, that's probably not a bad speech.

On Tuesday I had to give a speech at the local grammar school to nine-year-olds. I said, "Go ahead, pick any subject you want." They wanted to hear about hippies. My 16-year-old kid, America, heard me give this speech about how you can't have political and social change without cultural change as well, and he said, "Daddy, you're not gonna bring back the hippies, are you? The hippies go to Van Halen concerts, get drunk, throw up on their sweatshirts and beat up all the punks in town." I said, "Okay, no hippies." That was last year, this year he's changed his mind. His mother and I were activists in the sixties, and he heard all the anti-war stories over and over again, never believed any of it. Then one night last spring he saw the documentary "Twenty Years Ago Today" about the effect of the Beatles' *Sergeant Peppers Lonely Hearts Club Band* on us all. It's about the only thing I'm ever going to recommend to anybody about the sixties, a simply brilliant documentary. He sat there watching cops fight with young people in the streets, people put flowers at the Pentagon in the soldiers' bayonets, and the Pentagon rise in the air, he saw it move just like we said it did.

Tears came streaming out of his eyes, and he called up and said, "Daddy, why was I born now? I should have been a hippie."

When I went to college long ago there was a ritual that we all had to go through at freshman induction. We were herded into a big room and the dean of admissions came and gave us a famous speech, "Look to your right, look to your left, one of you three won't be here in four years when it comes time to graduate." I'm going to say to you, "Look to your right, look to your left, two of you three aren't going to be here in four years." That's about the attrition rate of the Left. I'm sure that many of the people who want to organize interplanetary space connections have got everything worked out with Shirley MacLaine, and it's okay with me that they become moonies and yuppies and then born-again Mormons. They're not the ones that keep me up at night. But I worry about the good organizers, the successful organizers. You're the ones who know that you can actually get better at this, that you can get good at it. You know that being on the side of the angels, being right, isn't enough. To succeed you also have to work very hard with lots of cooperation from those around you. You have to have your wits about you continuously, show up on time, and follow through. These are the things that take place behind the scenes that keep you aimed at a goal, at victory, at success. And I worry because somehow on the Left, all too often, it's like three people in a phone booth trying to get out. Two are really trying to kick the third one out, and that's how they spend all their time. The third one's always called some dirty name that ends in an "ist." It's been a movement that devours its own. I look out at you and I think of my comrades, not the people you saw in *The Big Chill*, but people that were great movement organizers. You know some of their names and many others you don't know. They risked not just their careers, marriage plans and ostracism from their family, but their lives. They faced mobs with chains and brass knuckles, the clubs of the police, the dirty tricks and infiltrations of the FBI, the CIA, Army intelligence, Navy intelligence, and local red squads all around the country. They had pressure put on their families. They were prepared for all of this from the moment they decided to go against the grain and take on the powers that be. They were not prepared for the infighting. They were not prepared for a movement that devours itself. That has got to cease. I remember a very free and open democratic meeting in a room in New York City in 1971. All the various strains were there. There was one group that disagreed with the decision-making structure that had been set up. They wanted to settle their differences with the majority so they came armed with baseball bats. I can't remember the group's name—it was The National Labor Committee or Caucus—but I do remember the name of its leader, Lynn Marcus, better known today as Lyndon LaRouche.

The movement has had its share of other problems. We are too issue-oriented and not practical enough. We debate issues endlessly, deciding whose issue is more important than whose other issue, and so letting the moment of opportunity in history pass. By that time there's another issue there that's outstripped the other two. We debate which "ism" is more important than which other "ism," and I agree that all the isms lead to schisms which lead to wasms. We need a new language as we enter the next century.

We need to be rid of false dichotomies. There's been a big discussion going on for the last couple of days here about whether the organizing focus should be local, regional, national or interplanetary. I have never seen a national issue won that wasn't based on grassroots organizing and support. On the other hand, I have never ever seen a local issue won that didn't rely on outside support and outside agitators. Another false dichotomy is one that I call "In the System/out of the System." Between inside the system and outside it is a semipermeable membrane. And either-or is only a metaphysical question, not a practical one. The correct stance, especially now in these times, is one foot in the street—the foot of courage, that gets off the curbstone of indifference—and one foot in the system—the intelligent foot, the one that learns how to develop strategies, to build coalitions, to negotiate differences, to raise money, to do mailing lists, to make use of the electronic media. You need that foot, too. The brave foot goes out into the street to strike out against the enculturation process that says: "Stay indoors," "Don't go out in the street," "There's crime in the street," "It's bad in the street," "You lose your job in the street," "You'll be homeless," "It's terrible," "Yecch." Civil disobedience—blocking trucks, digging up the soil, occupying buildings, chaining yourself to fences (I spent my summer vacation chained to a fence)—can be a necessary act of courage, but it doesn't take a hell of a lot of brains.

Decision making has been a problem on the Left. In the sixties we always made decisions by consensus. By 1970, when you had 15 people show up and three were FBI agents and six were schizophrenics, universal agreement was getting to be a problem. I call it "The Curse of Consensus Decision Making," because in the end consensus decision making is rule of the minority: the easiest form to manipulate, the easiest way to block any real decision making. Trying to get everyone to agree takes forever. Usually the people are broke, without alternatives, with no new language, just competing to see who can burn the shit out of the other the most. There must be a spirit of agreement and in this way most decisions *are* made by consensus, but there must also be a format whereby you can express your differences. The democratic parliamentary procedure—majority rule—is the toughest to stack, because in order to really get your point across you've got to get cooperation, and to go out and get more people to come in to have those votes the next time around.

My vision of America is not as cheery and optimistic as it might be. I agree with Charles Dickens, "These are the worst of times, these are the worst of times." Look at the institutions around us. Financial institutions, bankrupt; religious institutions, immoral; communications institutions don't communicate; educational institutions don't educate. A poll yesterday showed that 48% of Americans want someone else to run than the current candidates. The last election in 1987 had the lowest turnout since 1942. There are people that say to a gathering such as this—students taking their proper role in the front lines of social change in America, fighting for peace and justice—that this is not the time. This is not the time? You could never have had a better time in history than right now.

My fingers are crossed because I hope that you won't let the internal differences divide you. I hope that you'll be able to focus on the real enemies that are out there. In the late sixties we were so fed up we wanted to destroy it all. That's when we changed the name of America and stuck in the "k." The mood today is different, and the language that will respond to today's mood will be different. Things are so deteriorated in this society, that it's not up to you to destroy America, it's up to you to go out and save America. The same impulse that helped us fight our way out of one empire 200 years ago must help us get free of the Holy Financial Empire today. The transnationals—with their money in Switzerland, headquarters in Luxembourg, ships in tax-free Panama, natural resources all over the emerging world, and their sleepy consumers in the United States—do not have the interest of the United States at heart. Ronald Reagan and the CIA are traitors to America, they have sold it to the Holy Financial Empire. The enemy is out there, he's not in this room. People are allowed to have different visions and different views, but you have to have unity.

You also have to communicate a message and to do that you need a medium. We know television as the boob tube. We know educational television is an oxymoron, a contradiction in terms. We know it from reading fake intellectuals like Alan Bloom and his *Closing of the American Mind*, or from reading good ones like Neil Postman, whose *Amusing Ourselves to Death: Public Discourse in the Age of Showbiz* is a wonderful book. Bloom wants us to shut off the t.v. and start reading the Bible, and Postman just wants us to shut off the t.v. They are critics of t.v., but they are not organizers. A lot of people say, "Abbie, you just perform for the media, that's your duty, you manipulate," a lot of things like that. This is a misconception. I have never in my life done anything for the media. I'm speaking to you through a microphone because my voice is soft, and I couldn't reach all of you unless I used it. That's why I use the microphone. But my words are not for this goddamn microphone. If you want to reach hundreds of thousands or millions of people, you have to use the media and television. Television has an immense impact on our lives. We don't read, we just look at things. We don't gather information in an intellectual way, we just want to keep in touch.

As bad as it is, television has the ability to penetrate our fantasy world. That's why the images are at first quick and action-packed, very short, very limited and very specific, and afterward vague, blurry, and distorted. How can these images not be very important? They determine our view of the world. We in New England would not have known there was a civil rights movement in the South. We would not have known racism existed, that blacks were getting lynched, that blacks were not getting service at a Woolworth counter, if it hadn't been for television. We weren't taught it in our schools or churches. We had to see it and feel it with our eyes. You have to use that medium to get across the image that students have changed. You have to show it to them. Let the world watch, just like we watch students in the Gaza strip fight for their freedom and justice, students in Johannesburg, in El Salvador, in Central America, in the Philipines fight for their freedom.

One hundred and thirty schools represented here today out of 5,000 colleges and universities in America reminds us that going against the grain at the University of South Dakota or Louisiana State is a very tough, lonely job. You have to feel that you're part of something bigger. You want to know that there's a movement out there. That's where the role of a national student organization becomes so important, giving hope and comfort to people that are out there trying to make change at a grassroots level.

The student movement is a global movement. It is always the young that make the change. You don't get these ideas when you're middle-aged. Young people have daring, creativity, imagination and personal computers. Above all, what you have as young people that's vitally needed to make social change, is impatience. You want it to happen now. There have to be enough people that say, "We want it now, in our lifetime." We want to see apartheid in South Africa come down right now. We want to see the war in Central America stop right now. We want the CIA off our campus right now. We want an end to sexual harassment in our communities right now. This is your moment. This is your opportunity.

Be adventurists in the sense of being bold and daring. Be opportunists and seize this opportunity, this moment in history, to go out and save our country. It's your turn now. Thank you.

QUESTIONS FROM THE AUDIENCE

Question: What's so revolutionary about something like MTV?

Abbie: Actually, the initials stand for moron television, if you ask me. I wasn't praising it. When you have an image in your head, like the ruling class runs the media, too often this can serve as an excuse not to learn how to fight it—not to learn who the assignment editor is on the local newspaper, or how to write an effective letter to the editor, or how to write effectively in general, or how to compose or sing a song effectively, or how to produce a videogame—when, if you think about it, how else are you going to change people's imaginations and consciousnesses around the world. At the same time as you're putting the media down, you have to learn how to use it. In fact, I don't believe you have the right to criticize it unless you've gone in there and tried to really do it.

Q: How do you think students of the sixties compare to us right now, students of the eighties coming into the nineties?

Abbie: You're about the same size, shape. What can I say? I think that you are faced with the same decisions. The decision to be blindly obedient to authority versus the decision to try and change things by fighting the powers that be is always, throughout history, the same decision. Each individual has to make it. The only difference today is that we in the sixties left you a legacy which says that you can do it. No matter what people think about the sixties, they know that young people were there in the streets taking on the strongest government in the world, and winning, making change. Making change that is so permanent in our country that not Reagan, not Jesse Helms, Pat Robertson or Anal Roberts can turn back the clock. Women are simply not going to go back, gay people are not going back and black people are not going back. It's just not going to happen. There are trends that have been put in motion. The word is out. Liberation is out. So yes, I'll give advice. I give advice all the time in my newspaper column anyway—Dear Abby, I don't know if you read it—but it's only advice. It's you that have to make the decisions and change, and it's you that have to supply the leadership. Student empowerment means you have to learn how to handle the word power. Before you say power is a bad thing, or that people are on power trips, you should remember that the first guy that said that power corrupts and absolute power corrupts absolutely was a British Lord speaking to people that had no power. It's like Michael Jackson saying money doesn't count. There are problems with power. But if you have the proper structure you can correct those problems. You can change what happens. You have a vehicle that's continuously changing as the times change and people change. Right now you have powerlessness, and powerlessness, just like poverty, is a much bigger problem than having power and wealth, I guarantee you.

Q: You mentioned a lot of problems in the sixties resulting from the infighting. In my experience a lot of problems come from excessive drug and alcohol use. Wouldn't you advise students today to be more health-minded?

Abbie: It's more complex than that. There are 300,000 drug products listed in *The Physician's Desk Reference*. Every time you turn on a commercial on t.v. it's about instant relief. We are the most drugged-out culture in the history of the world. Try to tell an American not to take drugs. You drive across town to a doctor and the doctor says, "Well, we don't know much about it, it's going around, why don't you get some rest and drink some fruit juice." You gonna pay $75 for that? No! You want some drugs! It's the American way.

Now drug abuse is not the same as drug use. But let's be a little more specific. Last year, according to the U.S. Bureau of Mortality statistics, 300,000 Americans died from a drug called nicotine. One hundred and fifty thousand died from a drug called alcohol. These are all drug-related deaths. Eight to ten thousand died from the misuse of prescription drugs. Thirty-five hundred or less died from the use of all recreational drugs. Those are U.S. Bureau of Mortality statistics. Don't go freaking out like Nancy Reagan, making this the number one problem in the country.

There were excesses in the sixties. Let's name them: irresponsible meddling in world affairs, the rise of conservatism. Those were the excesses of the sixties. Focus on the excesses of the government during the period, forget about the excesses of the people in the street, and you'll have a far better idea of what really was going on.

Q: I've been out of school for five years, working in the American business world. How can you appeal to people my age, into their thirties, who are out of the student scene and settled in their jobs? How can you appeal to them to become involved in this movement, which will need to reach out beyond the campuses. To succeed, won't it need the participation of people in business?

Abbie: Well, I think that much of the expertise of the business world, in terms of the way problems are explored and solved, could benefit the movement enormously. I mean we just couldn't imagine people at an Amway convention standing up and saying, "Nobody listens," "We don't have any money," "No one cares about what we've got to say," "They can't get it together," and all that kind of stuff. It just doesn't go on out there. The ability to turn problem presenters into problem solvers is an enormously significant and useful aspect of business thinking.

Also, the whole problem of money is very different today from what it was in the sixties. Economics are a big thing now; we didn't have to deal with that as much. There was so much affluence in the sixties, and if you had to get by on 40 dollars a week, that was fine. You all chipped in, got a crash pad, and just worked it out. But now money is a reality and you have choices to make about your money. There are organizations like Working Assets. If you want to have a VISA card, that's okay, don't make that an issue. When one of the delegates here wanted to know if they could put the $25 admission fee on their Mastercard, I thought that was kind of cute. If you get your VISA card from Working Assets and your health insurance from Co-Op America, your money isn't being invested in corporations that have holdings in South Africa, or in corporations that are ruining the earth, or corporations that are involved in the defense industry. There are many alternatives that are being put into action so that people can actually have concepts like good money and can do good things with their talents as business people.